"Since the 'new perspective' burst on the center of the ensuing debate has been Paul's 'works of the law.' A flood of studies examining the phrase in its Pauline contexts and in Jewish literature has engulfed the world of Pauline scholarship. Matthew Thomas has taken a refreshingly new approach, looking carefully at the way theologians in the first centuries of the church approached the issues about the law that are tied to the meaning of the phrase. His study finds points of continuity and discontinuity with both the 'new perspective' and the 'old perspective.' He describes accurately and fairly the views of the scholars he chooses to highlight. His study will not settle the ongoing debate about the phrase and the issues associated with it, but anyone engaged in this debate needs to take account of his work."

Douglas J. Moo, Wessner Chair of Biblical Studies at Wheaton College

"What Paul meant by 'works of the law' has been hotly debated for years. When we allow the second-century writers to have their say, the balance suddenly shifts—in favor of what has been called the 'new perspective,' but should now, it seems, be called the 'original perspective.' Matthew Thomas has put us all in his debt with this detailed, patient, historically careful, and theologically explosive study."

N. T. Wright, research professor of New Testament and early Christianity at the University of St. Andrews, senior research fellow at Wycliffe Hall, Oxford

"Through careful analysis of the textual data, Matthew Thomas argues persuasively that the early reception of Paul on 'works of the law' was far closer to the 'new perspective' on Paul than to the so-called old! This important book thus demonstrates again the value of reception-history and makes a genuinely fresh contribution to a long debate."

John M. G. Barclay, Lightfoot Professor of Divinity at the University of Durham

"Matthew Thomas's cogent and compelling argument moves the stalled discussion between 'old' and 'new' perspective views forward. His thorough, nuanced, and even-handed presentation illuminates second-century writings on the topic of law and works, and brings their analyses into conversation with current scholarship. If the reader's goal is to better understand Paul's thought, then Thomas's thesis deserves serious consideration."

Lynn H. Cohick, provost/dean at Denver Seminary

"Matthew Thomas has done a rare thing. This book is a stellar contribution to patristic studies that, by examining the early reception of Paul in light of the 'old' and 'new' perspectives on Paul, makes an equally important—or perhaps even more important given the heat of the controversy—contribution to biblical studies. Thomas directs us to the early Fathers' view: Paul is insisting that the 'law of Christ' has replaced the Torah. As a Catholic theologian, my hope is that this stimulating book will rekindle dormant discussions among Catholic theologians about justification and the life of grace."

Matthew Levering, James N. and Mary D. Perry Jr. Chair of Theology, Mundelein Seminary

PAUL'S "WORKS OF THE LAW"

IN THE

PERSPECTIVE OF SECOND-CENTURY RECEPTION

MATTHEW J. THOMAS

FOREWORD BY
ALISTER E. McGRATH

ivp
Academic

An imprint of InterVarsity Press
Downers Grove, Illinois

InterVarsity Press
P.O. Box 1400, Downers Grove, IL 60515-1426
ivpress.com
email@ivpress.com

First published by Mohr Siebeck GmbH & Co. KG, Tübingen, Germany

InterVarsity Press® is the book-publishing division of InterVarsity Christian Fellowship/USA®, a movement of students and faculty active on campus at hundreds of universities, colleges, and schools of nursing in the United States of America, and a member movement of the International Fellowship of Evangelical Students. For information about local and regional activities, visit intervarsity.org.

All Scripture quotations, unless otherwise indicated, are the author's own translation.

Cover design and image composite: David Fassett
Interior design: Jeanna Wiggins
Images: black slate: © xamtiw / iStock / Getty Images
*   gold texture background: © Katsumi Murouchi / Moment Collection / Getty Images*

ISBN 978-0-8308-5526-1 (print)

Printed in the United States of America ∞

InterVarsity Press is committed to ecological stewardship and to the conservation of natural resources in all our operations. This book was printed using sustainably sourced paper.

Library of Congress Cataloging-in-Publication Data
A catalog record for this book is available from the Library of Congress.

P	25	24	23	22	21	20	19	18	17	16	15	14	13	12	11	10	9	8	7	6	5	4	3	2	1
Y	39	38	37	36	35	34	33	32	31	30	29	28	27	26	25	24	23	22	21	20					

For Nabeel Qureshi

(1983–2017)

CONTENTS

PART IV: CONCLUSIONS

FOREWORD

ALISTER E. MCGRATH

IT IS A GREAT PLEASURE to write the foreword to this very important piece of scholarly writing, which casts much light on early Pauline reception, as well as making some wise and cautionary comments on more recent debates about how best to understand Paul's theology of justification. Dr. Thomas's work is a landmark in historical scholarship, which no interpreter of Paul should be allowed to overlook.

The New Perspective on Paul, which emerged in response to works such as E. P. Sanders's *Paul and Palestinian Judaism* (1977), led to intense scholarly interest being focused on how early Christian writers understood the Pauline phrase "works of the law." Sanders was critical of what he considered to be a Christian caricature of Judaism as a religion of legalistic works-righteousness, a stereotype that he held to be perpetuated by the Lutheran interpretation of Paul.

The rise to prominence of the New Perspective on Paul has generated significant new research questions, not least the need to clarify the way in which key biblical phrases—such as the "works of the law"—were interpreted in the pre-Reformation traditions. Did earlier Christian writers understand such works as general human achievements or as more specifically cultic actions or obligations? This debate has created an increased awareness of the need to establish precisely what early Christian writers understood by this phrase rather than assimilating it to what later writers such as Luther understood by the term.

This is the task that Dr. Thomas undertakes in this groundbreaking work. What did second-century writers understand by Paul's phrase "works of the law," and how was this understanding incorporated into their wider understanding of salvation history? This meticulous piece of analysis considers a range of second-century writers, aiming to identify what we are to understand by "works of the law," paying particular attention to two associated questions: What does practicing these "works" signify, and why are Christians no longer under any obligation to practice them? In exploring these themes in writers such as Ignatius of Antioch, Irenaeus of Lyons, and Melito of Sardis, Dr. Thomas is able to open up a rich interpretive tradition focusing on the belief that, for Paul, justification proceeds completely on the basis of grace apart from works of any sort, and that the final judgment is based on the subsequent outworking of this grace.

Yet this is not simply a study of the reception of some core Pauline ideas in the second century. Although this study is of considerable importance as an intellectually rigorous and objective exercise in clarifying how Paul's early Christian readers understood him, it also plays into more recent debates about how Paul's theology of justification is to be understood, particularly in relation to Christian understandings of Judaism. Dr. Thomas shows that these early Christian interpreters of Paul interpret "works of the law" in terms of the cultic requirements of Judaism—not some presumed ethic of self-justification or achievement. These writers understood Paul's opposition to such works as arising from the promised "new law" or "new covenant" resulting from the coming of Christ. This new law is transformative in nature and universal in scope, thus putting to an end any obligation to observe these "works of the law," in that they are linked to the specifics of the older dispensation.

I have no reason to believe that E. P. Sanders read many second-century Christian interpreters of Paul, or that he was familiar with the complex and rich interaction with the Pauline corpus associated with early Protestant writers such as Martin Luther, Philip Melanchthon, Martin Bucer, and John Calvin. The so-called Lutheran perspective on Paul, as presented by Sanders, is of little scholarly value, and is best set to one side in these discussions as a polemical construction. Dr. Thomas has made it clear that today's interpreters of Paul often have an inadequate grasp of the long Christian tradition of engagement with Paul, at times leading them to draw questionable conclusions about the interpretation of Paul in the past and to project these on their interpretation of Paul in the present.

Paul's "Works of the Law" in the Perspective of Second-Century Reception based on Dr. Thomas's recent Oxford doctoral thesis, brings its readers up-to-date with the significant shifts in our understanding of how Paul was received and understood in the early Christian period. For example, it highlights the historical vulnerability of the influential notion of a "Pauline captivity," popularized during the 1970s by writers such as Krister Stendahl, which held that Paul was marginalized in the early church. Yet the book's most significant achievement is to force a recalibration of our understanding of how early Christian interpreters of Paul understood his doctrine of justification, undermining any simplistic contrast between old and new perspectives on Paul.

As Dr. Thomas makes clear, the discussion of the implications of Paul's theology of justification continued after the second century, perhaps reaching its apex in the theology of Augustine of Hippo. Yet, as I found when researching the latest edition of my *Iustitia Dei: A History of the Christian Doctrine of Justification* (Cambridge University Press, 2020), the lines of thought emerging from the second-century readers of Paul discussed in Dr. Thomas's work proved to be highly significant for later Christian Pauline interpretation and the increasingly sophisticated theologies of justification based on this foundation.

This major work of scholarship, happily now available in this new edition, is an invitation to rediscover what early Christian readers of Paul found in his letters. Yet it is also a powerful reminder that contemporary reflection on Paul must be informed *about*—and informed *by*—how earlier generations understood him.

PREFACE TO THE IVP EDITION

I AM GRATEFUL FOR THE OPPORTUNITY to republish this book with
InterVarsity Press, and I hope that the early sources presented here will
help fellow readers of Paul as much as they have helped me. As articulated by Irenaeus at the beginning of part III and C. S. Lewis in part IV,
this book is based on the idea that evaluating early reception is an integral part of historical inquiry and that reconstructions that ignore or
dismiss such evidence are not more historically rigorous but less. My
hope is that these early perspectives will prove to be of value for those
trying to navigate contemporary Pauline interpretation, and if this work
provides any original contribution to these discussions, it has come about
only by attempting to be as unoriginal as possible.

There are three areas where readers have most frequently asked for
elaboration on portions of this book, and (without inundating the reader
with details before the book begins) I hope to briefly offer a few comments on them here. The first is on the broader patristic framework of
salvation, described on p. 279: that "initial justification is completely by
grace apart from works of any sort, and that final judgment (or final
justification) is based on the outworking of this grace in one's subsequent
life." These two sides of this patristic framework can be well illustrated
using Jesus' parable of the unmerciful servant as an analogy: while the
servant is granted an inconceivable gift simply by his petition, without
being able to give anything, this gift is meant to be transformative in the
servant's life. When the servant is judged according to his deeds, which
have manifestly not been transformed by the king's mercy, all that
remains for the servant is severe judgment.

A helpful example of this framework is found in Irenaeus's *Against Heresies* 4.27. Irenaeus describes how Old Testament figures merited less punishment for their sins since they acted apart from the Spirit's empowerment, and those in the new covenant should not despise them for their faults since neither they nor we are justified by ourselves, but rather by Christ's advent. On the other hand, those in the new covenant are now held accountable at a higher level, having now been the recipients of this saving power to which the patriarchs only looked forward. Recognizing that most will be demanded of those to whom Christ has given the most, Irenaeus counsels his readers to not judge these prior figures, but rather to fear lest we be cut off, which he illustrates using Paul's image of the olive tree from Romans 11. Such a framework underlies discussions on salvation in patristic sources, in which statements of "salvation by grace" and "judgment by works" are regularly presented with great emphasis in the same sources, and even in the same passages. (Along with the examples noted in the book, *1 Clement* 30–35 and *Polycarp* 1–2, see also the striking passage in the earliest preserved Christian homily, *2 Clement* 1–4). The lack of tension between these principles becomes clear when it is recognized that these sources regard God's grace as transformative, so that one is enabled to live in a way that will be judged favorably at the last day. To paraphrase a later line from Augustine that corresponds with the testimony of these early sources, God's justifying grace turns an ungodly man into a godly one (cf. *Spir. et Litt.* 45), and one who disregards this power will be held more strictly accountable than one who has never known it. Within this broader soteriological framework, early patristic sources regard the Mosaic law's distinctive works as having no decisive role, "either as bearers of the grace of salvation (or somehow prerequisites for it), or as criteria that will have any kind of significance at the last judgment" (279).

The second area is how the writings of the broader Pauline corpus such as Ephesians and the Pastorals relate to the early patristic sources in this study. The brief response is that these epistles seem to correspond closely with the paradigm described above (which given the Pauline influence on early patristic soteriology should come as little surprise). As

with Romans and Galatians, the Pauline writings elsewhere are clear that
the source of saving grace is not any work of our own but God
(cf. Eph 2:8-9; 2 Tim 1:9; Titus 3:5). At the same time, these Pauline texts
are also clear that believers remain accountable for the grace that has
been given (1 Cor 3:13-15; 2 Cor 5:10, 11:15; Eph 6:8-9; Col 3:22-25). To use
a helpful distinction from John Barclay, God's grace for Paul is *uncondi-
tioned*, but not *unconditional*; while given without regard to prior worth,
this grace is not without obligations on the recipient's subsequent life,
precisely because Christ's justifying gift enables an obedience that is
otherwise impossible. Within this paradigm, while the Torah is a witness
to the arrival of Christ's saving power, the "works of the law" are not the
source of God's grace, nor do they form the criteria by which humanity
will be judged as righteous or unrighteous—for which the familiar example of Abraham, who was righteous by faith prior to the Torah and
even the sign of circumcision, is key.

The third is on the relation of Augustine's ideas to the early perspectives presented in this book. As is outlined in the lengthy footnote on
p. 280, within the context of the Pelagian controversy, Augustine interprets "works of the law" as any works done apart from God's grace,
which he contrasts with meritorious works that are empowered by this
grace. While this reading is distinct from the preceding tradition (and
both old and new perspectives), it is important to recognize the degree
to which Augustine's interpretative moves are conditioned by the specific circumstances of the controversy with Pelagius. For example, in the
thirty-three books of his disputation with Faustus (ca. 397–398), both
Augustine and his opponent regard the works of the law as physical
circumcision, Sabbaths and festival days, food laws, and sacrifices,
which serve as identifiers for the Jewish nation and covenant. Augustine's arguments regarding why these works are no longer observed
focus on *type* and *time*: such practices had a typological significance that
foreshadowed coming realities in the new covenant and are no longer
observed because the time of these realities that were signified has now
arrived (cf. *Faust.* 10, 12, 15-19, 25, 32). Interestingly, this interpretation
is not discarded by Augustine following the Pelagian controversy. In

An Answer to the Jews—written near the end of his life circa 428–429, well after his major anti-Pelagian works like *On the Spirit and the Letter* (ca. 412)—Augustine continues presenting the points in conflict as the "ancient sacraments" of circumcision, food laws, Sabbaths and festivals, and sacrifices, which he again counters with the logic of type and time, showing how the Old Testament attests to the new sacraments that would come with Christ's advent. Augustine's continuity with the preceding tradition can be witnessed in his interpretative parallels with a figure like Irenaeus. Both closely link faith and good works: as Augustine writes in his treatise *On Faith and Works*—also written in the midst of the Pelagian controversy around 412–413—"a good life is inseparable from faith which works through love; indeed, rather faith itself is a good life" (*Fid. et op.* 23.42; cf. *Haer.* 4.6.5). Similarly, both Irenaeus and Augustine identify the Jews' infidelity to the law (rather than an undue focus on it) as their reason for rejecting Christ; as Augustine writes, "[t]he reason why the Jews did not believe in Christ, was because they did not observe even the plain literal precepts of Moses" (*Faust.* 16.32; cf. *Haer.* 4.2.8). Thus, while the Pelagian controversy prompts distinct interpretative moves from Augustine (as Luther rightly observed), these moves should not be regarded as discontinuous with the preceding tradition or his earlier views, since Augustine himself continues articulating them after his major anti-Pelagian works in contexts where Pelagius is not a target.

But this is to take us far beyond our present focus, which is on the earliest reception of these Pauline ideas. May these early perspectives benefit the reader as much as they have the author!

PREFACE

THIS BOOK IS A LIGHTLY revised version of my doctoral dissertation at the University of Oxford, and my family and I are indebted to many individuals for their encouragement to pursue the project and helping to bring it to completion. I am grateful for the guidance of my three supervisors: Prof. Mark Edwards, the constant support and encouragement behind this study from start to finish; Dr. David Lincicum, who believed in the project and helped to shape it in the initial stages; and Prof. Jenn Strawbridge, whose feedback has been so valuable in making it into a finished product. Prof. Markus Bockmuehl has also played a critical role in guiding me and refining my work through the examination process, along with offering guidance in publishing this material, for which I am greatly in his debt. Prof. Alister McGrath and Prof. John Barclay provided encouragement to pursue this topic during the initial stages of formulating the project, which played a key role in helping it to become a reality. Prof. Barclay and Prof. Johannes Zachhuber have also contributed valuable feedback in their examination of the thesis, which has made this a far stronger book than it would have been otherwise. At Regent College, we are indebted to Dr. Hans Boersma and Dr. Iwan Russell-Jones for their tremendous support and their encouragement to move to England to pursue this project. Thanks are also due to our friend Dr. Don Lewis, who originally had the idea to put an unknown graduate student together with Prof. McGrath in 2011, and who has been a deep source of encouragement to so many at Regent.

My family and I also offer our thanks to our friends Nabeel, Michelle, and Ayah Qureshi for giving us a place to stay during last stages of writing the dissertation, and to Prof. Graham Ward, who has been so generous in taking us in and offering his support for this project. I am deeply indebted to Dr. Ben Edsall, who generously volunteered himself as my IT manager for both the thesis and publishing process, and to Dr. Alex "Shifty" Garabedian, who served as our family's butler off and on throughout the writing of the original thesis.

This project would not have been possible without the very generous financial support from the Clarendon Fund, Christ Church, the American Friends of Christ Church, and the Institute for Religion and Culture (in the legacy of James Houston), as well as the constant love and support from my parents throughout the writing process. Thank you as well to Prof. Jörg Frey and Katharina Gutekunst for accepting the thesis into WUNT II, and to everyone at Mohr Siebeck for their guidance in publishing this volume.

I am grateful for a number of friends who have offered feedback on sections of the original thesis, including Lauren Thomas, Barnabas Aspray, Jimmy Tran, Dr. Hans Boersma, Dr. Douglas Moo, Prof. James Dunn, Prof. James Carleton Paget, Dr. Jim Prothro, Dr. Peter Gurry, and Dr. Bobby Jamieson. I am especially indebted to three individuals—Jacob Imam, Simeon Burke, and my incredible wife Leeanne—who took on the task of reading through the entire thesis before its submission. Thanks are also due to Charles Homer and Buz Hannon, who provided helpful advice in drafting the book's summaries. This book has also benefited from the valuable feedback of subsequent readers, including Dr. Thomas Scheck, Rev. Dr. Richard Ounsworth, Rev. Dr. Andrew Louth, and Rev. Fr. Dustin Lyon, for which I offer my sincere thanks. Any errors that remain are my own.

This book is dedicated to our friend Nabeel, a true witness of Jesus Christ.

ABBREVIATIONS

Abbreviations of primary and secondary sources in this volume conform to Society of Biblical Literature, *The SBL Handbook of Style*, second edition, Atlanta: SBL Press, 2014. Additions and alterations to these guidelines are as follows:

ActPl	Acts of Paul
Arist.	Aristides, *Apology*
Comm. Gal.	John Calvin. *Commentary on Galatians*. Edited by T. H. L. Parker. Grand Rapids, MI: Eerdmans, 1996.
Comm. Rom.	John Calvin. *Commentary on Romans*. Edited by Ross Mackenzie. Grand Rapids, MI: Eerdmans, 1995.
Didasc.	*Didascalia Apostolorum*
Inst.	John Calvin. *Institutes of the Christian Religion*. Edited by Ford Lewis Battles. Philadelphia: Westminster Press, 1960.
JP	Aristo of Pella, *Dialogue of Jason and Papiscus*
KP	*Preaching of Peter*
LW	Martin Luther. *Luther's Works*. Edited by J. Pelikan and H. L. Lehmann. 55 vols. St. Louis: Concordia; Philadelphia: Fortress Press, 1955–1986.
PP	Melito of Sardis, *On Pascha*
Ref.	Hippolytus, *Refutation of All Heresies*
Ser. Gal.	John Calvin. *Sermons on Galatians*. Edited by Kathy Childress. Edinburgh: Banner of Truth Trust, 1997.
WA	Martin Luther. *Dr. Martin Luthers Werke*. 69 vols. Weimar: Böhlau, 1883–1993.

PART I

INTRODUCTION

◘

It is a matter of doubt, even among the learned,
what the works of the law mean.

JOHN CALVIN, COMMENTARY ON ROMANS[1]

---

[1] *Comm. Rom.* 3.20, trans. Owen, 130.

1

INTRODUCTION, THEORY, AND METHODOLOGY

◻

INTRODUCTION

In Paul's epistles to the Romans and the Galatians, the apostle famously declares that one is considered righteous by faith, and not by works of the law. This antithesis, forcefully stated in the context of disputes regarding Jews and the law, has induced a number of theological aftershocks in Christian history; for some it represents the definitive articulation of Christianity itself, providing the interpretive lens through which the rest of the Scriptures are to be read. But what exactly is Paul opposing? What works of what law are these? What is the significance of practicing them, and why are they rejected by Paul? The answers to such questions will necessarily influence one's conception of what Paul means by faith, justification, and indeed the Christian gospel itself.

These questions have been asked with renewed interest since 1977, when E. P. Sanders's *Paul and Palestinian Judaism* introduced a picture of Paul and his context that differed considerably from the prevailing image in New Testament studies. As attested by Luther and Calvin in the sixteenth century and the majority of interpreters in Sanders's time, these works were viewed as any and all actions that one might perform in order to be justified before God and earn salvation. According to Sanders, such a scenario was without historical foundation in the Judaism of Paul's time, being instead a projection of Reformation-era critiques of the late medieval church onto Paul's interlocutors. Rather, according to Sanders, Paul was reacting against the imposition of a particular law—the Torah—and within it specific works such as circumcision, Sabbath, and food laws, which were performed not on an individual basis to accord merit with God, but to become part of God's people, the Jews. Sanders's view soon found defenders in figures such as James Dunn and N. T. Wright, and became known as the "new perspective" on Paul, with those holding to the traditional view in the vein of the Reformers being called the "old perspective."

The debate between "old" and "new" perspectives has continued unabated since the early 1980s, spurring a variety of offshoots from the two frameworks and an enormous amount of research in Paul's epistles and Second Temple Jewish sources on both sides. Such efforts have nevertheless been unable to draw the debate to resolution, with questions regarding what precisely Paul is objecting to by "works of the law" remaining a central point of division between these two camps in New Testament studies. Within such discussions, however, a potentially useful body of material has gone largely unexamined: the witness of the early patristic figures who followed Paul, who stand in close proximity to the apostle's debates and are among the earliest known readers of his epistles. In what ways might these early figures have understood the works of the law to which Paul was objecting? How might their early perspectives relate to the "old" and "new" perspectives on this issue? And what might their collective witness suggest about Paul's own meaning?

This study seeks to answer these three questions. For the first task, this book attempts to identify how the phenomena of works of the law were understood in early patristic sources up to the time of Irenaeus in the late second century. As is outlined below, this search does not focus exclusively on the phrase ἔργα νόμου, but traces lexical overlap with this phrase within a broader examination of patristic discussions that are similar to Paul's in this period. This examination assesses the works and law that are rejected in similar conflicts with Jewish parties, and the patristic usage of Paul's epistles and specific works of the law passages in such disputes.[1] It evaluates these works in terms of "meaning," "significance," and "opposition," asking which particular works of what law are under discussion, what the practice of these works appears to signify (e.g., to earn salvation, to become a Jew), and why these works are not necessary for the Christian in each author's perspective. Following from this analysis, this study's second aim is to evaluate how these second-century perspectives relate to the conceptions put forward by the old and new perspectives in New Testament debates. As part two of this book illustrates, such assessments must be properly nuanced: while the views of figures within these categories are sufficiently consistent to make the classifications intelligible, there is diversity within both the old and new perspectives on this subject. The third aim of this study—to assess what these early perspectives would suggest regarding Paul's own meaning by works of the law—must be stated the most tentatively, but is also potentially the most significant. While Paul's meaning is not to be decisively settled by early reception, tradition, or memory alone, this book seeks to identify what the early patristic evidence would suggest about how the burdens of proof should be borne in contemporary debates on this subject.

THEORY: EFFECTIVE HISTORY AND LIVING MEMORY

A model for how early patristic sources can be of use in New Testament interpretation is found in the work of Markus Bockmuehl, whose 2006 book *Seeing the Word* presents the case for utilizing early reception to engage contested areas of interpretation. Building on the work of Ulrich Luz,[2] Bockmuehl's proposal for providing a way through impasses in

---

[1]Such an approach holds correspondence with Barclay's recent study on grace, which similarly attempts to analyze a concept behind the words rather than simply the usage of words themselves, cf. John M. G. Barclay, *Paul and the Gift* (Grand Rapids, MI: Eerdmans, 2015), 3: "Hence, our study is confined to no single term (and certainly not to χάρις); its focus is on concepts, not words."

[2]Cf. e.g. Ulrich Luz, *Matthew in History: Interpretation, Influence, and Effects* (Minneapolis: Fortress Press, 1994), 23-38; Luz, *Matthew 1–7: A Commentary*, ed. Helmut Koester, trans. James E. Crouch (Minneapolis: Fortress Press, 2007 [1989]), 60-66. Luz himself is dependent on Hans-Georg Gadamer's *Truth and Method* (New York: Crossroad, 1975), cf. particularly 268-74, though he recognizes his work cuts against Gadamer's intentions. See Luz, *Matthew 1–7*, 62; Gadamer, *Truth and Method*, 305.

contemporary New Testament scholarship is "that New Testament scholars explicitly adopt the history of the influence of the New Testament as an integral and indeed inescapable part of the exercise in which they are engaged."[3] As Bockmuehl comments,

> The meaning of a text is in practice deeply intertwined with its own tradition of hearing and heeding, interpretation and performance. Only the totality of that tradition can begin to give a view of the New Testament's real historical footprint, the vast majority of which is to be found in reading communities that, for all their diversity, place themselves deliberately "within the living tradition of the church, whose first concern is fidelity to the revelation attested by the Bible." And conversely, that footprint, for good and for ill, can in turn serve as a valuable guide to the scope of the text's meaning and truth.[4]

Of course, such attention to reception or effective history (*Wirkungsgeschichte*)[5] runs the risk of engaging a cacophony of contemporary New Testament interpretation by simply introducing a second cacophony of historical reception, which Bockmuehl acknowledges: "The further the effects are removed in time from their causes, the more tenuous their connection becomes," so that "Wirkungsgeschichte increasingly turns into the story of serendipitous echoes and often arbitrary canons of intertextual association, rather than a continuity of demonstrable effects."[6]

---

[3]Markus Bockmuehl, *Seeing the Word: Refocusing New Testament Study* (Grand Rapids, MI: Baker Academic, 2006), 64-65.

[4]Bockmuehl, *Seeing the Word*, 65, citing *The Interpretation of the Bible in the Church* in Joseph A. Fitzmyer, *The Biblical Commission's Document "The Interpretation of the Bible in the Church": Text and Commentary*, Subsidia Biblica 18 (Rome: Pontifical Biblical Institute Press, 1995), §3.

[5]Luz distinguishes between reception history (*Auslegungsgeschichte*) and effective history (*Wirkungsgeschichte*), with the former referring to commentaries and the latter to reception elsewhere ("verbal media such as sermons, canonical documents, and 'literature,' as well as in nonverbal media such as art and music, and in the church's activity and suffering, that is, in church history"; Luz, *Matthew 1–7*, 61). These distinctions do not play a role in Bockmuehl's model, and for the purposes of this study the two terms are taken as essentially coterminous, though effective history is preferred in emphasizing the potential of influence in this period beyond strictly textual interpretation (and since none of the sources here are commentaries in the strict sense; cf. similarly Alexander N. Kirk, *The Departure of an Apostle: Paul's Death Anticipated and Remembered*, WUNT 2:406 [Tübingen: Mohr Siebeck, 2015], 34).

[6]Bockmuehl, *Seeing the Word*, 168. Alternatively, as Räisänen notes, *Wirkungsgeschichte* can risk being used for the construction of echo chambers, with theologians "keen on appealing to the 'effective history' of the Bible as a norm which they use in defending their particular vision of biblical study" (Heikki Räisänen, "The Effective 'History' of the Bible: A Challenge to Biblical Scholarship?," *Scottish Journal of Theology* 45 [1992]: 306).

However, between the original texts and events and later interpreters, there is "a third set of voices, uniquely placed to mediate between primary and secondary sources": the early witnesses that follow within a period of "living memory," who "retain a personal link to the persons and events concerned."[7] According to Bockmuehl, such a period of living memory continues beyond the New Testament into the second century, with there being "a uniquely privileged window of up to 150 years . . . when there were still living witnesses of the apostles or of their immediate students,"[8] and within which "tradition inhabits a narrative world that is still colored, and at least potentially subject to correction, by what is remembered."[9] Bockmuehl's proposal is that effective history be employed in this particular period of living memory "to privilege the *earlier* over the more remote effects for a historical understanding of Christianity's texts, persons, and events."[10]

This proposal is further developed in Bockmuehl's subsequent prosopographic studies on Simon Peter.[11] As Bockmuehl writes, "it is a matter of historical record that during the limited window of a generation or two, the New Testament aftermath includes a unique group of people who retained a personal link to the persons and events concerned," which was claimed both by the figures themselves and affirmed by their younger contemporaries.[12] Bockmuehl suggests that privileging the testimony of these early witnesses can lead to real exegetical and historical gains, as "the individual and communal memory of that early period offers us an interpreted appropriation of the past by people who personally retain experiential and cultural links to the events—historical links that are

---

[7]Bockmuehl, *Seeing the Word*, 168.

[8]Bockmuehl, *Seeing the Word*, 170.

[9]Bockmuehl, *Seeing the Word*, 172. This 150-year window incorporates three generations: "(1) sources dating roughly from the lifetime of the apostles (ca. 1–70); (2) younger contemporaries like Polycarp, who personally remembered either the apostles or their close associates (ca. 70–130); and (3) people like Irenaeus, who in turn were taught by these students (ca. 130–200)" (Bockmuehl, *Seeing the Word*, 178).

[10]Bockmuehl, *Seeing the Word*, 169 (italics original).

[11]Markus Bockmuehl, *The Remembered Peter*, WUNT 262 (Tübingen: Mohr Siebeck, 2010); Markus Bockmuehl, *Simon Peter in Scripture and Memory* (Grand Rapids, MI: Baker Academic, 2012).

[12]Bockmuehl, *The Remembered Peter*, 20.

closer than ours can ever be, even with the best historical methods."[13] While such evidence "of course must be taken with considerable caution—read critically and *dialectically*, i.e. sifting and discerning between the differing contexts, commitments and agendas,"[14] this period of living memory is nevertheless available for inquiry for New Testament scholars up to "the passing of the church father Irenaeus (ca. 130–200)."[15] His death "signals the demise of those who remembered the apostles' last surviving disciples,"[16] with discussions thereafter taking on a more distinctly archival character without similar appeals to memory; as Bockmuehl notes, "we find no such claims made in the third century."[17]

This study follows Bockmuehl's recognition of the distinct value of testimony in this period, and sets the scope of its inquiry to the time of Irenaeus, the last figure recognized to be writing within a window

---

[13]Bockmuehl, *The Remembered Peter*, 20.

[14]Bockmuehl, *The Remembered Peter*, 20 (italics original).

[15]Bockmuehl, *The Remembered Peter*, 17.

[16]Bockmuehl, *The Remembered Peter*, 17.

[17]Bockmuehl, *The Remembered Peter*, 24. One objection to Bockmuehl's methodology comes from Paul Foster, whose study on Simon Peter in the apocryphal New Testament writings concludes that the representation of Peter in these sources "is both diverse and highly contested" (Paul Foster, "Peter in Noncanonical Traditions," in *Peter in Early Christianity*, ed. Helen K. Bond and Larry W. Hurtado [Grand Rapids, MI: Eerdmans 2015], 260). These traditions "are largely literary reinventions of Peter," and their "vastly differing representations reflect the theological concerns of the authors of the texts . . . rather than stemming from historically reliable traditions concerning Peter" (Foster, "Peter in Noncanonical Traditions," 260). Targeting Bockmuehl's claim that later sources preserve memories that can contribute to historical questions, Foster asks whether the canonical NT writers and patristic sources "are any less likely to be prone to the same forces of reinvention, which serve the legitimation of theological positions" (261). Foster concludes his analysis on a skeptical note: "So who is the Peter of the noncanonical texts? Probably the simple answer is whoever the authors wanted, or needed him to be" (262).

In this particular case, I believe Foster understates the level of coherence found in the Petrine picture that Bockmuehl assembles from the diverse body of sources within this early period, which is less clear in a study such as Foster's, which is limited in scope to apocryphal texts. Nevertheless, in our own case, one can neither prove nor rule out a priori whether a search for Paul's "works of the law" in the second century will find a jumble of self-interested literary inventions; the evidence has to be examined to discover whether this is the case. Even in Foster's worst-case scenario, however, his own study does not absolutely negate Bockmuehl's methodology, as he himself attests to have discovered two consistent pieces of testimony from his noncanonical sources: "Peter was the leader or spokesperson of the Twelve, and he was present during the revelatory events of the transfiguration" (Foster, "Peter in Noncanonical Traditions," 260). Such findings may be modest, but they are not insignificant; and if the present study were to find only a few key consistent testimonies amid an array of otherwise discordant Pauline reinventions, these would nevertheless serve as valuable data for the question at hand. (I am indebted to Simeon Burke for the reference to Foster.)

of apostolic "living memory." The function of this early testimony can be illustrated by borrowing and adapting an analogy from Bockmuehl regarding smoke and fire. This book attempts to identify how the "smoke" of early effective history might help us adjudicate between competing accounts of the "fire"—the conflicts over works of the law—that Paul and his congregations were engaged in.[18] While this smoke of second-century testimony might be so widely dispersed as to only create a fog, if at all concentrated, it will constitute valuable evidence in evaluating whether the fire of these conflicts is located in one of the areas identified by the old and new perspectives—or it may perhaps lead us places that neither perspective currently identifies. Complicating this task, of course, is the fact that identifying influence of a given text or event in later discussions is often an inexact science; and further, unlike Bockmuehl's prosopographical study (where the "fire" ends with the individual's death), disputes with Jewish parties appear to have continued throughout this period, and one cannot be certain that these conflicts would have remained identical in the years following Paul, either from Paul's side or that of his interlocutors. While these concerns can be alleviated somewhat by prioritizing sources that are more clearly influenced by Paul, they nevertheless illustrate how the task of relating the smoke of patristic reception to Pauline fire must remain at the level of relative probabilities rather than certitude.

Such challenges notwithstanding, however, there remains considerable potential in accounting for early interpretation and effective history within a historical investigation of works of the law. A useful point in this regard is made by Schreiner, who notes that "the preservation of Paul's letters by the churches implies that his arguments were related to actual views in the religious world of his readers."[19] If this is indeed the case, then identifying the actual views in the religious world of Paul's early readers should also be of historical value in shedding light back onto his arguments, where these happen to be in dispute. The reflexive connection between text and effects is reflected on by Luz, who writes that effective

---

[18]Cf. Bockmuehl, *The Remembered Peter*, 8.
[19]Thomas R. Schreiner, "'Works of Law' in Paul," *Novum Testamentum* 33 (1991): 242.

history is "an expression of the texts' own power," which "belongs to the texts in the same way that a river flowing away from its source belongs to the source."[20] Thus, just as studying a river can tell us about the source from which it originates, so too can these effects tell us about the original texts and events, with effects in close proximity to the source being of particular value. Such an approach does not deny that early patristic sources engage the apostle and his writings with an eye to their own contexts and circumstances, of course, but rather maintains that such engagements are not pure reinventions. As White argues in his study on Paul in this period, "memory is not *just* a product of present needs, though it certainly is this, but is also constrained by the past—molded by the force of tradition."[21] This constraining quality of the past signals the value of early testimony for such an investigation, for as Kirk observes, "Paul, like any other great historic figure, exerted such influence and created such a lasting impression while alive that the contours of his historical footprint could not be so easily reshaped a generation or two after his death."[22] As such, an examination of effective history within this generation or two following the apostle represents a promising witness to the debates in which he engaged.

THE EARLY RECEPTION OF PAUL

The recent interest in reception and effective history, witnessed in proposals like Bockmuehl's,[23] has coincided with a renewed appreciation for

---

[20]Luz, *Matthew in History*, 24.

[21]Benjamin L. White, *Remembering Paul: Ancient and Modern Contests over the Image of the Apostle* (Oxford: Oxford University Press 2014), 17 (italics original), siding with Schwartz and Hutton over Halbwachs. Cf. 96-97, 167-68.

[22]Kirk, *Departure of an Apostle*, 20, arguing against an overly "presentist" perspective represented in Richard I. Pervo, *The Making of Paul: Constructions of the Apostle in Early Christianity* (Minneapolis: Fortress Press, 2010). For "presentist" and "continuity" perspectives on memory (the latter represented by White and Kirk), cf. e.g. Chris Keith, *Jesus' Literacy: Scribal Culture and the Teacher from Galilee* (New York: T&T Clark, 2011), 57-58.

[23]On this interest in recent biblical studies more broadly, cf. e.g. Mark Knight, "Wirkungsgeschichte, Reception History, Reception Theory," *Journal for the Study of the New Testament* 33 (2010): 137-46; Ian Boxall, *Patmos in the Reception History of the Apocalypse* (Oxford: Oxford University Press, 2013), 209-29; Robert Evans, *Reception History, Tradition and Biblical Interpretation: Gadamer and Jauss in Current Practice* (London: Bloomsbury T&T Clark, 2014); and Emma England and William John Lyons, eds., *Reception History and Biblical Studies: Theory and Practice* (London: Bloomsbury T&T Clark, 2015).

the early patristic period as a source for Pauline reception. This renewal can be traced to the late 1970s and early '80s, when the studies of Andreas Lindemann, Ernst Dassmann, and David Rensberger overturned previously influential notions of a "Pauline captivity,"[24] in which Paul's influence in mainstream Christian circles in the second century was thought to have diminished, usually due to supposed connections with Marcion and the Gnostics.[25] Against this idea, these studies on the engagement with Paul in the first and second centuries found that while "gnostics and Marcionites are opposed on matters of substance" by early orthodox writers, "Paul himself—like Jesus and like other apostles—is never the issue; no one disavows his authority or doubts his orthodoxy when opponents appeal to him."[26] As Lindemann observes, within the writings of the apostolic fathers from the late first to mid-second century, Paul is the most frequently mentioned figure apart from Jesus, and his epistles are the most referenced New Testament sources for engaging contemporary debates.[27] Paul's popularity is such that the title of "the apostle" becomes his own personal epithet in the second century, with Paul being the only figure to whom it applies "absolutely and without need for further specification";[28] for whatever their disagreements

---

[24]Andreas Lindemann, *Paulus im ältesten Christentum: das Bild des Apostels und die Rezeption der paulinischen Theologie in der frühchristlichen Literatur bis Marcion* (Tübingen: Mohr Siebeck, 1979); Ernst Dassmann, *Der Stachel im Fleisch: Paulus in der frühchristlichen Literatur bis Irenäus* (Münster: Aschendorff, 1979); David Rensberger, "As the Apostle Teaches: The Development of the Use of Paul's Letters in Second-Century Christianity" (PhD diss., Yale University, 1981). See also the important volume of Maurice Wiles, *The Divine Apostle: The Interpretation of St. Paul's Epistles in the Early Church* (London: Cambridge University Press, 1967), which, while dealing primarily with later patristic sources, nevertheless reached similar conclusions about Paul's distinct influence in early Christianity.

[25]This idea has roots in the work of F. C. Baur (cf. Baur, *The Church History of the First Three Centuries*, trans. Allan Menzies [London: Williams and Norgate, 1878], 147n1), and is influentially developed in W. Bauer's *Orthodoxy and Heresy in Earliest Christianity*, ed. Robert A. Kraft and Gerhard Krodel (Philadelphia: Fortress Press, 1971 [1934]), 215-28. An excellent overview of the development of this narrative from the time of Baur to its downfall with these studies is found in White, *Remembering Paul*, 20-48. On "Pauline captivity," see particularly chapter 9, "Justin and Paul," on Justin Martyr in this volume.

[26]Rensberger, "As the Apostle Teaches," 363; cf. Lindemann, *Paulus im ältesten Christentum*, 402.

[27]Cf. Andreas Lindemann, "Paul in the Writings of the Apostolic Fathers," in *Paul and the Legacies of Paul*, ed. William S. Babcock (Dallas: Southern Methodist University Press, 1990), 28-29, 45.

[28]William S. Babcock, "Paul in the Writings of the Apostolic Fathers," in *Paul and the Legacies of Paul*, ed. William S. Babcock (Dallas: Southern Methodist University Press 1990), xiv.

elsewhere, this singular designation is agreed on by an "entire range of ideological adversaries," being employed by Basilides, the author of *Diognetus*, Heracleon, and Irenaeus alike.[29] Even Justin Martyr—whose failure to employ this title or any other explicit references to Paul had made him the key evidence for a Pauline captivity—was argued by Lindemann to make considerable tacit use of Paul, and a majority of contemporary studies now regard Justin as indeed drawing on the apostle's writings.[30] As Babcock writes in a 1990 essay, rather than being derived from the patristic evidence, the notion of Paul's captivity seems to have been fundamentally rooted in a tendency among biblical scholars to assume that if their own conceptions of Paul's theology could not be found in the early patristic sources, Paul must not have been read at all.[31] Whatever judgments are rendered on these conceptions, the theory that Paul was unengaged by the patristic sources is untenable as a support for them: "[Paul] was simply too vast a presence in the early history of Christianity to permit such a notion."[32]

This recognition of Paul's early influence has been further explored in a wide range of studies since this time, of which major works include the edited volumes of Babcock (*Paul and the Legacies of Paul*, 1990) and Bird and Dodson (*Paul and the Second Century*, 2011), the recent monographs of White (*Remembering Paul*, 2014) and Strawbridge (*The Pauline Effect*, 2015), and the volumes on Paul in the Evangelisch-Katholischer Kommentar zum Neuen Testament, Blackwell Bible Commentaries, and Ancient Christian Commentary on Scripture series. While this book is unique in its aims of determining the early patristic understanding of works of the law and relating it to contemporary debates,[33] it builds on the work of these and similar recent studies on early Pauline reception, and engages with them where relevant in its

---

[29]White, *Remembering Paul*, 7; cf. the table of references in 7-8.

[30]See Lindemann, *Paulus im ältesten Christentum*, 353-67; cf. the broad survey in ch. 9, "Knowledge and Use of Paul" in this volume.

[31]Cf. Babcock, "Paul in the Writings," xiii-xv.

[32]Babcock, "Paul in the Writings," xv.

[33]Following from my earlier brief study in Matthew J. Thomas, "Paul and Works of the Law: Perspectives Old and New," *Canadian Theological Review* 1 (2012): 81-86.

analysis.[34] In addition to these works, the earlier studies of Barnett (*Paul Becomes a Literary Influence*, 1941), Massaux (*The Influence of the Gospel of Saint Matthew on Christian Literature Before Saint Irenaeus*, 1950), and Hagner (*The Use of the Old and New Testaments in Clement of Rome*, 1973) are engaged in tracing the usage of specific Pauline texts in the early patristic writings. This study also interacts with the broader context of scholarship on Jews and Christians in this period where relevant (including the "Parting of the Ways" literature), such as the studies of Wilson (*Related Strangers: Jews and Christians, 70–170 C.E.*, 1995), Lieu (*Image and Reality: The Jews in the World of the Christians in the*

---

[34]Such studies include Graham Stanton, "The Law of Moses and the Law of Christ: Galatians 3.1–6.2," in *Paul and the Mosaic Law*, ed. J. D. G. Dunn, WUNT 89 (Tübingen: Mohr Siebeck 1996), 99-116; Kathy L. Gaca and L. L. Welborn, *Early Patristic Readings of Romans* (New York: T&T Clark, 2005); Andrew F. Gregory and Christopher M. Tuckett, eds., *The Reception of the New Testament in the Apostolic Fathers* (Oxford: Oxford University Press, 2005); Gregory and Tuckett, *Trajectories Through the New Testament and the Apostolic Fathers* (Oxford: Oxford University Press, 2005); David Rylaarsdam, "Interpretations of Paul in the Early Church," in *Rereading Paul Together: Protestant and Catholic Perspectives on Justification*, ed. David Aune (Grand Rapids, MI: Baker Academic, 2006), 146-68; James W. Aageson, *Paul, the Pastoral Epistles, and the Early Church* (Grand Rapids, MI: Baker Academic, 2007); Mikael Sundkvist, *The Christian Laws in Paul: Reading the Apostle with Early Greek Interpreters* (Joensuu: University of Joensuu, 2008); Pervo, *Making of Paul*; Kenneth Liljeström, *The Early Reception of Paul* (Helsinki: Finnish Exegetical Society, 2011); Brian John Arnold, "Justification One Hundred Years After Paul" (PhD diss., Southern Baptist Theological Seminary, 2013); Tobias Nicklas, Andreas Merkt, and Jozef Verheyden, *Ancient Perspectives on Paul* (Göttingen: Vandenhoeck & Ruprecht, 2013); Kirk, *Departure of an Apostle*, and James D. G. Dunn, *Neither Jew nor Greek: A Contested Identity*, vol. 3 of *Christianity in the Making* (Grand Rapids, MI: Eerdmans, 2015). See also the valuable earlier studies of René Kieffer, *Foi et justification à Antioche: Interprétation d'un conflit (Ga 2, 14-21)* (Paris: Cerf, 1982); Heikki Räisänen, *Paul and the Law*, WUNT 29 (Tübingen: Mohr Siebeck, 1983); and Robert B. Eno, "Some Patristic Views on the Relationship of Faith and Works in Justification," *Recherches Augustiniennes et Patristiques* 19 (1984): 3-27. While engaging different periods, this book holds correspondence with the work of Athanasios Despotis, *Die "New Perspective on Paul" und die griechisch-orthodoxe Paulusinterpretation* (St. Ottilien: EOS-Verl., 2014), which looks at the work of later Greek interpreters (such as Chrysostom) in relation to the new perspective on Paul. The recent volume on Tertullian and Paul (Todd D. Still and David E. Wilhite, eds., *Tertullian and Paul* [New York: Bloomsbury T&T Clark, 2013]) similarly falls outside this study's immediate scope. Many older evaluations of sources in this period (such as Eva Aleith, *Paulusverständnis in der alten Kirche* [Berlin: A. Töpelmann, 1937]; Victor Hasler, *Gesetz und Evangelium in der alten Kirche bis Origenes, eine auslegungsgeschichtliche Untersuchung* [Zürich: Gotthelf, 1953]; Thomas F. Torrance, *The Doctrine of Grace in the Apostolic Fathers* [Grand Rapids, MI: Eerdmans, 1959]; and Wilhelm Schneemelcher, "Paulus in der griechischen Kirche des zweiten Jahrhunderts," *ZKG* 75 [1964]: 1-20), are strongly colored by the presupposition of what is now termed the "old perspective," rendering their studies less useful in contexts where this viewpoint is itself under analysis.

Second Century, 1996), Horbury ("Jewish-Christian Relations in Barnabas and Justin Martyr," 1998), Becker and Reed (*The Ways That Never Parted: Jews and Christians in Late Antiquity and the Early Middle Ages*, 2003), Murray (*Playing a Jewish Game: Gentile Christian Judaizing in the First and Second Centuries CE*, 2004), Boyarin (*Border Lines: The Partition of Judaeo-Christianity*, 2004), Buell (*Why This New Race? Ethnic Reasoning in Early Christianity*, 2005), Dunn ("The Acts of Paul and the Pauline Legacy in the Second Century," 2006), Skarsaune and Hvalvik (*Jewish Believers in Jesus: The Early Centuries*, 2007), and Robinson (*Ignatius of Antioch and the Parting of the Ways: Early Jewish-Christian Relations*, 2009).

METHODOLOGY

A number of methodological difficulties present themselves in searching for the early patristic understanding of works of the law. The first relates to the phrase *works of the law*, which is not frequently used in second century sources, and within the scope of this study is found only in Irenaeus (*Haer.* 4.21.1). Second, even if this phrase were more commonly used, how would one know if the phenomena denoted by these words—which are quite general—matches with the phenomena that Paul is discussing in his epistles? Even with complete lexical overlap with Paul's phrase, it would only be on the basis of other considerations, such as contextual parallels and broader Pauline influence, that correspondence with the phenomena of works of the law could be identified with confidence.[35]

In light of these considerations, this study adopts a two-part strategy in seeking to identify the understanding of works of the law in the early patristic writings. First, it searches through these writings to examine the

---

[35]On the importance of context and situation in semantics, cf. Thiselton (citing Lyons): "Any meaningful linguistic unit, up to and including the complete utterance, has meaning in context. The context of the utterance is the situation in which it occurs. . . . The concept of 'situation' is fundamental for semantic statement. . . . Situation must be given equal weight with linguistic form in semantic theory" (John Lyons, *Structural Semantics* [Oxford: B. Blackwell, 1963], 23-24, in Anthony C. Thiselton, "Semantics and New Testament Interpretation," in *Thiselton on Hermeneutics: The Collected Works and New Essays of Anthony Thiselton* [Grand Rapids, MI: Eerdmans, 2006 {1977}], 191).

law and works in conflict in the context of discussions that are similar to Paul's own in Romans and Galatians. Following from the context of the Pauline passages, it views similar discussions as material that shows evidence of conflict with Jewish parties regarding the law and works, whether specific practices or works in general. It searches for "works of the law" as the points in conflict that are rejected as unnecessary from the Christian standpoint within these contexts.[36] While not necessary for a patristic source to be included in the study, discussion of themes that are common in the context of Paul's arguments—such as justification, a contrast with faith, the relation of Jews to Gentiles, the figure of Abraham, and reception of the Spirit—serve as secondary indicators that a search for works of the law is on the right track.

Second, this study categorizes this material based on each source's usage of Paul and specific works of the law passages, according greater weight to those sources that are more clearly dependent on the apostle's writings. Category A sources ("direct evidence") are those that contain similar discussions to Paul's own, demonstrate usage of Romans or Galatians, and make reference to works of the law, either by using the phrase directly or referring to verses in Paul that do so.[37] Category B sources ("supporting evidence") also contain similar discussions and usage of Paul's epistles, including Romans or Galatians, without making use of the phrase *works of the law* or referring to specific verses that do so. Category C sources ("circumstantial evidence") have only minimal or unclear Pauline influence and do not use the phrase *works of the law*, but contain disputes with Jewish parties that appear to be similar to Paul's own. Classifying in this manner allows for sources to be prioritized that most clearly draw on relevant Pauline material, while also not overlooking others that, though not

---

[36]The precise identity of the Jewish parties and interlocutors in Paul's conflicts is disputed; Jewish Christians or Judaizing Gentiles are most commonly identified in Galatians, while Paul's referent appears to be more general in Romans ("a Jew," Gal 2:17-18). Similar ambiguities are found in discussions with Jewish parties in early patristic sources, and while seeking to identify the interlocutors in each source as closely as possible, this book does not attempt to limit its analysis to only one type of Jewish opponent.

[37]The phrase ἔργα νόμου is found in six verses in Paul's epistles: two in Romans 3 (Rom 3:20, 28), one in Galatians 2 (three times in Gal 2:16), and three in Galatians 3 (Gal 3:2, 5, 10). Note as well the B-rated variant at Rom 9:32, though this verse is not searched for in this analysis.

carrying certain usage of verses discussing works of the law (or even clear
Pauline dependency), nevertheless may be valuable as secondary or circumstantial witnesses to the phenomena in question.

While more labor intensive than a simple index or database search, an
examination of the early patristic material along these lines carries two
distinct advantages. First, such an approach is able to better account for
the way in which influence from NT texts is found in second-century
writings, which often takes the form of paraphrase or restatement rather
than exact reproduction.[38] Second, this approach allows one to avoid
falling into lexical-conceptual equation (or word-concept fallacy), in
which the only recognized instances of a particular reality are those tied
to a specific word or phrase.[39]

---

[38]On the highly flexible practices of reference and citation in antiquity and among early patristic
writers, see the excellent overviews of John Whittaker, "The Value of Indirect Tradition in the
Establishment of Greek Philosophical Texts or the Art of Misquotation," in *Editing Greek and
Latin Texts: Papers Given at the Twenty-Third Annual Conference on Editorial Problems, University
of Toronto, 6–7 November 1987*, ed. John N. Grant (New York: AMS Press, 1989), 63-95; Sabrina
Inowlocki, *Eusebius and the Jewish Authors: His Citation Technique in an Apologetic Context*
(Leiden: Brill, 2006), 33-73; and Charles E. Hill, "'In These Very Words': Methods and Standards
of Literary Borrowing in the Second Century," in *The Early Text of the New Testament*, ed.
Charles E. Hill and Michael J. Kruger (New York: Oxford University Press, 2012), 263-81.
Cf. Gregory and Tuckett, *Reception of the New Testament*, 67: "Modern academics are trained to
quote and acknowledge their sources with scrupulous accuracy, but this was not the practice of
the ancient world. Ancient writers appear to have used even authoritative sources with a great
deal of freedom, and often to have referred to them from memory, so it would be unrealistic to
demand too high a degree of identity between a potential quotation or allusion and its source
before allowing that appropriation of that source had taken place." As Young summarizes
(building on the work of Richard B. Hays, *Echoes of Scripture in the Letters of Paul* [New Haven,
CT: Yale University Press, 1989]), "If allusive use of scripture is more evident in the New Testament than has usually been observed, that is even more the case in the second century" (Frances M. Young, *Biblical Exegesis and the Formation of Christian Culture* [Peabody, MA: Hendrickson, 2002], 131; similarly Charles E. Hill, *The Johannine Corpus in the Early Church* [Oxford:
Oxford University Press, 2004], 70). Furthermore, a source being precisely cited and explicitly
acknowledged by patristic authors does not necessarily correspond with it being held in greater
esteem, as van den Hoek notes in her study on Clement of Alexandria: "It is particularly striking that Clement acknowledges the works of his gnostic adversaries in such an accurate way,
naming author and book," which "stands in sharp contrast to his practice in borrowing from
authors to whom he apparently felt a kinship, such as Philo, Tatian, and Pantaenus" (Annewies
van den Hoek, "Techniques of Quotation in Clement of Alexandria: A View of Ancient Literary
Working Methods," *Vigiliae Christianae* 50 [1996]: 233). Indeed, "good old Saint Paul" is Clement's most frequently cited author "by quite a wide margin," and of Clement's 1,273 "Pauline
borrowings," only 24 percent of these explicitly name or refer to Paul, with the specific epistle
cited in only 9 percent of instances (227, 230).

[39]On the pitfalls of an exclusively lexical approach, cf. Silva's example of the subject of hypocrisy in
relation to Is 1:10-15; while a key passage on hypocrisy, without usage of the word itself, "the

The way in which sources in the first two categories can serve as witnesses to the works of the law discussed by Paul is relatively straightforward, with those in category A engaging directly with the Pauline verses in question, and those in category B making use of the Pauline epistles in which they are discussed. By contrast, category C sources can offer only circumstantial support without a certain tie to Paul's texts, but may still be valuable as possible witnesses to Paul's meaning in one of two ways: either as bearing witness to a commonly held concept of works of the law, or to Pauline teaching that has simply become assimilated as early Christian doctrine. The first possibility, that of a commonly held concept, follows from Paul's discussions of works of the law in Romans and Galatians, in which the topic is engaged without any introduction or definition of his terms. In Galatians, Paul's appeal of "we know" (Gal 2:16) to Peter over the place of works of the law presupposes a shared understanding of the subject under discussion, as does Paul's interrogation of the Galatians over their reception of the Spirit by faith or works of the law (Gal 3:2, 5). The possibility of a commonly held concept seems even stronger in Romans, where Paul's referent not only requires no definition, but is evidently comprehensible without Paul having ever visited the church.[40]

The second possibility draws on the recognition of the influence of Paul's teaching, which, much like Jesus' teaching in the NT epistles,[41] can be restated without attribution as early Christian doctrine by patristic

---

student suckled at the concordance would never find it" (Moisés Silva, *Biblical Words and Their Meaning* [Grand Rapids, MI: Zondervan, 1983], 27). See also Osborne on "word fallacy," "a failure to consider the concept as well as the word, that is, the other ways the biblical writers could say the same thing," which applies similarly to early Christian writings in general. "We never dare study only occurrences of the particular term if our purpose is to trace the theology behind a word or phrase," as "none of us ever uses the exact same words to describe our thoughts. Rather, we use synonyms or other phrases to depict our ideas. Therefore, a truly complete picture must cluster semantically related terms and phrases" (Grant R. Osborne, *The Hermeneutical Spiral* [Downers Grove, IL: IVP Academic, 2010], 92-93). On the distinction between words and concepts, cf. James Barr, *The Semantics of Biblical Language* (London: Oxford University Press, 1961), 206-7.

[40]Cf. James D. G. Dunn, *The New Perspective on Paul* (Grand Rapids, MI: Eerdmans, 2005), 127 on Paul's odd introduction of the phrase in Rom 3:20 at the end of the first section of his argument: "The implication must be that its meaning or reference was either well known or self-evident."

[41]Cf. e.g. the allusions to Jesus' sayings identified by Dunn in Romans, 1 Corinthians, 1 Thessalonians, James, and 1 Peter (*Jesus Remembered*, vol. 1 of *Christianity in the Making* [Grand Rapids, MI: Eerdmans, 2003], 181-84).

sources.[42] This can be witnessed in the case of the *Epistle to Diognetus* (which, though in category B, is useful as a certain illustration of this particular practice): while Paul is "clearly the most formative intellectual force in the theology of the apologist," the author never explicitly mentions Paul's name or his letters.[43] As Dunn observes, such omissions suggest that "Paul's teaching . . . had become so much meat and drink to mid-second century catechesis and preaching that no such reference was deemed necessary to give the teaching added weight," a judgment that can conceivably apply to earlier sources, as well as those for which Pauline dependency is less certain.[44] While these possibilities do not mean these sources can bear weight on their own—a patristic source could be engaged in similar conflicts with Jewish parties that are independent of both a theorized common concept, and of Pauline teaching turned into common doctrine—they do illustrate the potential value of such sources as circumstantial evidence. An example of a source within this category would be the Epistle of Barnabas: though not exhibiting clear Pauline influence, commentators agree that the epistle at least shares traditions in common with Paul, which could point to engagement with a commonly held concept of works of the law.

This study proceeds chronologically through the early patristic sources up to the writings of Irenaeus in the late second century. Each source's analysis begins with an introduction that identifies its background and context, including author, date, provenance, and audience. It then presents an evaluation of the source's knowledge and use of Paul, classifying it in one of these three categories. Among sources with clear Pauline influence (A- and B-level sources), a brief overview of the place of Paul in their theology and their character as Pauline interpreters is presented as well.[45] It then analyzes the relevant material in each source, identifying

---

[42]On such cases, cf. Lindemann, *Paulus im ältesten Christentum*, 18.

[43]Michael F. Bird, "The Reception of Paul in the Epistle to Diognetus," in *Paul and the Second Century*, ed. Michael F. Bird and Joseph R. Dodson (London: T&T Clark 2011), 87.

[44]Dunn, *Neither Jew nor Greek*, 699. See also Theophilus of Antioch's *Apologia ad Autolycum* (ca. 180), which likewise never mentions Paul, and which attributes teachings from Rom 13 and 1 Tim 2 to "the divine word" that speaks similarly through the law and the prophets (*Autol.* 3.9-14).

[45]This study's focus on passages from the undisputed texts of Romans and Galatians means that broader questions regarding the authorship of Pauline texts are not engaged in depth here; when

the law and works in question, the significance of practicing these works, and the reasons they are rejected as unnecessary for the Christian. These sources are then grouped according to their categories in the final analysis in the conclusion, with primary weight granted to A-level sources (and so on).

REFERENCES AND TERMINOLOGY

In the foreword to Barnett's 1941 *Paul Becomes a Literary Influence*, E. J. Goodspeed writes that "no method in literary study is more objective or more fruitful than the comparison of one work with another to determine the question of literary indebtedness—which one shows acquaintance with the other, use of it, and dependence upon it."[46] While not entirely without basis, a survey of studies that trace literary dependence in patristic sources shows Goodspeed's estimation of the method's objectivity to be perhaps overly optimistic. Instead of being purely objective, such studies tend to map onto an individual scholar's broader ideas regarding the development of early Christianity (with Barnett's study being a clear example, dating various writings and tracing supposed influence in accordance with a broader hypothesized narrative of Paul's rise, fall, and return to popularity). Further, even in instances where usage of a Pauline text by a later author seems apparent, it is possible that this may be due to having heard the text read in congregations (rather than direct personal interaction with the text), oral traditions concerning Paul's teachings, or unknown intermediate sources (whether derived from Paul or shared with Paul).[47]

---

used in this study, "Pauline" describes the texts carrying Paul's name as author that the early church generally received as such, including disputed texts in contemporary scholarship (such as Ephesians and the Pastorals). For treatment of this term, cf. similarly White, *Remembering Paul*, 7n21, 12-13; Jennifer R. Strawbridge, *The Pauline Effect: The Use of the Pauline Epistles by Early Christian Writers* (Berlin: De Gruyter, 2015), 1n2.

[46] Albert Barnett, *Paul Becomes a Literary Influence* (Chicago: University of Chicago Press, 1941), vii.

[47] Cf. Lindemann, *Paulus im ältesten Christentum*, 18; Kirk, *Departure of an Apostle*, 28-30. See also David Lincicum, "Learning Scripture in the School of Paul: From Ephesians to Justin," in *The Early Reception of Paul*, ed. Kenneth Liljeström (Helsinki: Finnish Exegetical Society, 2011), 149-50 on our lack of knowledge regarding intermediate sources (such as *testimonia* collections) and our ignorance of compositional methods. However, note also Frances M. Young, *Biblical Exegesis and the Formation of Christian Culture* (Peabody, MA: Hendrickson, 2002), 133, who observes how the allusive manner of apparent textual references to the NT in the early patristic

While such considerations must temper confidence in our ability to map literary dependency and to know the precise manner in which teaching is transmitted in this period, Goodspeed nevertheless remains correct that this task is a fruitful one for interpretation, even if this tracing deals only in probabilities. In identifying the usage of Pauline texts in early patristic sources, this study relies on the wisdom found in a multitude of counselors, and engages extensively with both subject-specific and broader studies of reception for each source. For instances where usage is in dispute between studies, this study weighs arguments and makes judgments in accordance with standard (though admittedly subjective) criteria of lexical overlap, theological correspondence, and broader Pauline influence.[48] This task is as much an art as a science; as Hays notes in his classic study on this subject, identifying intertextuality "is less a matter of method than of sensibility . . . of tuning our ears to the internal resonances of the biblical text"—and here patristic texts as well.[49]

The terminology employed in tracing the usage of NT texts in later Christian writings is not currently standardized between various studies, with editions often including lists of references that do not differentiate between citations and possible allusions, and undefined terms carrying potentially different meanings between authors. Because this book engages heavily with studies that make use of terminology in this sometimes-ambiguous manner, it is not possible for all instances of each term to be used uniformly. In instances where the language is my own, the terminology is used in accordance with the simplified definitions given by Strawbridge in her study within this same period.[50] This divides citation types into two main categories: "reference" and "possible reference."

---

writings is consistent with long-standing literary conventions, meaning that theories regarding transmission via oral tradition (e.g., Helmut Koester, *Synoptische Uberlieferung bei den apostolischen Vätern* [Berlin: Akademie-Verlag Koester, 1957]) are not strictly necessary.

[48]On criteria in tracing early patristic NT references, cf. Gregory and Tuckett, *Reception of the New Testament*, 61-82; on Paul in particular, cf. Lindemann, *Paulus im ältesten Christentum*, 15-19. See similarly Hill, *Johannine Corpus in the Early Church*, 70, and the seven guidelines (Availability, Volume, Recurrence, Thematic Coherence, Historical Plausibility, History of Interpretation, Satisfaction) in Hays's study (*Echoes of Scripture*, 29-32).

[49]Hays, *Echoes of Scripture*, 21.

[50]Strawbridge, *Pauline Effect*, 21, 182-85.

A "reference" is "what many scholars might define as a quotation, direct attribution, or paraphrase," which has "a considerable degree of literality" but "need not be verbatim in the modern sense."[51] Within this category of "reference," I follow Bird in describing instances as either citation ("a *direct* and deliberate lifting of one text into another," often with a citation formula) or allusion (which "makes *indirect* extratextual references by activating awareness of a second text through its particular choice of subject, language and grammar" and "requires knowledge of a second text . . . in order to be discernible").[52] For this study, both are "references" in the sense of there being a high degree of confidence in dependency on the texts in question. The second category, "possible reference," refers to "a phrase or series of words where similarities between the Pauline passage and early Christian texts can be detected" in their general thematic coherence, but where "neither the context nor the content of the surrounding text allows certainty about whether it is a clear reference to and dependent on Pauline material."[53] "Possible references" correspond with what studies commonly identify as "echoes" or "reminiscences," and often "have few literal correspondences to the Pauline texts listed; they instead allude to the text in theme, thought, or through a few words."[54] Both categories involve subjective judgments, and decisions in individual cases are made in conversation with other commentators on each text.

SCOPE AND OUTLINE

This study proceeds in part two to an overview of the old and new perspectives on works of the law. For the old perspective, it examines the views of Martin Luther and John Calvin, as well as two influential modern representatives of the Lutheran and Reformed traditions, Rudolph Bultmann and Douglas Moo. For the new perspective, the views of E. P. Sanders, James Dunn, and N. T. Wright are examined. Part three presents an investigation of works of the law in the early patristic writings that

---

[51]Strawbridge, *Pauline Effect*, 183; cf. van den Hoek, "Techniques of Quotation," 229.
[52]Bird, "Reception of Paul," 74 (italics original); see similarly Gregory and Tuckett, *Reception of the New Testament*, 64-65; Lindemann, *Paulus im ältesten Christentum*, 17-18.
[53]Strawbridge, *Pauline Effect*, 184.
[54]Strawbridge, *Pauline Effect*, 184.

followed Paul within a period of living memory, stretching from the Didache to Irenaeus. Part four presents a synthesis of the study's findings on these early perspectives, as well as a brief overview of how these lines of interpretation continue up to Origen, the author of the earliest extant commentary on Romans. This is followed by an assessment of how these early perspectives relate to the views espoused by the old and new perspectives, and implications for what their collective witness suggests about Paul's own meaning.

In evaluating early patristic writings, this study follows the traditional categorical distinction between these and the writings that form the New Testament. While at least in some ways artificial, this distinction does mark a real separation in disciplines that has led to these sources being largely unexamined in contemporary debates on this issue, and it is this particular gap this study seeks to fill. Categorizing non-"orthodox" parties (such as Marcion and the Gnostics) in relation to patristics is a perennial difficulty, as one wishes to do justice to the significance of these sources without artificially homogenizing them into a broader ecclesial category, particularly in instances where their own self-understanding is one of distinction from the mainstream church.[55] These difficulties are often compounded in this period by a lack of sources, with much of our evidence coming from reports on their views by later heresiologists rather than their own writings. This study balances these considerations by attempting to reconstruct in an excursus the views of three parties— the Ebionites, Marcion, and the Gnostic Ptolemy—that appear to hold the most relevant parallels with Paul's works of the law debates, while recognizing that the fragmentary and often mirror-read nature of the evidence means these reconstructions must remain provisional.[56]

---

[55]This appears to be the case for the three parties engaged here: the Ebionites seem to hold that only ethnic Israelites (τοὺς σαρκίνους Ἰσραηλίτας) are included in the people of God (*Princ.* 4.3.8); Marcion fights against a Judaizing conspiracy that has overtaken "the whole main body of Christendom" (*Marc.* 1.20; cf. Adolf von Harnack, *Marcion: The Gospel of the Alien God*, trans. Lyle D. Bierma and John E. Steely [Durham, NC: Labyrinth Press, 1990 {1921}], 23); and Ptolemy appears to rely on a secret line of apostolic doctrine in contrast with the "ecclesiastic" masses (*Haer.* 3.15.1-2; *Pan.* 33.3.1, 33.7.9).

[56]On this task, cf. John M. G. Barclay, "Mirror-Reading a Polemical Letter: Galatians as a Test Case," *Journal for the Study of the New Testament* 10 (1987): 73-93.

This study also includes a short excursus on three second-century writings—the Preaching of Peter, Aristo of Pella's *Dialogue of Jason and Papiscus*, and the Acts of Paul—which, though only extant in small fragments, nonetheless merit analysis due to their early dates and relevant material.

With respect to limitations of scope, this study focuses its analysis on the early patristic sources and their relation to the old and new perspectives, and does not engage in detailed analysis in related areas (such as exegetical analysis of Romans and Galatians, possible reception of these debates in NT texts, correspondence in Second Temple Jewish sources, and wider history of reception).[57] While these early patristic sources are targeted as representing a distinct lacuna in scholarship on this topic, the absence of these other areas from the present study does not reflect an

---

[57]Volumes of literature can be produced for detailed exegesis of the NT texts. For a sampling of recent literature in other areas, see e.g. I. H. Marshall, "Salvation, Grace and Works in the Later Writings in the Pauline Corpus," *New Testament Studies* 42 (3): 339-58; James D. G. Dunn, "Whatever Happened to 'Works of the Law,'" in *Epitoayto*, ed. J. Kerkovsky (Praha: Mlyn, 1998), 107-20; Friedrich Avemarie, "Die Werke des Gesetzes im Spiegel des Jakobusbriefs: A Very Old Perspective on Paul," *ZTK* 98 (2001): 282-309; Daniel Marguerat, "Paul après Paul: une histoire de réception," *New Testament Studies* 54 (1997); Michael F. Bird and Joel Willitts, eds, *Paul and the Gospels: Christologies, Conflicts, and Convergences* (London: T&T Clark, 2011); David P. Moessner et al., *Paul and the Heritage of Israel*, (London: T&T Clark, 2012) on possible NT reception; Michael Bachmann, "4QMMT und Galaterbrief, התורה מעשי und ΕΡΓΑ ΝΟΜΟΥ," *Zeitschrift für die Neutestamentliche Wissenschaft und die Kunde der Älteren Kirche* 89 (1998): 91-113; D. A. Carson, Peter Thomas O'Brien, and Mark A. Seifrid, eds., *Justification and Variegated Nomism*, 2 vols. (Grand Rapids, MI: Baker Academic, 2001); Simon J. Gathercole, "A Law unto Themselves: The Gentiles in Romans 2.14-15 Revisited," *Journal for the Study of the New Testament* 24 (2002): 27-49; N. T. Wright, "Justification and Eschatology in Paul and Qumran: Romans and 4QMMT," in *History and Exegesis: New Testament essays in honor of Dr. E. Earle Ellis for his 80th birthday*, ed. Sang-Won Son (New York: T&T Clark, 2006), 104-32; Chris VanLandingham, *Judgment and Justification in Early Judaism and the Apostle Paul* (Peabody, MA: Hendrickson, 2006); Jacqueline de Roo, "*Works of the Law" at Qumran and in Paul* (Sheffield, UK: Sheffield Phoenix Press, 2007); Paul M. Sprinkle, *Paul and Judaism Revisited: A Study of Divine and Human Agency in Salvation* (Downers Grove, IL: IVP Academic, 2013); Ben C. Blackwell, John K. Goodrich, and Jason Maston, eds., *Reading Romans in Context: Paul and Second Temple Judaism* (Grand Rapids, MI: Zondervan, 2015) on Second Temple Jewish correspondence; and Robert Morgan, *Romans* (Sheffield, UK: Sheffield Academic Press, 1997); Stephen Westerholm, *Perspectives Old and New on Paul: The "Lutheran" Paul and His Critics* (Grand Rapids, MI: Eerdmans, 2004); Alister E. McGrath, *Iustitia Dei: A History of the Christian Doctrine of Justification*, 3rd ed. (Cambridge: Cambridge University Press, 2005); Mark Reasoner, *Romans in Full Circle: A History of Interpretation* (Louisville, KY: Westminster John Knox Press, 2005); John Riches, *Galatians Through the Centuries* (Oxford: Blackwell, 2007); Thomas Scheck, *Origen and the History of Justification: The Legacy of Origen's Commentary on Romans* (Notre Dame, IN: University of Notre Dame Press, 2008) for wider history of reception.

undervaluing of their importance for this subject.[58] In focusing on the early understanding of works of the law, this study engages broader questions of Pauline reception, memory, and imaging in this period only in so far as they relate to this particular subject.[59] With regards to the sources engaged, this study seeks to avoid admitting false positives into its analysis by only engaging contexts that, like Paul's discussions in Romans and Galatians, show evidence of conflict with Jewish parties regarding the law or works.[60] This means that texts such as 1 Clement and Polycarp's *Philippians* are not evaluated, which, though containing general material on justification, salvation, and works, show no evidence of conflict with Jews or dispute over the law.[61] It merits noting that the principle found in passages like 1 Clement 32.3-4 regarding the purely gracious nature of God's acceptance does not represent a point in

---

[58]On this lacuna of early NT reception more generally, cf. the comments of Meeks: "Practically speaking, we [New Testament scholars] have done rather well with the prehistory of texts, considerably less well with the history of their later reception and effects. The Wirkungsgeschichte of the NT—and of those non-canonical texts in its penumbra about which we have come to know so much more in recent years—remains a vast field still crying out to be explored in depth" (Wayne Meeks, "Why Study the New Testament?," *New Testament Studies* 51 [2005]: 165).

[59]In addition to Lindemann and Dassmann, cf. e.g. Donald N. Penny, "The Pseudo-Pauline Letters of the First Two Centuries" (PhD diss., Emory University, 1979); Anthony J. Blasi, *Making Charisma: The Social Construction of Paul's Public Image* (New Brunswick, NJ: Transaction Publishers, 1991); and the recent volume of Pervo, *Making of Paul*, on Pauline images in the second century. Note as well the earlier studies (largely focusing on NT reception) of C. K. Barrett, "Pauline Controversies in the Post-Pauline Period," *New Testament Studies* 20 (1974): 229-45; and Martinus C. de Boer, "Images of Paul in the Post-apostolic Period," *Catholic Biblical Quarterly* 42 (1980): 359-80. As White notes, such studies often rely on a seven-letter collection of Pauline *Hauptbriefe* as an Archimedean point for determining their "real" Paul, without recognizing that decisions for what constitutes this Paul "were often (if not always) made out of theological preference" within nineteenth-century German Protestant scholarship, making the Archimedean point itself in need of assessment (cf. White, *Remembering Paul*, 65-66). It bears noting that in identifying the early church as adding the deutero-Paulines to create for themselves a "safe" Paul, nineteenth-century exegetes largely failed to recognize the way in which their excising of these writings performed precisely the same function, leaving a two-dimensional apostle who would repeat favorite themes without troubling them about less important matters (such as ecclesiology); the "safe" Paul of one party can be a danger to the next.

[60]For old and new perspective agreement on this as the context of Paul's discussions, cf. e.g. Rudolf Bultmann, *Theology of the New Testament*, trans. Kendrick Grobel, 2 vols. (London: SCM, 1952), 1:280; Dunn, *New Perspective on Paul*, 126.

[61]As Grant notes, 1 Clement contains "no criticism of Judaism whatsoever," and Polycarp's epistle similarly bears witness to no such conflicts (Robert M. Grant, *The Apostolic Fathers: Introduction*, vol. 1 of *The Apostolic Fathers: A New Translation and Commentary* [New York: Thomas Nelson 1964], 97). On 1 Clement, cf. similarly Bultmann, *Theology of the New Testament*.

contention between old and new perspectives, much as it is a point of ecumenical agreement more broadly.[62] It remains to be seen in this study whether and to what degree such a principle is a point of conflict with Jewish parties in this period, and on these questions 1 Clement and Polycarp's *Philippians* are not able to offer any judgment.[63]

Finally, a brief note on terminology in relation to this book's title and scope. The title of this book is *Paul's "Works of the Law" in the Perspective of Second-Century Reception*, and though the sources engaged here are regularly categorized as belonging to the second century, debate will be found around the margins. While the astute reader will note that I suspect the first two sources may actually originate from the late first century, the evidence is so tentative either way that it does not seem a misnomer to have them grouped under the *Second Century* title.

It is customary to offer a brief summary of a study's conclusions at the outset, and the results of this analysis are surprising in light of the labels used in contemporary debates. While not uniform, the early perspectives on works of the law are found to be largely cohesive, with the Mosaic law being the law in question, and the specific points in conflict including the works of circumcision, Sabbath, regulations regarding food, sacrifices, observance of Jewish feasts and fasts, and a focus on the temple and Jerusalem. The practice of these works represents an identification with the Jewish people and the old covenant, as well as with humanity's juvenile state before Christ's advent. These works are opposed for a

---

[62]See, for example, the recent Lutheran-Catholic document *From Conflict to Communion*: "Even in the sixteenth century, there was a significant convergence between Lutheran and Catholic positions concerning the need for God's mercy and humans' inability to attain salvation by their own efforts. The Council of Trent clearly taught that the sinner cannot be justified either by the law or by human effort, anathematizing anyone who said that 'man can be justified before God by his own works which are done either by his own natural powers, or through the teaching of the Law, and without divine grace through Christ Jesus'" (Karlheinz Diez and Eero Huovinen, *From Conflict to Communion: Lutheran-Catholic Common Commemoration of the Reformation in 2017* [Leipzig: Evangelische Verlagsanstalt, 2013], 48).

[63]This judgment is reinforced by the recognition that the relevant passages in these epistles appear to be drawing from sources besides Romans and Galatians; as Hagner notes, 1 Clem. 32.3 bears closest resemblance to Titus 3:5 (D. A. Hagner, *The Use of the Old and New Testaments in Clement of Rome* [Leiden: Brill, 1973], 236), and Pol. *Phil*. 1.3 appears to be a citation of Eph 2:8. Other passages within this category include Gospel of Thomas 53 (which, while discussing the value of physical versus spiritual circumcision, does so outside a context of dispute with the Jews), and the passages on justification by grace in Odes Sol. 17.2-4; 25.12; 29.5-6.

variety of reasons, the most prominent of which are the arrival of Christ's law in the new covenant; the prophetic witness of Scripture; the universal scope of the new covenant; the heart transformation produced by Christ, which renders the Mosaic laws unnecessary; and the examples of Abraham and the righteous patriarchs, who were similarly justified apart from these practices. With respect to the works themselves and the significance of practicing them, the so-called new perspective is found to correspond quite closely with these second-century perspectives, while the old perspective lacks similar parallels; in early conflicts with Jewish parties, there is no evidence of Christian objections to a Jewish insistence on good works, nor are Jews critiqued for seeking to earn their salvation. This does not amount to a complete endorsement of the new perspective from these early witnesses, however. Among the new perspective writers, only Wright's reasoning for why these works are rejected aligns substantially with the patristic witnesses, and portions of the old perspective's anthropological reasoning for rejecting these works carries at least some correspondence with these early perspectives. Finally, in light of the proximity of these sources to Paul, their evident reliance on his writings, and the coherence of their testimony, these early perspectives would suggest that Paul rejects these works of the Torah not fundamentally for experiential reasons, nor because they are socially exclusive, but because a promised new law and covenant of universal scope have come in Christ.

PART II

OLD AND NEW PERSPECTIVES ON WORKS OF THE LAW

□

According to some New Perspective scholars, "works of the law"
refer to Sabbath observance, food laws, and circumcision—those things
that identified Jews. According to the Old Perspective, "works of the law"
represents the Judaizers' attempt to secure salvation through moral effort.[1]

J. V. FESKO, "OLD AND NEW PERSPECTIVES ON PAUL:
A THIRD WAY?"

---

[1]Fesko, J. V. "Old and New Perspectives on Paul: A Third Way?" *The Gospel Coalition*, January 6, 2016, www.thegospelcoalition.org/reviews/old-and-new-perspectives-on-paul-a-third-way/.

2

THE OLD PERSPECTIVE ON WORKS OF THE LAW

◘

THIS SECTION PRESENTS an introduction to the views of major figures that make up the old and new perspectives on works of the law. These overviews provide a synthesis of each figure's exegesis and theological reasoning on works of the law, showing both the common features that are shared within each perspective and the distinctive emphases found in each figure's reading of Paul.[1]

This chapter presents the views of the sixteenth-century reformers Martin Luther and John Calvin, as well as two modern representatives of their respective theological traditions, Rudolph Bultmann and Douglas Moo.

MARTIN LUTHER

Our introduction to the old perspective on works of the law begins with Martin Luther (1483–1546), the sixteenth-century reformer whose quest to find a gracious God led to his own climactic apprehension of the meaning of justification apart from works of the law, and sparked a religious and political revolution within Western Christendom.

---

[1]To provide a sense of these characteristic features, the third sections in particular (on opposition to works of the law) present the main arguments that are foregrounded in each scholar's reasoning, rather than simply providing a list of arguments noted in their writings. To take one example, while all these figures note the experiences of Christians as playing some role in arguments against observing the works of the law, it is only Sanders who foregrounds this category as providing the fundamental rationale for why Paul rejects these works.

Meaning: What works of what law? "The true meaning of Christianity," according to Martin Luther, is the teaching that "we are justified by faith in Christ, not by the works of the Law"[2]—and from Luther's standpoint, the church is indeed built "by this doctrine alone."[3] For Luther, while the Mosaic law serves as the inciting referent in Paul's controversy over works of the law,[4] the real issue Paul is addressing is the value of human actions in general in justification as opposed to the "merely passive" righteousness that comes by faith in Christ.[5] As a result, Luther holds that "these words, 'works of the Law,' are to be taken in the broadest possible sense," whether "the Civil Law, the Ceremonial Law, or the Decalogue."[6] Indeed, even love for God belongs in this category, for "even if you were to do the work of the Law, according to the commandment, 'You shall love the Lord your God with all your heart, etc.' (Matt 22:37), you still would not be justified in the sight of God; for a man is not justified by works of the Law."[7] These works include those performed both before and following justification,[8] and are not limited to the Mosaic law. As Luther writes, "many good men even among the pagans—such as Xenophon, Aristides, Fabius, Cicero, Pomponius Atticus, etc.—performed the works of the Law and accomplished great things."[9] Their laudable qualities like integrity and veracity were "very fine virtues and very beautiful works of the Law; but these men were not justified by these works."[10] Luther frequently contrasts his

---

[2]*LW* 26.136 (Jaroslav Pelikan and Helmut L. Lehmann, eds. *Luther's Works* [St. Louis: Concordia Publishing House, 1986 {1955}]). This survey makes primary reference to Luther's *Lectures on Galatians*, which provide the most expansive treatment of Luther's fully-formed thought on the issue, and which is one of the handful of writings that Luther identified as his "best work" (*WA* 5:323, no. 5694).

[3]*LW* 26.10.

[4]See e.g. *LW* 26.202-12.

[5]*LW* 26.4.

[6]*LW* 26.122. For Luther's objections to distinguishing between parts of the law, see his writings against Karlstadt (*LW* 40.92-94).

[7]*LW* 26.122. Cf. *LW* 26.147: "For if faith justifies only with love, then Paul's argument is completely false; for he says clearly that a man is not justified by works of the Law, but alone by faith in Jesus Christ."

[8]See e.g. *LW* 26.124: "After justification . . . Peter, Paul, and all other Christians have done and still do the works of the Law; but they are not justified by them either."

[9]*LW* 26.123. For "Law" in the OT as extending beyond the Mosaic legislation, cf. e.g. *LW* 26.138: "In addition, it was the Law when Abraham was commanded to sacrifice his son Isaac."

[10]*LW* 26.123-24. For the works of the law as virtues, see also *Bondage of the Will*, where works of the law are synonymous with practicing "moral righteousness" (*LW* 33.263).

position with that of Origen and Jerome, who misled the church into thinking that Paul was speaking of only the ceremonies of the Jewish law.[11] Rather, with the phrase *works of the law*, "Paul speaks of the law simply and in a total sense, but especially about the moral law or the decalogue,"[12] so as to reject "everything that can be done on the basis of the Law, whether by divine power or by human."[13] The rejection of works of the law is thus a "universal principle": "Enlarge on this by running through all the stations of life as follows: 'Therefore a monk shall not be justified by his order, a nun by her chastity, a citizen by his uprightness, a prince by his generosity, etc.'"[14] In short, Luther understands works of the law as any and all actions that one might perform to earn favor with God.

Significance: What does the practice of these works signify? For Luther, it is the significance of practicing the works of the law—man's attempt "to merit grace by his own righteousness" and thus attain his own justification—that is at the heart of Paul's disputes, and renders these works so pernicious.[15] According to Luther, to focus on the specific works of the law themselves (rather than their function) was the dreadful error that Jerome fell into:

> Therefore we must consider carefully what Paul has in mind, lest we speak foolishly, as Jerome did when he imagined that the issue under debate was the practice itself. In this he was wrong. *For the issue is not whether wood is wood or stone is stone, but what is attached to them, that is, how these things are used:* whether this wood is God, whether divinity resides in this stone. To this we answer that wood is wood, as Paul says that "neither circumcision counts for anything nor uncircumcision" (1 Cor. 7:19). But to attach righteousness, reverence, confidence in salvation, and the fear of death to such things is to attribute divinity to ceremonies.[16]

---

[11]See e.g. *LW* 26.121, 180, 275; *LW* 33.258.

[12]"Theses Concerning Faith and Law," on Rom 3:28, *LW* 34.114.

[13]*LW* 26.122. There appears to be tension between this definition and Luther's earlier 1522 preface to Romans (reprinted in 1546), where he defines the works of the law as "everything that one does, or can do, toward keeping the law of his own free will or by his own powers" (*LW* 35.367).

[14]*LW* 26.141; cf. *LW* 26.137.

[15]*LW* 26.180; cf. *LW* 26.119.

[16]*LW* 26.92, italics mine.

Luther explains that the problem with works of the law is not the works themselves—which can indeed be anything at all—and rather what they are used for. Luther identifies this function as "trying to merit grace,"[17] so as to establish a "righteousness of works" in place of Christ's righteousness.[18] This is clearly seen in Luther's comments on Galatians 5:4:

> Here Paul expounds himself by showing that he is not speaking simply about the Law or about the act of circumcision but about *the confidence or presumption of justification through it*, as though he were saying: "I do not condemn circumcision or the Law as such. I am permitted to eat, drink, and associate with Jews in accordance with the Law; I am permitted to circumcise Timothy, etc. What I do condemn is the desire to be justified through the Law, as though Christ had not yet come or as though, while present, He were not able to justify by Himself. This is being severed from Christ."[19]

As Luther here illustrates, the core issue is not circumcision or any other particular practice, but rather the desire to be justified though them. According to Luther, Paul's opponents—and his—are "unwilling to accept grace and eternal life from [God] freely," and rather "want to earn it by their own works."[20] For Luther, it is this reliance on one's own works for justification, rather than something essential to the law or works themselves, that captures the significance of works of the law, and leads to the reasons they must be rejected.

Opposition: Why are these works not necessary for the Christian? Though Luther presents a wide array of arguments against works of the law, the reformer understands Paul as fundamentally opposing such works for a set of three closely related reasons. The first of these is human inability: no one can do any amount of works so as to be justified before God, and thus any attempt to rely on them is futile. As Luther writes, "To keep the Law is to do what is commanded in the Law not only in appearance but in the Spirit, that is, truly and perfectly. But

---

[17] *LW* 26.126. Cf. *LW* 26.347: "This was why so many works were thought up—to merit grace and the forgiveness of sins."
[18] See e.g. *LW* 26.273.
[19] *LW* 27.16; italics mine. Cf. *LW* 26.118.
[20] *LW* 26.127.

where can we find someone who keeps the Law this way?"[21] Humanity's sinful condition is such that this is completely impossible, as the law reveals, saying, "You are an evil tree. Therefore everything you think, speak, or do is opposed to God. Hence you cannot deserve grace by your works. But if you try to do so, you make the bad even worse; for since you are an evil tree, you cannot produce anything except evil fruits, that is, sins."[22] As a result, humanity's attempt to merit grace to be justified "is trying to placate God with sins, which is nothing but heaping sins on sins, making fun of God, and provoking His wrath."[23] This remains the case following justification as well, as works performed under grace are imperfect due to the believer's still-imperfect nature, and are only accepted as perfect on account of Christ.[24] Any works performed by imperfect humanity, then, can never bring about justification before God, and must therefore be cast away so that one can rely instead on Christ through faith.

Second is what Luther identifies as an incorrect understanding of the necessity of works for salvation. According to Luther, while "God has various ordinances, laws, styles of life, and forms of worship in the world . . . these do not achieve anything to merit grace or attain eternal life." Rather, "as many as are justified . . . are justified, not on account of their observance of human or divine Law but on account of Christ, who has abrogated all laws everywhere."[25] Interestingly, Luther sees the rejection of circumcision as following from this incorrect understanding, writing that "if the believing Jews at [Paul's] time had observed the Law and circumcision under the condition permitted by the apostles, Judaism would have remained standing until now, and the whole world would have accepted the ceremonies of the Jews."[26] Their incorrect understanding of the role of such works, however, required them to be rejected: "because they insisted on the Law and circumcision as

---

[21]*LW* 26.253.
[22]*LW* 26.126.
[23]*LW* 26.126.
[24]Cf. *LW* 26.274.
[25]*LW* 26.355.
[26]*LW* 26.105.

something necessary for salvation and constructed an act of worship and some sort of god out of it, God could not stand for it," and thus "threw over the temple, the Law, the worship, and the holy city of Jerusalem, so that not one stone was left on another."[27] As Luther similarly writes in relation to Galatians 2:15, the problem is "not that the Law is wicked or damnable; for the Law, circumcision, worship, etc., are not condemned for their inability to justify." Rather, "Paul inveighs against them because the false apostles maintained that by the sheer performance of these acts, without faith, men are justified and saved."[28] This faulty understanding of works in relation to justification leads to an idolatry whereby the works become "some sort of god," which for Luther must be rejected in favor of Christ.

Third, and most importantly for Luther, not only do works hold the potential to become idols, but humanity's attempt to justify itself by works effectively displaces Christ and places itself in the role of savior, thus constituting a most terrible self-idolatry.[29] As Luther writes, "because my sins are so grave, so real, so great, so infinite, so horrible, and so invincible that my righteousness does me no good but rather puts me at a disadvantage before God, therefore Christ, the Son of God, was given into death for my sins, to abolish them and thus to save all men who believe."[30] Since it is God alone who can save us, any attempt to justify ourselves represents not just a denial of Christ, but effectively claims the role of God for our own. As Luther describes in commenting on Galatians 3:10, one who relies on works of the law

> refuses to be merely passive matter but wants actively to accomplish the
> things that it should patiently permit God to accomplish in it and should
> accept from Him. And so it makes itself the creator and the justifier through
> its own works. . . . Therefore no one can describe in words how horrible and
> dreadful a thing it is to seek righteousness apart from the blessing, in the Law

---

[27] *LW* 26.105.

[28] *LW* 26.122. Luther goes on to explain that even with faith, these works are futile, since faith alone justifies.

[29] The close link between these three reasons can be observed in Luther's reading of passages such as Gal 3:13 (*LW* 26:283).

[30] *LW* 26.36.

and in works. For this is the abomination standing in the holy place
(Matt. 24:15), which denies God and establishes a creature in the place of
the Creator.[31]

In Luther's perspective, this idolatrous self-reliance is the most abhorrent
quality of practicing works of the law, and represents the most fundamental reason why they must be rejected.

For Luther, this absolute contrast between God saving us through
Christ and humanity saving itself is the same as the absolute contrast
between faith and works. "To rely on the Law or on the works of the Law
and to be a man of faith are altogether contrary," as contrary "as the devil
and God,"[32] since those relying on works "deny faith and try to bless
themselves by their own works, that is, to justify themselves, to set themselves free from sin and death, to overcome the devil, and to capture
heaven by force—which is to deny God and to set oneself up in place of
God."[33] This arrogation of Christ's role in trying to save ourselves by
works of the law is fulfillment of his prophecy that "many will come in
My name, saying: 'I am the Christ'" (Mt 24:5).[34] As Luther summarizes,
those who rely on works of the law fall not only for the idolatry of works,
but turn themselves into idols:

> Whoever seeks righteousness apart from faith and through works denies
> God and makes himself into God. This is what he thinks: "If I do this work,
> I shall be righteous. I shall be the victor over sin, death, the devil, the wrath
> of God, and hell; and I shall attain eternal life." Now what is this, I ask you,
> but to arrogate to oneself a work that belongs to God alone, and to show
> that one is God? Therefore it is easy for us to prophesy and to judge with
> certainty about all those who are outside the faith that they are not only
> idolaters but idols who deny God and set themselves up in place of God
> (2 Thess. 2:4).[35]

Along with these reasons, Luther recognizes a handful of other arguments against works of the law, including the experiences of Christians

---

[31]*LW* 26.259.
[32]*LW* 26.253.
[33]*LW* 26.257.
[34]*LW* 26.258-59.
[35]*LW* 26.258.

in receiving the Spirit apart from the law,[36] Christ's identity as the abolisher of the law rather than a new lawgiver,[37] and the nature of the law as opposed to faith.[38] However, for Luther, it is these three reasons—the inability of humans to keep the law, an idolatrous misunderstanding of works as being able to justify, and the even worse idolatry of placing one's self in the role of savior—that constitute the primary basis for Paul's rejection of the works of the law.

JOHN CALVIN

Equally important for defining the old perspective on works of the law are the views of John Calvin (1509–1564), the second-generation reformer whose writings would become the primary theological lens for biblical interpretation within the Reformed tradition.

Meaning: What works of what law? John Calvin's understanding of the meaning of works of the law closely accords with that of Martin Luther. While holding that the inciting matters for Paul's conflict are the "ceremonies" of the Jewish law,[39] Calvin nevertheless sees these particular issues as the tip of an iceberg in a discussion that includes all possible meritorious works, whether those of the Jewish law or otherwise.[40] Calvin describes his position in contrast to earlier interpreters in his commentary on Romans, noting Chrysostom's, Origen's, and Jerome's view that Paul is referring to the ceremonial aspect of the Jewish law,[41] and Augustine's understanding that Paul rejects all works done prior to receiving the grace of regeneration (but not those done by believers

---

[36]Cf. *LW* 26.212.

[37]Cf. *LW* 26.150, 177-78, 347.

[38]See e.g. *LW* 26.113: "For nothing is more hostile to faith than the Law and reason; nor can these two enemies be overcome without great effort and work, and you must overcome them if you are to be saved."

[39]So rightly Douglas Moo, *Galatians* (Grand Rapids, MI: Baker Academic, 2013), 174n19; cf. *Comm. Gal.* 38-39.

[40]Cf. Calvin on Gal 2: "Yet [Paul] does not treat only of ceremonies, but disputes of works in general; otherwise the whole argument would be weak" (*Comm. Gal.* 6).

[41]Cf. as well *Inst.* III.11.19 on Rom 3:28: "Here [our opponents] have an ingenious subterfuge: even though they have not devised it themselves but have borrowed it from Origen and certain other ancient writers, it is still utterly silly. They prate that the ceremonial works of the law are excluded, not the moral works."

through Christ's grace).[42] Calvin allows for neither limitation, and argues that in rejecting works of the law, "the apostle includes all works without exception, even those which the Lord produces in His own people."[43] Paul's targeting of "works universally" sets up an absolute contrast between faith and works, without any sort of limitation to a certain law or practices: the Apostle speaks "not of ceremonial observances alone, nor specifically of any external works, but includes all the merits of works which can possibly be imagined."[44]

Significance: What does the practice of these works signify? Calvin similarly concurs with Luther regarding the significance of doing the works of the law: to practice them is to attempt to accrue merit, so that one might satisfy God and attain salvation by one's own efforts. As with Luther, the key issue in the conflict over works of the law is not the particular works themselves, but rather what is signified by practicing them, as "Paul was less worried about ceremonies than about the ungodly notion that we obtain salvation by works."[45] Because this function of obtaining merit for salvation represents Paul's true target, the significance of the phrase applies just as much to those in Calvin's own time, outside of the context of the Jewish law, to any works that one might try to perform to gain merit before God. As Calvin comments in a sermon on Galatians 2:15-16, "Those who regularly attend Mass, running from the alehouse to the chapel, buying pardons and other such things, observing fasts and feast days—they are puffed up with vain pride and believe that God owes them something," and such as these "Paul intends to stop . . . from trusting in their own merits."[46] In sum, by placing the Jews' folly regarding works of the law in antithesis to faith, Paul "shows that those who endeavour to obtain salvation by trusting in their own works are justly rejected."[47]

---

[42]*Comm. Rom.* 71, cf. *Inst.* III.11.14.

[43]*Comm. Rom.* 71.

[44]*Comm. Rom.* 78. Cf. *Inst.* III.11.20: "No cavils of [our opponents] can prevent us from holding to the exclusive expression as a general principle."

[45]*Comm. Gal.* 6.

[46]*Ser. Gal.* 182-83.

[47]*Comm. Rom.* 217.

Opposition: Why are these works not necessary for the Christian? For
Calvin, the works of the law are to be opposed because their merit can
never be sufficient to justify us before God. As Calvin writes in a sermon
on Galatians 2:15-16,

> when Paul declares here that "no flesh shall be justified," he means that un-
> believers are condemned in Adam and remain condemned, and that be-
> lievers, because they will always be imperfect and have many spots and
> blemishes, are condemned as much as the others. Indeed, this condem-
> nation is a general one, for whoever seeks to be justified by the works of
> the law will always find himself guilty—yes, even the holiest person that
> ever existed.[48]

Calvin understands that the law demands perfect obedience to be
fulfilled,[49] and because the nature of humanity—both prior to and following conversion—is such that one can never produce this perfect obedience, the only way to be reckoned as righteous before God is to have
Christ's righteousness count in one's stead.[50] To trust in one's own works
for justification either foolishly fails to account for the justice of God, or
pridefully overestimates humanity's ability to produce these works. Because of the reality of human sinfulness and the futility of our efforts to
obey the law, such "trust in works" represents "the chief obstacle to our
attainment of righteousness," and "it is necessary that we should renounce it, in order that we may put our trust in the goodness of God
alone."[51] Calvin does not follow Luther in emphasizing that the law would
not justify even if humanity could obey it,[52] nor does he develop the idea
that attempting to obey the law is itself sinful and idolatrous.[53] Rather, it
is fundamentally humanity's inability to perfectly fulfill God's righteous

---

[48]*Ser. Gal.* 183-84.
[49]See e.g. *Ser. Gal.* 173.
[50]Cf. *Inst.* III.11.23.
[51]*Comm. Rom.* 218, cf. *Inst.* III.11.13
[52]Cf. *Inst.* III.11.15: "Now we confess with Paul that the doers of the law are justified before God;
but, because we are all far from observing the law, we infer from this that those works which
ought especially to avail for righteousness give us no help because we are destitute of them." See
also *Inst.* III.17.13.
[53]For differences between Luther and Calvin on the place of works, cf. Steven Coxhead, "John
Calvin's Interpretation of Works Righteousness in Ezekiel 18," *WTJ* 70 (2008): 303-16.

requirements, either before or after conversion, that sets up an absolute contrast requiring a rejection of all our own works. "For when [Paul] tells us that we are justified by faith because we cannot be justified by works, he takes for granted what is true, that we cannot be justified through the righteousness of Christ unless we are poor and destitute of our own righteousness. Consequently we have to ascribe either nothing or every-thing to faith or to works."[54]

In summary, Calvin follows Luther in regarding works of the law as all possible works that one might perform to gain merit with God and earn salvation. Unlike Luther, Calvin does not denounce attempts to obey the law, and regards righteousness as indeed coming by perfect obedience to God. It is humanity's inability to perfectly fulfill the works of the law that makes it impossible to procure justification by them, so that they must be entirely rejected in favor of Christ's righteousness.

RUDOLPH BULTMANN

Rudolph Bultmann (1884–1976) offers a modern Lutheran perspective on works of the law that, while formulated in a way that reflects his own twentieth-century context, is still recognizable as kindred to Luther's own.[55] Bultmann is also significant for this study for his tremendous in-fluence in New Testament studies in the period immediately prior to the new perspective's emergence; as John Barclay notes, the new perspective on Paul is largely written against Bultmann.[56]

Meaning: What works of what law? Like Luther and Calvin, Bultmann is not ignorant of the Jewish context of Paul's arguments, though this is sometimes attributed to him; as Gathercole notes, "many scholars, perhaps, would be surprised to find that Bultmann asserts that the issue of works of the Law 'does not arise in relation to the Gentiles,'

---

[54]*Comm. Gal.* 39-40.

[55]Cf. Barth's observation: "Those who throw stones at Bultmann should be careful lest they acci-dentally hit Luther, who *is* also hovering somewhere in the background" (Karl Barth, "Rudolph Bultmann—an Attempt to Understand Him," in *Kerygma and Myth: A Theological Debate*, ed. Hans Werner Bartsch, vol. 2 [London: SPCK, 1962], 123). I am indebted to John Barclay's 2014 SBL presentation, "Interpretation, not Repetition: Bultmann on Paul," for this quote.

[56]This taken from Barclay at the "Beyond Bultmann" session at SBL 2014.

because the gentiles do not possess the law."[57] Nevertheless, as with Luther and Calvin, Bultmann sees the particular works engaged by Paul as only the inciting referent for a theological problem that goes far beyond debates on the law of Moses. Bultmann thus presents his view in contrast to that of Mundle, who holds that "when Paul rejects works, only the works demanded by the Mosaic law are meant," not the "rejection of absolutely every accomplishment that can get or earn something for the doer."[58] Instead, Bultmann argues that "the 'works *of the Law*,' on which Paul naturally concentrates in this discussion with the Jew, represent works in general, any and all works as works-of-merit," which he bases on Paul's absolute rejection of boasting and his opposition of "working" and "grace."[59]

Significance: What does the practice of these works signify? Bultmann concurs with Luther and Calvin regarding the significance of practicing works of the law, which represent man's attempt "to procure his salvation by his own strength,"[60] frequently denoted by Bultmann as "legalism."[61] As with the Reformers, Bultmann's interpretation emphasizes the function of performing these works rather than the identity of the works themselves, as Paul's polemic is "aimed not against the accomplishment of specific acts—viz. those required by the Mosaic Law—but against the attitude of that man who wants to pass muster before God on his own strength."[62] Bultmann explicates the nature of this legalism in distinct language, memorably describing the effort to earn salvation as "man's self-powered striving to undergird his own existence in forgetfulness of

---

[57]Simon J. Gathercole *Where Is Boasting? Early Jewish Soteriology and Paul's Response in Romans 1–5* (Grand Rapids, MI: Eerdmans, 2002), 3, citing Bernd Jaspert and and G. W. Bromiley, eds., *Karl Barth—Rudolf Bultmann: Letters, 1922–1966* (Grand Rapids, MI: Eerdmans, 1981), 5. Cf. Rudolf Bultmann, *Theology of the New Testament*, trans. Kendrick Grobel, 2 vols. (London: SCM, 1952), 1:259.

[58]Bultmann, *Theology of the New Testament*, 1:283; cf. Wilhelm Mundle, *Der Glaubensbegriff des Paulus* (Leipzig: M. Heinsius Nachfolger, 1932), 99–100.

[59]Bultmann, *Theology of the New Testament*, 1:283, italics original.

[60]Bultmann, *Theology of the New Testament*, 1:264.

[61]See e.g. Rudolf Bultmann 1955, "Christ the End of the Law" in *Essays Philosophical and Theological* (London: SCM, 1955 [1940]), 36–66.

[62]Bultmann, *Theology of the New Testament*, 1:284. Cf. Bultmann, "Christ the End of the Law," 45: "Acquiring credit in God's sight . . . is the great error, the illusion, in which the Jews are involved—that man can gain his recognition in God's sight by what he does."

his creaturely existence."[63] Such distinctive language aside, Bultmann remains essentially consistent with his predecessors on the significance of performing these works.

Opposition: Why are these works not necessary for the Christian? While not identical with Luther, Bultmann rearticulates key themes in Luther's argumentation for why Paul rejects works of the law. Bultmann begins with the common Reformation argument that works of the law are impossible for fallen man to produce so as to be justified in God's sight. As Bultmann comments on Romans 3:20, "The reason why man under the Law does not achieve 'rightwising' and life is that he is a transgressor of the Law, that he is guilty before God."[64] While affirming this traditional anthropological reasoning, it is significant that human inability does not function for Bultmann in precisely in the same way as it does for Luther. Indeed, Bultmann interestingly seems to anticipate Sanders in a 1940 essay, writing that Paul "does *not* argue . . . that *faith frees from the law as from an unbearable burden* under which the Jews sigh, a burden which inhibits life at every step. . . . Paul is easily confused with Luther, and we overlook the historical situation in which Paul is writing."[65] Nevertheless, the inability of fallen humanity to fulfill the law still represents an objection to its works in Bultmann's theology: while "the Law was given 'for life' (with life-giving intent) . . . [w]hat makes [man's] situation so desperate is the simple fact that prior to faith *there is no true fulfilment of the law*," since sinful humanity "cannot exhibit 'the works of the Law' in their entirety."[66]

However, as with Luther, humanity's inability to obey the law is not the whole story for Bultmann. Rather, this reasoning is consistently paired in his writing with the more fundamental reason why works of the law are rejected: that the attempt to obey the law is itself sin.[67] As Bultmann writes,

---

[63]Bultmann, *Theology of the New Testament*, 1:264.

[64]Bultmann, *Theology of the New Testament*, 1:263.

[65]Bultmann "Christ the End of the Law," 37, italics original. Cf. 39: "And as for the *question of being inwardly weighed down by the law*, it is absolutely clear that Paul never speaks of it. In its Lutheran form this question is, in any event, entirely foreign to Judaism" (italics original).

[66]Bultmann, *Theology of the New Testament*, 1:262-63, italics original. Luther's second line of reasoning (a misunderstanding of the role of works) does not play a similar role in Bultmann's theology.

[67]Cf. Bultmann, *Theology of the New Testament*, 1:264.

Of course, it goes without saying that transgression of the law for Paul is sin. And Jews are just as guilty of this sin as are Gentiles (Rom. 3:19) . . . but the antithesis, "faith" (πίστις) vs. "works of the law" (ἔργα νόμου) goes way beyond any such view . . . [Paul's] fundamental reproach is not that the way of the law is wrong because, by reason of transgressions, it fails to reach its goal (that is the position, say of IV Ezra), but rather that the *direction* of this way is perverse and, to be sure, because it intends to lead to "one's own righteousness" (Rom. 10:3; Phil. 3:9). It is not evil works or transgressions of the law that first make the Jews objectionable to God; rather the intention to become righteous before him by fulfilling the law is their real sin, which is merely manifested by transgressions.[68]

While humanity is indeed unable to fulfill the law, according to Bultmann, "Paul goes much further still; he says not only that man *can not* achieve salvation by works of the Law, but also that he is not even *intended* to do so,"[69] since such self-reliant striving only "finds its extreme expression in 'boasting' and 'trusting in the flesh,'" which are themselves the epitome of sin.[70] Indeed, "*real sin* does not consist in individual transgressions of the law at all, but in the *basic attitude of man—his striving to establish his own righteousness,* and to glorify himself in the presence of God."[71] For Bultmann, this self-glorifying, self-reliant attitude represents the fundamental reason why Paul rejects the works of the law, since man "can find his salvation only when he understands himself in his dependence upon God the Creator."[72]

Bultmann uses Paul's language of "boasting" to describe this fundamentally antifaith disposition of Paul's Jewish opponents, which parallels Luther's description of the Jews' self-idolatry.[73] As Bultmann

---

[68]Bultmann, "Romans 7 and the Anthropology of Paul," in *Existence and Faith: Shorter Writings of Rudolf Bultmann,* ed. Schubert Miles Ogden (New York: Meridian Books, 1960 [1932]), 148-49, italics original.

[69]Bultmann, *Theology of the New Testament,* 1:263, italics original.

[70]Bultmann, *Theology of the New Testament,* 1:264; cf. 1:268.

[71]Bultmann, "Christ the End of the Law," 46-47, italics original.

[72]Bultmann, *Theology of the New Testament,* 1:264.

[73]Cf. Bultmann, "Liberal Theology and the Latest Theological Movement," in *Faith and Understanding,* vol. 1 (London: SCM, 1969 [1924]), 46: "[Man's] moral transgressions are not his fundamental sin . . . *Man's fundamental sin is his will to justify himself as man,* for thereby he makes himself God" (italics original).

writes in the *TDNT* entry for καυχᾶσθαι, "For Paul, καυχᾶσθαι *discloses the basic attitude of the Jew* to be one of self-confidence which seeks glory before God and which relies on itself."[74] Such boasting in the law is "the fundamental attitude of the Jew" and "the essence of his sin," while "*'faith' is the absolute contrary of boasting*"[75] and represents "the radical renunciation of accomplishment."[76] By Paul's rejection of works of the law in favor of faith, then, "Judaism is vanquished and the law is disqualified as the means of winning acceptance in God's sight by one's own achievements."[77]

To summarize, Bultmann regards works of the law as any and all works of merit that are performed by humanity to earn salvation by their own strength. In addition to regarding these works as impossible to perform, Bultmann follows Luther in seeing the attempt to do so as sinful, as humanity can only find salvation in absolute dependence on God.

DOUGLAS MOO

We conclude this introduction to the old perspective with a contemporary representative of the Reformed tradition, Douglas Moo (1950–).[78] A prominent Pauline scholar, Moo is particularly relevant for this study for his attempts to engage constructively with the various new perspectives on Paul.[79]

---

[74]Bultmann, "Καυχᾶσθαι," in *Theological Dictionary of the New Testament*, vol. 3, ed. Gerhard Kittel and Geoffrey William Bromiley, 10 vols. (Grand Rapids, MI: Eerdmans, 1966), 648-49, italics original; cf. Bultmann, "Paul," in *Existence and Faith: Shorter Writings of Rudolf Bultmann*, ed. Schubert Miles Ogden (New York: Meridian Books, 1960 [1930]), 133.

[75]Bultmann, *Theology of the New Testament*, 1:281, italics original.

[76]Bultmann, *Theology of the New Testament*, 1:316.

[77]Bultmann, "Christ the End of the Law," 60; cf. 45.

[78]Cf. Douglas Moo, "Justification in Galatians," in *Understanding the Times: New Testament Studies in the 21st Century: Essays in Honor of D. A. Carson on the Occasion of His 65th Birthday*, ed. Andreas J. Köstenberger and Robert W. Yarbrough (Wheaton, IL: Crossway, 2011), 190. Though identifying with the Calvinist tradition, Moo is in some ways a hybrid figure, offering a 1993 chapter on the law of Christ as "a modified Lutheran view"; see "The Law of Christ as the Fulfillment of the Law of Moses," in *Five Views on Law and Gospel*, ed. Stanley Gundry (Grand Rapids, MI: Zondervan, 1993), 319.

[79]This is witnessed in the contributions of Dunn and Wright in Moo's recent Festschrift; cf. as well Wright in 2007: "One of the things I really respect about Doug Moo is that he is constantly grappling with the text. Where he hears the text saying something which is not what his tradition

Meaning: What works of what law? Moo is notable among contemporary old perspective proponents for his willingness to part ways with Luther and Calvin, which can be witnessed from the outset of his career in a 1983 article on the meaning of the law in Paul. As Moo writes, "the Reformers, as most theologians today, use 'law' to mean anything that demands something of us. . . . 'Law' is a basic factor in all of human history; and man is in every age, whether in the OT or NT, confronted with 'law.'"[80] According to Moo, "what is crucial to recognize is that this is *not* the way in which Paul usually uses the term *nomos*."[81] Rather, Moo agrees with the new perspective in holding that it is the law of Moses in particular, and the works it prescribes, that serves as Paul's target in rejecting works of the law: "What is vital for any accurate understanding of Paul's doctrine of the law is to realize that Paul uses *nomos* most often and most basically of the Mosaic law."[82] However, while viewing the Reformers as erring in interpreting "works of the law" apart from the context of Paul's disputes over the law of Moses, Moo also sees Paul as expanding and generalizing this phrase as simply "works," which for Moo "suggests the propriety of the application made by the Reformers."[83] Indeed, because Paul's intention is to exclude all works from justification, Moo lands in a traditional Reformed position, concluding that "the Reformers, we think, were entirely justified in viewing Paul's phrase 'the works of the law' as a synecdoche for the more general category 'works.'"[84]

Significance: What does the practice of these works signify? With regard to the significance of practicing works of the law, Moo offers a similarly nuanced view that nevertheless ultimately affirms the traditional Reformed position. As with his interpretation of the works themselves,

---

would have said, he will go with the text. I won't always agree with his exegesis, but there is a relentless scholarly honesty about him which I really tip my hat off to" (Wright, "Trevin Wax Interview with N. T. Wright," *The Gospel Coalition*, November 19, 2007, blogs.thegospelcoalition.org/trevinwax/2007/11/19/trevin-wax-interview-with-nt-wright-full-transcript/).

[80] Moo "'Law,' 'Works of the Law,' and Legalism in Paul," *Westminster Theological Journal* 45 (1983): 88.

[81] Moo "'Law,' 'Works of the Law,'" 88, italics original.

[82] Moo "'Law,' 'Works of the Law,'" 80, cf. 90. See also Moo, *Galatians*, 19-20.

[83] Moo "'Law,' 'Works of the Law,'" 99; cf. Moo, *Galatians*, 160.

[84] Moo, *Galatians*, 176; cf. Moo, "Justification in Galatians," 181.

Moo follows the new perspective in denying that Paul's opponents in Galatia were proto-Pelagians, writing that "the agitators were arguing not
that people get right with God by doing good works but that people can
have their right standing with God vindicated only by faithful observance
of God's covenant stipulations."[85] Nevertheless, Moo also holds that Paul's
usage of terms like *grace* suggests that from the apostle's perspective, his
argument is also against relying on human merit for justification, and
Moo maintains that this is the more fundamental significance that Paul
has in mind in rejecting works of the law. As Moo comments on
Galatians 3:3, it is "likely that [Paul] wants to tie the agitators' demand for
torah obedience to the broader issue of human 'achievement' as a contrast
to the utterly gracious character of God's justifying work in Christ."[86] Thus,
while it is true that "Galatians is not a polemic against semi-Pelagianism
(as N. T. Wright has often insisted)," Moo maintains that Paul "finds
behind the agitators' views a reliance on human achievement that, indeed,
has fundamental resemblances to semi-Pelagianism."[87]

Opposition: Why are these works not necessary for the Christian?
Concurring with the view that he sees as held by most contemporary
scholars, Moo affirms that Paul objects to works of the law on salvation-
historical grounds, as "the era of torah has ended with the coming of
Christ and any attempt now to require torah obedience for righteousness
is to turn the clock back and, in effect, deny that Christ has come."[88] Nevertheless, according to Moo, the logic of Paul's arguments "appears to move
beyond (or behind!) salvation history to more fundamental theological
issues, with anthropological and soteriological implications."[89] This means
that salvation-historical reasons are ultimately subsidiary to the real
reason Paul objects to works of the law, which is the reality of human
inability to fulfill the law, such that one can never produce sufficient works
to be justified before God. As Moo writes in his commentary on Romans:

---

[85]Moo, "Justification in Galatians," 180.

[86]Moo, "Justification in Galatians," 185-86.

[87]Moo, "Justification in Galatians," 186.

[88]Moo, "Justification in Galatians," 180; cf. 184.

[89]Moo, "Justification in Galatians," 186. Cf. Moo, *The Epistle to the Romans* (Grand Rapids, MI:
Eerdmans, 1996), 212.

"Works of the law" are inadequate not because they are "works of *the law*" but, ultimately, because they are "works." This clearly removes the matter from the purely salvation-historical realm to the broader realm of anthropology. No person can gain a standing with God through works because no one is able to perform works to the degree needed to secure such a standing. This human inability to meet the demands of God is what lies at the heart of Rom. 3. On this point, at least, the Reformers understood Paul correctly.[90]

This traditional Reformed conclusion has been a consistent refrain in Moo's writings on this topic. Beginning with his 1983 article, Moo argues that Paul's reasoning in Romans 3 and Galatians 3 "strongly supports the notion that 'works of the law' cannot justify, not because they are inherently *wrong* [*pace* Bultmann in a footnote],[91] nor only because a decisive shift in salvation-history has occurred, but fundamentally because no man is able to *do* them in sufficient degree and number so as to gain merit before God."[92] This inability to produce the works for justification remains humanity's condition before and after conversion, so that "faith is the means not only of entering into relationship with God but also of maintaining that relationship and of confirming that relationship on the day of judgment."[93] This means that an absolute contrast between faith and works always remains fundamental: as Moo argues, the "underlying issue in the failure of the law" in Galatians 3 is that "the torah . . . cannot be the means of justification because, by definition (for Paul), it involves 'doing' rather than 'believing.'"[94] This same point is made in relation to Paul's view of "reliance

---

[90]Moo, *Epistle to the Romans*, 217, italics original.

[91]Against the Lutheran view, Moo writes that "Paul affirms the principle that doing the law can lead to salvation," with Paul's denial being "(1) that anyone can so 'do' the law; and (2) that Jews can depend on their covenant relationship to shield them from the consequences of this failure" (Moo, *Epistle to the Romans*, 148).

[92]Moo "'Law,' 'Works of the Law,'" 98, italics original. Cf. also Moo, "Justification in Galatians," 182.

[93]Moo, "Justification in Galatians," 192. Here there appears to be tension in Moo's thought: while maintaining that any paradigm whereby one is "justified initially by faith, judged finally by faith plus works" is "ruled out," Moo also acknowledges that "labeling our Spirit-induced works simply as 'evidence' may not finally do justice to the fact that this evidence is something we are commanded to produce" (Moo, "Justification in Galatians," 194-95).

[94]Moo, "Justification in Galatians," 167. Moo positively cites the NIV's translation of Gal 3:3 in contrasting "the Spirit" with "*human effort*" (σάρξ), and continues, "Works are a problem in Galatians, therefore, not simply because they involve an outmoded torah; they are a problem also, and more fundamentally, because human inability renders them incapable of delivering people from sin" (185, italics original).

on doing the law ('works of the law') as bringing people under the curse," which is "not simply because the law belongs to a past stage of salvation history, but because the law is bound up with 'doing,' and 'doing' or 'works' in general are never able to justify a person before God."[95] As Moo summarizes his position by reference to Gundry (and *pace* Sanders), humanity's abiding inability to produce sufficient works means that "for Paul . . . getting in and staying in are covered by the seamless robe of faith as opposed to works."[96]

In summary, Moo places greater emphasis on the immediate context of Paul's discussions, noting that Paul was objecting to the works of Torah that were performed to remain within God's covenant with the Jews, but ultimately seeing these as a subcategory in a broader rejection of works or human achievements. While recognizing salvation-historical reasons for rejecting the Torah with Christ's advent, Moo sees humanity's inability to perform God's requirements—leading to an absolute contrast between works and faith, or "doing" and "believing"—as the more fundamental rationale for Paul's rejection of works of the law.

CONCLUSION

In conclusion, one can observe that the old perspective sees Paul's emphasis to be on *works* in rejecting works of the law. While acknowledging that the Torah appears to be Paul's immediate referent, these figures reject the idea that Paul's focus is on the Mosaic law or any particular works it prescribes. Rather, the old perspective regards Paul's target as human efforts or works in general, with the Mosaic law's practices representing a subset of a broader category of good works, and the law in question being God's requirements more generally. All four of these figures see the practice of these works as an individual's attempt to gain merit by their own achievements and earn salvation. There is variation among these old perspective figures with respect to why Paul rejects these works. While all four identify an anthropological argument

---

[95]Moo, "Justification in Galatians," 182; cf. Moo, *Galatians*, 27.
[96]Moo, "Justification in Galatians," 192n83, cf. R. H. Gundry "Grace, Works, and Staying Saved in Paul," *Biblica* 66 (1985): 12.

regarding sinful humanity's inability to fulfill the law, only Calvin and Moo regard this as Paul's central objection. Luther adds that the law would not justify even if it were obeyed, and—most fundamentally—that the attempt to do so is itself an act of self-idolatry, while Bultmann similarly identifies humanity's efforts to obey the law as sinful, self-glorifying attempts to establish their identity apart from God.

3

THE NEW PERSPECTIVE ON WORKS OF THE LAW

□

E. P. SANDERS

We begin this overview of the new perspective with E. P. Sanders (1937–), who, while preceded in important respects by figures such as W. D. Davies, Krister Stendahl, and George Howard, nevertheless inaugurated a revolution in New Testament studies with his 1977 monograph, *Paul and Palestinian Judaism*.[1] Sanders's revised picture of Palestinian Judaism led to a reevaluation of what Paul was reacting against by his rejection of works of the law, to which we now turn.

Meaning: What works of what law? For Sanders, the works of the law in Paul refer to deeds prescribed by "the *Tanak*, the Jewish Torah," which Sanders usually terms "the Mosaic law."[2] By Sanders's reading, it is the necessity for Gentiles to fully adopt the works of this law that represents Paul's major point of contention with his interlocutors in Galatians and Romans. While Paul's opponents held that "universal salvation . . . would be achieved by full proselytization to the Jewish messianic sect," including

---

[1]See W. D. Davies, *Paul and Rabbinic Judaism* (London: S.P.C.K., 1948); Krister Stendahl, "The Apostle Paul and the Introspective Conscience of the West," *The Harvard Theological Review* 56 (1963): 199-215; George Howard, "Romans 3:21-31 and the Inclusion of the Gentiles," *Harvard Theological Review* 63 (1970): 223-33. Parallels can be drawn further back to F. C. Baur, who similarly viewed Paul as objecting to "Jewish particularism"; cf. Baur, *The Church History of the First Three Centuries*, trans. Allan Menzies (London: Williams and Norgate, 1878), 72. I owe this reference to John M. G. Barclay, *Paul and the Gift* (Grand Rapids, MI: Eerdmans, 2015), 163n247.
[2]E. P. Sanders, *Paul, the Law, and the Jewish People* (Philadelphia: Fortress Press, 1983), 3.

"acceptance of the election of Israel, the law of Moses, and the saving death of the Messiah Jesus," Paul counters that "God required of Gentiles only acceptance of the God of Israel and of Jesus as saviour."[3]

Within the Mosaic law, according to Sanders, Paul specifically targets the works of "circumcision, rules governing eating, and observance of the sabbath ('days')" as not necessary for Christian observance.[4] Sanders contends that Paul does not mean to target the entire Mosaic law by such objections: "Once he excluded circumcision, food, and days from 'the commandments of God' (an exclusion which is explicit with regard to circumcision in 1 Cor. 7: 19), he could say, without contradicting himself, that his followers should observe 'the whole law.'"[5] According to Sanders, Paul's filtering out of certain works of the law does not follow a later-theorized pattern of distinguishing between "cultic" and "moral" law ("This is not an ancient Jewish categorization of the law. Paul did not invent it, nor would he have agreed with it"[6]), or use categories of his own day that distinguished between laws governing the relation of humans to God and those governing relations between humans.[7] Rather, Sanders holds that Paul "revised the law on an *ad hoc* basis, without offering theoretical principles for deleting part of the law which God had given."[8] This is not to say, however, that Paul abrogated laws at random; rather, "with the aid of hindsight . . . we can now apply a heading for the laws which he opposed in Galatians and which he either opposed or held to be optional elsewhere: those which, in the Diaspora, separated Jew from Gentile."[9]

---

[3]Sanders, *Paul* (New York: Oxford University Press, 1991), 51.

[4]Sanders, *Paul*, 90.

[5]Sanders, *Paul*, 91.

[6]Sanders, *Paul*, 86.

[7]Sanders, *Paul*, 86, 91. This appears to be in tension with Sanders's position in 1977: see *Paul and Palestinian Judaism* (Philadelphia: Fortress Press, 1977), 544.

[8]Sanders, *Paul*, 91. See also Sanders, *Paul, the Law*, 105: "We cannot get around the fact that Paul, while offering no theoretical basis for distinguishing among the commandments, did make de facto distinctions." Unlike Dunn and Wright, Sanders has no difficulty in charging Paul with inconsistency: "Those who want to make Paul a perfectly consistent thinker, whose words can be used to construct a perfect system of Christian theology, are doomed to lives of frustration and disappointment. So I hope that the reader does not want that too much" (Sanders, "Paul Between Judaism and Hellenism," in *St. Paul Among the Philosophers*, ed. John D. Caputo and Linda Alcoff [Bloomington: Indiana University Press, 2009], 88).

[9]Sanders, *Paul*, 90.

Significance: What does the practice of these works signify? Sanders asserts that the practice of these works of the law—principally circumcision, food laws and Sabbath keeping—signifies inclusion within the Jewish people, and correspondingly, the separation of Jew from Gentile. According to Sanders, the contested issue in the Galatian conflict is whether Gentiles must become Jews to be part of the people of God. While Paul's opponents in Galatia, the "preachers of circumcision," held along with Paul that "the God previously accepted only by Israel was God of the world, and that he intended to save the entire world," they also "wished the Gentile members, in the interim between Jesus' resurrection and his return, to become Jews."[10] By Sanders's reading, Paul's counter—"being righteoused by faith and not by works of law"—means that "Gentiles who have faith in Christ do not need to become Jewish and that even those who are already Jews in good standing are rightly related to God only by their faith in Christ."[11] In Romans as in Galatians, "the problem is, again, that of Gentile inclusion in the people of God," with the adoption of works of the law signifying Gentile admission on the basis of becoming a Jew.[12] According to Sanders, to adopt works of the law would not represent a sort of legalism or reliance on "working" per se, as Paul's objections relate specifically to "the aspects of the law which were against his own mission, those which separated Jew from Gentile in the people of God."[13] In contrast to certain older perspectives, Sanders holds that such "opposition to works of the law was not motivated by dislike of effort."[14]

Opposition: Why are these works not necessary for the Christian? According to Sanders, Paul shared in the "long-held Jewish expectation that, in the final days, Gentiles would come to worship the God of Israel," which indeed finds attestation across the Hebrew Scriptures, as Paul himself makes clear in contexts such as Romans 15.[15] However,

---

[10]Sanders, *Paul*, 54.
[11]Sanders, *Paul*, 63.
[12]Sanders, *Paul*, 66.
[13]Sanders, *Paul*, 91.
[14]Sanders, *Paul*, 102.
[15]Sanders, *Paul*, 3.

while Paul frequently appeals to these Scriptures as providing the rationale for why works of the Mosaic law are unnecessary for Gentiles in the inaugurated messianic era, the difficulty for Sanders is that such passages (such as Is 2) do not "give legal detail about precisely what the Gentiles should do when they turn to the God of Israel," or "specify what worship of the God of Israel entails—except, of course, abandoning the worship of other gods."[16] As such, despite what Sanders regards as Paul's ingenious usage of these Scriptures, he asserts that the prophetic texts themselves cannot represent the fundamental basis for Paul's opposition to works of the law.

This leaves one with a puzzle: If such scriptural evidence in the conflicts between Paul and his opponents—in Galatia, for example—were indeed debatable, "whence the passion and rage? Why did they not have a polite academic dispute about the meaning of Isaiah 2:3?"[17] Sanders makes clear that Paul's strong views cannot simply have been inherited from elsewhere: "There is no body of Jewish literature which expects the abolition of the law with the advent of the Messiah, nor do we know of any other Christian groups or theologians which drew Paul's conclusion about the law, as would be the case if the view were predetermined by his background."[18]

Rather, Sanders identifies three fundamental rationales that underlie Paul's various arguments for why works of the law are not necessary for the Christian. The first two are based in experience, and are bound up together: Paul's own experience of being called as apostle to the Gentiles; and his conviction, based on the experiences of his Gentile congregations who had received the Spirit, that they were equal members of the people of God in the messianic era. Drawing on W. D. Davies, Sanders holds that what is distinctive about Paul's understanding of the law (and indeed his theology as a whole) is a central conviction: "Christ saves Gentiles as well as Jews."[19] According to Sanders, "this was not only a theological view, but it was bound up with Paul's most profound

---

[16]Sanders, *Paul*, 50.
[17]Sanders, *Paul*, 53.
[18]Sanders, *Paul and Palestinian Judaism*, 496.
[19]Sanders, *Paul and Palestinian Judaism*, 496.

conviction about himself, a conviction on which he staked his career and his life: he was the apostle to the Gentiles."[20] From this first reason of Paul's own self-understanding, the second rationale follows naturally: "The salvation of the Gentiles is essential to Paul's preaching, and with it falls the law; for, as Paul says simply, Gentiles cannot live by the law (Gal 2.14).[21]" Just as the first rationale is autobiographical, the second follows the biographies of his converts, as "it was a matter of common Christian experience that the Spirit and faith come by hearing the gospel, not by obeying the law (Gal 3.1-5)."[22] Sanders asserts that it is following from this pair of convictions—and not the other way round—that Paul seeks to demonstrate from Scripture "that the biblical commandments about being Jewish did not need to be observed by Gentiles in the messianic age."[23]

With these two experiential reasons as a foundation, a third follows logically and involves not simply selected works, but the entire Mosaic dispensation. Since God has sent his apostle and his Spirit to save Gentiles apart from observing the Jewish law, there must have been something wrong or insufficient about that law, otherwise salvation would not have come about by another means.[24] In contrast to the first and second reasons for opposing such works, the third is not directly experiential, but "theological or dogmatic. The law must do something bad, since it was not intended by God to save—since God saves through Christ."[25] Here Sanders famously describes Paul as not moving from plight to solution, but solution to plight; having discovered that Christ is the answer, Paul is forced to venture a series of arguments regarding the problem

---

[20]Sanders, *Paul and Palestinian Judaism*, 496.

[21]Sanders, *Paul and Palestinian Judaism*, 496.

[22]Sanders, *Paul and Palestinian Judaism*, 496. From this follows the critique of Jewish exclusivity, as illustrated in passages such as Rom 10:3: "'Their own righteousness' is the righteousness peculiar to Jews as a group, not that earned by individuals. Jewish righteousness springs from loyalty to the law of Moses, which applies only to Jews, and which is thus 'their own' and is not 'for all'" (Sanders, *Paul*, 120; cf. Sanders, *Paul, the Law*, 38). However, Sanders does not contend that opposing an attitude of exclusivity per se is fundamental to Paul's opposition to works of the law (as does Dunn).

[23]Sanders, *Paul*, 55.

[24]See Sanders, *Paul and Palestinian Judaism*, 550.

[25]Sanders, *Paul*, 100.

itself. Such a situation presented Paul with "a problem in reconciling the two dispensations: the old, represented by Moses, and the new, given in Christ," and "his most basic instinct was to relate them by having the old lead up to the new negatively: the law condemned so that God subsequently could save through Christ."[26] This does not necessarily mean the law is a bad thing; indeed, "in itself obedience to the law is a good thing (Rom. 2.13), just as circumcision in itself is a good thing (2.25–3.2) and is faulted only when it seems to threaten the exclusiveness of salvation by faith in Christ (Galatians)."[27] Similarly, as Paul writes in Philippians 3:9, "there is such a thing as righteousness by the law," which is indeed "gain" in and of itself; this righteousness "becomes wrong only because God has revealed another one."[28] Because it is only by hearing Christ's gospel— and not by observing the Mosaic works—that the Spirit and faith have come about, the value of works of the law (and indeed the entire Mosaic dispensation) is absolutely negated in Paul's thought.[29]

In summary, Sanders regards the law in question for Paul as the Jewish Torah, with Paul objecting to the specific works of circumcision, rules governing eating, and the observance of Sabbath. According to Sanders, practicing these works represents identification with the Jewish people and separation from the Gentiles. Sanders sees Paul as rejecting the works of the law fundamentally for experiential reasons, based on his own experience in being called as apostle to the Gentiles, and the experience of his congregations in receiving the Spirit apart from these works. This leads Paul to a broader rejection of the Mosaic dispensation, not because of any prior plight he himself experienced, but because salvation has only come with Christ.

JAMES DUNN

The second representative of the new perspective is James Dunn (1939–), who, beginning with his 1982 Manson Memorial Lecture, "The New

---

[26]Sanders, *Paul*, 94-95.
[27]Sanders, *Paul and Palestinian Judaism*, 550.
[28]Sanders, *Paul*, 122.
[29]Cf. Sanders, *Paul and Palestinian Judaism*, 519.

Perspective on Paul," has spent over thirty years drawing out the implications of Sanders's work for a revised understanding of works of the law.

Meaning: What works of what law? James Dunn's views on works of the law are complex and have been subject to clarification over the years, and as a result they are difficult to summarize in a manner that does them justice. An important key to understanding his perspective is his view that Paul himself does not use terms like *works of the law* in a completely uniform way (though Dunn is reticent to fault Paul for inconsistency[30]). According to Dunn, "Paul worked with a differentiated concept of *nomos*" and "had different attitudes to the law of Israel, depending on what aspect or function of the law was in view."[31] Correspondingly, Paul's phrase *erga nomou* parallels this "flexible use of *nomos*," so that "ambiguity in his talk of 'works of the law' should occasion little surprise."[32]

In Dunn's first major lecture on works of the law in 1982, he suggested that the meaning of works of the law was more circumscribed than had been traditionally thought in Protestant contexts. In this lecture, Dunn asserts that "'works of the law' do *not* mean 'good works' in general, 'good works' in the sense disparaged by the heirs of Luther, works in the sense of self-achievement."[33] Rather, the phrase is "a fairly restricted one," referring to "*covenant* works—those regulations prescribed by the law which any good Jew would simply take for granted to describe what a good Jew did."[34] The law in question is thus the Jewish Torah, and the works in view are specific, as "to be a Jew . . . was to observe circumcision, food laws, and sabbath."[35] Dunn holds that Paul "intended his readers to think of [these] *particular observances of the law*" with his phrase,[36] and

---

[30]James D. G. Dunn, *The New Perspective on Paul* (Grand Rapids, MI: Eerdmans, 2005), 257.

[31]Dunn, *New Perspective on Paul*, 475.

[32]Dunn, *New Perspective on Paul*, 464.

[33]Dunn, *New Perspective on Paul*, 111, italics original. *Pace* e.g. Rudolf Bultmann, *Theology of the New Testament*, trans. Kendrick Grobel, 2 vols. (London: SCM, 1952), 1:283; cf. Dunn, *The Theology of Paul the Apostle* (Grand Rapids, MI: Eerdmans, 1998), 355.

[34]Dunn, *New Perspective on Paul*, 111, italics original.

[35]Dunn, *New Perspective on Paul*, 111. As Dunn notes elsewhere, these particular works had emerged since the Maccabean crisis as "crucial test cases on which Israel's identity as the people of God was seen to hang" (215, deitalicized).

[36]Dunn, *New Perspective on Paul*, 108, italics original.

finds fault with Sanders for his "failure to distinguish 'works of the law' from 'doing the law'" in general.[37]

Dunn soon clarified this view in response to a number of objections, writing in 1984 that "'works of the law' denote all that the law requires of the devout Jew," referring "not exclusively but particularly to those requirements which bring to sharp focus the distinctiveness of Israel's identity."[38] Within this definition, works like circumcision and food laws feature prominently "because they have such a crucial role in defining 'Jewishness,' membership of the covenant people."[39] This clarification is best stated in his 2005 essay on the new perspective:

> It has been a matter of regret to me that my initial formulation of the case I was making (regarding "works of the law") allowed it to be so readily dismissed. Let me make it quite clear, then: I have no doubt that "works of the law" refer to what the law requires, the conduct prescribed by the Torah; whatever the law requires to be done can be described as "doing" the law, as a work of the law.[40]

In this essay, Dunn makes clear that he does "not want to narrow 'the works of the law' to boundary issues," and that the works like circumcision that distinguished Jew from Gentile were simply the particular occasion for the first great statement of justification by faith alone.[41] Dunn illustrates in a 2013 essay how works of the law can refer both to particular works and to the whole law. Taking the example of

---

[37]Dunn, *New Perspective on Paul*, 119. Many commentators have continued to identify Dunn's position with this early articulation, including N. T. Wright, whose recent work on justification still attributes to Dunn this narrower view that works of the law are "the particular commandments and ordinances which kept Jew and Gentile separate from one another" (Wright, *Justification: God's Plan and Paul's Vision* [London: SPCK, 2009], 48). See also Wright, "Communion and Koinonia: Pauline Reflections on Tolerance and Boundaries," *NTWrightPage* (blog), 2002, ntwrightpage.com/Wright_Communion_Koinonia.htm., positively citing Dunn as developing the insight that works of the law are "circumcision, the food laws, and the sabbaths—the three things which every Jew in the ancient world, and many pagans in the ancient world too, knew were the boundary-markers between Jews and pagans." For Dunn's reaction, see Dunn, *Theology of Paul*, 358n97: "I do not (and never did!) claim that 'works of the law' denote only circumcision, food laws, and Sabbath."

[38]Dunn, *New Perspective on Paul*, 130.

[39]Dunn, *New Perspective on Paul*, 130.

[40]Dunn, *New Perspective on Paul*, 23-24. See also Dunn, *Theology of Paul*, 354-55: "The meaning of 'works of the law' is not much in dispute. It refers to what the law requires, the 'deeds' which the law makes obligatory."

[41]Dunn, *New Perspective on Paul*, 28.

Galatians, "the 'works of the law' to which Paul objected (as a requirement in addition to believing in Jesus Christ) were in this case the boundary markers, the laws which marked out Jews in their distinctiveness/separation from other nations," so that "'works of the law' and 'living like a Jew' overlap and are almost synonymous."[42] Works of the law nevertheless remains "a more general phrase, which refers to the principle of keeping the law in all its requirements," which in context of Paul's Gentile mission in Galatians just happens to refer "particularly to the law in its role as a wall dividing Jew from Gentile, the boundary markers which define who is 'inside' and who is 'outside.'"[43] For Dunn, "circumcision and food laws in particular come into play simply (!) because they provided the key test cases [of covenantal nomism] for most Jews of Paul's time."[44]

Nevertheless, Dunn still suggests that Paul's varied statements on the law may require a narrower target than critics of his early formulation may admit, since (as is discussed in the following sections) what Paul has in mind to critique is not the law per se, but rather "a particular *attitude* to the law as such, its social function as distinguishing Jew from Gentile."[45] This can be seen from how Paul speaks about other parts of the law. As Dunn comments,

> It is worth noting that Paul does not refer to avoidance of idolatry or porneia (sexual license) as "works of the law," even though such avoidance is "doing the law." This strengthens the suggestion that for Paul the phrase "works of the law" is not simply to be equated with "doing the law" but is a negative characterisation of the motivation for "doing the law" which so conflicted with his gospel for all who believe.[46]

If this is indeed the case, then works of the law are not so much the entire Torah or some subset of works from it, but rather any work carried out with motivation that conflicts with the gospel.

---

[42]Dunn, *New Perspective on Paul*, 174.
[43]Dunn, *New Perspective on Paul*, 174-75.
[44]Dunn, *New Perspective on Paul*, 214.
[45]Dunn, *New Perspective on Paul*, 131, italics original.
[46]Dunn, *New Perspective on Paul*, 86n362; cf. 464, 466.

Further, having acknowledged that works of the law in Paul refers to the whole law, Dunn still maintains that Paul's understanding of the gospel leads him to distinguish between commandments in the law. Commenting in relation to Paul's relativizing circumcision in favor of "keeping God's commandments" in 1 Corinthians 7:19, Dunn writes,

> Of course Paul would have been well aware that circumcision is one of the commandments (Gen 17:9-14). The point is that only someone who differentiated between commandments (works of the law) could make such an assertion. This obviously provides an explanation of how Paul could set aside or devalue commandments like circumcision and the laws of clean and unclean, while, at the same time, strongly reasserting the commandments against idolatry and sexual license.[47]

As Dunn writes elsewhere on this same 1 Corinthians passage, "*only someone who differentiated between the requirements of the law*, for some good reason, could write like this," though Dunn is noncommittal in identifying Paul's standard for distinguishing between these works.[48] He does venture, however, that such a standard "presumably involved a prioritizing of the multitudinous laws of the Torah, presumably in effect a recognition of the continuing force of the moral commandments in the decalogue (cf. Rom. 13.9) and a demotion of commandments regarding circumcision, sacrifice and clean and unclean as matters of indifference (at least as understood literally)."[49]

For Dunn, it is also essential to distinguish "works of the law" from "good works," as "in Galatians and Romans 'works of the law' do not signify 'good works' in general. Or to be more precise, when Paul criticizes 'works of the law' he was not attacking an attempt to achieve salvation by one's own efforts."[50] As Dunn writes,

> Had Paul's primary or even underlying polemic been directed against a prevalent view among Jews (and Christian Jews) that justification depended on

---

[47]Dunn, "A New Perspective on the New Perspective on Paul," *Early Christianity* 4 (2013): 179; cf. *New Perspective on Paul*, 86.

[48]Dunn, *New Perspective on Paul*, 55, italics original.

[49]Dunn, *New Perspective on Paul*, 337.

[50]Dunn, *New Perspective on Paul*, 386.

works of achievement, he is unlikely to have expressed himself so unguardedly as he does in commending good works to his readers. He is hardly likely to have spoken of a "work of faith," or of "the obedience of faith." Paul evidently did not associate "works of the law" with "good works." The two phrases operated within different substructures of his thought. To both commend "good works" and rail against "works of the law" was no inconsistency for Paul.[51]

However one understands the relation of good works to the requirements of the Torah, then, Dunn maintains that Paul's objections to works of the law are not directed against the performance of good works to attain salvation.

Finally, Dunn's later works are marked by a reticence to plant too firm a flag on the precise identity of works of the law. In a 2004 essay, for example, Dunn writes that "whatever else 'works of the law' signify" in Romans 3, "they attest or are particularly exemplified in Jewish insistence that the laws which set Israel apart from the nations have to be maintained."[52] Dunn similarly refrains from offering a strict judgment in a 2002 essay, where after establishing that in Galatians, "the 'works of the law' which Paul had particularly in mind were rules which, unless embraced by Gentiles, should prevent full acceptance of these Gentiles," he writes,

> It is certainly open to exegetes and interpreters to argue from these basic observations. (1) That "works of the law" must include all and any laws to which obedience is required as a necessary part of the salvation process. (2) That the principle articulated in Gal. 2.16 is deeper or broader than simply the issue of relations between Jewish and Gentile believers in Messiah Jesus. I would have no quarrel in either case.[53]

After raising the question of how works of the law can simultaneously be "the deeds prescribed by the law" and those "by reference to which final judgment shall be rendered," Dunn again prescinds from putting forth his own position.[54] Instead, Dunn simply remarks that "the issue, of course, is all the sharper for those who understand 'works of the law' to

---

[51]Dunn, *New Perspective on Paul*, 365.
[52]Dunn, *New Perspective on Paul*, 465.
[53]Dunn, *New Perspective on Paul*, 416.
[54]Dunn, *New Perspective on Paul*, 425.

refer to the whole range of conduct required by the law," as "then Paul's various statements on the subject of 'works' seem to fall into complete confusion."[55] It must be stated again, however, that this reticence does not necessarily imply a lack of conviction from Dunn; rather, it is consistent with his view that Paul's own usage of the phrase carries some ambiguity, with its precise meaning in any passage determined by the context of the argument.

In summary, Dunn views works of the law in Paul as referring particularly, though not exclusively, to the Torah's specific works of circumcision, food laws, and Sabbath. While the term is representative of all else that the law requires as well, the degree to which it can apply in the same way to other deeds prescribed by the Torah (such as those on idolatry and sexual ethics) is ultimately left uncertain.

Significance: What does the practice of these works signify? With regard to the significance of works of the law, Dunn is quite close to Sanders, holding that these works function as "boundary markers" that identify those who practice them as members of the Jewish people and participants in the Jewish covenant.[56] This identification as a Jew is simultaneously a move of separation from the other nations: as Dunn writes, such works are simply what "ought to characterize the good Jew and set him apart from the Gentile."[57] In his original 1982 lecture, Dunn identifies Paul's target as this "racial" expression of faith,[58] and in this regard his views have remained consistent. In his 1984 essay, Dunn cites Romans 9:32 as evidence that "'works of the law' are what Jews do to demonstrate and maintain their standing with God as something peculiar to Israel," which "bring to sharp focus the distinctiveness of Israel's identity" and have "a crucial role in defining 'Jewishness.'"[59] This

---

[55]Dunn, *New Perspective on Paul*, 425. This difficulty appears even more acute in a 2013 piece, cf. "A New Perspective," 179-81.

[56]Cf. Dunn on Rom 3: "The 'works of the law' must be a shorthand way of referring to that in which the typical Jew placed his confidence, the law-observance which documented his membership of the covenant, his righteousness as a loyal member of the covenant" (Dunn, *New Perspective on Paul*, 127).

[57]Dunn, *New Perspective on Paul*, 139; cf. Dunn, *Theology of Paul*, 363.

[58]Dunn, *New Perspective on Paul*, 115.

[59]Dunn, *New Perspective on Paul*, 130; cf. Dunn, *Theology of Paul*, 355.

is restated in 2002, where Dunn writes on Galatians 2 that "it still seems to me impossible to avoid the strong inference here that the works of the law in view were seen as important by the Jewish traditionalists for what I have called their 'boundary defining function,'" which "marked out the distinction between the chosen nation and all others (= Gentiles)."[60] Thus, *pace* the old perspective, Dunn writes that "when Paul said in effect, 'All are justified by faith and not by works,' he meant *not* 'Every individual must cease from his own efforts and simply trust in God's acceptance,' however legitimate and important an interpretation of his words that is."[61] Rather, Paul meant that "justification is not confined to Jews as marked out by their distinctive works; it is open to all, to Gentile as well as Jew, through faith."[62] For Dunn, it is this function of identifying their practitioner as one of the Jews, the people of God, that captures the significance of practicing the works of the law.

Opposition: Why are these works not necessary for the Christian? According to Dunn, Paul rejects works of the law not because of something inherent to the specific deeds, but rather because of the *attitude* that is represented by practicing them. This incorrect orientation that Paul rejects is not one of works righteousness (as the old perspective claims), as "there is no clear teaching in pre-Pauline Jewish documentation that acceptance by God has to be earned," and "the proposition that relationship with God is first and foremost a gift and not something earned, an act of grace and not reward for merit, would be axiomatic to any Jew who took the Torah and the Prophets seriously."[63] Rather, what Paul is objecting to in his Jewish interlocutors is an ethnocentric exclusivism: as Dunn states in his 1982 lecture, "it is *nationalism* which he denies not *activism*."[64] Such

---

[60]Dunn, *New Perspective on Paul*, 416.

[61]Dunn, *New Perspective on Paul*, 205, italics original.

[62]Dunn, *New Perspective on Paul*, 205.

[63]Dunn, *New Perspective on Paul*, 371; cf. 78. According to Dunn, this suggests that passages such as Eph 2:8-9; 2 Tim 1:9; and Titus 3:5 are affirming "Israel's own most fundamental theologoumenon (as in Deut. 9.5): that all salvation begins from God's grace and is dependent on God's grace from start to finish," rather than restating "Paul's more narrowly directed polemic" in Romans and Galatians (390-91).

[64]Dunn, *New Perspective on Paul*, 115, italics original; cf. 131. Nor does Dunn see Paul's relativizing of ethnic identity to be captured by a ritual/moral law distinction, cf. 330.

nationalism is indicative of a more general attitude of "excluding the other,"[65] and as Dunn writes in relation to Galatians 2:16, it is "exclusivism which is encapsulated in one degree or another in the phrase 'works of the law.'"[66] From Dunn's perspective, Paul was concerned that "covenant promise and law had become too inextricably identified with ethnic Israel as such," and thus was endeavoring "to free both the promise and law for a wider range of recipients, freed from the ethnic constraints which he saw to be narrowing the grace of God."[67]

Since exclusivism is the real target of Paul's objections to works of the law, it follows that while the "specific issues of circumcision and food laws" were brought into "sharp focus" as boundary markers in Paul's time, "all requirements could thus be manipulated by sin, could become 'works of the law.'"[68] This principle of an issue becoming an exclusive identity marker does not extend only to the Torah; rather, Dunn is also willing to allow that many contemporary matters would similarly draw Paul's ire as analogous to the works of the law that he encountered, since (here contra Wright) "the point . . . is not what constituted the boundary, but the boundary-drawing attitude itself."[69] As a result, Dunn holds that Paul's statements on works of the law can similarly be applied to all kinds of contemporary "factional shibboleths," such as "'inerrancy,' 'six-day creation,' 'Papal infallibility,' 'Sabbath observance,' 'penal substitution,' 'male headship,'" and the like.[70] As Dunn writes on the broader application of Paul's arguments,

> Equivalent defining issues within the history of Christianity have included
> believer's baptism, speaking in tongues, or apartheid. Today we might think
> of issues like abortion, women priests, scriptural inerrancy, or papal

---

[65]Dunn, *New Perspective on Paul*, 25n99.

[66]Dunn, *New Perspective on Paul*, 418. Cf. 417: "Paul in or as a result of his conversion reacted particularly against Jewish exclusivism," an attitude that "can only safeguard the correctness of its belief by persecuting those who disagree or by seeking to eliminate (through conversion or otherwise) those who hold divergent views," and which finds its extreme expression in events such as "the horrors of the Holocaust."

[67]Dunn, *New Perspective on Paul*, 150; cf. Dunn, *Theology of Paul*, 364.

[68]Dunn, *New Perspective on Paul*, 280.

[69]Dunn, *New Perspective on Paul*, 25n99.

[70]Dunn, *New Perspective on Paul*, 70; cf. 214-15.

infallibility. None of the disputants in such internal controversies would regard the point at issue as the whole of their faith or even as the most important element in their faith. But the issues have become *foci* of controversy to such an extent that the status of the opponent's confession as a whole can in fact be called into question.[71]

Dunn's position thus carries some parallels with the old perspective, in that both maintain that Paul's arguments can extend beyond his immediate conflict with the Torah to all kinds of other circumstances. However, while the old perspective understands Paul to be rejecting any works used to earn salvation, Dunn sees Paul as rejecting works that are used to exclude the other, thus violating God's more fundamental commandments regarding love.[72] Such exclusivism is a "misunderstanding of what the covenant law required,"[73] a "sectarian interpretation" that "attempt[s] to define, too narrowly in Paul's perspective, what membership of the seed of Abraham necessarily involved."[74] As Dunn concludes, "where requirements of the law were being interpreted in a way which ran counter to the basic principle of the love command, Paul thought that the requirements could and should be dispensed with."[75] Nevertheless, Paul holds that the law "still has a positive role to play in the expression of God's purpose and will," as long as it is not "misunderstood as defining and defending the prerogatives of a particular group."[76]

While such exclusivism is Paul's "chief target" in rejecting works of the law,[77] Dunn also identifies salvation-historical reasoning behind Paul's rejection of these works, though this plays a less prominent role in Dunn's understanding of Paul's theology. Dunn sees the law as holding

---

[71]Dunn, *Theology of Paul*, 358-59.

[72]Cf. Dunn, *New Perspective on Paul*, 54, 425.

[73]Dunn, *Theology of Paul*, 366. Contra Reformed perspectives that argue that the problem with works of the law is that no one can do them (such as Westerholm's identification of the "works of the law" as "the deeds of righteousness *not* done by sinners" [Stephen Westerholm, *Perspectives Old and New on Paul: The "Lutheran" Paul and His Critics* {Grand Rapids, MI: Eerdmans, 2004}, 445]). Dunn holds that the opposite is true: "the works of the law are (by definition!) '*doing*' what the law demands, but failing to realise that acceptance by God is not dependent on that doing" (Dunn, *New Perspective on Paul*, 45n178, italics original).

[74]Dunn, *New Perspective on Paul*, 235.

[75]Dunn, *Theology of Paul*, 656.

[76]Dunn, *New Perspective on Paul*, 184; cf. 457.

[77]Dunn, *New Perspective on Paul*, 184.

an "essentially positive role" as a "kind of guardian angel for Israel" before Christ's advent, with Paul's critique of his fellow Jews being their "failure to recognise that that role is now complete."[78] According to Dunn, the key event in this salvation-historical development is Christ's death,[79] which corresponds with the giving of the Spirit. While the law had "a temporary role for Israel," "the coming of Messiah and his Spirit marks the point in time/history at which Israel's transition from childhood to (young) adulthood takes place," and "for the (young) adult the inspiration and monitor of life is now more the Spirit than simply the law."[80] Thus, while "for Paul 'the whole law' was still an obligation for the believer, Gentile as well as Jew . . . 'the whole law' is not fulfilled by 'works of the law,' as in the time before Christ, but in the one word, the well-known, 'You shall love your neighbor as yourself' (Lev. 19.18), a love which is also the fruit of the eschatological Spirit (Galatians 5.22)."[81] According to Dunn, this salvation-historical reasoning explains "why circumcision was such a retrograde step for the Galatians to take," as it was "not merely the step of affiliation to another group, not merely the step from one ethnic identity to another; it was also a step back into another age, another world, one in which other powers were dominant and whose authority and influence had already been superceded [sic] by Christ on the cross."[82]

To summarize, Dunn identifies the works of the law in Paul as the requirements of the Torah, and particularly (though not exclusively) the practices of circumcision, food laws, and Sabbath. These practices are to be distinguished from "good works," which belong to a different category in Paul's thought, though it is ultimately unclear to what degree the

---

[78]Dunn, *New Perspective on Paul*, 52.

[79]For Dunn, Christ's death also relativizes the Jew-Gentile boundary; cf. Dunn, *New Perspective on Paul*, 192, 324-25.

[80]Dunn, *New Perspective on Paul*, 272.

[81]Dunn, *New Perspective on Paul*, 275.

[82]Dunn, *New Perspective on Paul*, 329. Though anthropological reasoning does not play a central role in what Dunn sees as Paul's objections to works of the law, such reasoning can be witnessed here as a subset of the salvation-historical category; see e.g. Dunn on transformation in 92-95. Dunn also allows that Paul's calling to the Gentiles may be related to his objections to the works that excluded them (as Sanders states), though "which of these two came first and gave rise to the other it is not possible now to say" (181).

phrase might be applied to the Torah's other requirements. These works of circumcision, food laws, and Sabbath serve as boundary markers, the practice of which signifies identification with the Jewish people and covenant, and separation from the Gentiles. For Dunn, Paul fundamentally objects to these works because of their social function, as mandating them amounts to a nationalistic exclusivism that prohibits God's grace from reaching all nations. Further, because this attitude of exclusivism is Paul's fundamental target in rejecting works of the law, the principle of rejecting requirements that "exclude the other" can be extended to all kinds of other issues as well. In addition to this, Dunn also recognizes salvation-historical reasoning for leaving behind these practices of the Torah in the messianic age.

N. T. WRIGHT

The final figure representing the new perspective is the Anglican bishop N. T. Wright (1948–), who has done arguably the most to popularize new perspective ideas. Usually sequentially ordered as the third major representative of this viewpoint (being about ten years junior to Sanders and Dunn), it is actually Wright who coined the *new perspective* term in a 1978 lecture (with Dunn himself present in the front row).[83] While not infrequently disagreeing with Sanders and Dunn, Wright identifies three new perspective ideas in particular as genuine insights: that first-century Judaism was not a system of Pelagian works righteousness; that "works of the law" were the markers separating Jew from Gentile; and that Paul critiques Israel not for moralism, but for limiting God to its own nation.[84]

Meaning: What works of what law? Like Sanders and Dunn, Wright insists that for Paul, the law in question in discussing works of the law *"always* means 'the Jewish Law, the Torah.'"[85] Wright similarly contends that in using the phrase, Paul is referring particularly to the works that marked Jew off from Gentile, which "were well known both to Jews and

---

[83]Cf. Wright, *Justification*, 12.
[84]Cf. Wright, "Communion and Koinonia."
[85]Wright, *Justification*, 95, italics original.

to non-Jews in the first century."[86] These are "the specific 'works of Torah' which consisted of circumcision, sabbath and the food laws," accompanied by "a geographical focus on Jerusalem and its Temple and a widely assumed (though no doubt often flouted) endogamy."[87] According to Wright, "every Jew in the ancient world" knew that these practices "were the boundary-markers between Jews and pagans," so that they would have been clear to Paul's audiences as the target of his objections.[88]

As with Sanders and Dunn, Wright notes that it is a mistake to understand "works of the law" as good works or moral principles in general, citing Dunn's "major breakthrough" in recognizing that "the 'works of the law' against which Paul warned were not . . . the moral good deeds done to earn justification (or salvation),[89] but the particular commandments and ordinances which kept Jew and Gentile separate from one another."[90] This can be observed by considering the function of the primary work that Paul cites as an example, circumcision, which "is not a 'moral' issue; it does not have to do with moral effort, or earning salvation by good deeds," but rather functioned as an "ethnic badge" to distinguish who was a Jew and who was not.[91] Unlike Sanders, who views Paul as distinguishing between the Torah's works on an ad hoc basis, Wright holds that Paul's objections to these particular works are guided by the promises given in Israel's covenant.[92] While Wright concedes that "Paul never spells out as precisely as we would like him to" the difference between these "works of Torah" that cannot justify and the "righteous requirement of the law" to be fulfilled in Christians (Rom 8:4),[93] he argues that works that "carried the connotations of ethnic boundary lines"—the practices of circumcision, Sabbath, and food laws—belong

---

[86]Wright, *Paul and the Faithfulness of God* (London: SPCK, 2013), 1034-35.

[87]Wright, *Paul and the Faithfulness*, 1034-35, cf. 364; Wright, *The New Testament and the People of God* (Minneapolis: Fortress, 1992), 237.

[88]Wright, "Communion and Koinonia."

[89]"The moral 'good works' which the Reformation loves to hate," as Wright polemically terms them (Wright, *Justification*, 96).

[90]Wright, *Justification*, 148.

[91]Wright, *Paul: In Fresh Perspective* (Minneapolis: Fortress Press, 2005), 120; Wright, *What Saint Paul Really Said* (Grand Rapids, MI: Eerdmans, 1997), 148.

[92]See Sanders, *Paul*, 3, 50.

[93]Wright, *Paul and the Faithfulness*, 1109.

in the former category, while those that marked "the difference between genuine, living, renewed humanity and false, corruptible, destructive humanity" fit in the latter.[94]

Significance: What does the practice of these works signify? Wright concurs with Sanders and Dunn in seeing these works as boundary markers that identify their practitioner with the Jewish people and covenant, and serve to separate them from the Gentiles.[95] Rather than the Reformation conception of "a legalist's ladder, up which one climbed to earn the divine favour," "the 'works of Torah' . . . were the badges that one wore as the marks of identity, of belonging to the chosen people in the present, and hence the all-important signs, to oneself and one's neighbors, that one belonged to the company who would be vindicated when the covenant god acted to redeem his people."[96] The function of these works as signifying membership in Israel can be witnessed in passages like Romans 3:28-39, where the "'boasting' which is excluded is not the boasting of the successful moralist," but rather "the racial boast of the Jew": "If this is not so, 3:29 ('Or is God the God of the Jews only? Is he not of Gentiles also?') is a *non sequitur*."[97] In practicing the works of the law, then, one sought to gain "not a treasury of moral merit, but the assured status of belonging to God's people, separated from the rest of humankind."[98] As Wright comments,

> Saul, I used to believe, was a proto-Pelagian, who thought he could pull himself up by his moral bootstraps. What mattered for him was understanding, believing, and operating a system of salvation that could be described as "moralism" or "legalism." . . . I now believe that this is both radically anachronistic (this view was not invented in Saul's day) and culturally out of line (it is not the Jewish way of thinking). To this extent, I am convinced,

---

[94]Wright, "Communion and Koinonia."

[95]Cf. e.g. Wright on Gal 2: "What, then, are the 'works of the law,' by which one cannot be 'justified' in this sense? Again, the context is pretty clear. They are the 'living like a Jew' of 2.14, the separation from 'Gentile sinners' of 2.15" (Wright, *Justification*, 96).

[96]Wright, *New Testament and the People*, 238; cf. Wright, "The Letter to the Romans: Introduction, Commentary, and Reflections," in *The New Interpreter's Bible*, ed. Leander E. Keck, vol. 10 (Nashville: Abingdon, 2001), 460.

[97]Wright, *What Saint Paul Really Said*, 129.

[98]Wright, "Letter to the Romans," 480.

Ed Sanders is right: we have misjudged early Judaism, especially Pharisaism, if we have thought of it as an early version of Pelagianism.[99]

"Legalism" or "works righteousness" are thus misidentifications of the significance of practicing these works, which Wright terms instead as "'national righteousness,' the belief that fleshly Jewish descent guarantees membership of God's true covenant people."[100] As Wright summarizes, this represents the heart of the paradigmatic conflict over works of the law in Antioch, where Paul rebukes Peter for "saying, in effect, to the ex-pagan Christians, 'if you want to be part of the real family of God, you are going to have to become Jewish.'"[101]

Opposition: Why are these works not necessary for the Christian? For Wright, the reasons that Paul objects to the works of the law are not based fundamentally in experience (Sanders) or social exclusivity (Dunn), but rather in the promises of Jewish Scriptures and covenant, which Paul understands to be now fulfilled in the Messiah.[102] One can identify three lines of reasoning under this covenantal heading, which are found in seed form as early as Wright's 1978 lecture. As Wright summarizes Paul's argument in Romans 2–3, "the one God has purposed and promised that he will create one worldwide family for Abraham, a family in whom the sin of Adam is reversed: and this he has achieved in the Messiah, Jesus."[103] Here three arguments against works of Torah can be drawn out (which, for clarity, we can term as the "universal," "anthropological," and "salvation-historical" arguments). First, the covenant promises to Abraham were universal in scope, not simply for the Jews, who are separated and demarcated as a single distinct nation by the

---

[99]Wright, *What Saint Paul Really Said*, 32; cf. 19; Wright, "Letter to the Romans," 460-61.

[100]Wright, "The Paul of History and the Apostle of Faith," *Tyndale Bulletin* 29 (1978): 71.

[101]Wright, *Justification*, 94; cf. 104-5; Wright, *The Climax of the Covenant: Christ and the Law in Pauline Theology* (London: T&T Clark, 1991), 173.

[102]Regarding covenant as a unifying Pauline theme, Wright comments that "it is surprising . . . that E.P. Sanders did not move in this direction, since he argued strenuously for a 'covenantal' reading of rabbinic and other forms of Palestinian Judaism, making the point as he did so that the reason the rabbis do not often use the word 'covenant' itself is because it is everywhere presupposed. The same point could, and in my view should, be made about Paul" (Wright, *Paul and the Faithfulness*, 781).

[103]Wright, "Paul of History," 66. On God promising one family (σπέρμα), see Wright on Gal 3:15-22 (Wright, *Climax of the Covenant*, 162-74).

Torah and its practices. Second, these promises were given to reverse the fundamental anthropological problem stemming from Adam's sin, which Israel's history shows that the Torah and its works cannot do. Third, these covenant promises have now been fulfilled in the Messiah, Jesus, bringing salvation history to its climax and inaugurating the new age in which the Torah's purposes have reached their end.

According to Wright, the first two arguments against works of the law—the universal and anthropological arguments, which he identifies as representing new and old perspective emphases[104]—interlock, as the "problem of Genesis 11 (the fracturing of humanity) is the full outworking of the problem of Genesis 3 (sin), and the promise to Abraham is the answer to both together."[105] For Wright, the universality of God's promises to Abraham, whose seed is promised to bless all nations on the earth and create a single worldwide family, is foundational for why becoming an ethnic Jew cannot be required in the new era when these covenant promises are fulfilled. As Wright comments on Romans 3:29, "what Israel has always been tempted to forget, from Paul's point of view, is that the God who made the covenant with Abraham is the creator of the whole world and that the covenant was put in place precisely in order that through Israel God might address the whole world."[106] As Wright comments elsewhere,

> Martin Luther saw the essence of sin as being "turned in on one-self"; Israel was acting out that primal sin through the attempt to carve out and cling on to a covenant membership which would be for Jews and Jews only, a national identity marked out by the "works of Torah" which proclaimed Jewish distinctiveness. That is what Paul means when he says that "they did not pursue the law by faith, but as though it was based on works" (9.32).[107]

---

[104]Cf. Wright, *Justification*, 186: "[Romans] 3.28 is saying: God declares a person to be 'righteous' on the basis of faith, apart from those 'works of Torah' which (a) would have established a status for Jews and Jews only and (b) were in any case impossible because Torah would then only have proved that Jews too were sinful. In other words, let's go beyond the new perspective/old perspective divide: both are necessary parts of what Paul is actually saying."

[105]Wright, *Justification*, 97-98. As Wright notes, "holding these two things together (Torah as separating Jew and gentile; Torah as condemning its possessors for failure to keep it) is vital to avoid reducing 'works of Torah' simply to the outward symbols, however important they are" (Wright, *Justification*, 1037n745). See also 195.

[106]Wright, "Letter to the Romans," 482.

[107]Wright, *Justification*, 215; cf. Wright, *Climax of the Covenant*, 240.

Against the idea that God is limited to the Jews alone, Wright sees Paul as insisting that the Jewish covenant itself promises "*a single worldwide people praising the God of Israel, the creator*," undoing the fracturing of humanity witnessed at Babel.[108] With covenant's fulfillment by the Messiah, the old walls of separation between nations must be made relative, with the way now "open for all, Jew and Gentile alike, to enter the family of Abraham."[109]

Though this argument holds some overlap with Dunn's reasoning, in which "exclusivism" is the target of Paul's objections, it is important to note that these arguments function in different ways for Dunn and Wright. While both figures identify Paul as objecting to Jewish nationalism in his rejection of works of the law, for Dunn nationalism is a subset of a more fundamental issue of exclusivity, meaning that while circumcision, food laws, and Sabbath were the particular divisive issues that Paul encountered, any other boundary-marking issues that serve to divide believers in Christ from one another (such as views on abortion, inerrancy, or apartheid) can be seen as equivalent defining issues.[110] Wright, on the other hand, sees this Jewish nationalism as problematic because it points to a deeper issue of inconsistency with Israel's covenant and its promises, which were always meant to be for all nations when brought to their fulfillment. This means that "works of the law" cannot be expanded beyond the specific markers of the Jewish people into a general category of "issues that exclude" (which, in Wright's view, degenerates Paul's reasoning into a "vague liberalism" that uses a supposed faith vs. works/law dichotomy "as a way of avoiding the sharp edges of every ethical issue in sight").[111]

According to Wright, the second reason that "'works of the law' will never justify" is anthropological, as "what the law does is to reveal sin," and "nobody can keep it perfectly."[112] Here Wright shows correspondence

---

[108]Wright, *Paul and the Faithfulness*, 399, italics original.

[109]Wright, "Paul of History," 71. Wright holds that this reasoning "goes back, if we are to believe the gospels, to John the Baptist and to Jesus himself. God can give Abraham children from these stones: many will come from East and West and sit at table with Abraham, while the sons of the kingdom are cast out" (71).

[110]Cf. Dunn, *Theology of Paul*, 358-59; Dunn, *New Perspective on Paul*, 70, 214-15.

[111]Wright, "Communion and Koinonia."

[112]Wright, *Justification*, 97.

with "old" Pauline perspectives that highlight human inability to keep the law, writing that "the problem was not with the law, but with the people to whom the law had been given . . . since Israel was precisely made up entirely of human beings who, themselves sinful, were as much in need of redemption as the rest of humankind."[113] This reality shows the fruitlessness of reliance on Jewish identity and possession of the Torah (which Israel's history shows to have not solved the problem of sin), and makes an "appeal to Torah . . . like calling a defense witness who endorses what the prosecution has been saying all along."[114] This problem of the underlying persistence of sin both outside and inside of Israel is Paul's point in Romans 2–3: "If 'the Jew' appealed to Torah to say 'This shows that I am different from the Gentiles,' Torah itself, according to Paul, would say 'No, it doesn't; it shows that you are the same as Gentiles.'"[115]

While both Wright and the old perspective recognize anthropological reasoning for why works of the law are to be opposed, here as well it should be noted that the reasoning does not operate in precisely the same way. For Luther, Calvin and their heirs, works of the law do not justify because (a) the all-pervasiveness of sin makes performing enough good works impossible, which is true even following conversion; and (b) because the law demands a perfect obedience, one that can only be won by Christ and imputed to the Christian's account. For Wright, the works of Torah do not justify because they do not solve the underlying problem of human sinfulness, which is the fundamental issue to be resolved due to humanity's fall in Adam, and which the covenant promises made to Abraham were meant to address. However, Wright differs from the old perspective at point (a) in that he sees the Holy Spirit given to Christians as making possible the works that will serve as the basis for their judgment on the last day,[116] and at point (b) in maintaining that Torah itself provides the means for repentance (which is how Paul can call himself "blameless" before the law in Phil 3:6),[117] so that Christ's

---

[113]Wright, *Justification*, 105; cf. Wright, *Climax of the Covenant*, 21-26.
[114]Wright, "Letter to the Romans," 459-60.
[115]Wright, "Letter to the Romans," 461.
[116]Cf. Wright, *Justification*, 163-67, 209-12.
[117]Cf. Wright, *Justification*, 124-25.

achievement does not consist in perfectly obeying the law and imputing the merits of this obedience toward Christians. As Wright states, "to think this way is to concede, after all, that 'legalism' was true after all—with Jesus as the ultimate legalist."[118] Rather, in passages such as Romans 3, "[Paul's] primary concern is not to analyze every single individual and to demonstrate somehow that he or she really is sinful, but rather to show that possession of Torah itself cannot sustain the claim that 'the Jew' is automatically in covenant with God, automatically a cut above the Gentiles," since both remain in the Adamic condition.[119]

Finally, because Wright sees Paul's theology as fundamentally guided by the covenant, the two arguments above are themselves dependent on salvation-historical (or eschatological) reasoning, whereby Jesus the Messiah represents the fulfillment of the Abrahamic covenant and ushers in the promised new age. According to Wright, Paul holds that the Torah "belongs to the age of preparation, the strange pre-Messiah period when it seemed as though God's worldwide promises to Abraham were never going to be fulfilled."[120] For Paul, then, the continued necessity of the works of Torah is actually dependent on the question of Jesus' messiahship: if Jesus is the Messiah, then he indeed fulfills the promises made to Abraham and inaugurates the new age, in which God's promised blessing is poured out to all nations; if he is not, then these promises are as-yet unfulfilled and the age of Torah remains. Paul's rejection of the works of Torah thus has "everything to do with covenantal eschatology: in the Messiah God has unveiled his long-awaited purpose, all preparatory stages are rendered indifferent, and to insist on them is to deny the Messiah himself and his achievement."[121]

Wright thus holds that it is incorrect to see Paul as redefining praxis apart from the Torah's identity markers because "[Judaism] was bad, shabby, second-rate, semi-Pelagian or concerned with physical rather than spiritual realities,"[122] or due to "a contrast between types or patterns

---

[118]Wright, *Justification*, 205.
[119]Wright, "Letter to the Romans," 461.
[120]Wright, *Justification*, 108.
[121]Wright, *Paul and the Faithfulness*, 363; cf. 444; Wright, *Justification*, 116.
[122]Wright, *Paul and the Faithfulness*, 1264.

of religion,"[123] or because "Paul was simply a born-out-of-due-time modern liberal when it came to scriptural commandments."[124] Rather, it is the fulfillment of salvation history that is essential for understanding why these Jewish symbols are now made relative:

> Paul's point was not that there was anything wrong with the original promise or symbol. Far from it. When you have arrived at your destination, you switch off the engine and park the car, not because it has not done its proper job but because it has. It is eschatology, not religious superiority, that forms the key to Paul the apostle's radical revision of the symbolic world of Saul of Tarsus.[125]

Wright similarly views it as a mistake to identify "works" or "working" in general as Paul's target, as this fails to account for why Paul maintains (and even strengthens) requirements for praxis elsewhere:

> Paul not only *redefined* the Jewish praxis, leaving behind elements that were now irrelevant in his Messiah-based inaugurated eschatology and unified ecclesiology: he also *intensified* it. What have often been called the "moral standards" or "ethical imperatives" in his key texts show no sign of a slackening of demand, and in fact indicate on the contrary a standard of perfection at which one might well blanch.[126]

As Wright argues, rather than holding to a fundamental dichotomy between faith and works, Paul presents those who have been given the Spirit with "*a fuller range of ethical behaviour as a new form of Torah-keeping.*"[127] This fuller range of ethical imperatives can be given because of the gift of the Spirit with the Messiah's advent, which fulfills the covenant's promises by blessing and uniting all nations in a new and transformed humanity. For Paul, then, the Jews' error is not rooted in legalism, or social exclusivity, but rather is "eschatological: Israel's God had kept his promises, but Israel had refused to believe it."[128]

---

[123]Wright, *Paul and the Faithfulness*, 363.

[124]Wright, *Paul and the Faithfulness*, 444, with a footnote noting Dunn as his target.

[125]Wright, *Paul and the Faithfulness*, 367. Wright notes that in light of this eschatological inbreaking, Paul sees that practices like physical circumcision held a typological significance as "advanced signposts" for the heart circumcision brought by the Messiah, though this typological reasoning is not weight bearing for Paul's objections in Wright's arguments (cf. 362-63).

[126]Wright, *Paul and the Faithfulness*, 445.

[127]Wright, *Paul and the Faithfulness*, 1037, italics original.

[128]Wright, *Paul and the Faithfulness*, 1264.

In summary, Wright concurs with Sanders and Dunn in seeing Paul as relativizing the Torah's works of circumcision, Sabbath keeping, and food laws (as well as endogamy and a focus on Jerusalem and the temple). These works are to be distinguished from good works in general, as the practices Paul targets are not related to moral effort. For Wright, the observance of these works signifies identification with Jewish people and covenant, and separation from the Gentiles. According to Wright, Paul rejects these works in accordance with the promises made in Israel's covenant, in which God purposed to bless and unite all nations (and not simply the Jews, who are demarcated by the Torah), and to repair humanity's sinful condition (which Torah is unable to do). The fulfillment of this covenant by the Messiah marks the inauguration of the new age, in which humanity's condition is restored, and these practices that separated Jews from the other nations are to be left behind.[129]

CONCLUSION

In summarizing the new perspective on works of the law, it can be seen that in contrast with the old perspective, these figures generally see Paul's emphasis by "works of the law" as on *the law*—and this a specific law, the Jewish Torah.[130] Within this law, the new perspective sees Paul's most prominent targets as circumcision, laws regarding food, and the observance of Sabbath. While these figures do not agree precisely on the way in which the rest of the Torah's requirements can be regarded as works of the law—indeed, there can appear to be internal tension among the authors on this question—all three agree that Paul does not mean to target "good works" in general, and that moral works belong in a different subcategory of Paul's thought than works of the law. In contrast to the old perspective, these practices are not performed on an individual basis to accord God's favor, but are rather adopted as group identity markers that signify one's membership in God's chosen people,

---

[129]Cf. Wright, *Climax of the Covenant*, 240.

[130]The partial exception to this is Dunn, who argues that the most fundamental matter is not the works of the Torah that made up the boundary between Jews and Gentiles, but rather "the boundary-drawing attitude itself" (Dunn, *New Perspective on Paul*, 25n99).

the Jews. The new perspectives diverge on Paul's reasons for rejecting these works. Sanders emphasizes the role of experience, with Paul rejecting these practices based on his own experience in being called to the Gentiles, and his Gentile congregations' experience of receiving the Spirit apart from these works. Dunn's emphasis can be identified as social, as he sees Paul as primarily rejecting these works due to their role in separating and excluding believers in Christ from one another, though he also acknowledges salvation-historical reasoning behind this rejection as well. Wright's emphasis can be regarded as covenantal, with Paul rejecting these works because of the universal scope of the covenant promises, the inability of Torah to repair the problem of humanity's sinfulness brought about by Adam, and the new age inaugurated by Jesus' fulfillment of the covenant.

In light of the considerable divergence between these old and new perspectives regarding the "fire" of Paul's conflicts over the works of the law, how might the "smoke" of second-century testimony help us adjudicate between these competing accounts? Like the old perspective, would these early patristic sources have seen the works of the law as works in general, performed on an individual basis to earn salvation? Or, conversely, would they align with the new perspective in seeing them as particular works of a specific law, the Torah, which function as group identity markers to signify membership in the chosen people, the Jews? Further, among the variety of arguments put forward by the old and new perspectives, why might these early figures have understood Paul to be rejecting these works? It is to these questions that our study now turns.

PART III

EARLY PERSPECTIVES
ON WORKS OF THE LAW

□

For how stands the case? Suppose there arise a dispute relative
to some important question among us, should we not have recourse
to the most ancient Churches with which the apostles
held constant intercourse, and learn from them what is certain
and clear in regard to the present question?

IRENAEUS, *AGAINST HERESIES* 3.4.1 (ANF)

4

THE DIDACHE (C)

◻

INTRODUCTION

Introduction and background. The first source in this study is the Teaching of the Twelve Apostles, commonly known as the Didache. A short compilation of early Christian doctrine, the Didache is difficult to date due to its lack of internal markers or references by outside sources, with the most common suggestions being the second half of the first century or the early decades of the second.[1] Presenting itself as the "teaching of the Lord to the Gentiles through the twelve apostles" (Did. 1.0), the Didache is often suggested to be of Syrian or Egyptian provenance, and its authorship, as with most issues related to the document, is a mystery. There are questions regarding the possible composite nature of the Didache, with Jefford and Milavec respectively arguing for multiple levels of redaction over time or composition by a single early community.[2] The paucity of evidence prohibits such

---

[1]Cf. Michael W. Holmes, ed., *The Apostolic Fathers: Greek Texts and English Translations* (Grand Rapids, MI: Baker Academic, 2007), 337. This situation is further complicated by the possibility that the Didache is composed of primitive materials and edited by a later source. Among other factors, guidance given regarding itinerant prophets and apostles have led many to date its material to a period preceding that of the more clearly established structures delineated in Ignatius's epistles in the early second century; however, no firm *terminus ante quem* exists prior to Clement of Alexandria's citation at the close of the second century.

[2]Clayton N. Jefford, *Reading the Apostolic Fathers: A Student's Introduction* (Grand Rapids, MI: Baker Academic, 2012), 33; Aaron Milavec, *The Didache: Faith, Hope, & Life of the Earliest Christian Communities, 50–70 C.E.* (New York: Newman Press, 2003), xii; cf. Kraft's designation of the Didache as "evolved literature" in Robert Kraft, ed. *Barnabas and the Didache*, vol. 3 of *The Apostolic Fathers: A New Translation and Commentary* (New York: Thomas Nelson, 1965), 9-16. For

questions from being settled with confidence, and in any case, it is generally agreed that the Didache represents one of the earliest witnesses to Christianity outside of the New Testament writings.[3] While the quantity of material in the Didache that shows evidence of works in dispute with Jewish parties is very small, the document's early date nevertheless makes it of interest as a possible witness to early discussions on this topic.

Text and translation. The Didache is primarily known via a single manuscript (the eleventh-century Codex Hierosolymitanus), with only minor fragments preserved elsewhere, though variations of the "Two Ways" section are incorporated into a number of later writings. This chapter uses the Holmes edition for both Greek text and English translation.[4]

THE DIDACHE AND PAUL

Knowledge and use of Paul. The Didache shows very few possible marks of Pauline influence. Tuckett's analysis of possible allusions to Romans, 1 Corinthians, and 1 Timothy concludes that "there is little if any evidence to support any theory that Didache knew or used the Pauline corpus of letters."[5] Lindemann's conclusions are essentially identical; while acknowledging that the Didache "zwar zeigen sich an einigen Stellen schwache Parallelen" with Pauline letters, particularly with 1 Corinthians, he nevertheless judges that the document "keine Kenntnis der paulinischen Briefe zeigt" and "ist von paulinischer Theologie nicht berührt."[6] Contemporary commentators offer few if any suggestions of

---

possible attribution of the Didache's "Two Ways" section to Peter, see Robert E. Aldridge, "Peter and the 'Two Ways,'" *Vigiliae Christianae* 53 (1999): 233-64.

[3]This is of course a later distinction, as Clement of Alexandria expressly cites it as Scripture (*Strom.* 1.20, citing Did. 3.5), as do Origen and Didymus; cf. Holmes, *Apostolic Fathers*, 334.

[4]Holmes, *Apostolic Fathers*.

[5]Christopher M. Tuckett, "The Didache and the Writings That Later Formed the New Testament," in *The Reception of the New Testament in the Apostolic Fathers*, ed. Andrew F. Gregory and Christopher M. Tuckett (Oxford: Oxford University Press, 2005), 93.

[6]Including the translated portion, this reads, "Didache indeed displays weak parallels in some places with Pauline letters, particularly with 1 Corinthians, he nevertheless judges that the document shows no knowledge of the Pauline letters and is not touched by Pauline theology," Andreas Lindemann, *Paulus im ältesten Christentum: das Bild des Apostels und die Rezeption der paulinischen Theologie in der frühchristlichen Literatur bis Marcion* (Tübingen: Mohr Siebeck, 1979), 174, 177; cf. David Rensberger, "As the Apostle Teaches: The Development of the Use of Paul's Letters in Second-Century Christianity" (PhD diss., Yale University, 1981), 69.

Pauline correspondence, and any possible connections would be minor at most.[7] Thus, while the Didache may potentially contain material that corresponds with a commonly held concept of works of the law, such material can bear no more weight than that of circumstantial evidence (C) as a witness to Paul's understanding.

THE LAW AND WORKS IN THE DIDACHE

Meaning: What works of what law? As a positive statement of Christian teaching, the Didache offers almost no engagement with or critique of groups outside of its own audience, and the general consonance of its teaching with Jewish thought is unanimously recognized by commentators.[8] A brief exception to this is chapter 8, where the author instructs that the fasts of Christians[9] not coincide with those of "the hypocrites" (οἱ ὑποκριταί); while these fast on Monday and Thursday, the Christian is to fast on Wednesday and Friday (Did. 8.1).[10] Along with fasting according to a different calendar, the hypocrites' manner of prayer is also to be rejected, in favor the thrice-daily practice of the Lord's prayer (8.2-3).

Commentators largely agree that "hypocrites" is in some way a reference to the Jews; though such days of fasting are not instituted by the Torah, they are attested in later rabbinic teaching (cf. *m. Ta'an.* 2.9; *Meg.* and *Ta'an.* 12), and may be referenced in Luke 18:12 in relation to the Pharisee

---

[7]Jefford, for one, identifies portions of the Didache as sharing "an affinity with the theology and language" of the Pauline letters and a general "Pauline consciousness" (seen in comments corresponding with 1 and 2 Thessalonians and Galatians), though the concerns of Paul are not identified with those of the Didachist (cf. Jefford, *Reading the Apostolic Fathers*, 39; Jefford, *The Apostolic Fathers and the New Testament* [Peabody, MA: Hendrickson Publishers, 2006], 22). See also Massaux, perhaps the only commentator who positively identifies a "literary relationship with the Pauline epistles," though the evidence presented is not decisive in his favor (Edouard Massaux, *The Influence of the Gospel of Saint Matthew on Christian Literature Before Saint Irenaeus*, ed. Arthur J. Bellinzoni, vol. 3 of 3 [Macon, GA: Mercer, 1993 {1950}], 177-79).

[8]The "Two Ways" section (ch. 1–5), to take one example, is often seen as a Jewish source that largely predates Christianity; among others, see Kurt Niederwimmer, *The Didache: A Commentary*, ed. Harold W. Attridge (Minneapolis: Fortress Press, 1998), 36. As Jefford writes, "at the core of the Didache there is little that is not Jewish in perspective or intention" (Jefford, *Apostolic Fathers and the New Testament*, 162).

[9]The designation here is not anachronistic, with Χριστιανός used in 12.4.

[10]The Jewish-Christian character of the document is also illustrated by its use of the Jewish (rather than Roman) calendar; see Milavec, *Didache*, 289.

who fasts twice weekly. Regarding the custom of daily prayer, Niederwimmer is likely correct in positing that "the prayer of the ὑποκριταί refers concretely to the *Shemoneh Esreh*, the *Tefillah* as such," which the Lord's prayer is meant to replace.[11] Beyond this, however, the brevity of the passage means that further inferences are difficult to establish. The term *hypocrites* does not appear to be a specific allusion to the Matthean Pharisees,[12] and most follow Audet's view that these are "tous ceux des Juifs, pharisiens ou autres, qui ont refusé et qui refusent encore de croire en l'evangile."[13] Rordof is more specific in identifying the hypocrites as Jewish Christians advocating "le retour aux observances judaïques dans les communautés chrétiennes"[14] and draws analogy with Galatians 2:13, wherein "les judaïsants sont effectivement appelés hypocrites,"[15] but this thesis has not gained great traction for lack of explicit evidence.[16]

An interesting variant of Rordorf's thesis is put forward by Milavec, who makes the case that the hypocrites refer to those Jews who "advocated temple piety for gentile converts."[17] Milavec interprets the designation of "hypocrites" through five points he sees as demonstrating a conscious attempt to displace the temple cult in the Didache: (1) the "ransoming of your sins" through alms without priest, temple, or animal sacrifice (Did. 4.6); (2) prayer that ignores Jerusalem and the temple cult (8.2); (3) the Eucharist as the "pure sacrifice" prophesied by Malachi 1:11

---

[11]Niederwimmer, *Didache*, 134; cf. Géza Vermès, *Christian Beginnings: From Nazareth to Nicaea* (New Haven, CT: Yale University Press, 2013), 141.

[12]So Jean Paul Audet, *La didachè: instructions des apôtres* (Paris: J. Gabalda, 1958), 368; Milavec, *Didache*, 302-03; Marcello Del Verme, *Didache and Judaism: Jewish Roots of an Ancient Christian-Jewish Work* (New York: T&T Clark International, 2004), 175; *pace* Massaux, *Influence of the Gospel*, 3:155.

[13]"All those of the Jews, Pharisees or others, who have refused and still refuse to believe in the gospel." Audet, *La didachè*, 368; cf. Niederwimmer, *Didache*, 131.

[14]"The return to Jewish observances in the Christian communities."

[15]"The Judiazers are effectively called hypocrites." Cf. Del Verme, *Didache and Judaism*, 183-84, who draws the same comparison.

[16]Willy Rordorf and André Tuilier, eds., *La doctrine des douze apôtres: Didachè*, Sources Chrétiennes 248 (Paris: Éditions du Cerf, 1998), 37n2; cf. 224. Vermès, *Christian Beginnings*, 141 also notes Gal 2:12-13, identifying the hypocrites as "Jewish-Christians who remained attached to Pharisaic customs."

[17]Milavec, *Didache*, 785. An underlying theme of replacing the temple system does not require the early dating posited by Milavec's specific narrative (according to which he places Didache at 50–70).

(14.1-3); (4) prophets as "your high priests" (13.3); (5) eschatology with no place for Jerusalem and the temple (16.3-8).[18] By Milavec's reading, the Didache is written by "Stephen Christians" persecuted and exiled from the temple, who have branded as hypocrites those whose self-definition does not similarly exclude "both the temple and its sacrificial system."[19] While Milavec's case for an underlying displacement of the temple and its cult in the Didache is compelling, the absence of explicit reference to the temple in relation to the "hypocrites" (or indeed elsewhere in the document) prevents it, like Rordorf's suggestion, from being established beyond the level of conjecture.[20]

Significance: What does the practice of these works signify? In the Didache, the practice of fasting on these particular days and praying in this manner appears to associate one with the "hypocrites," the Jews. As is discussed above, the precise identity of the Jewish opponents cannot be deduced with confidence, and the small amount of relevant material in the Didache means that little else can be said on the significance of practicing these works.

Opposition: Why are these works not necessary for the Christian? The Didachist rejects these works for their association with hypocrisy, which commentators regard as referring to their connection with the Jews who have largely failed to believe in the gospel, though this point is a common inference rather than an explicit statement in the Didache. Beyond the general charge of hypocrisy, the Didache presents these Jewish practices as being replaced by corresponding Christian ones, including different days

---

[18]Milavec, *Didache*, 786.

[19]Milavec, *Didache*, 795.

[20]Also to be noted is Did. 6.2 ("For if you are able to bear the whole yoke of the Lord, you will be perfect"), which Draper proposes to represent a call for the Gentiles to adopt the Torah, thereby becoming Jews (Jonathan A. Draper, "Torah and Troublesome Apostles in the Didache Community," *Novum Testamentum* 33 [1991]: 368; cf. David Flusser, "Paul's Jewish-Christian Opponents in the Didache," in *Gilgul: Essays on Transformation, Revolution and Permanence in the History Of Religions; Dedicated to R.J. Zwi Werblowsky*, ed. Shaul Shaked, David Shulman, and Gedaliahu A.G. Stroumsa [Leiden: Brill, 1987], 71-90). Following Milavec, this thesis (along with Draper's accompanying narrative of Paul as the lawless deceiver of 11.2 and 16.3-4) is difficult to maintain; the Didachist's yoke is more naturally understood as the lengthy "Way of Life" immediately preceding this passage, and no clear awareness of Paul is found in the Didache. See Milavec, *Didache*, 769-82.

of fasting and a differing manner of prayer. Apart from this, the Didache offers no explicit reasoning for why these works are not to be observed.

CONCLUSION

In summary, the practices in conflict with Jewish parties in the Didache include the keeping of Jewish days of fasting and the Jewish manner of daily prayer, with both founded on the traditions surrounding the Torah (though "law" itself is never used as a target). Though they cannot be conclusively demonstrated from the text, rejections of the temple and sacrificial system (or an underlying conflict with "Judaizers" like those attested in Galatians) may be implied as well. Little can be said about the significance of practicing these works or the reasons for opposing them, beyond that they appear to identify one with the Jews. The fact that these practices are replaced by similar Christian ones suggests that their objectionable aspect is not their nature as works, but rather their association with a rejected group or identity. However, while such observations are interesting as very early points of distinction between Jewish and Christian communities, broader questions of the law are only tangential to this text, and the brevity of the passage that holds possible correspondence with works of the law allows little by way of firm conclusions to be drawn. Further, because of the lack of clear overlap with Paul's discussions (besides the possible thematic correspondence with Gal 2:13) and the weakness of evidence suggesting knowledge of Paul's letters, the Didache can only offer general suggestions as to where some points of conflict with the Jews, perhaps nearly contemporary or only decades after Paul's own time, may have lain.

5

THE EPISTLE OF BARNABAS (C)

◻

INTRODUCTION

Introduction and background. The Epistle of Barnabas carries a reputation as a bit of a curiosity among the early Christian writings, with Vielhauer memorably calling it the "seltsamste Dokument der urchristlichen Literatur."[1] The epistle holds a fascinating reception history, with evidence of its popularity and usage as Scripture in the region around Alexandria found beginning in the second century. It does not appear to have become widely influential elsewhere, however, being classed variously among the disputed (ἀντιλεγόμενα) and spurious (νόθα) books by Eusebius in the fourth century,[2] and eventually falling into relative disuse until the rediscovery of the full Greek text in Codex Sinaiticus in the nineteenth century.[3] The relationship between Barnabas and Paul is also an intriguing one, for while much of the content of Barnabas's arguments seems reminiscent of Paul, usage of

---

[1]Translated as "Strangest document of early Christian literature," Philipp Vielhauer, *Geschichte der urchristlichen Literatur. Einleitung in das Neue Testament, die Apokryphen und die Apostolischen Väter* (Berlin: De Gruyter, 1975), 612, cited in Ernst Dassmann, *Der Stachel im Fleisch: Paulus in der frühchristlichen Literatur bis Irenäus* (Münster: Aschendorff, 1979), 225.

[2]See *Hist. Eccl.* 6.14.1, 3.25.4 (Eusebius, *The Ecclesiastical History*, ed. Kirsopp Lake and J. E. L. Oulton, 2 vols. [Cambridge, MA: Harvard University Press, 2014 {1926}]). As Carleton Paget notes, these designations do not make Barnabas unorthodox according to Eusebius, as he reserves heretical books for a fourth category; see James Carleton Paget, *The Epistle of Barnabas: Outlook and Background*, WUNT 2:62 (Tübingen: Mohr Siebeck, 1994), 252.

[3]Carleton Paget notes that "this decline in interest may in part be accounted for by the fact that a more fastidious approach to the canon emerged from the fourth century onwards" (Carleton Paget, *Epistle of Barnabas*, 256).

actual Pauline texts in the epistle is difficult to pinpoint, and the author himself has been identified on a range from a disciple (and even fellow worker) of Paul to a Pauline opponent.[4] Because of this, classifying the influence of Pauline texts in Barnabas is one of the more difficult decisions in this study, and arguments can be made for the both B- and C-level classifications. While acknowledging the merit of arguments that identify stronger Pauline influence in Barnabas, this study adopts a modest C-level standard below, making Barnabas's theology of interest for identifying a potentially broader category of works of the law, but not higher than the level of circumstantial evidence as a witness to Paul's own ideas.

Current scholarship on Barnabas offers a fairly wide range of possible dates for the epistle, which is further complicated by Kraft's suggestion that Barnabas represents "evolved literature" with multiple levels of redaction.[5] While commentators generally agree that a provenance of Alexandria seems most likely (though this too is conjectural),[6] a number of possible contexts and dates can be argued for following the *terminus a quo* of the temple's destruction in AD 70 (cf. Barn. 16.3-4). These include the view that the epistle reflects anxieties held in the 90s about a possible rebuilding of the Jewish temple under Nerva,[7] or that

---

[4]The early view of Barnabas ascribes it to Paul's fellow worker in Acts (for which see n9 below); for one recent example of Barnabas as a Pauline opponent, see James D. G. Dunn, *Neither Jew nor Greek: A Contested Identity*, vol. 3 of *Christianity in the Making* (Grand Rapids, MI: Eerdmans, 2015), 696. This view is less common and difficult to sustain as an argument from silence (which Dunn acknowledges).

[5]Robert Kraft, ed. *Barnabas and the Didache*, vol. 3 of *The Apostolic Fathers: A New Translation and Commentary* (New York: Thomas Nelson, 1965), 1-4, 19-22. In relation to this view (and the similar argument of Pierre Prigent, *Les testimonia dans le christianisme primitif: l'Épître de Barnabé I-XVI et ses sources* [Paris: J. Gabalda, 1961]), Carleton Paget persuasively argues that the author of Barnabas is better understood as a single original compiler of traditional materials; see Carleton Paget, *Epistle of Barnabas*, 183-85.

[6]Reasoning for this position includes a heavily allegorical interpretive method, reminiscent of Alexandrian authors like Philo, Clement, and Origen, and usage of the epistle that appears to be centered around the Alexandrian region (including Clement, Origen, Codex Sinaiticus, and Didymus the Blind). For discussion on Alexandrian provenance (and possible alternatives), see Kraft, *Barnabas and the Didache*, 45-56; Ferdinand Prostmeier, *Der Barnabasbrief* (Göttingen: Vandenhoeck & Ruprecht, 1999), 119-30.

[7]See William Horbury, "Jewish-Christian Relations in Barnabas and Justin Martyr," in *Jews and Christians in Contact and Controversy* (Edinburgh: T&T Clark, 1998), 132-33; Carleton Paget, "Paul and the Epistle of Barnabas," *Novum Testamentum* 38 (1996): 364. Carleton Paget later

it contains a reference to Hadrian's building of the temple of Jupiter in Jerusalem (whether before or in the wake of the Bar-Kochba revolt) in the 130s.[8] Even Tugwell's suggestion that the epistle may indeed represent the work of Paul's fellow laborer post-70 cannot be firmly discounted,[9] though this possibility is often dismissed out of hand by commentators,[10] a trend that is at least in some measure attributable to theological considerations.[11]

While the nature of the evidence is such that reasonable conclusions can be reached for a number of dates within this range,[12] in my view, the two strongest cases for dating Barnabas are under Vespasian in the 70s and under Hadrian in the 130s. In relation to the two primary passages used for dating the epistle, Barnabas 4.4-5's reference to the beasts and horns from Daniel 7 appears to best correspond with a fulfillment during the reign of Vespasian in the 70s,[13] and the enemies rebuilding the temple in 16.3-4 seem to fit most naturally as a reference to Hadrian's Jupiter

---

expands his suggested dating to "any time between the mid-90s CE and the 130s CE" (Carleton Paget, "The Epistle of Barnabas and the Writings that Later Formed the New Testament," in *The Reception of the New Testament in the Apostolic Fathers*, ed. Andrew F. Gregory and Christopher M. Tuckett [Oxford: Oxford University Press, 2005], 229), no doubt owing to the tentative nature of any conclusions on this question.

[8]For the former, see Reidar Hvalvik, *The Struggle for Scripture and Covenant: The Purpose of the Epistle of Barnabas and Jewish-Christian Competition in the Second Century*, WUNT 2:82 (Tübingen: Mohr Siebeck, 1996), 23; for the latter, see James N. Rhodes, *The Epistle of Barnabas and the Deuteronomic Tradition*, WUNT 2:188 (Tübingen: Mohr Siebeck, 2004), 75-80, 86.

[9]See Simon Tugwell, *The Apostolic Fathers* (Harrisburg, PA: Morehouse Pub., 1990), 44. Carleton Paget notes that the early attribution of Barnabas to the apostolic figure is strong, including Clement of Alexandria's *Strom.* 2.6.31, 2.7.35, 2.20.116, and 5.10.63; Vaticanus 859; Jerome's *Vir. ill.* 6, and Didymus the Blind's *Comm. Zach.* 259:21-24. See Carleton Paget, *Epistle of Barnabas*, 3n1.

[10]Among many examples, see Carleton Paget, "The Epistle of Barnabas," 229; Dassmann, *Der Stachel im Fleisch*, 224. As Carleton Paget notes, it is "extremely difficult to imagine that the Jew, and former Levite, Barnabas, could have argued that the Jewish ritual laws should never have been implemented literally," among other views of the author (Carleton Paget, *Epistle of Barnabas*, 4). It is relevant, however, that it seems similarly difficult to imagine a Pharisee claiming ὅσοι γὰρ ἐξ ἔργων νόμου εἰσίν, ὑπὸ κατάραν εἰσίν (Gal 3:10).

[11]Cf. Kraft, *Barnabas and the Didache*, 44: "Some of the reasons advanced have been less than 'scientific' (e.g., *Barn.* 10 is 'unworthy of an apostle'!)." See Kraft's lucid analysis on the question in 44-45. For the purposes of this chapter, Barnabas is used to refer to the epistle without making a judgment on authorship.

[12]Cf. Holmes, *Apostolic Fathers*, 373; Kraft, *Barnabas and the Didache*, 42.

[13]See J. B. Lightfoot, "The Epistle of Barnabas," in *The Apostolic Fathers* (London: Macmillan and Co., 1890), 506-12; cf. Hvalvik, *Struggle for Scripture and Covenant*, 25-26; Carleton Paget, *Epistle of Barnabas*, 18.

temple in the 130s.[14] Those persuaded by the weight of one passage are generally forced to argue for an atemporal interpretation of the other.[15] While the Nervan date (90s) has the advantage of splitting the difference, it is not the best explanation for either passage; as Carleton Paget concedes, Nerva is a less likely identification for the "little horn" than Vespasian,[16] and there is not clear evidence for the possibility of a temple under Nerva as is found in the time of Hadrian.[17]

Though there are weaknesses to both views, the periods of the 70s under Vespasian and the 130s under Hadrian seem the strongest candidates for dating Barnabas.[18] In assessing Barnabas's engagement with the writings that become the New Testament, however, three factors emerge as noteworthy for the present question: (1) Barnabas's zeal for citing texts as authorities, including those that are beyond the scope of the commonly recognized Jewish Scriptures; (2) themes and interests in the epistle that appear to be shared with the writings of the New Testament; and (3) a curious absence in Barnabas of citations of these writings.[19]

---

[14]See Hvalvik, *Struggle for Scripture and Covenant*, 21-23; Rhodes, *Epistle of Barnabas*, 83-87.

[15]See, respectively, the conclusions of Lightfoot, *The Apostolic Fathers*, ed. J. R. Harmer (London: Macmillian and Co, 1898), 241, who argues that the temple being rebuilt in Barn. 16.3-4 is the spiritual temple of Christians, so that "the passage has no bearing at all on the date," and Hvalvik, *Struggle for Scripture and Covenant*, 26, who argues that as an apocalyptic passage, the author in Barn. 4 "is eager to show that the end is at hand, but he is not concerned about the actual point in time," so that "4.3-6a has no bearing on the dating of Barnabas."

[16]Carleton Paget, *Epistle of Barnabas*, 28. In Lightfoot's thesis, the "little horn" is actually Nero *redivivus* in the time of Vespasian; see Lightfoot, "Epistle of Barnabas," 510-12.

[17]Carleton Paget, *Epistle of Barnabas*, 26. Carleton Paget infers that there may have been a rumor of such a rebuilding based on Nerva's revoking of the *Fiscus Judaicus*, but this seems a heavy inference without supporting evidence for this date elsewhere. As Hvalvik, *Struggle for Scripture and Covenant*, 20, notes, such a view undervalues the force of γίνεται and νῦν in 16.4; whether a spiritual or material temple, *something* appears to be underway. For the account of Hadrian's Jupiter temple in Jerusalem, see Dio Cassius's *Roman History* 69.12.1-2.

[18]That these two periods are judged by recent scholarship as the most likely candidates is similarly ceded by the Nervan-favoring Carleton Paget; see Carleton Paget, *Epistle of Barnabas*, 27.

[19]Cf. Carleton Paget, "The Epistle of Barnabas," 249. The major exception to this is Barn. 4.14 (προσέχωμεν, μήποτε, ὡς γέγραπται, πολλοὶ κλητοί, ὀλίγοι δὲ ἐκλεκτοὶ εὑρεθῶμεν), cf. Mt 22:14 (πολλοὶ γάρ εἰσιν κλητοί, ὀλίγοι δὲ ἐκλεκτοί). As Carleton Paget notes, although preceded by a *formula citandi*, many have sought alternative explanations for this passage besides reliance on Matthew (such as possible reference to written traditional materials or 4 Ezra 8.3 or 9.15), though "one senses that attempts to argue for independence from Matthew are partly motivated by a desire to avoid the implication of the *formula citandi* which introduces the relevant words: namely, that the author of Barnabas regarded Matthew as scriptural" (Carleton Paget, "The Epistle of Barnabas," 233). Though reliance on Matthew seems most plausible in this instance,

While some have sought to reconcile (1) with (3) by denying the middle term, asserting that the author's interests are so idiosyncratic that he does not find correspondence for them in the early Christian writings (and thus largely ignores them),[20] Rhodes and Carleton Paget argue persuasively that Barnabas's interests have far more correspondence with the NT writings than has sometimes been posited.[21] If this assessment is correct, it becomes difficult for one adopting a late Hadrianic date to explain why an author with such a penchant for citing texts is virtually silent on those associated with Christ and his apostles—who are positively referenced in Barnabas 8.3 as those given "authority over the gospel" (οἷς ἔδωκεν τοῦ εὐαγγελίου τὴν ἐξουσίαν)—particularly as other figures prior to the 130s who show less enthusiasm for citation, such as Ignatius and Polycarp, nevertheless appear to reference these writings freely.[22] By contrast, this combination of factors is well accounted for by a dating under Vespasian, in which many writings associated with Christ and the apostles would have been either unwritten or far less circulated than in later decades. Such a dating also better accounts for the veneration found for Barnabas toward the end of the second century, witnessed to by its inclusion in Clement of Alexandria's *Hypotyposeis*,[23] his commentary on the biblical writings, and Clement's repeated attribution of the epistle to the apostolic Barnabas. Even if such an identification is inaccurate, this

---

the *formula citandi* does not necessarily require the author of Barnabas to have understood Matthew as belonging to a defined set of authoritative writings, any more than Barnabas's similar citations of unknown apocryphal texts necessitate that they were understood in such a manner.

[20]See, for example, Dassmann, *Der Stachel im Fleisch*, 225.

[21]See particularly Rhodes, *Epistle of Barnabas*, 137-74, and Carleton Paget, *Epistle of Barnabas*, 200-30, 248-58, who emphasize how the reverence with which Barnabas is treated alongside other apostolic texts in early patristic sources suggests it would be incorrect to see the epistle as isolated from the rest of early Christian literature.

[22]The hypothetical "one" includes the present author: this chapter was originally written with a 130s date following Barn. 16.3-4, and later revised to the earlier date in light of the arguments mentioned in this section. As Rensberger notes, while fewer explicit appeals to Christian texts might be standard in apologetic literature, an absence of appeal to them is unexpected in a document clearly written for "insiders" such as Barnabas; cf. David Rensberger, "As the Apostle Teaches: The Development of the Use of Paul's Letters in Second-Century Christianity" (PhD diss., Yale University, 1981), 336-37.

[23]There is some debate as to whether Eusebius rightly identifies Barnabas as included in the *Hypotyposeis*, though the identification appears to be correct; see Carleton Paget, *Epistle of Barnabas*, 249n316.

status and ascription seem more easily attainable by a document commonly known to date back to an earlier age, than for one originating in the 130s.

In sum, while maintaining that any dating within the range of AD 70 and circa 135 is possible, this study finds the cumulative evidence for a 70s dating under Vespasian to be strongest among the various proposals (outweighing difficulties in interpreting the rebuilding of the temple in 16.3-4 in a spiritual manner),[24] and adopts this decade following the temple's destruction as the likeliest date for the epistle. If this identification is correct, it seems less likely that Barnabas was written within a context of renascent Judaism;[25] rather, Barnabas's wide variety of explanations regarding the true meaning of Israel's law can be seen as a reevaluation of the history of Israel in light of the catastrophic events of the Jewish war and the temple's destruction.[26] While not making a judgment on authorship (which cannot be settled with confidence in any case), it is interesting to consider whether the spirit of contemporary critical scholarship, so influenced by Bauer's conception of orthodoxy as a projection onto the past, would actually be most compatible with the idea that Barnabas was correctly remembered in the second century as the work of Paul's companion, with Pseudo- only added at a later date when the epistle's theology was in question and deemed unworthy of the apostolic designation.

Text and translation. The major witnesses to the text of Barnabas are Codex Sinaiticus (S) from the late fourth or early fifth century; Codex Hierosolymitanus (H), dated to 1056; a family of Greek manuscripts (G)

---

[24]While not necessarily the more obvious reading of Barn. 16.3-4, the temple as a spiritual reality represented by Christians is a strong motif in the epistle (cf. Barn. 4.11, 6.15, 16.6-10), with some commentators taking the spiritual interpretation of this passage as the more natural one. See Prigent, *Testimonia dans le christianisme primitif*, 77, who finds correspondence between this passage and Jesus' rebuilding of the temple in three days; J. V. Bartlet, "Barnabas," in *The New Testament in the Apostolic Fathers*, ed. Oxford Society of Historical Theology (Oxford: Clarendon Press, 1905), 3n1; Lightfoot, *Apostolic Fathers*, 241.

[25]*Pace* e.g. Carleton Paget, *Epistle of Barnabas*, 69, though this does not exclude Hvalvik's view that Judaism constituted a "living and real threat" for Barnabas; see Hvalvik, *Struggle for Scripture and Covenant*, 323-29.

[26]See, for example, Barnabas's stated purpose in the introduction to "cheer you up in the present circumstances" (Barn. 1.8), which moves to a reassurance that God does not need the sacrifices that were offered in the temple (Barn. 2.4-10).

beginning in the eleventh century in which Barnabas (beginning at 5.7) is appended to Polycarp's *Philippians* at 9.2; and a Latin translation (L) going back to the second or third century, and now preserved in the ninth-century Codex Corbeiensis, which contains only Barnabas 1–17. For this chapter, the Holmes Greek text and English translation are used (except where noted).[27]

THE EPISTLE OF BARNABAS AND PAUL

Knowledge and use of Paul. Assessing usage of Pauline writings in Barnabas is well recognized as a difficult undertaking,[28] with the task being hindered by the letter's free style of citation; as Bartlet notes, the author often "appears to trust to memory, and not to concern himself greatly about the words of his author," so that "even when preceded by a *formula citandi* his citations often wander far from the LXX, although they are clearly based on it."[29] As Lindemann notes, "Die Frage, ob Barn von paulinischer Theologie beeinflußt sei, wurde vor allem in der älteren Forschung weithin bejaht,"[30] and Carleton Paget's recent study notes the apparent thematic convergences between Paul and Barnabas: "Both, in broad terms, are concerned with the relationship between the new covenant in Christ and the old covenant with the Jews," and "take a keen interest in issues relating to the law and the history of Israel."[31] On the other hand, Barnabas never mentions Paul or his letters, and with one major exception, identification of specific verses in Paul that Barnabas may be drawing on is quite difficult, leading many to conclude that shared traditional materials explain the apparent affinities between the two authors.

---

[27]Holmes, *Apostolic Fathers.*

[28]On the difficulty of identifying Pauline influence in Barnabas (and more generally), see Carleton Paget, "Paul and the Epistle," 363. A helpful summary of older scholarship, representing the wide range of views on this question, can be found in Carleton Paget, "Paul and the Epistle," 367n33.

[29]Bartlet, "Barnabas," 1. Cf. Carleton Paget, *Epistle of Barnabas*, 86: "If B. was making use of the LXX when he composed his letter he was a lax copier. What is more he was inconsistent in his laxity."

[30]Translated as, "The question, of whether Barnabas was influenced by Pauline theology, was widely answered in the affirmative in older research," Lindemann, *Paulus im ältesten Christentum*, 274.

[31]Carleton Paget, "The Epistle of Barnabas," 239.

The strongest case for usage of Paul in Barnabas is at 13.7, where the author writes, "What, then, does [God] say to Abraham, when he alone believed and was established in righteousness? 'Behold, I have established you, Abraham, as the father of the nations who believe in God without being circumcised.'" Commentators generally view this passage as either directly drawing on Romans 4, or on traditional materials that are influenced by or shared with Paul. The case for the former view is based on the parallel between Barnabas's citation of Genesis 15:6 with Paul's in Romans 4:3 (cf. Gal 3:6), combined with the statement of Abraham as the "father of those believing through uncircumcision," which both Paul in Romans 4:11 and Barnabas insert into their references to Genesis 17:4-5.[32] The latter view holds that despite these similarities, the theological points in Barnabas 13.7 and Romans 4 are quite different (with Paul arguing for Gentile inclusion and Barnabas for Christian priority), and thus the similarities should be attributed to something other than direct reference.[33] The case is not easily settled either way, though the verbal parallels are strong enough that reliance on Romans seems perhaps the likelier of the two options,[34] with readers such as Bartlet, Muilenburg, and Hagner concluding that the passage represents usage of Paul's epistle.[35] At the same time, though the argument relies on a less tangible "traditional materials" category, the fact that so many commentators conclude from the passages' theological dissimilarities that Barnabas is relying on something other than Paul gives pause to the

---

[32] Barn. 13.7: πατέρα ἐθνῶν τῶν πιστευόντων δι᾿ ἀκροβυστίας τῷ θεῷ; Rom 4:11: πατέρα πάντων τῶν πιστευόντων δι᾿ ἀκροβυστίας.

[33] Cf. Carleton Paget, "The Epistle of Barnabas," 240-41; Dassmann, *Der Stachel im Fleisch*, 224-25.

[34] It is not necessary to postulate another source between Barnabas and Paul to explain the difference in theological points made by these texts (*pace*, e.g., Carleton Paget, "The Epistle of Barnabas," 245), as such differences are not uncommon in early patristic writings. For clear examples, see Diog. 12.5, where the author cites 1 Cor 8:1 not as a caution against knowledge without love, but supporting his assertion that life is through knowledge; and *Haer.* 5.22.1, where Irenaeus brings forward Rom 3:30 to demonstrate the oneness of God rather than the equality of Jew and Gentile.

[35] Bartlet, "Barnabas," 3-4 (who gives this a B rating); James Muilenburg, *The Literary Relations of the Epistle of Barnabas and the Teaching of the Twelve Apostles* (Marburg: Yale University, 1929), 89 ("Barnabas is also familiar with the Pauline Epistles, especially Romans and Ephesians"); D. A. Hagner, *The Use of the Old and New Testaments in Clement of Rome* (Leiden: Brill, 1973), 285 ("clear allusions to Romans").

supposition that clear usage of Pauline texts can be established from this passage alone.[36]

Carleton Paget's study on Barnabas and Paul identifies five other passages as potential candidates for Pauline dependency,[37] and though none of these are ultimately judged to conclusively demonstrate usage of Pauline texts, a few among them merit further discussion. In the case of Barnabas 2.6, following a citation of Isaiah 1:11-13 rejecting sacrifices and Sabbaths, the author writes, "Therefore he has abolished [κατήργησεν] these things, in order that the new law [ὁ καινὸς νόμος] of our Lord Jesus Christ, which is free from the yoke of compulsion [ζυγοῦ ἀνάγκης], might have its offering, one not made by humans." This verse can be seen as a composite of various Pauline elements, with καταργέω being used frequently in Romans in relation to the law (Rom 3:31; 4:14; 7:2, 6; cf. also 2 Cor 3:7, 11, 13), the reference to the law of Christ having parallels in Galatians 6:2 and 1 Corinthians 9:21, and the law as "yoke" corresponding with Galatians 5:1. Though the cumulative effect is compelling, Carleton Paget cautions that in this case the "weakness lies in the fact that we find no verse in Paul which contains all the component parts of *Barn.* 2. 6," which prevents this verse from conclusively demonstrating usage of Paul's writings.[38] Another example is Barnabas's use of ἄρα οὖν in *Barn.* 9.6, a distinctively Pauline phrase that, combined with Barnabas' usage of the similarly Pauline ἐπικατάρατος in Barnabas 7.7, leads Prostmeier to conclude, "Daß der Vf. paulinische Redeweisen und Theologie, wenn auch nicht unbedingt in Form der uns überlieferten kanonischen Paulusbriefe, bekannt war, ist in Anbetracht seiner Konzeption der Verfasserschaft oder des Verdikts ἐπικατάρατος in Barn 7,7 kaum zu bezweifeln."[39]

---

[36]See for example Kraft, *Barnabas and the Didache*, 123; Lindemann, *Paulus im ältesten Christentum*, 278-79; Hvalvik, *Struggle for Scripture and Covenant*, 34; Prostmeier, *Barnabasbrief*, 97; Dassmann, *Der Stachel im Fleisch*, 225; Carleton Paget, "Paul and the Epistle," 381. Cf. Carleton Paget's assessment: "What must be true is that at the very least knowledge of a tradition influenced by Paul is evidenced at this point" (Carleton Paget, "The Epistle of Barnabas," 241).

[37]Barn. 4.10 (cf. 1 Cor 4:8; 3:16-17); Barn. 2.6 (cf. Gal 5:1; 6:2; 1 Cor 9:21; Rom 3:31; 2 Cor 3:7, 11, 13; Eph 2:15); Barn. 7.7 (Gal 3:10, 13); Barn. 9.6 (Rom 4:11); Barn. 5.9 (1 Cor 15:8-9; Eph 3:8; 1 Tim 1:15).

[38]Carleton Paget, "The Epistle of Barnabas," 242.

[39]"That the author was familiar with Pauline ways of speaking and theology, even if not necessarily in the form of the canonical Pauline texts handed down to us, is hardly to be doubted when

Though this conclusion appears sound, for the purposes of this study it is uncertain whether such engagement is significant enough to demonstrate direct usage of Pauline texts.

While a few other possible areas of Pauline influence are identified by Bartlet and Hagner,[40] these are less weighty than the aforementioned examples, and we are ultimately left with a picture of Barnabas's use of Paul that is less than fully conclusive. In my view, the weight of the available evidence suggests that Barnabas's familiarity with Pauline letters is more probable than not, and that reliance on Romans seems to be a strong hypothesis in explaining correspondence with passages like Barnabas 13.7. At the same time, the nature of the evidence—both with respect to differences in the way similar phrases are used, suggesting the possibility of shared traditions as a source of Pauline parallels, as well as the challenges presented by Barnabas's allusive reference style—means that the influence of Pauline texts in Barnabas cannot be conclusively demonstrated beyond a minimal level.[41] As a result, the epistle is better classified in category C for this study than category B (which would denote secure usage of the relevant Pauline texts).

THE LAW AND WORKS IN THE EPISTLE OF BARNABAS

Meaning: What works of what law? In Barnabas, the law in question is the legislation given to the people of Israel, though this is not given definition beyond the designation of "their law" (τῷ ἐκείνων νόμῳ, Barn. 3.6). A number of specific works of this law are objected to throughout the

---

one considers his conception of authorship or of the verdict of ἐπικατάρατος in Barn. 7.7." Prostmeier, *Barnabasbrief*, 365n53.

[40]Bartlet (along with Hagner, *Use of the Old and New Testaments*, 285) identifies Barn. 6.11-12 as overlapping with new creation themes in Ephesians (and to a lesser extent 1 and 2 Cor), but as a composite it is difficult to classify as conclusively demonstrating textual reliance (as with Barn. 2.6); see Bartlet, "Barnabas," 6-7.

[41]Cf. Massaux, who while identifying a wide range of passages that hold correspondence with Paul, nevertheless concludes that "no passage can be found to have a definite literary contact with a Pauline text" (Edouard Massaux, *The Influence of the Gospel of Saint Matthew on Christian Literature Before Saint Irenaeus*, ed. Arthur J. Bellinzoni, vol. 1 of 3 [Macon, GA: Mercer, 1993 {1950}], 78). It is also possible that Barn. 13.7 points to oral familiarity with Paul's teaching, which Young has argued to be the primary mode of familiarity with Jesus tradition in the period prior to 2 Clement (cf. Stephen E. Young, *Jesus Tradition in the Apostolic Fathers: Their Explicit Appeals to the Words of Jesus in Light of Orality Studies*, WUNT 2:311 [Tübingen: Mohr Siebeck, 2011]).

letter, including various kinds of sacrifices (θυσιῶν, ὁλοκαυτωμάτων, προσφορῶν, 2.4), new moons and Sabbaths (τὰς νεομηνίας ὑμῶν καὶ τὰ σάββατα, 2.5; cf. also 15), fasts (3), circumcision (9), and regulations against eating various kinds of animals (10). The author also inveighs against the temple and how the people hoped in it (εἰς τὴν οἰκοδομὴν ἤλπισαν, 16.1) rather than God.

Barnabas contrasts these rejected works with "the righteous requirements of the Lord" (τὰ δικαιώματα κυρίου, Barn. 2.1; cf. Rom 2:26; 8:4), the pursuit of which the author commends before his rejection of sacrifices and Sabbaths in Barnabas 2.4-6. This language is repeated throughout the epistle,[42] along with similar endorsements of practicing the "commandments" of God.[43] Examples of these righteous requirements include not bearing a grudge or loving a false oath (2.8), the works commended in Isaiah 58:6-10 in lieu of fasting (such as breaking unjust bonds, setting free the oppressed, sharing bread with the hungry, clothing the naked, and sheltering the homeless, 3.3), pursuing "the things able to save us" (τὰ δυνάμενα ἡμᾶς σῴζειν) and rejecting works of lawlessness (4.1-2, 9-12), and avoiding the vices and performing the virtues signified by the Mosaic food laws (10). Such works are further elucidated by the "two ways" section at the end of Barnabas (18–21), which is largely shared in common with the similar section found in the Didache.[44]

Significance: What does the practice of these works signify? In Barnabas, the practice of the works of the law rejected by the author represents the adoption of the Jewish law, and thus identification with "those ones" (ἐκεῖνοι, cf. Barn. 2.9; 3.6; 4.6; 8.7; 10.12; 13.1, 3; 14.5), the people of Israel.[45] This people has gone astray from their calling from the time of the golden calf under Moses up to their rejection of Jesus,[46] and serves as the

---

[42]Cf. Barn 1.2; 4.11; 10.2, 11; 16.9; 21.1, 5.

[43]See Barn. 4.11, "let us strive to keep his commandments" (φυλάσσειν ἀγωνιζώμεθα τὰς ἐντολὰς αὐτοῦ), cf. 9.5; 10.11-12; 16.9; 19.2; 21.8. Cf. 1 Cor 7:19.

[44]See Did. 1.1–6.2. On the relationship between these sections, see Kraft, *Barnabas and the Didache*, 4-16; as Kraft notes, the "two ways" theme can be seen as present in the rest of Barnabas as well.

[45]Cf. Barn. 4.14; 5.2, 8; 6.7; 11.1; 12.5; 16.5.

[46]Barn. 4.6-8; 14.1-5; 5.11; 8.1. There is debate as to whether Barnabas understands Israel to have entirely lost the covenant at the golden calf incident, or whether this incident serves as a

counterexample throughout the epistle for how the "us" of Christians are to act and interpret Scripture.[47] As the author states in 2.9, "we ought to perceive... the gracious intention of our Father, because he is speaking to us; he wants us to seek how we may approach him, rather than go astray as those ones did" (translation adjusted; see also 4.14; 8.7; 10.9-12). There appears to have been at least some measure of temptation for Barnabas's audience to adopt this Jewish law,[48] with the author writing at the end of a chapter on true and false fasting that God, by his prophecies through Isaiah, has "revealed everything to us in advance, in order that we might not shipwreck ourselves as proselytes to their law" (ἵνα μὴ προσρησσώμεθα ὡς ἐπήλυτοι τῷ ἐκείνων νόμῳ, 3.6). There is also conflict over whether the covenant belongs to "those ones," the people of Israel, or the people redeemed by Christ (cf. 4.6-8;[49] 13.1; 14.4-9). As Barnabas interprets the stories of Rebecca's sons and Jacob's blessing, those that practice these works are "greater" of the two people, who are nevertheless destined in Scripture to serve "the lesser," the true heirs of the covenant (13.1-6, cf. Rom 9:10; Gen 25:21-23, 48:19).[50]

---

paradigmatic apostasy that is brought to consummation in the rejection of Jesus. While the former position constitutes the majority view (based on a straightforward reading of Barnabas's statement in 4.6 that "those ones lost it completely in the following way" [ἐκεῖνοι οὕτως εἰς τέλος ἀπώλεσαν αὐτὴν]), Rhodes offers a compelling argument that the logic of Barnabas's argument elsewhere necessitates that this statement be seen as in some way hyperbolic, drawing analogy to Paul's εἰς τέλος language in 1 Thess 2:14-16, and 1 Jn 2:19's statement that those who depart from the community never actually belonged to it. See Rhodes, *Epistle of Barnabas*, 1-32.

[47]The term *Christian* is not used in Barnabas, with the "us" party being defined in various ways as the people God has prepared, cf. Barn. 3.6: ὁ λαὸς ὃν ἡτοίμασεν ἐν τῷ ἠγαπημένῳ αὐτοῦ; 5.7: αὐτὸς ἑαυτῷ τὸν λαὸν τὸν καινὸν ἑτοιμάζων.

[48]Cf. Carleton Paget, *Epistle of Barnabas*, 262; Tugwell, *Apostolic Fathers*, 23. While Lindemann comments regarding the "us"/"them" polarity that "Der Text setzt voraus, daß die Scheidung zwischen Christentum und Judentum vollständig ist" ("The text assumes that the separation between Christianity and Judaism is complete"), it is possible that the frequent use of this language is meant to reinforce border lines that may not be universally observed (Lindemann, *Paulus im ältesten Christentum*, 273).

[49]The text of Barn. 4.6 is "notoriously corrupt" (Rhodes, *Epistle of Barnabas*, 24), with the emendation of Rhodes (followed by Holmes) reading ἡμῶν μενει, S reading ἡμῶν μεν, C reading ὑμῶν ὑμιν μενει, L reading *illorum et nostrum est nostrum est autem*, and Kraft/Prigent reading ἡμῶν ἡμιν μενει ἡμων μεν. See Holmes, *Apostolic Fathers*, 388-89. In my view, Rhodes's emendation of S constitutes the best explanation of the variants; see Rhodes, *Epistle of Barnabas*, 24-28.

[50]It is important to note that despite the consistent "us"/"them" language in Barnabas, to see the author as simply slandering the "other" as a long-rejected people to buffet his own group's identity would be reductionistic, as the author's critiques of Israel are themselves drawn from and firmly rooted within Israel's own tradition (cf. Rhodes, *Epistle of Barnabas*), and despite their

Opposition: Why are these works not necessary for the Christian? A
great deal of Barnabas is devoted to why the works of Israel's law are not
to be practiced by Christians, and Barnabas's reasons for this opposition
are manifold. Indeed, one may be forgiven for thinking of Barnabas's
methodology as a version of "throw everything at the wall and see what
sticks," as it is challenging to place all of the reasons for why these works
are to be rejected into consistent categories. Instead of beginning with
such categories, this section will proceed sequentially through the letter
and detail the reasons given for rejecting the particular works mentioned
in each section, and then collate these reasons as far as possible at
the conclusion.

At the outset of the epistle, Barnabas cites God's testimony through the
prophets as a reason for rejecting sacrifices, new moons and Sabbaths.
Following his statement that "the Master has made known to us through
the prophets things past and things present, and has given us a foretaste
of things to come" (Barn. 1.7), Barnabas continues, "For he has made it
clear to us through all the prophets that he needs neither sacrifices nor
whole burnt offerings nor general offerings" (2.4). This is followed by a
citation of the paradigmatic text of Isaiah 1:11-13 (2.5):

> "What is the multitude of your sacrifices to me?" says the Lord. "I am full of
> whole burnt offerings, and I do not want the fat of lambs and the blood of
> bulls and goats, not even if you come to appear before me. For who demanded
> these things from your hands? Do not continue to trample my court. If you
> bring fine flour, it is in vain; incense is detestable to me; your new moons and
> sabbaths I cannot stand."

Such works are now displaced by Christ's new law and new sacrifice, with
God having "abolished" (κατήργησεν) these former works "in order that
the new law of our Lord Jesus Christ, which is free from the yoke of compulsion, might have its offering, one not made by humans" (2.6). This new
law is elucidated by citation of Jeremiah and Zechariah—"Let none of you
bear a grudge in his heart against his neighbor, and do not love a false

---

failings, Barnabas portrays Christ's approach to Israel as one of love, cf. Barn. 5.8: "Furthermore,
by teaching Israel and performing extraordinary wonders and signs, he preached and loved them
intensely."

oath'" (2.8; Jer 7:22-23 LXX; Zech 8:17 LXX)—as well as a citation from the Psalms that is spoken by God "to us": "To us, therefore, he says this: 'A sacrifice to God is a broken heart; an aroma pleasing to the Lord is a heart that glorifies its Maker'" (2.10; Ps 50:19 LXX).

The testimony of the prophets is similarly brought forth as the reason for rejecting Israel's fasts, with one prophetic passage being directed "to them," declaring Israel's fast with sackcloth and ashes as unacceptable (3.1-2, Is 58:4-5 LXX), and the next commending just and moral behavior directed "to us." "'Behold, this is the fast I have chosen,' says the Lord: 'break every unjust bond, untie the knots of forced agreements, set free those who are oppressed, and tear up every unjust contract'" (3.3-5; Is 58:6-10).[51] This prophetic word has (paradoxically) been given to Christians beforehand to keep them from observing Israel's law: "So for this reason, brothers and sisters, the one who is very patient, when he foresaw how the people whom he had prepared in his beloved would believe in all purity, revealed everything to us in advance, in order that we might not shipwreck ourselves as proselytes to their law" (Barn. 3.6). While Barnabas explains more precisely in other contexts why various works are not to be practiced, here the author does not elaborate on why adopting Israel's law is to suffer this fate.[52]

In chapters 7 and 8, Barnabas engages various rites of atonement in the Scriptures, arguing that these rites were actually types of realities fulfilled in Christ, with the implication (made explicit elsewhere, cf. 2.4-10) that their literal interpretation is not binding. These include the sacrifice of the goats from Leviticus 16:7-9, thrice cited as typologically corresponding with Jesus (7.7, 10-11), and the red heifer (8.1-7, cf. Num 19:1-10). Such types, according

---

[51]This principle of different statements in Scripture speaking to the different parties can be found elsewhere in the epistle, cf. Barn. 5.2: "For the scripture concerning him [Christ] relates partly to Israel and partly to us."

[52]Though arguments here are based on silence, one suggestion from Rhodes is of an underlying reference to the temple's destruction, so that "by keeping its distance from '*their* law,' a religious praxis tied closely to cultic observances, the author's community has been spared the devastation of sharing in Israel's national disaster. Assimilation to Jewish praxis would have meant assimilation to Israel's fate" (Rhodes, *Epistle of Barnabas*, 43, italics original). While not made explicit, a related reason for not observing these works may be the invalidity of Israel's covenant as discussed in Barn. 4, though no specific works are mentioned in this section, and the logic behind such an argument (if intended) would be unclear.

to the author, "are clear to us, but to them are covered in darkness, because they did not listen to the voice of the Lord" (8.7, translation adjusted).

In Barnabas 9, physical circumcision is rejected in favor of the spiritual circumcision of the ears and heart (cf. Rom 2:29), which is similarly presented as foretold in the prophets with a string of scriptural citations.[53] In addition to the testimony of the prophets, the author adds what is a very striking claim in 9.4: "But the circumcision in which they have trusted has been abolished, for he [God] declared that circumcision was not a matter of the flesh. But they disobeyed, because an evil angel 'enlightened' them" (ὅτι ἄγγελος πονηρὸς ἐσόφιζεν αὐτούς).[54] Barnabas immediately returns to prophecy in 9.5, citing Jeremiah 4:3-4 ("Do not sow among thorns, be circumcised to your Lord"), Deuteronomy 10:16 ("Circumcise your hardheartedness, and stop being stiff-necked"), and Jeremiah 9:25 LXX ("Behold, says the Lord, all the nations have uncircumcised foreskins, but this people has an uncircumcised heart"), before adding another new argument in 9.6: "But you will say: 'But surely the people were circumcised as a seal!' But every Syrian and Arab and all the idol-worshiping priests are also circumcised; does this mean that they too belong to their covenant? Why, even the Egyptians practice circumcision!" Following this pragmatic argument about the impossibility of physical circumcision as the distinguishing feature of the covenant, the author closes the section by arguing that numerical typology reveals the true significance of Abraham's household being circumcised, with the Greek numerals for "ten [I] and eight [H]" and "three hundred [T]" men taken to represent Jesus (IH, an abbreviation for Ιησους seen in the later manuscript tradition) and the cross (T) (9.7-9).[55]

Chapter 10 discusses the true meaning of Mosaic food laws, and again the author of Barnabas begins by taking a scriptural text as a prophetic

---

[53]Cf. Ps 17:45 LXX; 2 Sam 22:45; Is 33:13; Jer 4:4; 7:2-3; Ps 33:13 LXX; Is 50:10; Ex 15:26; Is 1:2; Mic 1:2; Is 1:10; 28:14; 40:3. As elsewhere, Barnabas's citation style is allusive and often matches imprecisely with the texts that are drawn on.

[54]For discussion of Barnabas's possible reliance on other angel traditions in Judaism, see James Carleton Paget, "Barnabas 9.4 a Peculiar Verse on Circumcision," in *Jews, Christians and Jewish Christians in Antiquity*, WUNT 251 (Tübingen: Mohr Siebeck, 2010 [1991]), 81-83. On Barn. 9.4 and Paul in Gal 3:19, see 81n21.

[55]Cf. Holmes, *Apostolic Fathers*, 409.

basis for his interpretation: "Furthermore, he says to them in Deuteronomy, 'I will set forth as a covenant to this people my righteous requirements'" (10.2; cf. Deut 4:10, 13). Because physical eating does not pertain
to righteousness, Barnabas understands this passage to indicate that in
relation to food laws, "it is not God's commandment that they should not
eat; rather Moses spoke spiritually" (10.2).[56] Starting with this premise,
Barnabas proceeds to show the spiritual meaning of various laws regu-
lating food, such as the prohibition from eating pigs representing a
command to not be ungrateful in pig-like fashion (10.3), and the injunction to eat the animals with divided hoof representing a commendation of the righteous person who "not only lives in this world but also
looks forward to the holy age to come" (10.11).[57] While Moses spoke
spiritually (10.9) and indeed excellently ("See how well Moses legislated!,"
10.11, translation adjusted), the people took such commandments as referring to actual food on account of the desires of their flesh (10.9).
Indeed, the author acknowledges the apparent difficulty of understanding
such commandments rightly ("But how could those people grasp or understand these things?"), but maintains that Christians indeed do so,
having had their ears and hearts circumcised by the Lord, and thus
leaving behind the literal practice of such works (10.12).

In chapter 15 Barnabas begins again with an argument from prophecy
in rejecting the Sabbath, twice repeating the injunction given to Moses
in the Decalogue to "sanctify the Lord's sabbath, with clean hands and a
clean heart" (15.1, 6; cf. Ex 20:8; Deut 5:12; Ps 23:4 LXX). Such an action
is impossible according to Barnabas, for if "anyone now is able, by being
clean of heart, to sanctify the day that God sanctified, we have been de-
ceived in every respect" (Barn. 15.7). Rather, this can happen only "after
being made righteous (δικαιωθέντες) and receiving the promise; when
lawlessness no longer exists, and all things have been made new by the
Lord, then we will be able to sanctify it, because we ourselves will have

---

[56]The author cites David as an example of one who understands Moses rightly; cf. Barn. 10.10; Ps 1:1.
[57]As commentators have noted, while a similar interpretive methodology can be found in Philo
(QG 3.45-46; QE 2.2; Agr. 39; Somn. 2.25; cf. Carleton Paget, "Barnabas 9.4," 78-79), Philo also
inveighs against those who use the spiritual meaning of the law to disregard the literal (for which
see Migr. 92; cf. Carleton Paget, "Barnabas 9.4," 79). Cf. also Let. Aris. 150-51.

been sanctified first" (15.7, translation adjusted).[58] Because of this, it is not the "present sabbaths" (τὰ νῦν σάββατα) of the seventh day that are to be observed, which God expressly rejects in Isaiah ("I cannot stand your new moons and Sabbaths," Is 1:13). Rather, this true Sabbath is the eighth day celebrated by Christians, the day that Jesus rose from the dead and ascended, and the first day of the new creation (15.8-9; cf. 6.11-14).

Finally, chapter 16 offers a rejection of the physical temple, which is now replaced by the temple of the heart (cf. also 6.5). Interestingly, while the destruction of the temple is brought up in this section (16.3-4), it is not articulated as a reason for not observing works of the law or temple service. Rather, this too is presented as being an illustration of the prophetic witness of Scripture (Is 40:12, 66:1; Barn. 16.2).

In summarizing Barnabas's arguments, three categories of reasoning can be identified for why the works in question are not necessary for the Christian:

(1) The most prominent category in Barnabas for rejecting these works of Israel's law is the prophetic witness of Scripture, a grouping within which many kinds of arguments are presented. Even while many of the texts cited may not seem to carry an obvious "prophetic" sense,[59] Barnabas is consistent in appealing to them as the first word for each practice that is discussed, and though sometimes haphazard in citation accuracy, Barnabas's appeals to Scripture as the basis for current practice (and nonpractice) are extensive. As part of this prophetic witness, Barnabas identifies certain parts of Scripture that are specifically directed to the "us" of God's new covenant people, and others that pertain specifically to "those ones" of disobedient Israel (cf. 5.2; 6.6-19). A subset of this category is the typological nature of Scripture, as Barnabas identifies a number of scriptural stories and practices as types that point to realities that are now present in Christ (such as Israel's sacrificial practices and the circumcision of Abraham's household, cf. 7–8; 9.7-9). Though not discussed in sections rejecting

---

[58]Δικαιωθέντες is translated in the factitive sense ("made righteous"), as Barnabas's argument in this context relates to whether one actually is (or is not) καθαρός and ἅγιός.

[59]As an example of this practice elsewhere, see Paul's usage of the Hagar and Sarah story in Gal 4:21-31.

particular works, the practice of these works is also inveighed against because they serve to identify one with Israel, which Scripture prophesies to
be the "greater" people that will nonetheless serve the "lesser" that God has
now established, the true heir of the promises to Abraham (13).[60]

(2) The new law of Christ, while not recurring explicitly throughout
the epistle, stands in a foundational position as the first reason Barnabas
gives for not observing these works following the initial summary rejection of sacrifices, Sabbaths, and new moons (2.6). In addition to its
institution as the reason for displacing these practices, the law of Christ
also appears to be the logical tie that explains the frequent commendations of the "righteous requirements" and "commandments" of God
throughout the letter (which are themselves prophesied as the true basis
of the covenant, cf. Barn. 10.2; Deut 4:10, 13), as well as the celebration of
the eighth day in lieu of the Sabbath (15.8-9).

(3) Third is that the renewing power of God, described variously as the
new birth and the circumcision of the ears and heart (Barn. 6.11-14; 9.1-4;
cf. Rom 2:29), makes one able to understand the true spiritual meaning
of Scripture (10.2, 12). This transformation occurs with baptism and the
forgiveness of sins (6.11; 11.1, 11; 16.8), and with it the literal (mis)under-
standing of various laws falls away, such as those regarding sacrifices and
circumcision in Barnabas 8 and 9. Conversely, disobedience and lust
create an inability to understand the law's commandments rightly
(cf. 8.7; 10.9), as some that were never meant to have been practiced in a
fleshly sense were nevertheless interpreted as such by "those" fleshly
people.[61] This need for the transformation wrought by God can also be
seen as the basis for chapter fifteen's arguments, which describe the need
to be made righteous to be able to rightly obey Scripture's spiritual
meaning and sanctify the Sabbath as God intends (15.6-9).

In addition to these categories, Barnabas offers arguments that we can
only describe as ad hoc: they do not appear to be theologically connected

---

[60]Cf. again Gal 4:21-31 as analogous to Barnabas's argument. See also Rom 9:7-13, though different
points are drawn from Gen 25:23; cf. Carleton Paget, "The Epistle of Barnabas," 240n40.

[61]Cf. Carleton Paget, "Paul and the Epistle," 367: "Barnabas believes that there is one revelation
and that is the Christian revelation which is no more than the Old Testament interpreted as it
always should have been."

to his arguments elsewhere, and are not sustained throughout his epistle, being moved on from as soon as they are offered. The two clear examples of such arguments are those made in his rejection of circumcision: that of the "evil angel" deceiving the people into thinking circumcision was a matter of the flesh (9.4), and of the impossibility of physical circumcision—a practice with wider adoption among heathen nations—being the distinguishing feature of God's covenant people (9.6).

CONCLUSION

The works objected to in the Epistle of Barnabas are those of Israel's law, including the specific works of sacrifices, new moons and Sabbaths, fasts, circumcision, and dietary regulations, which Barnabas sets in contrast with God's "righteous requirements" (τὰ δικαιώματα κυρίου, Barn. 2.1; cf. Rom 2:26; 8:4). The practice of these works represents the adoption of Israel's law, and thus identification with "those ones," the disobedient people of Israel. Barnabas contrasts this people throughout the letter with "us," the new people foreshadowed throughout Scripture (13) who are the beginning of God's new creation (15; cf. 6.11-14). These works of Israel's law are to be rejected due to the diverse prophetic witness of Scripture, the new law now instituted by Christ, and the true spiritual understanding and obedience that are now enabled by God's renewing power. While Barnabas seems to make little to no direct use of Paul's epistles, and thus can serve only as circumstantial evidence for determining Paul's own meaning by works of the law, there is widely held recognition of shared traditions between Barnabas and Paul, suggesting that such a conception of works of the law may also have been held in common between the two authors.

6

IGNATIUS OF ANTIOCH (B)

Epistle to the Magnesians
and *Epistle to the Philadelphians*

◻

INTRODUCTION

Introduction and background. The next sources to be considered are the letters of Ignatius of Antioch, which Eusebius attests to have been written en route to his martyrdom in Rome under Trajan (AD 98–117), and among which two (*Magnesians* and *Philadelphians*) contain material of interest for the current study.[1] The textual history of the Ignatian letter collection is complex, with longer recensions and larger collections of letters being commonly used in the Middle Ages until the hypothesis and discovery of a shorter "middle" recension in the late seventeenth century.[2] At the close of the nineteenth century, the work of Zahn and Lightfoot served to vindicate the authenticity of the middle recension,[3] and challenges to this consensus in recent decades have not served to displace the now-traditional view.[4] The authenticity of the middle

---

[1]*Hist. Eccl.* 3.36.2-4.

[2]The story of the various recensions is well told in Allen Brent, *Ignatius of Antioch* (London: T&T Clark, 2009), 1-9; cf. Paul Foster, "Epistles of Ignatius of Antioch," in *The Writings of the Apostolic Fathers*, ed. Paul Foster (London: T&T Clark, 2007), 82-84. The "short" recension (S) is an abridged Syriac version of the middle recension of three letters (*Ephesians, Romans,* and *Polycarp*).

[3]Theodor Zahn, *Ignatius von Antiochen* (Gotha: Perthes, 1873); J. B. Lightfoot, *S. Ignatius, S. Polycarp*, vol. 2 of *The Apostolic Fathers*, 2nd ed (London: Macmillan and Co, 1889).

[4]See Mark Edwards, "Ignatius and the Second Century: An Answer to R. Hübner," *Zeitschrift für Antikes Christentum* 2 (1998): 214-26, contra Reinhard Hübner, "Thesen zur Echtheit und Datierung der sieben Briefe des Ignatius von Antiochien," *ZAC* 1 (1997): 44-72.

recension is assumed for this study, with a provenance from Smyrna for the first four epistles (including *Magnesians*) and Troas for the last three (including *Philadelphians*) during Trajan's reign circa AD 107–115.[5] These epistles constitute B-level evidence for this study: while specific verses discussing works of the law are not referenced, the letters bear witness to conflicts with Jews that are reminiscent of Pauline discussions on this topic, and Paul is commonly recognized to hold considerable influence in Ignatius's theology.

Holmes writes of Ignatius's life that "just as we become aware of a meteor only when after traveling silently through space for untold millions of miles, it blazes briefly through the atmosphere before dying in a shower of fire, so it is with Ignatius, bishop of Antioch in Syria."[6] Eusebius identifies Ignatius as the second bishop of Antioch,[7] with Theodoret later claiming this appointment to have come from Peter himself,[8] and Ignatius appears to have been held in high esteem within the church long after his death.[9] However, most of our biographical details for Ignatius (including the account of his martyrdom) come from centuries after his life and are not generally recognized to be of historical value, which leaves us almost entirely dependent on Ignatius's epistles for our knowledge of him. Nevertheless, these letters paint a vivid picture of the bishop; as Foster writes, "although the epistles may have been written in as little as a few weeks, they provide a remarkable insight into the nature of the person facing martyrdom, as well as conveying much about the beliefs and theological positions he held."[10]

Ignatius's epistles frequently counter teachings of his time that he regards as heretical, including sections against "Judaizing" in *Magnesians*

---

[5] Eusebius dates Ignatius's martyrdom in AD 107–108 (*Chron.* 194) and Malalas places his arrest in 115, with suggested dates for the epistles generally clustering around these periods; cf. Paul Hartog, *Polycarp and the New Testament*, WUNT 2:134 (Tubingen: Mohr Siebeck, 2002), 57-60.

[6] Michael W. Holmes, ed., *The Apostolic Fathers: Greek Texts and English Translations* (Grand Rapids, MI: Baker Academic, 2007), 166.

[7] *Hist. Eccl.* 3.22.

[8] See Theodoret's *Eranistes* 1 ("The Immutable").

[9] See *Hist. Eccl.* 3.36.2: "Ignatius . . . whose fame is still celebrated by a great many."

[10] Foster, "Epistles of Ignatius of Antioch," 81.

8–10 and *Philadelphians* 6–9 that bear resemblance to passages discussing works of the law in Galatians and Romans. There is long-standing debate regarding the precise identity and argumentation of Ignatius's Judaizing opponents, as well the degree to which these opponents correspond with those of Paul. The fragmentary evidence in Ignatius's letters makes firm conclusions on these questions impossible to reach, and Donahue notes that "even more than is customary in historical study, we must content ourselves when discussing Ignatius's opponents and their beliefs with probability rather than certitude."[11]

Ignatius writes against both Docetists and Judaizers in his letters, and scholars dispute whether or not there is overlap between these groups. On one side, many have interpreted the close proximity of anti-Judaizing and anti-Docetic statements in Ignatius's letters to indicate that his target is "Doceto-judaism" (as coined by Lightfoot),[12] with Molland and Barrett following the conclusion that the two heresies are linked.[13] On the other side, Richardson argues that while Ignatius does not "expressly distinguish" between these errors, "no record of 'Judaistic docetism' has ever come down to us," and "the very presuppositions which led to the docetic point of view were keenly opposed to those of the Judaisers."[14] The weight of the external evidence supports the idea of a separation between these views: Richardson rightly notes that even when accounting for mutual influence of Hellenistic and Hebrew thought on one another, "according to our records of early heresies, docetism with its high Christology is never found connected with Jewish practices, and the invariable concomitant of those heresies that are inclined to Hebrew rites is a view of Christ which stresses his humanity more than his divinity."[15] From an

---

[11]Paul J. Donahue, "Jewish Christianity in the Letters of Ignatius of Antioch," *Vigiliae Christianae* 32 (1978): 81.

[12]Lightfoot, *S. Ignatius, S. Polycarp*, 124-25.

[13]Cf. Einar Molland, "The Heretics Combatted by Ignatius of Antioch," *Journal of Ecclesiastical History* 5 (1954): 1-6; C. K. Barrett, "Jews and Judaizers in the Epistles of Ignatius," in *Jews, Greeks and Christians: Essays in Honour of W. D. Davies*, ed. R. Hammerton-Kelly and R. Scroggs (Leiden: Brill, 1976), 237: "This view [of Lightfoot] is probably in essence correct."

[14]Cyril Richardson, *The Christianity of Ignatius of Antioch* (New York: Columbia University Press, 1935), 51.

[15]Richardson, *Christianity of Ignatius of Antioch*, 52.

internal standpoint, while it is true that Ignatius does not specifically delineate between these groups in his letters,[16] one would anticipate Judaizing practices to be more consistently mentioned were the two views linked; instead, Docetism is engaged in nearly all the letters, and Judaizing only in two.[17] The analysis of Donahue is most persuasive in arguing for a delineation between these two groups, and it is assumed for this study that Ignatius's Judaizing opponents in Magnesia and Philadelphia are distinct from docetic parties.[18]

In comparing Ignatius's opponents with those of Paul in Romans and Galatians, Barrett issues the warning that "we must not assume that for Ignatius 'to judaize' meant exactly what it did for Paul."[19] However, while Barrett himself does not correlate Ignatius's and Paul's attacks on Judaizing, his represents a minority position on this issue.[20] Lightfoot, for one, sees Ignatius's use of ἰουδαϊσμός as corresponding with Paul's circumstances in Galatians 1–2, and writes regarding Ignatius's appeal against adopting Judaism in *Magnesians* 8 that "Ignatius doubtless had in his mind Gal. v. 4."[21] Donahue similarly sees Ignatius's argument in *Magnesians* as echoing "the classic Pauline dichotomy between faith and the Law," suggesting that "at Antioch he represented the Pauline school" and

---

[16]Cf. Richardson, *Christianity of Ignatius of Antioch*, 52: "[Ignatius] does not trouble with fine distinctions, nor does he elaborate the points at issue. Fundamentally in his mind all heresy is one—no matter from what philosophic presupposition it may spring, it is division." See also Donahue, "Jewish Christianity," 81: "Ignatius does not catalogue the opposing groups, or describe the precise points at which they have gone astray, as Irenaeus did later in the century."

[17]Cf. Richardson, *Christianity of Ignatius of Antioch*, 53-54.

[18]Donahue, "Jewish Christianity." For this view, see also Robert M. Grant, *Ignatius of Antioch*, vol. 4 of *The Apostolic Fathers: A New Translation and Commentary* (Camden, NJ: Thomas Nelson, 1967), 22; Foster, "Epistles of Ignatius of Antioch," 92; Matti Myllykoski, "Wild Beasts and Rabid Dogs: The Riddle of the Heretics in the Letters of Ignatius," in *The Formation of the Early Church*, ed. Jostein Ådna, WUNT 1:183 (Tübingen: Mohr Siebeck, 2005), 358; Michele Murray, *Playing a Jewish Game: Gentile Christian Judaizing in the First and Second Centuries CE* (Waterloo, Ontario: Wilfrid Laurier University Press, 2004), 83-84. Marshall, while rejecting Lightfoot's "implausible 'judaizing, gnosticizing Christian Jew,'" argues for a single Jewish-Christian group that understands Jesus to be an angel. While the small amount of angel language in Ignatius (with none in Ign. *Phld.* or *Magn.*) ultimately renders this reading less persuasive than the two-group thesis, the view seems preferable to Lightfoot's (John W. Marshall, "The Objects of Ignatius's Wrath and Jewish Angelic Mediators," *J. Eccles. Hist.* 56 [2005]: 4; see also Mark Edwards, "Ignatius, Judaism, Judaizing," *Eranos* 93 [1995]: 69-77).

[19]Barrett, "Jews and Judaizers," 221.

[20]Barrett, "Jews and Judaizers," 244.

[21]Lightfoot, *S. Ignatius, S. Polycarp*, 125.

"confronted those like Peter who followed the advice which James sent from Jerusalem."[22] Jefford likewise sees Paul and Ignatius as fighting similar battles:

> What is particularly interesting in the case of Ignatius . . . is the theme that he adopted most prominently from the perspective of Paul: the need to resist those who wanted to return Christianity to a faith of Jewish traditions. What Paul considers to be the "circumcision party," Ignatius labels as "Judaizers." The specifics of each group's perspective have been the focus of much speculation and are not clearly understood, but we may generally assume that each author is addressing roughly the same perspective, that is, a movement to return to the church's Jewish roots.[23]

Grant concurs with this assessment, writing of *Philadelphians* 6.1-2 that "Ignatius seems to have Gentile converts to Jewish Christianity in mind, not unlike those whom Paul describes as not keeping the law but advocating circumcision (Gal. 6:13),"[24] and similarly identifying Ignatius's argument that "to live in conformity with Judaism, after the incarnation, means acknowledging that grace has not been received" as "clearly Pauline" (Ign. *Magn.* 8.1-2).[25] In light of these parallels in argumentation, this study assumes a general correlation between Paul and Ignatius's "Judaizing" opponents, while recognizing that the precise level of correspondence between them cannot be identified definitively.[26]

Texts and translations. For the middle recension of the authentic Ignatian epistles (save for Romans, which has a different textual history), the Greek text survives only in the eleventh-century Codex Mediceo-Laurentianus (G), along with an early Latin translation (L, Caiensis 395, fifteenth century) and Syriac (Sf), Coptic (C), Armenian (A) and Arabic

---

[22]Donahue, "Jewish Christianity," 85.

[23]Clayton N. Jefford, *The Apostolic Fathers and the New Testament* (Peabody, MA: Hendrickson Publishers, 2006), 167.

[24]Grant, *Ignatius of Antioch*, 103.

[25]Grant, *Ignatius of Antioch*, 62.

[26]See also Carl Smith, "Ministry, Martyrdom, and Other Mysteries: Pauline Influence on Ignatius of Antioch," in *Paul and the Second Century*, ed. Michael Bird and Joseph Dodson (New York: T&T Clark, 2011), 47. In relation to the broader thesis that the distinction between Jews and Christians in Ignatius's time was largely imaginary, see Thomas Robinson, *Ignatius of Antioch and the Parting of the Ways: Early Jewish-Christian Relations* (Peabody, MA: Hendrickson, 2009).

fragments. In addition, the longer recension of the Greek texts (g) often provides a valuable textual witness, as well as (to a lesser degree) the Syriac abridgment (S). This study uses the Holmes edition for the Greek texts of Ignatius and English translations.[27]

IGNATIUS AND PAUL

Knowledge and use of Paul. As Jefford writes, "scholars have long recognized that Ignatius holds the apostle Paul as something of an inspiration and hero of the faith," and there is general agreement that Paul is the most significant apostolic influence in Ignatius's theology. Paul is twice mentioned within the epistles, with Ignatius calling him "the one who was sanctified, approved, deservedly blessed" and stating his wish to "be found in his steps when I reach God" in *Ephesians* 12.2, as well as mentioning him together with Peter in *Romans* 4.3 ("I do not give you orders like Peter and Paul"). Beyond these explicit references, Grant writes that "[Ignatius's] own letters are crowded with allusions to those of Paul," and in identifying himself with Paul's life and death, "he hopes that he himself, like Paul, will become a sacrificial offering on behalf of the Church" (cf. e.g. Phil 2:17; Ign. *Rom.* 2.2).[28] Jefford identifies Ignatius as consciously modeling himself after the apostle, witnessed in his practice of writing letters to churches in what he terms "the apostolic manner" (Ign. *Trall.* 1.0), his similar insistence on freedom from Judaism, and a literary style that is similar to Paul's.[29] As Schoedel similarly concludes, "of all [the biblical] material Paul seems to have exercised the profoundest formative influence on Ignatius."[30]

While Ignatius's knowledge of Paul and his letters is sure, the scope of the letters known to him is a matter of some debate. As is the tendency with other early patristic sources, Ignatius's knowledge of Paul's letters "is evident by similarities in terminology, style, and critical concepts" instead of direct copying from texts, which presumably would have been

---

[27]Holmes, *Apostolic Fathers.*
[28]Grant, *Ignatius of Antioch*, 1.
[29]Jefford, *Apostolic Fathers and the New Testament*, 138.
[30]William R. Schoedel, *Ignatius of Antioch: A Commentary on the Letters of Ignatius of Antioch* (Philadelphia: Fortress Press, 1985), 10.

impossible as a prisoner under armed transport.[31] Foster's analysis, which openly adopts a minimalist position, takes Ignatius's comment in his letter to the Ephesian church that Paul "in every epistle makes mention of you" (Ign. *Eph.* 12.1) as an indication that Ignatius only knew of the letters in which such mention is present: 1 Corinthians, Ephesians, and 1 Timothy and 2 Timothy.[32] While these letters do appear to be known by Ignatius, the view that the bishop of Antioch is speaking hyperbolically in this passage seems more plausible,[33] particularly in light of Ignatius's florid rhetoric elsewhere.[34] Inge's earlier study (which is closer to a maximalist reading) detects influence from the aforementioned epistles, along with Romans and 2 Corinthians, and potentially Galatians and Philippians as well.[35] This view that Ignatius was familiar with a broader set of Pauline writings shares company with Barnett[36] and Grant.[37]

Ignatius's knowledge and use of Romans and Galatians is of greatest interest to this study, and since these texts are unlikely to have been available en route to his execution, Ignatius's dependency on these epistles can only be measured by evaluating possible allusions. Nevertheless, there is strong evidence of allusions to the former epistle, and it seems that Ignatius at least knows the content and events discussed in the latter.[38] The

---

[31]Smith, "Ministry, Martyrdom, and Other Mysteries," 39.

[32]Paul Foster, "The Epistles of Ignatius of Antioch and the Writings That Later Formed the New Testament," in *The Reception of the New Testament in the Apostolic Fathers*, ed. Andrew F. Gregory and Christopher M. Tuckett (Oxford: Oxford University Press, 2005), 172.

[33]See Lightfoot, *S. Ignatius, S. Polycarp*, 65-66; a "pardonable exaggeration" in the words of Inge (W. R. Inge, "Ignatius," in *The New Testament in the Apostolic Fathers*, ed. Oxford Society of Historical Theology [Oxford: Clarendon Press, 1905], 69).

[34]See, for example, Ignatius's predilection for identifying things than which "nothing is better": "There is nothing better than peace" (Ign. *Eph.* 13.2); "Focus on unity, for there is nothing better" (Ign. *Poly.* 1.2); ". . . and of faith and love, to which nothing is preferable" (Ign. *Magn.* 1.2); "Jesus Christ, than whom nothing is better" (Ign. *Magn.* 7.1).

[35]Inge, "Ignatius," 69-71.

[36]"It is clear that Ignatius knew 1 Corinthians, Romans and Ephesians and that he probably knew Galatians, Philippians, and Colossians. He may also have known 2 Corinthians, 1 and 2 Thessalonians, and Philemon" (Albert Barnett, *Paul Becomes a Literary Influence* [Chicago: University of Chicago Press, 1941], 170).

[37]"Though for Ignatius 1 Corinthians was the most meaningful of the Pauline epistles, it is quite clear that he was acquainted with a larger collection which apparently included Romans, 1 Corinthians, Galatians, Ephesians, Philippians, Colossians, 1 Thessalonians, and 2 Thessalonians" (Robert M. Grant, *The Formation of the New Testament* [New York: Harper & Row, 1965], 94).

[38]While Aageson notes that "the elaborate arguments about the law, circumcision, faith, and works found in Paul's letters to the Romans and Galatians are not replicated by Ignatius," this does not

case for dependency on Romans is fairly straightforward, with a majority of commentators identifying correspondence between various passages in Ignatius's writings and Paul's epistle,[39] the strongest allusions being *Ephesians* 8.2 to Romans 8:5, 8-9,[40] *Ephesians* 18.2 to Romans 1:3-4,[41] and the possible reference of *Ephesians* 19.3 to Romans 6:4.[42] Beyond these, there are parallels between the introductions of the respective letters to the Romans (with Jefford seeing Ignatius's as "clearly . . . patterned upon Paul's own expression of doctrine and faith as stated in Rom 1:1-6"[43]), as well as a less-discussed possible allusion to Romans 4:25 at *Romans* 6.1.[44] Further parallels in argumentation are discussed in the analysis section below, and in light of Paul's broader influence in Ignatius's writings and the verbal and thematic correspondence between the passages noted, this study regards it as highly likely that Ignatius knows and alludes to this epistle.[45]

The case for Ignatius's knowledge and use of Galatians is more complex, as lexical overlap with specific passages in the epistle is more difficult to

---

necessarily constitute an objection to Ignatius's use of these letters, as the circumstances of Ignatius's writing are such that elaborate arguments on any topic are rare in his epistles (James W. Aageson, *Paul, the Pastoral Epistles, and the Early Church* [Grand Rapids, MI: Baker Academic, 2007], 128).

[39]See Inge, "Ignatius," 69-70; Grant, *Ignatius of Antioch*, 24; Schoedel, *Ignatius of Antioch*, 9n54; Richardson, *Christianity of Ignatius of Antioch*, 66; Heinrich Rathke, *Ignatius von Antiochien und die Paulusbriefe* (Berlin: Akademie-Verlag, 1967), 65; D. A. Hagner, *The Use of the Old and New Testaments in Clement of Rome* (Leiden: Brill, 1973), 283.

[40]Ign. *Eph.* 8.2: Οἱ σαρκικοὶ τὰ πνευματικὰ πράσσειν οὐ δύνανται οὐδὲ οἱ πνευματικοὶ τὰ σαρκικά; Rom 8:5, 8-9: Οἱ γὰρ κατὰ σάρκα ὄντες τὰ τῆς σαρκὸς φρονοῦσιν, οἱ δὲ κατὰ πνεῦμα τὰ τοῦ πνεύματος . . . οἱ ἐν σαρκὶ ὄντες θεῷ ἀρέσαι οὐ δύνανται.

[41]Ign. *Eph.* 18.2: Ἰησοῦς ὁ Χριστὸς ἐκυοφορήθη ὑπὸ Μαρίας κατ' οἰκονομίαν θεοῦ ἐκ σπέρματος μὲν Δαυὶδ πνεύματος δὲ ἁγίου; Rom 1:3-4: τοῦ γενομένου ἐκ σπέρματος Δαυὶδ κατὰ σάρκα, τοῦ ὁρισθέντος υἱοῦ θεοῦ ἐν δυνάμει κατὰ πνεῦμα ἁγιωσύνης ἐξ ἀναστάσεως νεκρῶν, Ἰησοῦ Χριστοῦ τοῦ κυρίου ἡμῶν. Lindemann, who holds to an ultraminimalist position that Ignatius knows only 1 Corinthians, nevertheless also notes the similarity between Ign. *Eph.* 18.2 and Rom 1:3-4, though he attributes this to common traditions (Andreas Lindemann, "Paul in the Writings of the Apostolic Fathers," in *Paul and the Legacies of Paul*, ed. William S. Babcock [Dallas: Southern Methodist University Press, 1990], 37). See also the parallel with Ign. *Smyrn.* 1.1: ἐκ γένους Δαυὶδ κατὰ σάρκα, υἱὸν θεοῦ κατὰ θέλημα καὶ δύναμιν θεοῦ.

[42]Ign. *Eph.* 19:3: θεοῦ ἀνθρωπίνως φανερουμένου εἰς καινότητα ἀϊδίου ζωῆς; Rom 6:4: καὶ ἡμεῖς ἐν καινότητι ζωῆς περιπατήσωμεν. See also Ign. *Magn.* 9.1-2: οἱ ἐν παλαιοῖς πράγμασιν ἀναστραφέντες εἰς καινότητα ἐλπίδος ἦλθον.

[43]Jefford, *Apostolic Fathers and the New Testament*, 138.

[44]Ign. *Rom.* 6.1: τὸν ὑπὲρ ἡμῶν ἀποθανόντα . . . τὸν δι' ἡμᾶς ἀναστάντα; Rom 4:25: ὃς παρεδόθη διὰ τὰ παραπτώματα ἡμῶν καὶ ἠγέρθη διὰ τὴν δικαίωσιν ἡμῶν.

[45]Note as well Ignatius's statement that he does not give the Romans orders like Peter and Paul (Ign. *Rom.* 4.3); if Ignatius knows Paul gave the Romans orders, this suggests his knowledge of the letter to the church (cf. Rom 15:15). I owe this point to Markus Bockmuehl (personal communication).

identify, with the strongest allusion being Galatians 1:1 with *Philadelphians* 1.1.[46] However, two factors suggest that Ignatius was very likely to have been familiar with the events described in the epistle, and more likely than not with the epistle itself as well. The first is Ignatius's background: as Smith notes, Ignatius's own city of Antioch was "a center for Pauline activity," where Paul was mentored by Barnabas and commissioned for mission, and was ground zero for the conflicts over Jews, Gentiles, and the law that are attested in Galatians. As Smith comments, "it seems reasonable to assume that the bishop was aware of at least some of this history."[47] The second factor is the number of close parallels in argumentation found in Ignatius's letters and Galatians, particularly within the passage of *Magnesians* 8–10 (further discussed below), which is striking even to those who do not believe Ignatius to have known the epistle. Within this passage, both Grant and Lightfoot identify Ignatius in *Magnesians* 8:1-2 as drawing on Paul's argument in Galatians 5:4,[48] and Donahue, himself agnostic on Ignatius's knowledge of Galatians, similarly holds that Ignatius "echoes the classic Pauline dichotomy between faith and the Law" found in Galatians 5:2-6.[49] Even Lindemann, who views it as "highly unlikely . . . that Ignatius was acquainted with Paul's epistle to the Galatians," nevertheless acknowledges that Ignatius "uses surprisingly similar arguments" in *Magnesians* 8–9, and concedes that "the theological structure of the Ignatian thinking in this passage does seem to recall Paul, in whose theology it may have originated."[50] Indeed

---

[46]Ign. *Phld.* 1.1: Ὃν ἐπίσκοπον ἔγνων οὐκ ἀφ᾽ ἑαυτοῦ οὐδὲ δι᾽ ἀνθρώπων κεκτῆσθαι τὴν διακονία . . . ἀλλ᾽ ἐν ἀγάπῃ θεοῦ πατρὸς καὶ κυρίου Ἰησοῦ Χριστοῦ; Gal 1:1: Παῦλος ἀπόστολος οὐκ ἀπ᾽ ἀνθρώπων οὐδὲ δι᾽ ἀνθρώπου ἀλλὰ διὰ Ἰησοῦ Χριστοῦ καὶ θεοῦ πατρός. Cf. Inge, "Ignatius," 70; Schoedel, *Ignatius of Antioch*, 196: "The authority of the (unnamed) bishop of Philadelphia is expressed in Pauline terms (cf. Gal 1:1) that emphasize his responsibility directly to God." Schoedel, *Ignatius of Antioch*, 10n56 also notes the possible reference to Gal 1:10 (Ἄρτι γὰρ ἀνθρώπους πείθω ἢ τὸν θεόν; ἢ ζητῶ ἀνθρώποις ἀρέσκειν; εἰ ἔτι ἀνθρώποις ἤρεσκον, Χριστοῦ δοῦλος οὐκ ἂν ἤμην) in Ign. *Rom.* 2.1: Οὐ γὰρ θέλω ὑμᾶς ἀνθρωπαρεσκῆσαι, ἀλλὰ θεῷ ἀρέσαι, ὥσπερ καὶ ἀρέσκετε.

[47]Smith, "Ministry, Martyrdom, and Other Mysteries," 40; cf. Acts 11:25-26; 13:1-3; 15:36-41; Gal 2:11-21.

[48]Grant, *Ignatius of Antioch*, 62; Lightfoot, *S. Ignatius, S. Polycarp*, 125. See also Murray, *Playing a Jewish Game*, 84.

[49]Donahue, "Jewish Christianity," 85.

[50]Lindemann, "Paul in the Writings," 37-38.

for Lindemann, this allusive quality points instead to the depth of Paul's influence on Ignatius: "Ignatius, we might say, was making an entirely unforced use of Paul, implicit rather than explicit, without rather than with any special thought or attention. If this view is correct, however, the allusions to Paul are all the more remarkable; they demonstrate just how far-reaching the Pauline influence on Ignatius apparently was."[51]

For the purposes of this study, it appears very likely from Ignatius's evident allusions that he knew the text of Romans, and thus would have been familiar with Pauline discussions on works of the law. While knowledge and use of Galatians is more difficult to establish based on the extant evidence—it is possible, for example, that Ignatius may have been familiar with Paul's arguments in Antioch without knowing the particular way they were articulated in the Galatian epistle—the parallels in argumentation between Galatians and *Magnesians* nevertheless make such dependency appear probable. In either case, it seems unlikely that the bishop of Antioch would have been unaware of the apostles' dispute over works of the law that took place in this very city.

Ignatius as Pauline interpreter. While Richardson notes that "the surest evidence of literary dependence in Ignatius is his indebtedness to Paul,"[52] critiques of Ignatius as a Pauline interpreter have not been infrequent over the past centuries (often owing to his significance in post-Reformation polemics), with common areas of criticism including an insufficient theology of the Holy Spirit,[53] and conflating the Pauline distinction between σῶμα and σάρξ.[54] A number of factors make it difficult to evaluate Ignatius's interpretive ability, of which some are common to sources in this period, and others specific to Ignatius's situation. First, as is the case with all patristic interpreters, contemporary assessments of

---

[51]Lindemann, "Paul in the Writings," 40. See also James D. G. Dunn, *Neither Jew nor Greek: A Contested Identity*, vol. 3 of *Christianity in the Making* (Grand Rapids, MI: Eerdmans, 2015), 691: "The impression is hard to escape that Ignatius had so steeped himself in Paul's letters that his own thought and concerns, perhaps unconsciously, were shaped by Pauline language and imagery."

[52]Richardson, *Christianity of Ignatius of Antioch*, 60.

[53]Cf. Richardson, *Christianity of Ignatius of Antioch*, 61-62; Grant, *Ignatius of Antioch*, 25.

[54]Dunn, *Neither Jew nor Greek*, 692. For one recent assessment of areas of continuity and discontinuity, see Smith, "Ministry, Martyrdom, and Other Mysteries."

the correspondence between Ignatius and Paul presuppose a set understanding of Paul's theology (and which epistles reflect the "real" Paul), with the numerous areas of divergence among contemporary Pauline exegetes producing a similarly wide range of evaluations of Ignatius's interpretive ability. Second, as is commonly the case in this period, Ignatius is making use of Pauline texts and ideas to engage his own circumstances rather than conducting standalone Pauline exegesis, and the degree of overlap between Ignatius's circumstances and those of Paul (such as in their encounters with Judaizers) can only be determined within the realm of probability. Third, both positive and negative evaluations of Ignatius as an interpreter are problematized by the occasional nature of his letters and the extreme conditions under which they were penned. While it is possible that the absence of any particular Pauline theme in Ignatius may point to a deficiency in his understanding of the Apostle's thought, for example, the fragmentary evidence provided by Ignatius's letters means that this cannot necessarily be assumed. As Lindemann notes, "es wäre jedoch ungerecht, wollte man die notgedrungen in Eile geschriebenen Ignatius mit den überaus sorgfältig ausgestalteten Paulusbriefen vergleichen, nur um dann ihre geringere theologische Qualität zu konstatieren."[55]

As the case stands, it seems safest to avoid strong positive or negative pronouncements on Ignatius's "Paulinism." Rather, in light of the close historical (and indeed geographical) proximity of the two figures, and Ignatius's own aims to imitate Paul and "to be found in his steps" (Ign. *Eph.* 12.2),[56] one can regard Ignatius's epistles as a distinctly valuable, if not necessarily infallible, witness to Paul's own teaching. As Smith and Dunn note, it is fair to consider Ignatius a protégé of Paul,[57] and one

---

[55]"It would, however, be unfair if one were to compare the (necessarily) hastily written letters of Ignatius with the extremely carefully crafted letters of Paul, in order thereafter to note their lower theological quality." Andreas Lindemann, *Paulus im ältesten Christentum: das Bild des Apostels und die Rezeption der paulinischen Theologie in der frühchristlichen Literatur bis Marcion* (Tübingen: Mohr Siebeck, 1979), 84.

[56]Cf. the strongly worded conclusion of Lindemann: "Paulus ebenso wie „die Apostel" für Ignatius unantastbare Autorität ist" ("Paul, just like 'the Apostles,' is an inviolable authority for Ignatius"). Lindemann, *Paulus im ältesten Christentum*, 87.

[57]Smith, "Ministry, Martyrdom, and Other Mysteries," 56; Dunn, *Neither Jew nor Greek*, 692.

would expect Ignatius's engagement with issues regarding Jewish insistence on law observance to draw on the apostle's thought and example.[58]

THE LAW AND WORKS IN *EPISTLE*
TO THE MAGNESIANS AND *EPISTLE*
TO THE PHILADELPHIANS

Meaning: What works of what law? In Ignatius's *Epistle to the Magnesians*, the term *law* appears in some manuscripts of 8.1, where Ignatius writes that "if we continue to live in accordance with Judaism, we admit that we have not received grace." While Holmes follows the Latin text (which suggests only Ἰουδαϊσμόν to be read), "law" is found in the extant Greek manuscript (νόμον Ἰουδαϊσμόν) and in g and A (νόμον Ἰουδαϊκόν).[59] The textual question is difficult, though however one resolves it, the works discussed by Ignatius are those corresponding with the Jewish law. In *Magnesians* 8–10, the particular works objected to are the "ancient practices" (παλαιοῖς πράγμασιν) and keeping the Sabbath, which are placed in contrast with "newness of hope" and keeping the Lord's day (Sunday) (9.1). Such deeds were previously practiced by the "most holy prophets" (8.2) who were waiting on Christ as their

---

[58]See as well Bultmann's positive assessment of Ignatius's Paulinism: "It seems to me that, with the exception of Ignatius, none of the Christian writers after Paul (and John)—either among the authors of the later New Testament writings or the Apostolic Fathers—has understood the Christian faith as an *existentiell* attitude . . . none of them, with the exception of Ignatius, has so clearly recognized the unity of indicative and imperative that for Paul characterizes Christian existence" (Bultmann, "Ignatius and Paul," in *Existence and Faith: Shorter Writings of Rudolf Bultmann*, ed. Schubert Miles Ogden [New York: Meridian Books, 1960 {1953}], 267-68).

[59]Commentators differ on which reading should be given priority, with Zahn and Camelot following the reading of G, and Lightfoot, Schoedel, and Holmes following the Latin reading. Defending L, Schoedel writes that "the reading of G (preserved by Zahn), κατὰ νόμον Ἰουδαϊσμὸν ζῶμεν 'we live Judaism according to the law,' is unlikely Greek. The reading of gA, κατὰ νόμον Ἰουδαϊκόν 'according to the Jewish law,' represents an effort to correct G" (Schoedel, *Ignatius of Antioch*, 119n7). Lightfoot's preference for L, however, departs from his stated principles elsewhere, whereby "the combination Ag is, as a rule, decisive in favour of a reading" (Lightfoot, *S. Ignatius, S. Polycarp*, 5). In my view the *lectio difficilior* of G seems the slightly more probable reading, particularly as traces of the awkward rendering are preserved (with some alteration) in the weighty combination of gA. Elsewhere in the Ignatian corpus, "law" appears in Ign. *Smyrn.* 5.1 in reference to those who are not persuaded by the prophets or the law of Moses (ὁ νόμος Μωϋσέως), but this context does not appear to involve Judaizing or objections to works of the law (*pace* Barrett, "Jews and Judaizers," 239). In Ign. *Magn.* 2:1, νόμος is positively used in relation to the law of Christ (νόμῳ Ἰησοῦ Χριστοῦ); cf. similarly Ign. *Rom.* 1.0.

teacher, but are now practiced by them no longer (9.1-2). Ignatius also objects to "heterodoxies" and "antiquated myths" in this context, (8.1) though these are not works per se.

In the *Epistle to the Philadelphians* 6–9, there are no specific works objected to, though some are relativized and others are made subordinate to Christ. Circumcision appears to be relativized in a rather oblique way when Ignatius states that "it is better to hear about Christianity from a man who is circumcised than about Judaism from one who is not" (6.1).[60] The logic of this challenging passage appears to be that it is Jesus Christ that is of importance, not circumcision, so that the performance (or non-performance) of this work is irrelevant as long as one speaks of Christ. As Ignatius continues in 6.2, "but if either of them [the circumcised or uncircumcised] fails to speak about Jesus Christ, I look on them as tombstones and graves of the dead, upon which only the names of people are inscribed." In addition, Ignatius writes that while both the "archives" (which are almost universally taken to refer to the Hebrew Scriptures[61]) and the Jewish priests were good, they are subordinate to Christ and his high priesthood (8.2; 9.1). The "archives" appear to correspond with the Scriptures that constitute the Jewish law, and though no clear practices can be

---

[60]Considerable debate is found over the identity of the "uncircumcised preaching Judaism" and the nature of the Philadelphian heresy. Lightfoot held such teachers to be "Gentile Christians with strong Judaic tendencies," speculating that "though circumcision was insisted upon by the earliest Judaizers, this requirement was soon dropped as impracticable. . . . Thus the heresy combated by Ignatius was only an ἰουδαϊσμὸς ἀπὸ μέρους, as Epiphanius describes the Judaism of Cerinthus" (Lightfoot, *S. Ignatius, S. Polycarp*, 264). Though most commentators follow some version of Lightfoot's reading (cf. Foster, "Epistles of Ignatius of Antioch," 91; Barrett, "Jews and Judaizers," 234), Donahue provides an alternative thesis: rather than witnessing to uncircumcised Judaizers, "Ignatius means no more than that the law-free gospel does not permit distinctions among Christians. . . . This group might well have adopted the Jewish Christian view of Gentile Christianity mentioned above: Gentiles can join the church as Gentiles, but they occupy a position in the church inferior to that of Jews. Ignatius, like Paul, found this distinction invidious and fights against it" (Donahue"Jewish Christianity," 90). Despite Myllykoski's rebuttal ("Wild Beasts and Rabid Dogs," 354n44), the speculative quality of the ἰουδαϊσμὸς ἀπὸ μέρους thesis still renders Donahue's view more plausible in my judgment, though Myllykoski's observation on the entire enterprise of identifying Ignatian opponents is (unfortunately) astute: "Strictly speaking, there is no agreement on anything" (351).

[61]Cf. Lightfoot, *S. Ignatius, S. Polycarp*, 262, 270-71; Smith, "Ministry, Martyrdom, and Other Mysteries," 46; Schoedel, *Ignatius of Antioch*, 208. As Myllykoski writes, "it is hard to imagine that this meant something other than the Jewish scriptures used by Christians in general" ("Wild Beasts and Rabid Dogs," 355).

deduced from the reference to the Jewish priesthood, it is possible that there is an implied relativizing of the sacrificial system and temple piety in which these priests serve as functionaries.

Significance: What does the practice of these works signify? In *Magnesians* 8–10, the observance of these practices represents Judaism, the Jews' pattern of life and worship according to the Torah,[62] which Ignatius makes clear is the real target of his objections: "For if we continue to live according to Judaism, we admit that we have not received grace" (8.1).[63] Ignatius's objections are not raised as a wholesale rejection of the Jews as such (cf., for example, Ign. *Smyrn*. 1.2: "so that [Christ] may raise a banner for the ages through his resurrection for his saints and faithful people, whether among Jews or among Gentiles"), but oppose Judaism insofar as it does not point to Christianity and Christ. This is clear in 10.3: "It is utterly absurd to profess Jesus Christ and to practice Judaism. For Christianity did not believe in Judaism, but Judaism in Christianity, in which every tongue believed and was brought together to God."

In *Philadelphians* 6–9, no clear significance is attached to the work of circumcision, though common usage and the context following 6.1 ("But if anyone expounds Judaism to you, do not listen to him") make it clear that it is connected with the Jews and the adoption of Judaism. The appeal to the archives also appears to represent an adherence to Judaism,[64] as does the system of the Jewish priesthood (9.1).

Ἰουδαϊσμός: A brief digression

There is vigorous debate in contemporary scholarship as to what Ἰουδαϊσμός would have represented in this period, sparked not least by the influential essay of Steve Mason in 2007, which takes its impetus from the relatively infrequent usage of the term before the third century AD. Against the traditional view (represented by Hengel) that "the word means both political and genetic association with the

---

[62]Similarly Judith Lieu, *Neither Jew nor Greek? Constructing Early Christianity* (Edinburgh: T&T Clark, 2002), 25.

[63]On Ἰουδαϊσμός, see the brief digression below.

[64]"If I do not find it in the archives, I do not believe it in the gospel," which Ignatius also associates with a "spirit of contentiousness" (8.2).

Jewish nation and exclusive belief in the one God of Israel, together with observance of the Torah given by him,"[65] Mason contends that no category of "Judaism" existed in this period. Rather, Ἰουδαϊσμός was a specialized term "usable only in the special context of movement toward or away from Judaean law and life, in contrast to some other cultural pull,"[66] with the verbal usage indicating that this involves identifying with a people or culture besides one's own.[67]

Novensen's study on the term in Galatians offers a variation of Mason's thesis, taking Ἰουδαϊσμός as having a specialized force as "the defense and promotion of Jewish customs by Jewish people,"[68] which he sees (contra Mason) as practiced by Jews themselves rather than non-Jews. This is not the general practice of such Jewish customs: "not all Jews practice Ἰουδαϊσμός. Virtually all Jews follow the ancestral traditions, but only a subset fight for the cause of judaization, defending the traditions even to the point of harassing other Jews whom they suspect of endangering those traditions, as both Judah Maccabee and Paul did. It is this kind of political activism that goes by the name Ἰουδαϊσμός in ancient sources."[69]

These pieces serve well as reminders that Ἰουδαϊσμός does not function as a "religion" in a post-Enlightenment sense of the term within this period,[70] a false impression that may be given by a simple reading of the term as "Judaism." It is telling, however, that neither piece is able to comfortably integrate the Ignatian instances of Ἰουδαϊσμός into their arguments. Mason's piece simply leaves out Ignatius's use of Ἰουδαϊσμός in *Magnesians* 8.1, which in its context gives no impression of being a specialized term, and while Mason asserts Ignatius to have a "narrowly restricted" use of Ἰουδαϊσμός, he does not identify from an internal standpoint why such an understanding better fits the Ignatian

[65]Hengel, *Judaism and Hellenism*, trans. J. Bowden (Philadelphia: Fortress, 1974), 1-2, in Steve Mason, "Jews, Judaeans, Judaizing, Judaism: Problems of Categorization in Ancient History," *Journal for the Study of Judaism* 38 (2007): 465.

[66]Mason, "Jews, Judaeans, Judaizing, Judaism," 511.

[67]Mason, "Jews, Judaeans, Judaizing, Judaism," 462.

[68]Matthew Novensen, "Paul's Former Occupation in Ioudaismos," in *Galatians and Christian Theology: Justification, the Gospel, and Ethics in Paul's Letter*, ed. Mark W. Elliot, Scott J. Hafemann, N. T. Wright, and John Frederick (Grand Rapids, MI: Baker Academic, 2014), 33.

[69]Novensen, "Paul's Former Occupation," 37.

[70]Cf. Mason, "Jews, Judaeans, Judaizing, Judaism," 482.

uses of the term than the traditional sense.[71] Novensen brackets Ignatius's uses of the term as not relevant to his study ("in patristic usage
from Ignatius onward, Ἰουδαϊσμός takes on a new, stereotyped sense,
which is beyond the scope of the essay"[72]). This approach is surprising
given the close proximity of Ignatius to Paul (whose usage is the topic
of his study) and the important role played by Paul's writings in Ignatius's theology, and no argument is offered as to why this term would
have suddenly taken on a new meaning in Ignatius's letters.

Moreover, it is not clear that such a revised reading of Ἰουδαϊσμός
is necessary—or even plausible—by the term's usage in the Maccabean accounts. To take the example of 4 Macc, likely the nearest oc-
currence of the term to Paul's time, Mason concedes that "a tolerable
sense" can be achieved by the traditional reading of Ἰουδαϊσμός.[73]
But the text does not appear to serve as a friendly witness for Mason's
counterproposal: in 4:26, Antiochus seeks to have everyone in the
nation renounce Ἰουδαϊσμός, and when one looks immediately before this to see the activities summarized by the term in 4:19-26—the
way of life, system of government, temple worship, observing the
ancestral law, circumcision, food regulations—it is difficult to follow
Mason's confident assertion that this "is not then 'Judaism' as a system of life," and rather only "a newly coined counter-measure against
Ἑλληνισμός."[74] Nor does it make sense to read Ἰουδαϊσμός in this
passage as signifying "the adoption of Jewish customs by non-Jewish
people" (the summary of Mason's view given by Novensen, which he
similarly rejects).[75]

To be sure, questions regarding the frequency of the use of the
term Ἰουδαϊσμός in this period merit continued exploration, but the
fragmentary nature of our extant evidence from antiquity must be
recognized to avoid the oversimplification of holding that the usage
(or nonusage) of a particular word necessarily corresponds with the
prevalence (or even existence) of a phenomenon in a certain period.

---

[71]Mason, "Jews, Judaeans, Judaizing, Judaism," 461.
[72]Novensen, "Paul's Former Occupation," 32n46.
[73]Mason, "Jews, Judaeans, Judaizing, Judaism," 468.
[74]Mason, "Jews, Judaeans, Judaizing, Judaism," 467.
[75]Novensen, "Paul's Former Occupation," 29; cf. Mason, "Jews, Judaeans, Judaizing, Judaism," 463-64.

To take a similarly odd case by way of analogy, a TLG search for Χριστιανισμός finds extant evidence of the term being used 132 times in the second century—but in the third century, this usage drops off dramatically to a mere eight instances. While a straightforward analysis of this data could produce theories of the dramatic third-century demise of the phenomenon of Christianity, we have good reasons to believe such ideas would be misguided, and such an example should temper assertions that the limited extant evidence for Ἰουδαϊσμός points to the nonexistence of "Judaism" as a category,[76] particularly when the evidence that does exist is not sufficiently accounted for.

Therefore, while the view of Ἰουδαϊσμός as a post-Enlightenment "religion" is to be rightly rejected, the traditional view of the term represented by Hengel (which includes what can be categorized as religious, political, and cultural dimensions of Jewish life) still makes the greatest sense of the term's meaning in our extant texts. As such, while some tempering of certitude may be called for, the views of older commentators on Ἰουδαϊσμός in Ignatius still have value, such as Donahue:

> We can be quite sure that [the Magnesians] would have known what living according to Judaism was. Judaism was an institution familiar to Ignatius's audience quite apart from Christianity; most of the large cities of Roman Asia had substantial Jewish populations. To Ignatius's audience, to live according to Judaism meant to adopt those customs which enabled an observer to distinguish the life of the Jew from that of the non-Jew. When Ignatius denigrates "living until now according to Judaism," he warns his epistles against adopting the ritual observances of the Mosaic law.[77]

See also Schoedel: "What mainly concerns the bishop is the fact that some still ('until now') wish to 'live according to Judaism.' The term 'Judaism' at this time stood for the whole system of belief and practice of the Jews (cf. 2 Macc 2:21; 8:18; 14:38; 4 Macc. 4.26); and 'living Jewishly' in Christian polemic meant insisting especially on the ritual requirements of that system (Gal 2:14; cf. 1:13)."[78]

---

[76]Mason, "Jews, Judaeans, Judaizing, Judaism," 457.
[77]Donahue, "Jewish Christianity," 84.
[78]Schoedel, *Ignatius of Antioch*, 118.

Opposition: Why are these works not necessary for the Christian? In *Magnesians* 8–10, five reasons can be identified for why Ignatius objects to works of the Jewish law.

(1) First, continuing to live according to Judaism is to "confess that we have not received grace" (8.1). The logic of this statement appears to parallel Paul's reasoning in Galatians 5:4: just as for Paul's audience, returning to the law constitutes a falling away from grace, so for Ignatius's audience a turn to Judaism is a de facto denial of having received grace apart from observing the Jewish law.[79] The parallel between these passages is strengthened by the common usage of a yeast metaphor,[80] and while Schoedel notes the echoes of Paul's argument with "Judaism" in place of "the law,"[81] the resemblance is even closer if the reading preserved by G (νόμον Ἰουδαϊσμόν) is original (for which see n59 above). Because grace has indeed been given, Ignatius exhorts the Magnesians, "Therefore, let us not be unaware of his goodness" (10.1).

(2) The second reason is that the godly prophets of the Old Testament were expecting Christ as their teacher (9.2) and lived in accordance with him instead of Judaism, which is manifest in that they themselves were similarly persecuted by the Jews (8.2). The Magnesians are to follow the example of such prophets who were "disciples in the Spirit" (9.2), who left behind the ancient practices and were raised from the dead at Christ's coming (9.1).[82]

(3) Third is the emphasis Ignatius places on the ultimate priority of Jesus Christ, and particularly his role as teacher. References to learning from Christ abound in this passage,[83] and contra the Jews, Ignatius's aim

---

[79]Cf. Grant, *Ignatius of Antioch*, 62.

[80]As Paul warns regarding the law that "a little yeast leavens the whole lump" (Gal 5:9), so Ignatius writes to "throw out . . . the bad yeast, which has become stale and sour, and reach for the new yeast, which is Jesus Christ" (10.1).

[81]Cf. Schoedel, *Ignatius of Antioch*, 119.

[82]Cf. Donahue on Ign. *Magn.* 8-9: "Ignatius, sharing Paul's general outlook, if not reproducing his argumentation, objects to these ritual practices. Only Christ can save, he insists; even for the prophets, the ritual practices of Judaism had no value. They too were saved as Christians" ("Jewish Christianity," 88).

[83]" . . . disciples of Jesus Christ, our only teacher" (9.1); "of whom the prophets were disciples, awaiting him as a teacher in the spirit" (9.2); "having become his disciples, let us learn to live according to Christianity" (10.1). On the "law of Christ" elsewhere in Ignatius, cf. Ign. *Magn.* 2.1; Ign. *Rom.* 1.0.

is that "we may be found to be disciples of Jesus Christ, our only teacher" (9.1), who is asserted to have been the teacher of the prophets as well (9.2). The priority of Christ also explains the rejection of Sabbath and its replacement with the Lord's day (μηκέτι σαββατίζοντες ἀλλὰ κατὰ κυριακὴν ζῶντες, 9.1), as this is the day on which Christ was raised and "our life also arose through him and his death" (9.1).

(4) Fourth is a sequential (or salvation-historical) argument, with the characterization of Judaism as old and of Christianity as new. In 9.1, Ignatius writes that the prophets left the "ancient deeds" and "came to newness of hope" in Christ, a possible allusion to Romans 6:4. Similarly in 10.1, the practices of Judaism are identified as "bad yeast" to be cast out, not because they are bad in themselves, but because they have "become stale and sour" (παλαιωθεῖσαν καὶ ἐνοξίσασαν), and are replaced with the new (νέαν) yeast of Christ. This sequential point is also evident in 10.3: "For Christianity did not believe in Judaism, but Judaism in Christianity."[84]

(5) Finally, the closing point in Ignatius's argument is the universality of Christianity over the ethnically delimited Judaism. Following his statement that "Christianity did not believe in Judaism, but Judaism in Christianity," Ignatius provides the reason: "in which every tongue believed and was gathered together to God" (10.3).[85] This reasoning may also correspond with the category of accordance with the prophets, as Ignatius's statement echoes the prophecies of Isaiah in 66:18 ("I am coming to gather all nations and tongues") and Isaiah 45:23 ("To me every knee shall bow, every tongue shall swear"), texts that are similarly picked up by Paul in Romans 14:11 and Philippians 2:10-11.[86]

In *Philadelphians* 6–9, Ignatius's arguments against Judaism can be placed into three categories:

(1) First, the "archives" and their accompanying works are primarily objected to insofar as they constitute a devaluation of Christ's work and

---

[84]Cf. Schoedel, *Ignatius of Antioch*, 126.

[85]Cf. Lightfoot, *S. Ignatius, S. Polycarp*, 134: "i.e., 'not the Jews only, but every race upon the earth'"; Barrett, "Jews and Judaizers," 236: "Christianity has supplanted Judaism as the means by which mankind as a whole (πᾶσα γλῶσσα) is to be brought to God (10.3)."

[86]Cf. Schoedel, *Ignatius of Antioch*, 127.

teaching, which for Ignatius makes all other things of secondary importance. Ignatius objects that those who reject teachings not found in the
"archives" are not placing Christ first: "But for me, the 'archives' are Jesus
Christ, the unalterable archives are his cross and death and his resurrection and the faith that comes through him," and it is "by these things
I want, through your prayers, to be justified" (8.2). Though only mentioned once in this context at the end of the argument, the use of
δικαιωθῆναι carries interesting parallels with Paul, as there is a clear resemblance in the structure of Ignatius's argument to Paul's in Galatians 2
and Romans 3. Here "the archives"—the Old Testament law, the Torah—
hold the place of works of the law, which Ignatius subordinates to Christ
and his actions and faith, which are the true hope for justification (8.2).[87]
Such parallels are only based on possible allusions, of course, but this is
the case for nearly all of Ignatius's references, and the thematic correspondence between this passage and the relevant Pauline texts is noteworthy. Ignatius's only other use of δικαιόω in his letters is a Pauline
allusion,[88] and given the parallels observed elsewhere between Ignatius's
arguments against Judaizers and Paul's writings, it seems likely that Paul's
arguments serve as Ignatius's inspiration in this passage.

(2) Though Ignatius does not explicitly spell out the logic, the context
of this passage also indicates that the unity of the church is an underlying
reason such works are not necessary for the Christian. Following his objection to Judaism and relativizing of circumcision in 6.1, Ignatius exhorts
the Philadelphians to "gather together with an undivided heart" (6.2). Ignatius then recalls his appeal to the Philadelphians to maintain unity
("the Spirit itself was preaching, saying these words . . . 'Love unity. Flee
from divisions,'" 7.2), and writes, "I was doing my part, therefore, as a
man set on unity. But God does not dwell where there is division and
anger. The Lord, however, forgives all who repent, if in repenting they
return to the unity of God and to the council of the bishop (συνέδριου

---

[87]Cf. Grant, *Ignatius of Antioch*, 106: "Ignatius desires to be 'justified' by the saving events and by
faith (a Pauline idea), along with the community's common prayer"; see also Donahue, "Jewish
Christianity," 89.

[88]Ign. *Rom.* 5.1: ἀλλ' οὐ παρὰ τοῦτο δεδικαίωμαι; 1 Cor 4:4: ἀλλ' οὐκ ἐν τούτῳ δεδικαίωμαι;
cf. Holmes, *Apostolic Fathers*, 231.

τοῦ ἐπισκόπου)" (8.1). After discussing Christ's superiority to the archives
and the Jewish priesthood, he concludes that Christ is the door to God
for the patriarchs, prophets, apostles alike, who "all . . . come together in
the unity of God" (9.1). For Ignatius in this passage, the church's unity is
not rooted in the archives and their accompanying works, but rather in
Christ, his apostles, and their episcopal successors (7.1–8.1).[89]

(3) Ignatius also presents a subtle argument in this passage for
Christian continuity with the prophets as being a reason for not reverting
to Judaism. Just before his warning against Judaism in 6.1 ("But if anyone
expounds Judaism to you, do not listen to him"), Ignatius writes, "And
we also love the prophets, because they anticipated the gospel in their
preaching and set their hope on him and waited for him; because they
also believed in him, they were saved, since they belong to the unity centered in Jesus Christ, saints worthy of love and admiration, approved by
Jesus Christ and included in the gospel of our shared hope" (5.2). This
argument for continuity is also seen in 9.1, where Christ is identified as
"the door of the father, through which Abraham and Isaac and Jacob and
the prophets and the apostles and the church enter in." This is continued
at the end of the section in 9.2, using the same language of anticipation
as 5.2: "For the beloved prophets preached in anticipation of him, but the
gospel is imperishable finished work." Ignatius closes with an exhortation
for the prophets and the gospel to be received together: "All these things
together are good, if you believe with love" (9.2).

CONCLUSION

In his epistles to the *Magnesians* and the *Philadelphians*, Ignatius objects
to the works of Sabbath and "ancient practices" and relativizes the work
of circumcision. The observance of these works represents Judaism—the
Jews' system of belief and practice as contained in "the archives" of the
Jewish law—which Ignatius makes clear is the real target of his objections.[90] A number of reasons are presented for not adopting such works,

---

[89]Donahue suggests that adherence to purity regulations in "the archives" would necessitate separate Jewish and non-Jewish Eucharistic celebrations; cf. Donahue, "Jewish Christianity," 89-90.

[90]Schoedel, *Ignatius of Antioch*, 118.

foremost among which are the primacy of Jesus Christ and his teaching—
who introduces new practices like keeping the Lord's day, and in whom
is the hope of justification—and the continuity of the prophets and their
prophecies with the new dispensation in Christ. In addition, the Christian
reception of grace apart from Judaism, the salvation-historical argument
of Judaism giving way to Christianity, the universal scope of Christianity,
and the unity of the church also emerge as reasons for not observing
these works. While not utilizing the phrase *works of the law* or directly
referencing verses in Paul that do so, Ignatius's epistles show considerable
influence from Paul's writings and contain disputes that parallel the apostle's own on this topic, and thus constitute supporting evidence for how
"works of the law" debates were received and understood in the early
second century.

SECOND-CENTURY FRAGMENTS

Preaching of Peter, Dialogue of Jason and Papiscus, and Acts of Paul

This excursus examines the fragments of three writings from the second century that are largely nonextant: the *Preaching of Peter, Dialogue of Jason and Papiscus,* and Acts of Paul. Because these works remain in only fragmentary form, it is difficult to identify how closely their content corresponds with Paul's discussions on works of the law, or to give a clear assessment of their Pauline influence. Nevertheless, portions in each of these writings show evidence of conflict with Jewish parties regarding the law or works, and due to their early date and potential relevance for this topic, these sections are briefly analyzed here.

PREACHING OF PETER

The first source is the *Preaching of Peter* (or *Kerygma Petri, KP*), a writing that has been suggested to be the oldest Christian apology,[1] and is primarily known through sections preserved in Clement of Alexandria's *Stromata*.[2] Usually dated to the first half of the second century, *KP* appears to be treated as Scripture by Clement, though Origen's writings contain some discussion questioning its authenticity (noting its usage by Heracleon), and Eusebius and Jerome reject it.[3] Cambe suggests that *KP*

---

[1] Joseph Nicholas Reagan, *The Preaching of Peter: The Beginning of Christian Apologetic* (Chicago: The University of Chicago Press, 1923), 46. This section uses Cambe's Greek text and numbering and Elliott's translation (J. K. Elliott, ed., *The Apocryphal New Testament: A Collection of Apocryphal Christian Literature in an English Translation* [Oxford: Clarendon Press, 1993]).

[2] *Kerygma Petri* is to be distinguished from *Kerygmata Petrou,* the hypothetical source for the Pseudo-Clementine homilies in the third or fourth century.

[3] Cf. Origen, *Comm. Jo.* 13.17; Eusebius, *Hist. Eccl.* 3.3.2; Jerome, *Vir. ill.* 1. Origen's comments dismissing a passage from *Doctrina Petri* in *Princ.* 1.pr.8 may also refer to this work.

may have been written "pour faire suite aux *Actes* lucaniens, ou pour compléter l'*Évangile de Marc* par un manifeste apostolique," though no firm conclusions can be drawn from the small portions of text that remain.[4] The witness to the document in Clement and Origen suggests an Alexandrian provenance,[5] and parallels with *Diognetus* and *Aristides* have been noted among its extant passages, though here as well the fragmentary evidence makes it is difficult to establish either the fact or direction of dependency with confidence.[6] Pauline influence in *KP* is similarly difficult to assess, and while Cambe identifies parallels with Galatians 3:19-20; 4:1-11 in Fragment 3-5,[7] no dependency on Paul can be securely demonstrated.

The most relevant section for this study is Fragment 3-5 (*Strom.* 6.5.4; cf. Origen *Comm. Jo.* 13.17), where *KP* contrasts the worship of the Greeks and Jews with that of Christians. Following an exposition of the idolatrous folly of the Greeks, Peter continues,

> Neither worship him as the Jews do [κατὰ Ἰουδαίους σέβεσθε] for they, who suppose that they alone know God, do not know him, serving angels and archangels, the month and the moon: and if no moon be seen, they do not celebrate what is called the first sabbath, nor keep the new moon, nor the days of unleavened bread, nor the feast of tabernacles, nor the great day [of atonement]. (Fr. 4a)

According to Clement, Peter then "adds the finale of what is required":

> So then learn in a holy and righteous manner that which we deliver to you, observe, worshipping God through Christ in a new way. For we have found in the Scriptures, how the Lord said, "Behold, I make with you a new covenant,

---

[4]"To follow up on the Lucan Acts, or to complete the Gospel of Mark with an apostolic manifesto." Michael Cambe, *Kerygma Petri: Textus et commentarius* (Turnhout: Brepols, 2003), 3.

[5]Cambe, *Kerygma Petri*, 6.

[6]Cf. Bernard Pouderon, trans., *Aristide: Apologie*, Sources Chrétiennes 470 (Paris: Éditions du Cerf, 2003), 77-82; see *Aristides* n11 below.

[7]"Les parallélismes de pensée entre l'*Épître aux Galates* et le *KP* sont assez remarqables pour que certains chercheurs se soient prononcés pour une dépendance littéraire de l'écrit pétrinien; ces rapprochements ont du moins l'intérêt de mettre en évidence la présence d'un même modèle de référence." ("The parallels of thought between the Epistle to the Galatians and the *KP* are sufficiently remarkable that certain researchers have declared the Petrine writing to hold a literary dependence; these connections have at least the benefit of highlighting the presence of a same model of reference.") Cambe, *Kerygma Petri*, 172.

not as the covenant with your fathers in mount Horeb." He has made a new one with us: For the ways of the Greeks and Jews are old, but we are Christians who worship him in a new way as a third race [τρίτῳ γένει]. (Fr. 5a, translation adjusted)

The other relevant passage is Fragment 1, which is cited three times by Clement (here *Strom.* 1.29.182; cf. *Strom.* 2.15.68; *Ecl.* 58): "And in the Preaching of Peter you may find the Lord called 'Law and Word.'"

From the first fragment, it can be seen that the practices rejected by *KP* are the Torah's calendar observances, including the "first sabbath," the new moon, the feast of unleavened bread, the feast of tabernacles, and "the great day" (the day of atonement).[8] To practice these works identifies one with the Jews and their erroneous practices of worship, just as the practices of worshipping the elements and animals characterize the Greeks in the previous section. These practices also correspond with the old covenant given at Mount Horeb. Buell notes how this passage serves as an example of the overlap between racial and religious categories in this period, with the three γένη being distinguished by their religious practices. As Buell writes, "So what are these groups? Religions? Races? Clement's use of this text defies this oppositional framing; for him, ethnic distinctions consist especially of differences in how one worships."[9] Such practices thus signify both ethnic identity and intended piety, with the observance of these particular practices of worship being what defines one as part of each γένος. Observing these days is rejected as not constituting true worship of God, but rather worship of "angels and archangels, the month and the moon," which *KP* contrasts by his instructions to learn to worship "in a holy and righteous manner" (ὁσίως καὶ δικαίως). This "new way" has been prophesied in the Scriptures and corresponds with the promised new covenant, which establishes a "third race" (τρίτῳ γένει) that contrasts with the old ways of the Greeks and the Jews. As with Ignatius, there is a sequential emphasis in *KP*'s argument, with the

---

[8]The meaning of "first sabbath" (σάββατον . . . τὸ λεγόμενον πρῶτον) is debated; see the detailed discussion in Cambe, *Kerygma Petri*, 249-55.
[9]Denise Kimber Buell, "Rethinking the Relevance of Race for Early Christian Self-Definition," *Harvard Theological Review* 94 (2001): 461.

author noting the newness of Christianity four times in the closing paragraph. Finally, the brief statement in Fragment 1 may correspond with a common theme in this period, that of Christ bringing—and himself being—the new law (e.g. *Barn.* 2.6; Ign. *Magn.* 2.1; *Dial.* 11.2-4). Though it is impossible to know the proximity of Fragment 1 to Fragment 3-5, the usage of "new law" reasoning in other sources in this period (as well as *KP*'s appeal to the new covenant in Fr. 5) suggests that this identification of Christ as the law may similarly have been used as an objection to these former Jewish practices.[10]

In summary, the works rejected in the fragments of *KP* are the Torah's calendar observances, which correspond with the Jewish people and their erroneous worship, as well as the old covenant. These practices are rejected due to their not constituting true worship of God. Instead, a new and righteous way of worship has been revealed to Christians in the new covenant, which establishes them as a third race in relation to the Greeks and Jews. While there is no clear Pauline influence in the fragments of *KP*, parallels can be suggested that may point to a common theological framework.[11]

DIALOGUE OF JASON AND PAPISCUS

The *Dialogue of Jason and Papiscus* (*JP*), if extant, would conceivably represent one of this study's most important sources. Written in the first half of the second century and attributed to Aristo of Pella,[12] *JP* is first noted

---

[10]Here Stanton suggests that the author of *KP*, like Justin, offers a "profoundly christological interpretation" of Paul's "law of Christ" in seeing Christ as the law himself (Gal 6:2; cf. Graham Stanton, "What Is the Law of Christ?," in *Studies in Matthew and Early Christianity*, ed. Markus N. A. Bockmuehl and David Lincicum, WUNT 309 [Tübingen: Mohr Siebeck, 2013], 317).

[11]See e.g. Gal 4:8-11, cf. Cambe, *Kerygma Petri*, 171-72.

[12]Celsus's *True Discourse* (ca. AD 178) represents a *terminus ante quem*, and because Eusebius notes Aristo as his source for Hadrian's banishment of the Jews from Jerusalem, this often leads to a suggested *terminus post quem* of 135 (with ca. 140 being a commonly suggested date). However, it is not known if Eusebius's information is drawn from Aristo's *Dialogue*, and Clement of Alexandria's surprising attribution of the work to Luke the Evangelist in his *Hypotyposeis* (noted by John of Scythopolis, who is himself the source for Aristo's authorship) may suggest a date earlier in the second century. On Clement's attribution, cf. Harry Tolley, "Clement of Alexandria's Reference to Luke the Evangelist as Author of Jason and Papiscus," *Journal of Theological Studies* 63 (2012): 523-32. Text and translation are drawn from Bovon and Duffy: Aristo of Pella, *Dialogue of Jason and Papiscus*, trans. François Bovon and John M. Duffy, "A New Greek Fragment from Ariston of Pella's Dialogue of Jason and Papiscus," *Harvard Theological Review* 105 (2012): 457-65.

by Origen in his defense of the work against Celsus, which he says narrates a Christian debating with a Jew and "showing that the prophecies about the Messiah fit Jesus."[13] A third-century preface to a Latin translation (attributed to Celsus Africanus) identifies Jason as a Jewish Christian and describes Papiscus, an Alexandrian Jew, as eventually being persuaded of Jesus' messiahship and requesting the seal of baptism.[14] It has been suggested that Jason may be modeled on Paul's convert in Acts 17,[15] and sections of the writing are thought to be preserved in a number of similar later dialogues, though these cannot be identified without the original text.[16] Though Origen gives *JP* a somewhat reserved endorsement against Celsus (who derides its simplicity, a charge Origen grants while still arguing for its value),[17] the work appears to have enjoyed fairly wide popularity into the third century.[18] *JP* also seems to have held at least some thematic correspondence with Paul's letter to the Galatians, with Jerome citing it in his commentary on the epistle.[19] While nothing could be said on the topic of works of the law from the previously known excerpts, this situation changed with a newly discovered fragment published in 2012.

The fragment is preserved in a homily of Sophronius, the seventh-century patriarch of Jerusalem, who (like Clement of Alexandria) attributes *JP* to Luke the Evangelist. In the fragment, Sophronius writes that Luke has Papiscus inquire "'why you (Christians) hold the first day of the

---

[13]*Cels.* 4.52 (Origen, *Contra Celsum*, trans. Henry Chadwick [Cambridge: Cambridge University Press, 1953]).

[14]Celsus Africanus, in Pseudo-Cyprian, *De iudaica incredulitate* (PG 5.1285).

[15]Cf. Lawrence Lahey, "Evidence for Jewish Believers in Christian-Jewish Dialogues Through the Sixth Century (excluding Justin)," in *Jewish Believers in Jesus: The Early Centuries*, ed. Oskar Skarsaune and Reidar Hvalvik (Peabody, MA: Hendrickson Publishers, 2007), 586.

[16]On *JP*'s possible use and influence in later sources, see Lahey, "Evidence for Jewish Believers." Skarsaune argues that Justin draws on *JP* for his *Dialogue*; while possible, it is difficult to demonstrate this from a nonextant source. See Oskar Skarsaune, *The Proof from Prophecy: A Study in Justin Martyr's Proof-Text Tradition* (Leiden: Brill, 1987), 234-42.

[17]Cf. *Cels.* 4.52-53.

[18]Cf. the comments of Celsus Africanus, identifying *JP* as "splendid and remarkable and renowned" (*praeclarum atque memorabile gloriosumque*).

[19]Jerome cites the words Λοιδορία θεοῦ ὁ κρεμάμενος at *Comm. Gal.* 3.13; cf. William Varner, "On the Trail of Trypho: Two Fragmentary Jewish-Christian Dialogues from the Ancient Church," in *Christian Origins and Hellenistic Judaism: Social and Literary Contexts for the New Testament*, ed. Stanley E. Porter and Andrew W. Pitts (Leiden: Brill, 2013), 556-57.

week in greater honor'" (τὴν μίαν τῶν σαββάτων τιμωτέραν ἔχετε).[20] To this, Jason replies,

> God ordained this through Moses, when he said, "Behold I make the last things as the first." The Sabbath comes at the end, while the first of the week is the first; for it was on this day that the beginning of the whole world took place through the Word of God, as we are informed also by the book of Moses, when God says, "'Let light come into being,' and light came into being." And the Word which proceeded from God and created the light was Christ, the son of God through whom all the other things as well came to be.
>
> . . . So you should know from this, sir, that we are completely justified in honoring the first of the week as the beginning of all creation, because on this day Christ was manifested on earth, where in obedience to the commands and the Scriptures he suffered, and following his Passion he arose from the dead; and he rose again on this day, and having appeared to his disciples, i.e., to the Apostles, he proceeded to heaven; and that this day is the day of the ages, falling on the eighth and destined to dawn for the just in incorruption, in the kingdom of God, as a light eternal for the ages, amen. For the Sabbath falls on a day of rest, since it is <the last day> of the week. It is for this reason, then, that we honor the first of the week, as the day that brings us a great wealth of good things.[21]

From this passage, it can be seen that the practice that is made relative is the Jewish Sabbath, with Papiscus inquiring why the Christians hold another day in greater honor than this one. There is little that explicitly indicates the significance of observing the Sabbath, beyond that it corresponds with a former period (represented by the seventh day), and is associated with the Jewish party in the dialogue. By contrast, observing the first day of the week is associated with the Christians and corresponds with both an earlier period—the beginning at the first day, when God made the world through Christ—and a later one, the eighth day, when God brings the dawn of new creation and the inauguration of his eternal kingdom. The bulk of the passage is given to explaining why this new day takes precedence over the former, and here first place is given to the argument from prophecy, with Jason appealing to God's

---

[20]Bovon and Duffy, "A New Greek Fragment," 462.
[21]Bovon and Duffy, "A New Greek Fragment," 462.

words through Moses that "I will make the last things as the first," an
agraphon shared with Barnabas (Barn. 6.13). Though the logic of the
passage is difficult to follow (perhaps illustrating the simplicity for which
Celsus derides the work[22]), Jason proceeds along salvation-historical
lines in arguing that God has replaced this seventh day with a new one,
the eighth day, identified as ἡ μία τῶν σαββάτων and ἡ τῶν αἰώνων
ἡμέρα. This day corresponds with the birth and resurrection of Christ
and has thus brought "a great wealth of good things," making it more
worthy of honor than the Sabbath, an argument that parallels Ignatius's
similar replacement of the Sabbath with the κυριακήν in *Magnesians* 9.1.

In summary, the work in dispute in this fragment is Sabbath observance, which is relativized because God, following from the prophetic
witness of Scripture, has replaced it with a new day with Christ's advent.
Though no Pauline influence can be detected in this brief passage, thematic correspondence with Paul elsewhere in *JP* is suggested by Jerome's
citation of the dialogue in his Galatians commentary. As will be seen, the
manner in which debate over a particular work—here the Sabbath—
leads to a broader discussion about Jesus and his fulfillment of the Scriptures holds parallels with later Christian apologetic writings toward the
Jews, including Justin's *Dialogue with Trypho* and Tertullian's *Against
the Jews*.

ACTS OF PAUL

Tertullian provides the earliest attestation to the "falsely so named" Acts
of Paul (ActPl), which he says was authored by a presbyter in Asia.
"Thinking to add of his own to Paul's reputation," Tertullian writes that
the presbyter was deposed when his work was found out, "though he
professed he had done it for love of Paul."[23] ActPl is cited twice by Origen
(*Princ.* 1.2.3; *Comm. Jo.* 20.12) and was possibly known to Clement of
Alexandria (*Strom.* 6.43.1-2) and Hippolytus (*Dan.* 3.29), with Eusebius

---

[22]Cf. Bovon and Duffy, "A New Greek Fragment," 464: "Jason's first argument is easy to understand, though not quite logical."

[23]Tertullian, *Bapt.* 17.5. This section follows Pervo's numbering.

eventually classing it among the νόθοι (*Hist. Eccl.* 3.25.4, cf. 3.3.5).[24] P.W. Dunn's study identifies ActPl as written between approximately AD 120 (Thecla's death) and 200 (Tertullian's attestation), and settles for an early to mid-second century date.[25] Most studies prefer a date closer to Tertullian, though Jerome's odd note that it was the apostle John himself who convicted the presbyter suggests that an earlier date in this range should not be ruled out.[26] While there appears to be Pauline influence in ActPl—as Dunn notes, for example, Paul's conversion story in 9.5-6 appears to be based on Galatians 1–2 rather than the canonical Acts[27]— Rensberger rightly maintains that usage of the epistles is limited and no great interest in expositing them can be identified.[28] Various suggestions have been made regarding the purpose of ActPl, such as a continuation of Acts or creative reworking of it,[29] but little can be said with confidence beyond Tertullian's concession that it was inspired out of love for the apostle.

Unfortunately, the primary relevant section of the extant ActPl is a disconnected and poorly preserved fragment of the Heidelberg Coptic papyrus (copl 68e). Schmidt has attempted to reconstruct the passage, which James brings into the English as follows:

> Again I say unto you . . . I, that do the works . . .
>
> that a man is not *justified by the Law*, but that he is justified *by the* works of righteousness, and he . . .[30]

---

[24]Cf. Peter Wallace Dunn, "The Acts of Paul and the Pauline Legacy in the Second Century" (PhD diss., University of Cambridge, 2006), 11.

[25]Dunn, "The Acts of Paul," 11.

[26]*Vir. ill.* 7; cf. Dunn, "The Acts of Paul," 9. See also Snyder's recent argument that *ActPl* is actually a composite of several independent texts that were grouped together over the centuries (Glenn E. Snyder, *Acts of Paul: The Formation of a Pauline Corpus*, WUNT 2:352 [Tübingen: Mohr Siebeck, 2013]).

[27]Dunn, "The Acts of Paul," 16-17, 43-44, 192-94.

[28]Cf. David Rensberger, "As the Apostle Teaches: The Development of the Use of Paul's Letters in Second-Century Christianity" (PhD diss., Yale University, 1981), 305.

[29]See Richard Bauckham, "The Acts of Paul as a Sequel to Acts," in *The Book of Acts in its Ancient Literary Setting*, ed. Bruce Winter and Andrew Clarke (Grand Rapids, MI: Eerdmans, 1993), 105-52, and Daniel Marguerat, "The Acts of Paul and the Canonical Acts: A Phenomenon of Rereading," *Semeia* 80 (1997): 169-84, respectively.

[30]M. R. James, *The Apocryphal New Testament* (Oxford: Clarendon Press, 1924), 286; cf. Carl Schmidt, ed., *Acta Pauli, aus der Heidelberger koptischen Papyrushandschrift Nr. 1.* (Leipzig: J. C.

Schmidt and James place this fragment in Tyre, where Paul is attested to encounter "a multitude of Jews" on his arrival, with discussion regarding Moses taking place in the heavily fragmented pages preceding this passage. However, while Schmidt identifies this section as corresponding with Pauline passages on justification (albeit now with an incorrect interpretation),[31] a number of subsequent studies have viewed Schmidt's restoration of the text as overly ambitious.[32] Schneemelcher's edition simply omits the fragment altogether.[33] Rordorf and Cherix place the fragment in Jerusalem and leave out any mention of the law: "De nouveau, je vous dis [. . .] C'est moi qui fais [. . .] moi [. . .] [. . .] parce que l'homme sera justifié [. . .] mais parce qu'il sera justifié < . . . les> oeuvres de la justice et qu'il [. . .]."[34] Pervo's recent edition similarly places the encounter in Jerusalem and notes "the frequency of allusions to Galatians 1-2 and Acts 15" in this passage (with "Israel," "necessity," "freedom," and "the yoke" mentioned in the surrounding context), though it should be noted that the chapter itself is a reconstruction of fragments.[35] Pervo follows Rordorf and Cherix in leaving the blanks unfilled, translating the passage as the following: "Again, I tell you [. . .] I am the one who does [. . .] me [. . .] [. . .] because the person will be justified [. . .] but because he will be justified [. . . the] deeds of righteousness and he [. . .]" (ActPl 8.10).[36]

Hinrichs, 1904), 65: "Wiederum (πάλιν) sage ich euch (?) . . . ich, der ich tue die *Werke* . . . mich . . . daß der Mensch *nicht gerechtfertigt* werde *durch das Gesetz* (νόμος), sondern (ἀλλά) daß er gerechtfertigt werde *durch die* Werke der Gerechtigkeit (δικαιοσύνη) und er . . ." (italics original).

[31]Here "die paulinische Glaubensgerechtigkeit hatte . . . jede Bedeutung verloren" ("the Pauline righteousness of faith had . . . lost all meaning") Schmidt, *Acta Pauli*, 190.

[32]Cf. Dunn, "The Acts of Paul," 181; Snyder, *Acts of Paul*, 193.

[33]Cf. W. Schneemelcher, ed., *New Testament Apocrypha*, vol. 2., trans. R. McL. Wilson (Cambridge: James Clarke & Co, 1992), 224-25.

[34]"Again, I say to you . . . It's me who does . . . me . . . because the man will be justified . . . but because he will be justified . . . [the] works of justice and that he . . ." Willy Rordorf and Pierre Cherix, eds., *Actes de Paul*, in *Écrits apocryphes chrétiens*, vol. 1, 1117-88 (Paris: Gallimard, 1997), 1150.

[35]Richard I. Pervo, *Acts of Paul: A New Translation with Introduction and Commentary* (Cambridge: James Clarke & Co, 2014), 211. Both Rordorf and Pervo make use of Nicetas of Paphlagonia's ninth-century *Panegyric to Paul* for their reconstructions, which uses ActPl as a source.

[36]Pervo, *Acts of Paul*, 209.

If one regards Schmidt's ambitious reconstruction as accurate, this passage would represent a rejection of the law (which in context appears to be Israel's Torah) in favor of works of righteousness. Little could be said about the significance of practicing the law, which ostensibly would be rejected because, unlike works of righteousness, it does not justify. While easily derided,[37] such an interpretation could potentially be viewed as a reading of Paul that foregrounds passages like Romans 2 (particularly Rom 2:25-29), which are often relegated to the background of modern readings.[38] Nevertheless, Schmidt's study indeed goes beyond the evidence into conjecture, and little can be safely asserted from the less ambitious reconstructions of the Heidelberg fragment. From the editions of Rordorf and Pervo, the only secure observation is that, within a context that parallels Paul's conflicts with the Jews in Galatians 1–2 and Acts 15, the author appears to have Paul saying that one will be justified by works of righteousness.

CONCLUSION

Though fragmentary and of unknown proximity to Paul, the extant portions of these three writings can still serve as minor witnesses to the works and law in conflict between Jews and Christians in this period. Within such conflicts, the works that are rejected by Christians include the Sabbath and other Jewish calendar observances, which are replaced in the new covenant by practices such as observing the eighth day (the Lord's day). These works associate one with Jewish people and their manner of worship (which are closely linked), as well as the old covenant and the period prior to Christ's advent. According to the Preaching of Peter, such works are unnecessary for the Christian because they do not represent true worship of God, which is instead contained in the

---

[37]Cf. Rensberger, "As the Apostle Teaches," 304: "This suggests a reading, but not a very penetrating one, of Galatians and Romans"; Schneemelcher, *New Testament Apocrypha*, 236: "This shows clearly how far removed the author is from the historical Paul." For a positive evaluation of ActPl's Paulinism, see Dunn, "The Acts of Paul," 191-99.

[38]This extends to the new perspective as well as the old, with Sanders famously identifying Romans 2 as a synagogue sermon that does not cohere with the rest of the letter; see E. P. Sanders, *Paul, the Law, and the Jewish People* (Philadelphia: Fortress Press, 1983), 123, 129.

promised new covenant given by Christ. In *Jason and Papiscus*, Sabbath observance is unnecessary due to the witness of the prophets, and because God has now replaced this day with a new one, the eighth day, in accordance with Christ's work. The fragments of Acts of Paul unfortunately can add very little to this picture, besides an evident portrayal of Paul stating that one is justified by works of righteousness in an encounter with the Jews.

7

THE EPISTLE
TO DIOGNETUS (B)

◻

INTRODUCTION

Introduction and background. It is difficult to imagine how a previously unattested epistle, preserved in a fragmented manuscript and discovered by chance in the fifteenth century among wrapping papers in a fishmonger's shop, could come to be identified by no less an authority than J. B. Lightfoot as "the noblest of early Christian writings."[1] Such is the case of the Epistle to Diognetus, a remarkable and enigmatic work that is especially interesting for the "erstaunliche Intensität" of its usage of Pauline theology.[2] While the epistle is rightly identified as "full of the Pauline spirit"[3] and contains both material objecting to Jewish practices and a section that commentators commonly identify as a rearticulation of Pauline justification theology in Romans 3, the separation of these sections from one another in the epistle, along with an absence of references to "works of the law," makes a B rating for Diognetus most appropriate for this study.

---

[1]J. B. Lightfoot, *Saint Paul's Epistles to the Colossians and to Philemon* (London: Macmillan and Co., 1879), 156, cited in Henry G. Meecham, *The Epistle to Diognetus* (Manchester, UK: Manchester University Press, 1949), 3.

[2]Translated as "astonishing intensity," Ernst Dassmann, *Der Stachel im Fleisch: Paulus in der frühchristlichen Literatur bis Irenäus* (Münster: Aschendorff, 1979), 254.

[3]Alexander Roberts and James Donaldson, eds., *The Ante-Nicene Fathers: Translations of the Writings of the Fathers down to A.D. 325*, vol. 1, *The Apostolic Fathers with Justin Martyr and Irenaeus* (Peabody, MA: Hendrickson, 1994 [1885]), 23.

Among the early Christian writings, few are more challenging to identify with respect to dating and authorship than the Epistle to Diognetus, and while most contemporary commentators believe it to have originated in the second century, the fact that the document is unmentioned under the present title before the fifteenth century makes it difficult to place with any greater precision. This has not prevented commentators from attempting to do so, and Marrou and Lona's commentaries contain multipage lists of theories ranging from identifications with Apollos or Clement of Rome before AD 70 at one end, to an unknown sixteenth-century forger at the other.[4] While the observation that scholarly efforts have produced such a wide variety of suggestions must temper any hopes to resolve this question conclusively, in light of this epistle's importance for the current study, this introduction will present a number of contemporary views on Diognetus's origins and attempt to identify the most plausible among current proposals.

The one known manuscript of the Epistle to Diognetus was preserved with the heading πρὸς Διόγνητον at the end of a collection of five works attributed to Justin Martyr, and though an identification with Justin is almost universally rejected due to discrepancies in style and content, no consensus on its authorship has emerged over the centuries to take its place. Jefford's recent commentary groups positions on the question into three schools of thought: first, a broad group holding that the epistle emerges in the mid-second to early third centuries, most likely in Alexandria, with figures such as Pantaenus (the teacher of Clement of Alexandria) suggested as possible authors;[5] second, the theory suggested by Dorner and advanced most prominently by Andriessen that the epistle is actually the lost *Apology of Quadratus*, delivered to emperor

---

[4]See Henri-Irénée Marrou, *À Diognète*, Sources Chrétiennes 33 (Paris: Éditions du Cerf, 1951), 242-43; Horacio E. Lona, *An Diognet* (Freiburg: Herder, 2001), 64-66.

[5]For example, Marrou, *À Diognète*, 244-68; Rudolf Brändle, *Die Ethik der "Schrift an Diognet"* (Zürich: Theologischer Verlag, 1975), 230-35; Lona, *An Diognet*, 63-69; Marco Rizzi, *La questione dell'unità dell' "Ad Diognetum"* (Milan: Vita e pensiero, 1989), 170-73. Jefford also mentions as a subgrouping those who hold to a mid–second-century date without making specific identification as to the author, such as Markus N. A. Bockmuehl, *Jewish Law in Gentile Churches: Halakhah and the Beginning of Christian Public Ethics* (Edinburgh: T&T Clark, 2000), 216; L. W. Barnard, *Studies in the Apostolic Fathers and Their Background* (New York: Schocken Books, 1966), 172-73; and Meecham, *Epistle to Diognetus*, 19.

Hadrian in Athens in AD 125/126;[6] and third, the recent argument by Hill that the epistle represents a previously unknown work of Polycarp, the bishop of Smyrna, during the early to mid-second century.[7] While Jefford himself is agnostic on which of these schools is correct, further analysis may allow us to determine more and less probable ways that the puzzle of Diognetus's origins can fit together.[8]

One important study in this respect is that of Nielsen, which asks whether Diognetus appears to have been written before or after the church came under the threat of Marcionism in the middle of the second century.[9] Nielsen recalls by reference to Cross and Harnack that "the sect which [Marcion] called into being spread rapidly and was the greatest challenge that Catholic Christianity ever had to face," and that "in the last third of the second century every teacher in the church who could lift a pen seems to have written against Marcion and his church."[10] However, not only does Diognetus not give positive evidence of belonging to this

---

[6]See I. A. Dorner, *History of the Development of the Doctrine of the Person of Christ*, trans. W. L. Alexander, vol. 1 (Edinburgh: T&T Clark, 1889); Paul Andriessen, "L'Apologie de Quadratus conservée sous le titre d'Épître à Diognète," *Recherches de Théologie Ancienne et Médiévale* 13 (1946): 5-39, 125-49, 237-60; Andriessen, "The Authorship of the Epistula ad Diognetum," *Vigiliae Christianae* 1 (1947): 129-36. Dorner raises the point that in Diognetus, "the Jews are represented as still sacrificing and unswervingly adhering to the religion of their fathers," which would seem to be nonsensical in a post-135 apologetic context (*History of the Development*, 374). Though sacrifices are often thought to have ceased following the temple's destruction in AD 70, see Kenneth W. Clark, "Worship in the Jerusalem Temple After A.D. 70," *New Testament Studies* 6 (1960): 269-80, who presents evidence that worship in the temple precincts may have continued in some diminished form before the final prohibition and supplanting of the Jewish cult in 135.

[7]See Charles E. Hill, *From the Lost Teaching of Polycarp*, WUNT 186 (Tübingen: Mohr Siebeck, 2006); cf. P. F. Beatrice, "Der Presbyter des Irenäus, Polykarp von Smyrna und der Brief an Diognet," in *Pléroma: Salus carnis: homenaje a Antonio Orbe, S.J.*, ed. Eugenio Romero-Pose (Santiago de Compostella: Aldecoa, 1990), 179-202. For all the above, see Clayton N. Jefford, trans., *The Epistle to Diognetus (with the fragment of Quadratus)* (Oxford: Oxford University Press, 2013), 15-29.

[8]Jefford, *Epistle to Diognetus*, 28.

[9]Rejecting assumptions of a later dating based on linguistic quality, Lindemann similarly identifies the Marcion question as critical (which he implicitly answers by including Diognetus in his volume examining "der frühchristliche Literatur bis Marcion" ["the early Christian literature up to Marcion"]); cf. Andreas Lindemann, *Paulus im ältesten Christentum: das Bild des Apostels und die Rezeption der paulinischen Theologie in der frühchristlichen Literatur bis Marcion* (Tübingen: Mohr Siebeck, 1979), 343.

[10]Charles M. Nielsen, "The Epistle to Diognetus: Its Date and Relationship to Marcion," *Anglican Theological Review* 52 (1970): 78, 81, citing F. L. Cross, *The Early Christian Fathers* (London: G. Duckworth, 1960), 40; Adolf von Harnack, *Marcion: das Evangelium vom fremden Gott*, 2nd ed. (Leipzig: J. C. Hinrichs, 1924), 315.

apologetic context (in which the first school of thought on its authorship places it), but many have noted the "obvious and important areas of agreement between the first ten chapters of *Ad Diognetum* and the theology of Marcion"[11]—such as its near-complete lack of engagement with the Old Testament and its dismissive attitude toward the Jewish dispensation—that seem difficult to imagine for an orthodox apologist of the late second century.[12] Such qualities are sufficiently distinct that Marcion himself is occasionally suggested as the epistle's author, and while there are obvious flaws to this suggestion,[13] it is nevertheless the case that an address with significant areas of correspondence with Marcion seems difficult to place among the virulently anti-Marcionite apologists. As Nielsen writes,

> If *Ad Diognetum* 1–10 does come from the years 190–200, it is a strange document indeed. . . . Surely one might reasonably expect that a document supposedly written during a high point in the reaction against "the most vigorous heretical movement within the ancient church"[14] might reflect the controversy in some way. *Ad Diognetum* 1–10 does not. But even more important, the author writes in such a way that it is quite difficult to believe that he could ever have heard of Marcion.[15]

Instead of these later apologists, Nielsen identifies the closest analogues to Diognetus as Polycarp's *Epistle to the Philippians* and the *Apology of*

---

[11]Nielsen, "Epistle to Diognetus," 77; cf. Meecham, *Epistle to Diognetus*, 35, 37-38: "The condemnation of Judaism is downright but superficial and warped. . . . Our author's temper is Marcionite in its ignoring of the historical link between Judaism and Christianity." See also Dassmann, *Der Stachel im Fleisch*, 257.

[12]Cf. Nielsen, "The Epistle to Diognetus," 79: "The Greek Apologists after Marcion most certainly do not ignore the Old Testament. The first of these is Justin Martyr, and it would be difficult to over-estimate the place of Old Testament prophecy in his writings. . . . The argument from prophecy is maintained with varying degrees of emphasis in Tatian, Athenagoras, Theopilus of Antioch (who composed a work Against Marcion) and Melito of Sardis, but it is not to be found in Aristides or *Ad Diognetum* 1–10."

[13]Nielsen comments that this identification goes "much too far," as Marcion "could hardly speak about the supreme God as *pantoktistēs* as *Ad Diognetum* does (7:2)" (Nielsen, "The Epistle to Diognetus," 77). On this, see particularly Meecham, *Epistle to Diognetus*, 16-17; *pace* Jefford, *Epistle to Diognetus*, 17n14, 18n22, who attributes to Nielsen the view that Marcion authors Diognetus.

[14]John Knox, *Marcion and the New Testament* (Chicago: University of Chicago Press, 1942), 1.

[15]Nielsen, "The Epistle to Diognetus," 81; similarly Meecham, *Epistle to Diognetus*, 19. See also Bockmuehl, *Jewish Law*, 215-16, noting that *Diognetus* appears "without as yet any obvious awareness of the views of Marcion or indeed of Gnosticism more broadly."

Aristides, two pieces from earlier in the second century that precede the crisis with Marcion.[16] While similarly not Marcionite themselves, these writings nevertheless exhibit no anxiety in needing to closely correlate the Christian and Jewish dispensations, an anxiety that appears as widespread as Marcion's church by the time of Justin's *First Apology* in the 150s.[17]

Nielsen's argument is compelling and shows a provenance following the outset of the crisis with Marcion to be less probable,[18] leaving two schools of thought: Andriessen's thesis that the address is actually the lost *Apology of Quadratus*, and Hill's argument that Diognetus is an otherwise unattested address of Polycarp.[19] At first glance, Andriessen's thesis

---

[16]Cf. Meecham on the parallels between *Diognetus* and Aristides: "In both . . . no element of revelation is credited to the Jewish religion. Both ignore the Old Testament as far as actual citation is concerned, and neither uses the argument from prophecy," though "Aristides's almost friendly tone" towards the Jewish religion "is in sharp contrast to *Digonetus's* severity and contempt" (Meecham, *Epistle to Diognetus*, 59). See also Lindemann, who identifies Diognetus's closest analogues as Polycarp and the even-earlier Ignatius (Lindemann, *Paulus im ältesten Christentum*, 350).

[17]Nielsen, "The Epistle to Diognetus," 78, 81, 89-90; cf. Justin, *1 Apol.* 26. According to Nielsen, a date prior to Marcion also "helps to explain why a document as attractive as *Ad Diognetum* 1-10 survived in only one manuscript and why it is never mentioned in antiquity," as "these chapters had so many dangerous points of contact with Marcionism" that "the Catholics could not be expected to preserve them" (82). Nielsen also argues that chapters 11-12 are a later addition meant to protect the address from Marcionite interpretation, though these arguments are not as convincing as his argument for a general pre-Marcion provenance. On the compatibility of these sections with regard to the Jews, see Hill, *From the Lost Teaching*, 116-17.

[18]A strong objection to Nielsen's thesis comes from Rensberger, who counters that neither Theophilus or Athenagoras mention Marcion in their later second-century apologies. Two points are to be noted in response: (1) neither of these two apologies, which both make numerous explicit appeals to the Hebrew Scriptures, seem to leave themselves open to possible correspondence with Marcion's theology in the ways observed in Diognetus; (2) rather than introducing the Christian religion, these two apologies engage with rather more circumscribed questioning, with Theophilus responding to the specific objections raised by Autolycus, and Athenagoras to pagan accusations of atheism, cannibalism, and incest. By contrast, Diognetus's curiosity regarding the correspondence between the Christians and the Jews provides a natural opportunity for the speaker to provide clarification in distinguishing the true church from that of Marcion (one that is eagerly taken up by other second-century authors when the opportunity is present), and his failure to do so—instead offering a position that seems strangely close to Marcion's—is striking. See David Rensberger, "As the Apostle Teaches: The Development of the Use of Paul's Letters in Second-Century Christianity" (PhD diss., Yale University, 1981), 287; for a more appreciative engagement with Nielsen's argument, see Dassmann, *Der Stachel im Fleisch*, 257-59.

[19]A number of commentators similarly recognize these two possibilities as most noteworthy among contemporary theories, such as Michael F. Bird, "The Reception of Paul in the Epistle to Diognetus," in *Paul and the Second Century*, ed. Michael F. Bird and Joseph R. Dodson (London: T&T Clark 2011), 72; Michael W. Holmes, ed., *The Apostolic Fathers: Greek Texts and English*

appears the weaker of the two, as (1) Quadratus's apology is attested to have been given to the Emperor Hadrian, not "Diognetus," and (2) the extant fragment we do possess from Quadratus's *Apology* via Eusebius is not found in our current text of Diognetus. While these factors would seem to rule out Andriessen's identification, however, a close examination of his argument reveals a more complex picture. With respect to the recipient of the address, Andriessen notes that the title of Diognetus ("Son of Zeus") may be related to Hadrian's initiation into the Eleusinian mysteries at this time in Athens,[20] by which "one was raised to the race of the gods," and that the name appears so common among the archons of Athens (of which Hadrian was one) that "one is inclined to ask whether this name is not a title of honour especially for those magistrates."[21] Andriessen further notes that Marcus Aurelius appears to call Hadrian by this name in his *Meditations*, as "wherever we should expect the name of the emperor, we find the name of Diognetus, the one and only unknown in the series of persons mentioned."[22] Regarding the fragment of Quadratus's *Apology* that is not found in the extant text of Diognetus, Andriessen draws attention to the fact that the copyist of the original manuscript notes two places where sections of the text are missing (between 7.6-7 and 10.8–11.1). Within the first of these lacunae—which begins with discussing the benevolent arrival of the Son into the world, and ends in praise of works that are the power of God and signs of his presence—the extant fragment of Quadratus's *Apology*, which discusses

---

Translations (Grand Rapids, MI: Baker Academic, 2007), 688. The nature of Diognetus's inquiry similarly suggests an early dating among the apologists, as Andriessen notes, with the author answering the seemingly introductory question of "en quoi consiste précisément la religion des chrétiens (ch. I)" ("in what the religion of the Christians consists precisely") rather than responding to specific charges or objections (Andriessen, "L'Apologie de Quadratus," 8). Though seldom discussed, Dorner's observation regarding the Jewish sacrificial system still merits attention in considering Diognetus's authorship (see n6 above, cf. Heinrich Ewald, *The History of Israel*, trans. J. F. Smith, vol. 8 (London: Longmans, Green, and Co, 1869), 174; Dassmann, *Der Stachel im Fleisch*, 258).

[20] Cf. Eusebius, *Chron.* 199; Jerome, *Vir. ill.* 19.

[21] Andriessen, "Authorship of the Epistula," 133. Cf. Jefford, *Epistle to Diognetus*, 22: "The name Diognetus and the title 'most excellent' (κράτιστος) were widely employed in Athens, especially for persons of high honor." See also Andriessen, "L'Apologie de Quadratus," 238.

[22] Andriessen, "Authorship of the Epistula," 134; cf. Andriessen, "L'Apologie de Quadratus," 253-60 for the full argument.

the Savior's miraculous works in healing and raising from the dead, would appear to fit quite well.[23]

If these two significant difficulties can be explained, one finds a surprising number of pieces fitting together to correspond with Andriessen's thesis. Foremost among these is the mystery of how to account for the complete lack of reference in all of patristic and medieval history to a text that is later called "indisputably, after Scripture, the finest monument we know of sound Christian teaching, noble courage, and manly eloquence."[24] If Diognetus is identified as the *Apology of Quadratus*, early Christian history would render it similar acclaim: Eusebius writes that the address "is still in the hands of a great many of the brethren, as also in our own, from which it is possible to see radiant proofs of the man's intellect and of his apostolic orthodoxy."[25] Jerome extols the apology as "indispensable, full of sound argument and faith and worthy of the apostolic teaching,"[26] and writes that "so great was the admiration caused in everyone by [Quadratus's] eminent ability that it stilled a most severe persecution."[27]

---

[23]"But the works of our Savior were always present, for they were true; those who were healed and those who rose from the dead were seen not only when they were healed and when they were raised, but were constantly present, and not only while the Savior was living, but even after he had gone they were alive for a long time, so that some of them survived to our own time" (Holmes, *Apostolic Fathers*, cf. Eusebius, *Hist. Eccl.* 4.3.2). Andriessen draws attention to how Jesus similarly points to his healings as evidence of his advent in response to John the Baptist's inquiry (Mt 11:4): "Jésus lui-même n'avait pas énuméré d'autres signes de sa venue" ("Jesus himself did not list other signs of his arrival") (Andriessen, "L'Apologie de Quadratus," 19). The suggestion of placing Quadratus's fragment in this lacuna was first made by Kihn (Heinrich Kihn, *Der Ursprung des Briefes an Diognet* [Freiburg: Herder, 1882], 97), though he dropped it in favor of arguing for Aristides as author. Andriessen identifies Irenaeus's *Haer.* 2.31-32 as an analogy for the full argument of this reconstructed passage (Andriessen, "L'Apologie de Quadratus," 31).

[24]C. K. J. Bunsen, *Christianity and Mankind*, vol. 1 (London: Longman, Brown, Green, and Longmans, 1854), 170, cited in Meecham, *Epistle to Diognetus*, 3.

[25]*Hist. Eccl.* 4.3.1 (translation adjusted). As McGiffert observes, "the importance of Quadratus' Apology in the mind of Eusebius is shown by his beginning the events of Hadrian's reign with it, as well as by the fact that he gives it also in his Chronicle, year 2041 of Abraham (124 to 125 A.D.). . . . Eusebius gives few events in his Chronicle, and therefore the reference to this is all the more significant" (Arthur Cushman McGiffert, *Eusebius* [New York: The Christian Literature Co, 1890], 175n983).

[26]Jerome, *Vir. ill.* 19 (E. C. Richardson, ed., *Nicene and Post-Nicene Fathers: A Select Library of the Christian Church*, vol. 3, *Jerome* [Peabody, MA: Hendrickson, 1999 {1892}]).

[27]Jerome, *Ep.* 70.4, cited in Andriessen, "Authorship of the Epistula," 132. Jerome mentions Quadratus's *Apology* in discussing the use of classical sources and styles in Christian writings, and Andriessen notes that "no Christian work deserves such admiration for its classic form as Dg" (Andriessen, "Authorship of the Epistula," 132).

Andriessen details how Diognetus also corresponds well with the allusions to Quadratus's *Apology* elsewhere in Photius,[28] Bede,[29] and the apocryphal Letter of James to Quadratus,[30] and the author's identification as ἀποστόλων γενόμενος μαθητής (Diog. 11.1) would correspond with the description of Quadratus as ἀποστόλων μαθητής in Jerome.[31] While Andriessen's claim that "almost every word reminds us of Hadrian" is overstated, interesting links can nevertheless be proposed between the person of Hadrian and Diognetus.[32] In Diognetus 3–4, for example, commentators have noted that the criticisms of Jewish practices are "in a vein which suggests that the speaker knew he could play into Diognetus' own prejudices,"[33] an observation that would correspond strikingly with

---

[28]"Photius (PG 103, 456) tells us that a certain monk Andreas, who favoured a sort of aphthartodocetism and, among other things, regarded Christ's Body as immortal, impassible, and incorruptible by nature, had recourse, among others, to Quadratus." See Diog. 9.2: "God has given His only Son for us as ransom, the Saint for the sinners, the Innocent for the guilty, the Incorruptible for the corruptible, the Immortal for the mortals" (Andriessen, "Authorship of the Epistula," 132). Here and in the following two footnotes, I have preserved Andriessen's translations to make clear the connections drawn.

[29]As Bede writes in his *Martyrology*, "Apud Athenas beati Quadrati episcopi, discipuli apostolorum. Hic firmavit ut nulla esca a Christianis repudiaretur quae rationalis et humana est" ("In Athens, of blessed Quadratus the bishop, a disciple of the apostles. He confirmed that no food was rejected by the Christians which is reasonable and humane.") (for May 26th, PL 94, 927). See Diog. 4.1-2: "How can it be justified to make a distinction between the food which God has created for the use of men and to repudiate the other as useless and contemptible?" (Andriessen, "Authorship of the Epistula," 133).

[30]"James, bishop of Jerusalem, to Quadratus, faithful disciple of Christ, salvation.—I have heard with joy the zeal which you show for the preaching of the Gospel of Christ, with what enthusiasm you receive those who are devoted to justice and truth and how you combat Jews and pagans." See Diog. 1.1-2: "I see, mighty Diognetus, how zealous you are to know the faith of the Christians and how accurately you inquire after the God they worship, whilst they neither honour the gods worshipped by the pagans, nor observe the formal worship of the Jews. . . . I readily accede to your desire" (Andriessen, "Authorship of the Epistula," 133). Lieu similarly recognizes the thematic correspondence between the Letter of James to Quadratus and the content of Diognetus, commenting that the hypothesis of identifying Diognetus with Quadratus's apology is "highly attractive for our purposes because of the strong anti-Jewish tone of that *Epistle*," though she demurs that Diognetus "probably belongs to the end of the second century" (Judith Lieu, *Image and Reality: The Jews in the World of the Christians in the Second Century* [London: T&T Clark, 1996], 156). If Nielsen is correct that Diognetus does not fit within this period, however, then Lieu's intuition is indeed relevant.

[31]Jerome, *Vir. ill.* 19 (Jerome, *De viris inlustribus in griechischer Übersetzung [der sogenannte Sophronius]*, trans. Oscar von Gebhardt [Leipzig: J. C. Hinrichs, 1896]); cf. Quadratus as "*discipulus apostolorum*" in Eusebius, *Chron.* 199.

[32]Andriessen, "Authorship of the Epistula," 134.

[33]Hill, *From the Lost Teaching*, 116; cf. Diog. 4.1: "I doubt that you need to learn from me that [these practices] are ridiculous and not worth discussing."

Hadrian, the emperor who famously forbade Jewish circumcision.[34] Diognetus's acknowledged inquisitiveness (1.1) would correspond with Hadrian's well-known intellectual and religious curiosity,[35] and the description of Christians in Diognetus 5 could also be articulated in such a way as to appeal to Hadrian, who similarly "adopte les moeurs, les costumes, les dignités des peuples qu'il visite."[36] A number of allusions to the Eleusinian mysteries can be suggested under such a reading as well, such as the speaker's commencing with the directive in 2.1 to "cleanse yourself" (καθάρας σεαυτόν), paralleling the first act of the mysteries, ἡ κάθαρσις.[37] The speaker also makes repeated references to the Christian "mysteries" (4.6; 7.1, 2; 8.10; 10.7; 11.2, 5), which, in contrast to "merely human mysteries" (7.1), Diognetus should "not expect to be able to learn from a human being" (4.6).[38]

In turning to Hill's thesis for authorship by Polycarp, one similarly finds a number of cogent arguments set forth, including his analysis

---

[34]Cf. Spartianus, *Vita Hadriani* XIV: "Judaei . . . vetabantur mutilare genitalia"; cf. Andriessen, "Authorship of the Epistula," 134.

[35]Cf. Diog. 1.1: "Since I see, most excellent Diognetus, that you are extremely interested in learning about the religion of the Christians and are asking very clear and careful questions about them . . ." (Andriessen, "Authorship of the Epistula," 134). Barnard, *Studies in the Apostolic Fathers*, 137 identifies Hadrian as "an unparalleled example of a man of relentless energy, curiosity and intellectual enthusiasm," and Tertullian calls him "curiositatum omnium explorator" (*Apol.* 5). Cf. Andriessen, "L'Apologie de Quadratus," 244: "Est-il alors étonnant qu'un tel homme, qui selon S. Jérôme se faisait initier à presque tous les mystères, voulût aussi savoir exactement en quoi consistait le christianisme?" ("Is it therefore surprising that such a man, who according to St. Jerome initiated himself into nearly all mysteries, would also want to know in what exactly Christianity consists?")

[36]"Adopts the manners, the customs, the dignities of the peoples he visits." Paul Allard, *Histoire des persécutions*, vol. 1 (Paris: V. Lecoffre, 1885), 201, in Andriessen, "L'Apologie de Quadratus," 239. Cf. Diog. 5.4: "They [Christians] live in both Greek and barbarian cities, as each one's lot was cast, and follow the local customs in dress and food and other aspects of life."

[37]Andriessen, "L'Apologie de Quadratus," 242.

[38]Additional areas of correspondence posited by Andriessen include the similar style of Quadratus's fragment and Diognetus (such as the common usage of short phrases "de *façon antithétique*" ["in antithetic fashion"]) (Andriessen, "L'Apologie de Quadratus," 33-39, at 37, italics original). See also Andriessen's linking of the Eleusinian mysteries, the title "Diognetus," and the author's deification language in Diog. 10, whereby Quadratus employs Hadrian's Athenian title of "Diognetus," "fils de Zeus, descendant du Très-Haut, pour lui montrer à la fin de son Apologie que ce titre n'est pas nécessairement quelque chose de vide, mais qu'on peut être réellement de la race de Dieu" ("son of Zeus, descendant of the Most High, to show him at the end of his Apology that this title is not necessarily something empty, but that we can really be of the race of God") (cf. Diog. 10:4-6; Andriessen, "L'Apologie de Quadratus," 241).

favoring the unity of the document,[39] the fascinating identification of an
aristocratic Diognetus in Smyrna who could correspond with the epistle's addressee,[40] and his reminder that Polycarp would fit the description
of a "disciple of the apostles" (11.1) just as well as Quadratus.[41] Interestingly, however, a number of Hill's more compelling arguments appear to
substantiate the thesis of Andriessen just as well as his own. Hill persuasively argues that Diognetus represents an "oral address outside a judicial
context" that was "undertaken at the request of Diognetus, who was
probably a pagan of high social or political standing, as is indicated by
the address, κράτιστος."[42] Rather than an epistle, the text "gives every
indication of being the transcript of an oral address," seen by the author's
frequent references to his speaking and the audience's hearing,[43] with the
preserved copy being either a transcription or the speaker's own written
text. This scenario corresponds closely with Andriessen's argument for a
similarly nonjudicial address in response to Hadrian's inquiry at Athens,
as well as his observation that "le style est parfaitment celui d'un discours,
et non pas celui d'une lettre."[44] With respect to the breaks in the text of
Diognetus, Hill argues that the missing text is likely due to a leaf falling
out of the codex, and writes of having discovered after the fact that this
was the same thesis of Andriessen,[45] with his conclusion that at least two
pages are missing in each lacuna corresponding with Andriessen's contention that the break at 7.6-7 is large enough to fit the Eusebian fragment
and its surrounding context.[46] While persecution is certainly within the
lived memory of both the speaker and the audience, Hill notes that the
overall tone of the epistle points away from its being written in the

---

[39]Hill, *From the Lost Teaching*, 106-27; cf. also Rizzi, *La questione*. In my view the arguments in
favor of the authenticity of 11–12 are stronger than those against; as Hill and others note, a similarly marked break in the document is found at 7.6, but virtually no one argues that 7.7–10.8
represents a different work (as is often assumed for 11–12). See Hill, *From the Lost Teaching*, 108-9.

[40]Hill, *From the Lost Teaching*, 160-65.

[41]Hill, *From the Lost Teaching*, 133n15.

[42]Hill, *From the Lost Teaching*, 101.

[43]Cf. Diog. 1.1-2; 2.1; 3.1; 11.1, 8; 12.1; see Hill, *From the Lost Teaching*, 104-6.

[44]"The style is perfectly that of a speech, and not that of a letter." Andriessen, "L'Apologie de Quadratus," 237.

[45]See Andriessen, "L'Apologie de Quadratus," 22-24.

[46]Hill, *From the Lost Teaching*, 109-14.

context of immediate persecution, and the "very fact that the speaker is addressing 'the most excellent Diognetus,' who is evidently a man of some rank, implies that the author was in no immediate danger of penalty or execution for owning his Christianity."[47] However, while Hill appeals to Frend in arguing that this points to a dating between 135 and 150, Frend's own analysis is even more congenial to a slightly earlier dating under Hadrian, whose decree that Christians be given protection against "slanderous attacks" around 124–125 was significant enough to be appended by Justin to his own apology in the 150s.[48] As Frend describes, this period under Hadrian was "the nearest to toleration that the Christians were to attain before the end of Valerian's persecution in 260."[49]

Further, whereas Andriessen's thesis is able to explain a number of outstanding questions—the most significant of which being how "la plus belle apologie du christianisme" is completely unmentioned in Christian history[50]—Hill's thesis does not offer these benefits, with the apology still being curiously unnoticed before the fifteenth century under his proposal. Hill's proposed dating of the epistle also risks making him subject to Nielsen's critique: though Nielsen himself finds affinities between the author of Diognetus and Polycarp, a dating after the Marcionite crisis has begun in earnest would nullify any advantage gained by identifying the two figures. Hill indeed argues that "certainly by the late 140's and the

---

[47]Hill, *From the Lost Teaching*, 102; cf. similarly Meecham, *Epistle to Diognetus*, 43. The candor with which Diognetus is addressed also corresponds with what is known of Hadrian, cf. Andriessen, "L'Apologie de Quadratus," 256: "Hadrien avait la réputation . . . que tout le monde pouvait l'aborder facilement, même lui signaler ses défauts et qu'il aimait à entendre le jugement d'autrui" ("Hadrien had the reputation . . . that everyone could approach him easily, even to point out his faults to him and that he loved to hear the judgment of others").

[48]On Hadrian's rescript, cf. Dennis Minns, "The Rescript of Hadrian," in *Justin Martyr and His Worlds*, ed. Sara Parvis and Paul Foster (Minneapolis: Fortress Press, 2007), 38-49.

[49]W. H. C. Frend, *Martyrdom and Persecution in the Early Church* (Eugene, OR: Wipf and Stock, 2014 [1965]), 225, cf. Barnard, *Studies in the Apostolic Fathers*, 137-50. It is possible that Jerome's later identification of Quadratus as stopping a "persecutionem gravissimam" is associated with Hadrian's rescript, delivered in this same period. Note as well that just as no hatred is attributed to "Diognetus," but only to the audience more broadly (διὰ τοῦτο μισεῖτε Χριστιανούς, Diog. 2.6), Jerome similarly distances Hadrian from the hate of those opposing the Christians, writing that his arrival δέδωκεν ἀφορμὴν ἐπὶ τὸ τοὺς μισοῦντας τούς Χριστιανούς, καὶ δίχα βασιλικῆς κελεύσεως κολάσαι (*Vir. ill.* 19). See as well Eusebius, who attributes malice only to τινες πονηροὶ ἄνδρες (*Hist. Eccl.* 4.3.1).

[50]"The most beautiful apology for Christianity." Andriessen, "L'Apologie de Quadratus," 6.

early 150's Marcionism was well known in Asia Minor," and surprisingly places himself directly in Nielson's sights by suggesting that "some of the language of the speech *presupposes* the Marcionite controversy," so that "a date after about 145 would be necessary" for the address.[51] If Hill's dating is correct, one is left with a curious scenario in which Polycarp concurrently identifies Marcion as "the first-born of Satan,"[52] and presents a defense of the faith that some have suspected to be the work of Marcion himself!

To be sure, questions remain about Andriessen's thesis, particularly regarding the various options for identifying "Diognetus" with Hadrian, each of which remain a step away from being demonstrated conclusively.[53] But when Jefford writes on consecutive pages that "the benefits of this argument are truly appealing," and "the picture that Andriessen paints is truly seductive," his repetition is understandable: Andriessen's thesis is simply able to account for more data with greater explanatory force than the other current theories.[54] Therefore, while recognizing that such conclusions deal with relative probabilities and thus must remain provisional, this thesis identifies the strongest case for Diognetus's

---

[51]Hill, *From the Lost Teaching*, 74, 168, italics mine.

[52]Irenaeus, *Haer*. 3.3.4.

[53]For critique of Andriessen's argument, see e.g. Marrou, *À Diognète*, 256-59. Andriessen's full eighty-four-page thesis in French from 1946 is not translated into English, and many appraisals of his argument consult only his eight-page English summary article from 1947. In addition to the suggestions regarding Hadrian as the "Diognetus" of Marcus's *Meditations* and the name as an Athenian honorific title, evidence can be found of both the deities and participants taking on new names in Eleusinian mysteries: "In the Lesser Mysteries, Persephone was known as Pherrephatta, and in the Greater Mysteries she was given the name of Kore. Everything was, in fact, a mystery, and nothing was called by its right name" (Dudley Wright, *The Eleusinian Mysteries and Rites* [London: Theosophical Publishing House, 1919], 29). See also Wright's citation of Lucian: "Lucian refers to this in one passage in Lexiphanes: 'The first I met were a torch-bearer, a hierophant, and others of the initiated, hailing Deinias before the judge, and protesting that he had called them by their names, though he well knew that, from the time of their sanctification, they were nameless, and no more to be named but by hallowed names'" (40; *Lex.* 10). It would be surprising to find Hadrian exempt in this regard, as the former Athenian archon appears to have taken the mysteries quite seriously: "Hadrian is the only imperial initiate, so far as is known, who persevered and passed through all three degrees. Since he remained at Eleusis as long as it was possible for him to do so after the completion of his initiation, it is not rash to assume that he was inspired by something more than curiosity or even by a desire to show respect" (Wright, *Eleusinian Mysteries*, 68).

[54]Jefford, *Epistle to Diognetus*, 21-22.

provenance to be that which identifies it as the "lost" *Apology of Quadratus*, addressed to Emperor Hadrian in Athens in 125/126.[55]

Text and translation. The text of Diognetus is notoriously poor, being preserved in only one fragmented thirteenth- or fourteenth-century manuscript (Codex Argentoratensis Graecus ix), which was itself destroyed in the Franco-Prussian War in 1870. The text is now reconstructed from previously copied versions of this manuscript and suggested emendations from commentators. This study follows the reconstructed Greek text and English translation of Jefford,[56] supplemented with the Holmes translation where noted.[57]

THE EPISTLE TO DIOGNETUS AND PAUL

Knowledge and use of Paul. While the origins of Diognetus are much disputed, substantial consensus is found regarding the influence of Paul's theology in the document. Bird's recent study echoes the judgment of commentators over the centuries by concluding that "Paul is the chief source for the theological fabric of the letter,"[58] and Nielsen notes that "Pauline influence appears not only very often but also at crucial points where the actual definition of Christianity is at stake."[59] Examples of such assessments

---

[55]This general conclusion is similarly supported by Fairweather, E. R. "The So-Called Letter to Diognetus: Introduction and Books," in *Early Christian Fathers*, ed. Cyril Richardson (Philadelphia: Westminster Press, 1953), 209-10. Meecham also offers a favorable assessment of Andriessen's argument (Meecham, *Epistle to Diognetus*, 148-52). Barnard, while maintaining that Andriessen's theory "goes beyond the evidence," nevertheless holds it as the "most learned and exhaustive recent study of the problem," praising his "immense thoroughness" and dating the epistle (1–10) within the same period of "not later than c. A.D. 130" (Barnard, *Studies in the Apostolic Fathers*, 172-73). The editors of the *Ante-Nicene Fathers* reached similar conclusions prior to Andriessen: while not making a connection with Quadratus, they place the epistle ca. 130, identifying the recepient as Marcus's tutor and the author as "perhaps the first of the apologists" (Roberts and Donaldson, *Apostolic Fathers*, 23-24). Cf. also Bockmuehl, *Jewish Law*, 215-16 who, while tentatively placing the epistle mid-century, states that "there is nothing to rule out a date rather closer to Hadrian." For discussion on the precise dating of Quadratus's *Apology*, see Marco Galli, "Hadrian, Eleusis, and the Beginning of Christian Apologetics," in *Hadrian and the Christians*, ed. Marco Rizzi (New York: De Gruyter, 2010), 78-83.

[56]Jefford, *Epistle to Diognetus*.

[57]Holmes, *Apostolic Fathers*.

[58]Bird, "Reception of Paul," 73.

[59]Nielsen, "The Epistle to Diognetus," 88.

can be multiplied,[60] and Lindemann's conclusion summarizes the case well: "Richtig ist aber, daß sich seine Paulus-Rezeption auf einem Niveau bewegt, das vor ihm kein anderer uns bekannter christlicher Autor . . . erreicht hat und daß insofern Dg in der ältesten Theologiegeschichte ohne Vorbild ist."[61]

With respect to knowledge of specific Pauline epistles, Bird's analysis finds strongest influence coming from Romans, 1 Corinthians, and Titus.[62] While the text's only direct citation is of 1 Corinthians 8:1 at Diognetus 12.5, allusions to Pauline letters abound, and Meecham's analysis excludes only 1 and 2 Thessalonians and Philemon from representation in Diognetus.[63] With respect to Romans, an allusion to Romans 8:12 on not living according to the flesh is found at Diognetus 5.8,[64] and Diognetus 9.1 alludes to the present revelation of God's righteousness in Romans 3:26.[65] Possible references include those to Jewish boasting in Romans 2:17; 11:28 at Diognetus 4.4,[66] the mystery of God's plan in Romans 16:25 at Diognetus 8.10,[67] and the "collage of echoes of Pauline texts" in the section on justification at Diognetus 9.2-5.[68] For Galatians, Diognetus 4.5 alludes to

---

[60]"L'auteur, sans doute, utilise constamment l'Écriture (et avant tout les Épitres pauliniennes)" ("the author, without doubt, constantly utilizes Scripture (and above all the Pauline epistles)") (Marrou, *À Diognète*, 102n5); cf. similarly Meecham, *Epistle to Diognetus*, 57; Lona, *An Diognet*, 54; Jefford, *Epistle to Diognetus*, 86.

[61]"It is true, however, that his Pauline reception rose to a level that no other Christian author that is known to us before him . . . reached and that in this respect Dg is without precedent in the earliest theological history." Andreas Lindemann, "Paulinische Theologie im Diognetbrief," in *Kerygma und Logos: Beiträge zu den geistesgeschichtlichen Beziehungen zwischen Antike und Christentum*, ed. Carl Andresen and Adolf Martin Ritter (Göttingen: Vandenhoeck & Ruprecht [1979]), 350.

[62]Bird, "Reception of Paul," 77.

[63]Meecham, *Epistle to Diognetus*, 57.

[64]Diog. 5.8: ἐν σαρκὶ τυγχάνουσιν, ἀλλ' οὐ κατὰ σάρκα ζῶσιν; Rom 8:12: ὀφειλέται ἐσμὲν οὐ τῇ σαρκὶ τοῦ κατὰ σάρκα ζῆν.

[65]Diog. 9.1: τὸν νῦν τῆς δικαιοσύνης δημιουργῶν; Rom 3:26: πρὸς τὴν ἔνδειξιν τῆς δικαιοσύνης αὐτοῦ ἐν τῷ νῦν καιρῷ.

[66]Diog. 4.4: τὸ δὲ καὶ τὴν μείνωσιν τῆς σαρκὸς μαρτύριον ἐκλογῆς ἀλαζονεύεσθαι ὡς διὰ τοῦτο ἐξαιρέτως ἠγαπημένους ὑπὸ θεοῦ; Rom 2:17: Εἰ δὲ σὺ Ἰουδαῖος ἐπονομάζῃ καὶ ἐπαναπαύῃ νόμῳ καὶ καυχᾶσαι ἐν θεῷ; Rom 11:28: κατὰ δὲ τὴν ἐκλογὴν ἀγαπητοὶ διὰ τοὺς πατέρας.

[67]Diog. 8.10: ἐν ὅσῳ μὲν οὖν κατεῖχεν ἐν μυστηρίῳ καὶ διετήρει τὴν σοφὴν αὐτοῦ βουλήν; Rom 16:25: κατὰ ἀποκάλυψιν μυστηρίου χρόνοις αἰωνίοις σεσιγημένου.

[68]Here Bird identifies possible references to Rom 2:4; 6:23; 3:25-26; 5:6-8; and 8:3, 32 ("Reception of Paul," 85; cf. Jefford, *Epistle to Diognetus*, 85-86). While engaging with Bird's helpful study, I differ from his judgments in viewing the Romans allusions in Diog. 4.4 and 8.10 as weaker "possible references," and counting Diog. 9.1 as a full allusion. For Galatians, I regard the Gal 5:17

the rejection of days, months, seasons, and years in Galatians 4:10,[69] and Diognetus 6.5 represents an allusion to Paul's opposition of flesh and spirit in Galatians 5:17 (though with "soul" used in place of "spirit").[70] Further possible references to Galatians include the dramatic statement of God's justifying action at the fulfillment of time in Diognetus 9.2 (cf. Gal 4:4),[71] and taking up the neighbor's burden at Diognetus 10.6 (cf. Gal 6:2).[72] For the purpose of this study, Diognetus's usage of both Romans and Galatians is taken as secure. Further, Bird notes that the section in Diognetus that engages the Jews is particularly full of Pauline content, with 4:1-5 containing "by far the most abundant and densely packed allusions to Pauline phrases, expressions, and ideas" in the address, including allusions and echoes of Romans, 1 Thessalonians, Galatians, Philippians, Colossians, and 1 Corinthians.[73]

Diognetus as Pauline interpreter. One need not look far to find acclamations of the author of Diognetus as a Pauline interpreter, such as Ewald's assertion that "his mind lived wholly in the Christianity which Paul had first preached to the world; indeed, in him there seemed to be no other than Paul himself come back to life to speak to this age."[74] Such assessments, however, should not be affirmed without qualification. On the one hand, Dassmann notes that Diognetus's reception of Paul is remarkable not only in the abundance of Pauline expressions that are cited or paraphrased,

---

reference at Diog. 6.5 as a full allusion, and the echo at Diog. 1.1 (cf. Gal 6:15) as too minor to note. For Bird's full analysis, see "Reception of Paul," 75-87.

[69]Diog. 4.5: τὸ δὲ παρεδρεύοντας αὐτοὺς ἄστροις καὶ σελήνῃ τὴν παρατήρησιν τῶν μηνῶν καὶ τῶν ἡμερῶν ποιεῖσθαι, καὶ τὰς οἰκονομίας θεοῦ καὶ τὰς τῶν καιρῶν ἀλλαγὰς; Gal 4:10: ἡμέρας παρατηρεῖσθε καὶ μῆνας καὶ καιροὺς καὶ ἐνιαυτούς. Cf. Jefford, *Epistle to Diognetus*, 82.

[70]Diog. 6.4: μισεῖ τὴν ψυχὴν ἡ σὰρξ καὶ πολεμεῖ μηδὲν ἀδικουμένη, διότι ταῖς ἡδοναῖς κωλύεται χρῆσθαι; Gal 5:17: ἡ γὰρ σὰρξ ἐπιθυμεῖ κατὰ τοῦ πνεύματος, τὸ δὲ πνεῦμα κατὰ τῆς σαρκός, ταῦτα γὰρ ἀλλήλοις ἀντίκειται, ἵνα μὴ ἃ ἐὰν θέλητε ταῦτα ποιῆτε. Cf. Jefford, *Epistle to Diognetus*, 84: "An obvious dependence on Gal. 5.17 . . . the author of *Diognetus* makes no use of the term 'spirit' throughout the text and thus may consciously have chosen to alter that term here."

[71]Diog. 9.2: ἦλθε δὲ ὁ καιρὸς ὃν θεὸς προέθετο λοιπὸν φανερῶσαι τὴν ἑαυτοῦ χρηστότητα καὶ δύναμιν; Gal 4:4: ὅτε δὲ ἦλθεν τὸ πλήρωμα τοῦ χρόνου, ἐξαπέστειλεν ὁ θεὸς τὸν υἱὸν αὐτοῦ.

[72]Diog. 10.6: ὅστις τὸ τοῦ πλησίον ἀναδέχεται βάρος; Gal 6:2: Ἀλλήλων τὰ βάρη βαστάζετε; cf. Lona, *An Diognet*, 53.

[73]Bird, "Reception of Paul," 75. Bird identifies allusions to 1 Cor 8:4; Col 2:16; Phil 3:2, 4-5; Rom 2:17; 11:28; 1 Thess 1:4; and Gal 4:10 in this passage (though I regard the Romans texts as possible references).

[74]Ewald, *History of Israel*, 174.

but also the author's own responsiveness to central concerns of Pauline theology in the epistle.[75] It is important to recognize areas of distinction as well, however, such as in relation to the apologist's restatement of Pauline justification theology in Diognetus 9. Although Brändle is correct that "die Worte des unbekannten Theologen fast wie eine Paraphrase der zentralen Römerbriefstelle anmuten" in this passage,[76] Lindemann makes the following observations: "die Gesetzelehre klingt nur an; das Problem der Werke ist lediglich am Rande erwähnt; der Zusammenhang mit der πίστις ist kaum erkennbar."[77] While some of these elements appear to be present in the author's critique of the Jews in Diognetus 3–4, the Diognetus 9 passage clearly addresses a different context than Paul's in Romans; no mention of the law or Jews can be found, and instead one encounters what Lindemann identifies as "der Versuch des Vf, die Substanz der paulinischen Soteriologie in den Kategorien der hellenistichen Umwelt und Religiosität auszusagen, ohne dabei die paulinische Begrifflichkeit preiszugeben."[78] Though such clear category distinctions are overstated by Lindemann (and in any case he regards the author's transposition as successful), his observations show that the author of Diognetus is better regarded as both less and more than *Paulus redivivus.*

Other areas of distinction, if not necessarily contradiction, can be identified between Paul and the apologist, and these should qualify any simplistic notions of the author as a link to a pure and unprocessed sort of Paulinism.[79] With such qualifications stated, however, one can affirm with Bird that Paul is "clearly the most formative intellectual

---

[75]Dassmann, *Der Stachel im Fleisch*, 255.

[76]"The words of the unknown theologian seem almost like a paraphrase of the central passage of the epistle to the Romans."

[77]"The doctrine of the law is only touched upon; the problem of works is only mentioned in passing; the connection with faith is hardly recognizable." Lindemann, *Paulus im ältesten Christentum*, 348.

[78]"The author's attempt to state the substance of Pauline soteriology in the categories of the Hellenistic environment and religiosity, without thereby giving up the Pauline terminology." Lindemann, *Paulus im ältesten Christentum*, 348.

[79]Cf., for example, Dassmann, *Der Stachel im Fleisch*, 256-57 in discussion of the different overtones of Pauline terms such as σάρξ, σῶμα, and ψυχή in Diognetus, and Bird's assessment of the use of Paul against the Jews in Diog. 3–4, which "fails to affirm . . . the place of Israel in God's future plans" ("Reception of Paul," 88).

force in the theology of the apologist,"[80] and that engagement with Pauline theology, already substantial in earlier sources like Clement of Rome, Ignatius, and Polycarp, indeed reaches a previously unreached level in Diognetus.

THE LAW AND WORKS IN THE EPISTLE TO DIOGNETUS

Meaning: What works of what law? In Diognetus 3–4, the speaker follows a rejection of Greek worship by answering the question of why Christians "do not worship as do Jews" (κατὰ τὰ αὐτὰ Ἰουδαίοις θεοσεβεῖν, 3.1). Though not utilizing the phrase *works of the law*, a number of specific works of the Jewish law are mentioned and rejected in this context. These include animal sacrifices (θυσίας αὐτῷ δι᾽ αἵματος καὶ κνίσης καὶ ὁλοκαυτωμάτων, 3.2-5; cf. Is 1:12 LXX[81]), qualms regarding foods (περὶ τὰς βρώσεις αὐτῶν ψοφοδεές, 4.1-2), observance of Sabbaths (4.1, 3), and circumcision (4.1, 4). The speaker also rejects the observances of the Jewish calendar (τὴν παρατήρησιν τῶν μηνῶν καὶ τῶν ἡμερῶν, 4.5), such as its new moons and feasts and fasts, which are based on the stars and the moon (4.1, 5).[82]

Such works are contrasted in the following section with those of the Christians, who "are not distinguishable from other people either by country, language, or customs" (5.1). These works include not exposing their offspring (5.6), sharing food (5.7), obeying and transcending the established laws (5.10), loving all people (5.11), and blessing when they are cursed (5.15). For their rejection of the former works and the practice of the latter, Christians are "attacked as foreigners" by the Jews (ὑπὸ Ἰουδαίων ὡς ἀλλόφυλοι πολεμοῦνται, 5.17).

Significance: What does the practice of these works signify? At the outset of the address, the author of Diognetus distinguishes Christianity from "the superstition of the Jews" (τὴν Ἰουδαίων δεισιδαιμονίαν, 1.1), a fair generalization of what the author understands the observance of these

---

[80]Bird, "Reception of Paul," 77.

[81]This allusion at Diog. 3.4 is noted in the manuscript's marginalia; cf. Jefford, *Epistle to Diognetus*, 110. See also Barn. 2.5.

[82]On the parallels between Aristides and Diognetus in rejecting these Jewish practices, cf. Jefford, *Epistle to Diognetus*, 215.

works to signify.[83] In 3.3, the apologist identifies sacrifices as "folly" (μωρίαν) rather than worship (θεοσέβειαν, which is ostensibly what the Jews understand such works to represent). In chapter 4, Sabbath observance is associated with superstition, impiety and slander of God (4.1, 3), food laws with unlawfulness (4.2),[84] circumcision with pride (and not, as the Jews think, a sign of God's election and special love, 4.1, 4), and the Jewish calendar system with imprudence (4.5). The author concludes that Christians "do well to keep away from the general silliness and deceit, officiousness and arrogance of the Jews" (4.6). In sum, the apologist associates these practices with the Jewish people and their misguided system of worship (1.1; 3.3).

As Bockmuehl notes, it is "interesting that [the author's] criticism centres on the 'boundary markers' which Jews themselves not infrequently stressed as distinctive, and which had played a significant part in the 'Judaizing' disputes in the Pauline churches."[85] The role of these works as boundary markers for the Jews can be seen in the apologist's contrasting of Jewish piety with that of the Christians in chapter 5: unlike the Jews who adopt these peculiar markers, the speaker portrays Christians as not distinguished from others by customs or "an eccentric way of life" (βίον παράσημον, 5.2).[86] The Jewish critique of Christians in this regard at the end of chapter 5 is telling, with Christians "attacked as foreigners" by the Jews for their rejection of these identity markers (5.17). From the Jewish standpoint, the logic appears to run that by rejecting these works that signify identification with the Jewish nation—while simultaneously affirming the same God, who has established the nation and its boundaries—Christians commit treason, making themselves rightly subject to Jewish aggression.

Opposition: Why are these works not necessary for the Christian? Along with their negative associations with qualities like pride and foolishness, Diognetus presents short arguments for why each of these Jewish practices are not to be observed, which, as Bockmuehl notes, "remain

---

[83]Though echoing popular pagan critiques, the characterization of these Jewish practices as superstition is not foreign to Christian literature; see, for example, Origen's description of law-observant Peter prior to his vision in Acts 10:9-15 as ἔτι δεισιδαιμονοῦντα (Cels. 2.1-2).

[84]Following Jefford and Holmes' emendation of οὐκ ἀθέμιστον for ου θεμις εστι.

[85]Bockmuehl, Jewish Law, 217n134.

[86]Trans. Holmes, Apostolic Fathers.

well within the generalities of standard Graeco-Roman critiques of Judaism."[87] According to Diognetus, by their animal sacrifices, the Jews fail to recognize that "the one who made heaven and earth and all that is in them and provides us with all that we need cannot need anything that he himself provides" (3.4). The Jews indeed imitate the foolish idolatry of the Greeks by such sacrifices, for "the latter make offerings to things unable to receive the honor, while the former think they offer something to the one who is in need of nothing" (3.5).[88] Jewish food regulations wrongly "accept some things that God made for human use as created good," but "reject others as worthless and unnecessary," and Sabbath observance "malign[s] God by saying that he forbids that anything good be done on the sabbath" (4.2-3, cf. Col 2:16). Circumcision is rejected as a "mutilation of the flesh" (4.4, cf. Phil 3:2), and Jewish calendar observances are made "as they [the Jews] are inclined," offering proof of their imprudence rather than their reverence (4.5, cf. Gal 4:10-11). Perhaps most provocatively, the supernatural origins of these practices seem implicitly denied in the apologist's conclusion that "as for the mystery of the Christian's own religion, do not expect to be able to learn this from a human being" (4.6, cf. Gal 3:19-20).[89]

Beyond these brief statements, Diognetus has surprisingly little to say on why these Jewish works are to be rejected. As Foster notes, the epistle's next section portrays Christians as "good citizens in that they do not separate themselves from the rest of society (5.1-2), which is surely a thinly veiled criticism of Judaism."[90] This carries the evident implication that the universal and universally beneficent quality of Christianity renders the nationally limited Jewish practices superfluous,[91] though this

---

[87]Bockmuehl, *Jewish Law*, 217n134. On the curious brevity of these arguments, cf. Marrou, *À Diognète*, 117-18.

[88]Trans. Holmes, *Apostolic Fathers*.

[89]Trans. Holmes, *Apostolic Fathers*. Cf. Meecham, *Epistle to Diognetus*, 36-37. The force of Nielsen's thesis is felt at this point, as such a choice of words is difficult to imagine from the later anti-Marcionite apologists; cf. Nielsen, "The Epistle to Diognetus," 81.

[90]Paul Foster, "The Epistle to Diognetus," in *The Writings of the Apostolic Fathers*, ed. Paul Foster (London: T&T Clark, 2007), 152.

[91]Cf. Bockmuehl, *Jewish Law*, 217: "Christians, by contrast, offer their life, 'publicly' lived before the world, as their form of religion."

argument is not made explicit. As the apologist states in the introduction, the establishment of Christians as a "new race or way of life" (καινὸν τοῦτο γένος ἢ ἐπιτήδευμα, 1.1) may explain why the old race of the Jews and their way of life are now rejected, though this argument is not explicitly stated in the address either. Much more striking are the arguments that are absent: unlike other early sources like Barnabas and the Ignatian epistles, no arguments from prophecy or the Old Testament at all are adduced against these works, no mention is made of Christ as the new lawgiver, and no appeal is made to the sequence of salvation history.[92] While Paul is drawn on in the rejection of these works—as Bird notes, this section contains the greatest density of Pauline allusions in the address[93]—the broader theological reasoning offered by Paul for this rejection seems largely unstated in the treatise.

One possible explanation for this is the address's nature as what Meecham calls "to some extent an *argumentum ad hominem*."[94] If the identification between "Diognetus" and Hadrian is correct, the epistle's audience would be the emperor who, despite initial signs of favor, would turn out to be the Jews' great antagonist; under his provocations, "Jewish revolt broke out again . . . during the tour of the eastern provinces which Hadrian undertook from 128 onwards," ultimately culminating in the mass slaughter of Jews and the prohibition of Jewish religious practices.[95] Though the date of his prohibition of circumcision is unknown, it seems likely that Hadrian's low estimation of Jewish practices would have been evident by 125/126, which would give context for the apologist's introductory statement in chapter 3 that "I expect that you are particularly anxious to hear about why they [Christians] do not worship as do Jews" (3.1). Rather than presenting an outsider with detailed theological argumentation for why Christian practice differs from that of the Jews, it appears that the speaker simply makes clear the fact of Christian disassociation from these distinctive practices by employing reasoning that held correspondence with common

---

[92]Cf. Nielsen, "The Epistle to Diognetus," 83; Marrou, *À Diognète*, 112-13.

[93]Bird, "Reception of Paul," 75; cf. n73 above.

[94]Meecham, *Epistle to Diognetus*, 43.

[95]William Horbury, *Jewish War Under Trajan and Hadrian* (Cambridge: Cambridge University Press, 2014), 278. Cf. Spartianus, *Vita Hadriani* XIV; Cassius Dio, *Historia Romana* LXIX.12-13.

Greco-Roman critiques, which would have been comprehensible to (and likely resonated with) Hadrian himself. Indeed, such a conclusion is suggested by the speaker's acknowledgment that "Diognetus" is already of the opinion that these practices are "absurdities unworthy of discussion" (4.1). Such a scenario would explain Diognetus's one-sidedness in emphasizing the discontinuities between the two parties, and with the Christians successfully and dramatically distinguished from the Jews by the apologist—as Hill notes, using a "play into Diognetus' own prejudices"[96]—Hadrian's desire to know the differences between Jewish and Christian piety would be met (3.1). From a later standpoint, such dissociative tactics would indeed leave an open door for Marcion's advance; but if we have correctly identified the dating of the address, then the apologist would not have been in a position to foresee this development.

CONCLUSION

In Diognetus, the works objected to in the context of conflict with Jews are those of the Jewish law, including animal sacrifices, food regulations, Sabbath observance, circumcision, and the new moons and fasts of the Jewish calendar. The author dismisses these works as representing the superstition, pride, and ignorance of the Jews and their worship, while from the Jewish standpoint they constitute signs of God's favor and identification with the Jewish nation. Because Christians worship the same God without observing such practices, they are "attacked as foreigners" by the Jews. Beyond a handful of brief arguments that echo pagan critiques and possible implied arguments for the universality of Christianity and the establishment of Christians as a new race, Diognetus is rather slim on reasoning for rejecting these works, though this may have as much to do with the context and recipient of the address as the speaker's own views. While not directly referencing works of the law, the influence of Paul's epistles is remarkably strong in Diognetus, making this address a valuable supporting witness to the understanding of works of the law in this period.

---

[96]Hill, *From the Lost Teaching*, 116.

8

THE *APOLOGY OF ARISTIDES* (C)

◻

INTRODUCTION

Introduction and background. Remembered in the early church as a companion to the illustrious *Apology of Quadratus*,[1] the *Apology of Aristides* is a fascinating document in its own right, offering its readers a comparison of the beliefs and practices of second-century Christians with those of other peoples in the Greco-Roman world. While not showing clear usage of Paul's epistles, Aristides's *Apology* contains a section that contrasts erroneous Jewish practices with the true piety of Christians, which holds sufficient correspondence with Paul's "works of the law" debates to be analyzed as circumstantial evidence (C) for this study.

Aristides's *Apology*, recorded by Jerome as the work of an "Atheniensis philosophus eloquentissimus" who served as an example for Justin, was thought to be lost until the late nineteenth century.[2] The first two chapters were found in Armenia in 1878, followed by a full Syriac text being discovered at St. Catherine's on Mount Sinai in 1889, from which came the surprising recognition of the Greek text as already extant within *Barlaam and Josaphat,* the popular eighth-century Greek novel attributed to John of Damascus.[3] Like the *Apology of Quadratus*, Eusebius and Jerome

---

[1] Cf. Eusebius, *Hist. Eccl.* 4.3.3.

[2] Jerome, *Vir. ill.* 20; *Ep.* 70.4.

[3] *Barlaam* is a Christian retelling of the story of Buddha, with the climactic section coming when a rousing defense of Christianity—which is in fact Aristides's *Apology* in the mouth of another character—leads all parties to conversion.

identify Aristides's *Apology* as addressed to Hadrian in 125/126, which corresponds with the text's address in the Armenian tradition.[4] However, the Syriac text appears to address the apology to *both* Hadrian and Antoninus Pius, Hadrian's successor, which has led Grant to propose the theory of a double publication, with a first under Hadrian in 125/126 and a second (expanded) version under Antoninus (140–145).[5] Others, notably Harris, look past the Syriac's initial reference to Hadrian and identify the apology as written solely to Antoninus Pius soon after his ascension in 138.[6] This study follows Pouderon's judgment that the dating under Hadrian carries the strongest case, with the variation in the Syriac address explained as a confusion of titles by a later scribe; as Pouderon notes, "de pareilles erreurs étaient fréquentes, même chez les meilleurs auteurs; on confondait ainsi Antonin et Marc-Aurèle sous le nom d'*Antoninus*, Marc-Aurèle et Caracalla sous le nom de *Marcus Aurelius*, etc."[7] This Hadrianic dating is similarly preferred by Alpigiano's Italian edition, though she rightly maintains that the variations above mean any date between roughly 124 and 140 remains possible.[8]

There are significant divergences between the Syriac and Greek versions of the *Apology*, and though the Syriac is usually preferred, identifying the primitive text in any given passage is difficult.[9] Fortunately,

---

[4]Cf. Eusebius, *Hist. Eccl.* 4.3.3; *Chron.* 199; Jerome, *Vir. ill.* 20.

[5]Cf. Robert M. Grant, *Greek Apologists of the Second Century* (Philadelphia: Westminster Press, 1988), 38-39.

[6]J. Rendel Harris and J. Armitage Robinson, eds., *The Apology of Aristides on Behalf of the Christians: From a Syriac MS. Preserved on Mount Sinai*, vol. 1, 1st ed. (Cambridge: Cambridge University Press, 1891), 7-17. This was the original position of Grant, cf. "The Chronology of the Greek Apologists," *Vigiliae Christianae* 9 (1955): 25. See as well Robinson, who disagrees with Harris (in favor of the Eusebius/Armenian date) within the same volume at Harris and Robinson, *Apology of Aristides*, 75n2. O'Ceallaigh (following Geffcken) argues that the *Apology* is simply a Jewish document reappropriated for Christian use, though this has not won a wide following; cf. G. C. O'Ceallaigh, "'Marcianus' Aristides, on the Worship of God," *Harvard Theological Review* 51 (1958): 234-35.

[7]"Similar errors were frequent, even among the best authors; Antoninus and Marcus Aurelius were thus confused under the name of Antoninus, Marcus Aurelius and Carcalla under the name of Marcus Aurelius, etc." Bernard Pouderon, trans., *Aristide: Apologie*, Sources Chrétiennes 470 (Paris: Éditions du Cerf, 2003), 35n1. See also the arguments in Judith Lieu, *Image and Reality: The Jews in the World of the Christians in the Second Century* (London: T&T Clark, 1996), 165n47.

[8]Carlotte Alpigiano, *Aristide di Atene, Apologia* (Florence: Nardini, 1988), 10.

[9]Cf. Goodspeed's opinion (as the apology's editor) that the problem of the text is virtually insoluble, noted in Robert Lee Wolff, "The Apology of Aristides: A Re-examination," *Harvard Theological Review* 30 (1937): 241.

commentators are uniform in agreeing that the passage in question for this chapter (*Arist.* 14), which is found only in the Syriac version, belongs to the earliest form of the *Apology*.[10] This judgment is followed by this study, with further divergences in the Syriac and Greek texts discussed where relevant below.[11]

Text and translation. Aristides's *Apology* is reconstructed from five sources: the seventh-century Syriac manuscript (usually considered the strongest witness), the Greek extract from *Barlaam and Josaphat*, Georgian and Armenian fragments, and fragments from Greek papyri. This study follows the Sources Chrétiennes critical edition (which gives priority to the Syriac MS) for the text and chapter/verse divisions, and supplements this with the SC Greek text where relevant.[12]

THE *APOLOGY OF ARISTIDES* AND PAUL

Knowledge and use of Paul. While Aristides mentions the apostolic writings a number of times, and indeed refers the emperor to them on three occasions,[13] the *Apology* itself contains few clear references to Scripture, which Rensberger suggests may be due to its genre as apologetic literature.[14] Nevertheless, as Robertson observes, while *Aristides* contains no direct biblical citations, "the Apologist's diction is undoubtedly coloured at times by the language of the Apostolic

---

[10]Cf. Lieu, *Image and Reality*, 169; Markus N. A. Bockmuehl, *Jewish Law in Gentile Churches: Halakhah and the Beginning of Christian Public Ethics* (Edinburgh: T&T Clark, 2000), 203n78. Under Grant's theory, the relevant passage for this study (*Arist.* 14) containing "the relatively favorable picture of Judaism" would be dated "well before 132" (Grant, *Greek Apologists*, 39).

[11]In addition to these textual questions, Robinson posits that *Aristides* draws on the Didache and (with Diognetus) is based on the Preaching of Peter (Harris and Robinson, *Apology of Aristides*, 84-97). Pouderon's analysis nuances these assertions: it is possible that *Aristides* draws on either the Didache or Barnabas, though all three may be influenced by shared "Two Ways" traditions. Similarly, a literary relationship between *Aristides*, Diognetus, and Preaching of Peter is possible, though determining the direction(s) of possible influence is difficult, and shared traditional materials may also lie behind all three (Pouderon, *Aristide: Apologie*, 77-82). For more on the Preaching of Peter, see Excursus I above.

[12]Pouderon, *Aristide: Apologie*. The Sources Chrétiennes edition represents the best current witness to the text, and the French translation of this version is used in this section in lieu of the older English translations.

[13]Cf. *Arist.* 2.4; 16.3-4; as Bockmuehl notes, such comments represent "an intriguingly early defence of unrestricted public access to the Bible!" (Bockmuehl, *Jewish Law*, 213).

[14]David Rensberger, "As the Apostle Teaches: The Development of the Use of Paul's Letters in Second-Century Christianity" (PhD diss., Yale University, 1981), 106-7.

writers."[15] Among such instances, Robertson's analysis of the Greek text finds echoes of Pauline passages to be among the most common, including *Aristides* 1.2 with Colossians 1:17,[16] *Aristides* 3.1 with Romans 1:25,[17] and *Aristides* 8.1 [Gk] with Romans 1:22.[18] Pouderon similarly notes the resemblance between Romans 1:25 and *Aristides* 3.1 with respect to worshiping creation rather than the Creator,[19] and identifies Aristides's reference to God being "all in all" at *Aristides* 13.3 as a "formule sans doute inspirée de Paul,"[20] though both phrases could have become common expressions (and not necessarily drawn directly from Paul) at the apologist's time.[21] In addition, Pouderon notes the resemblances with Pauline language in Aristides's creedal offering at *Aristides* 15.3, though this too may be more easily attributed to shared traditional materials than direct Pauline influence.[22] Massaux notes the same passages and offers the strongest affirmation of Pauline influence, writing that in light of the correspondences with Romans 1, Paul is "the only author about whom it can be said with certainty that he has had a literary influence on some passages of the Apology of Aristides."[23] Kay, in contrast to these commentators, remarks that *Aristides* makes "no reference . . . to the distinctive ideas of the Apostle Paul," and registers the only Pauline parallel as *Aristides* 3.1 with Romans 1:25 and Colossians 2:8 (the latter due to *Aristides's* mention of τῶν στοιχείων).[24]

---

[15]Harris and Robinson, *Apology of Aristides*, 82.

[16]*Arist.* 1.2: δι᾽ αὐτοῦ δὲ τὰ πάντα συνέστηκεν; Col 1:17: καὶ τὰ πάντα ἐν αὐτῷ συνέστηκεν.

[17]*Arist.* 3.1: καὶ ἤρξαντο σέβεσθαι τὴν κτίσιν παρὰ τὸν κτίσαντα αὐτούς; Rom 1:25: καὶ ἐσεβάσθησαν καὶ ἐλάτρευσαν τῇ κτίσει παρὰ τὸν κτίσαντα.

[18]*Arist.* 8.1 [Gk only]: σοφοὶ λέγοντες εἶναι ἐμωράνθησαν; Rom 1:22: φάσκοντες εἶναι σοφοὶ ἐμωράνθησαν. Cf. Harris and Robinson, *Apology of Aristides*, 83.

[19]Pouderon, *Aristide: Apologie*, 193n2. Cf. Constantino Vona, *L'apologia di Aristide: Introduzione versione dal Siriaco e Commento* (Rome: Faculta Theologica Pontificii Athenaei Lateranensis, 1950), 79: "Aristide poggia la sua asserzione sul testo di S. Paolo, *Rom.* 1,25" ("Aristides bases his assertion on the text of St. Paul, Rom. 1:25").

[20]"Formula without doubt inspired from Paul."

[21]Cf. 1 Cor 12:6; 15:28; Col 3:11; Pouderon, *Aristide: Apologie*, 229n1. Cf. Rensberger, "As the Apostle Teaches," 106 on *Arist.* 3.1: "The resemblance to Rom 1:25 is remarkable; yet this idea scarcely began or ended with Paul among critics of pagan religion, and the formula could perhaps be traditional."

[22]Cf. Rom 11:36; 1 Cor 8:6; Col 1:16; see Pouderon, *Aristide: Apologie*, 236n1.

[23]Edouard Massaux, *The Influence of the Gospel of Saint Matthew on Christian Literature Before Saint Irenaeus*, ed. Arthur J. Bellinzoni, vol. 3 of 3 (Macon, GA: Mercer, 1993 [1950]), 7-8.

[24]D. M. Kay, *The Apology of Aristides the Philosopher*, ed. Allan Menzies and Philip Schaff (Edinburgh: T&T Clark, 1897), 261.

In light of the observations above, one might say that Kay has overstated his case that *Aristides* contains no reference to Paul's distinctive ideas. At the same time, Kay would be correct in noting that *clear* influence from Paul—or indeed, from any other Christian sources—is difficult to demonstrate from the text of the *Apology*. While an author need not be explicitly mentioned for strong influence to be deduced (see, for example, the case of Justin below), there are few areas where clear overlap with Pauline texts can be posited in *Aristides*, and none that are inexplicable apart from direct usage of Paul's writings.[25] Further, within the Greek text taken from *Barlaam and Josaphat* (which contains more possible Pauline references than the Syrian MS), it is difficult to identify which areas of correspondence are original to *Aristides*, and which are a product of the text's readaptation centuries later, making (in Lindemann's words) "eine genaue Bestimmung des paulinischen Einflusses auf Aristides . . . letzlich unmöglich."[26] Rather, *Aristides*'s case seems similar to that of Barnabas, another document in which Pauline influence (and indeed influence from Romans) seems a very possible conclusion, but in which such influence cannot be securely demonstrated to reach beyond a minimal level.

For these reasons, *Aristides* is best placed within category C as representing circumstantial evidence for this study. Nevertheless, if *Aristides* is relying on traditional materials that are shaped by (or shared with) Pauline theology—as may be the case with his references to the God through whom all things are held together (*Arist.* 1.2), those claiming to be wise who are made fools (8.1 [Gk]), and worshiping creation rather than the Creator (3.1)—then the *Apology*'s objections to Jewish praxis

---

[25]As similarly judged by Dassmann ("keinen eindeutigen Reflex der paulinischen Schriften" ["no clear reflection of the Pauline writings"], Ernst Dassmann, *Der Stachel im Fleisch: Paulus in der frühchristlichen Literatur bis Irenäus* [Münster: Aschendorff, 1979], 244); Andreas Lindemann, *Paulus im ältesten Christentum: das Bild des Apostels und die Rezeption der paulinischen Theologie in der frühchristlichen Literatur bis Marcion* (Tübingen: Mohr Siebeck, 1979), 351-52; Rensberger, "As the Apostle Teaches," 106. See also Albert Barnett, *Paul Becomes a Literary Influence* (Chicago: University of Chicago Press, 1941), 221, who identifies six possible allusions to Romans and three to Colossians, none of which are strong enough to be classed as "C" for "reasonably probable."

[26]"A precise determination of the Pauline influence on Aristides . . . ultimately impossible." Lindemann, *Paulus im ältesten Christentum*, 351.

may also be passing on Paul-inspired teaching that has now become assimilated as common Christian doctrine.

THE LAW AND WORKS IN THE *APOLOGY OF ARISTIDES*

Meaning: What works of what law? Aristides's *Apology* introduces itself as addressing the fear of God, and how God is worshiped by the "quatre races d'hommes en ce monde: les barbares et les Grecs, les juifs et les chrétiens" (*Arist.* 2.1).[27] After a lengthy exposition of the follies of Barbarian and Greek worship, Aristides briefly describes the worship of the Jews before comparing it with that of the Christians, and thanks to the brevity of this passage it may be reproduced in full here:

> 1. Venons-en donc aussi, ô roi, à la question des juifs, et voyons qu'elle est leur conception de Dieu.[28]

> 3. Donc les juifs disent qu'il n'y a qu'un seul Dieu créateur de tout et tout-puissant, et qu'il ne convient pas d'adorer quoi que ce soit d'autre que ce seul Dieu. Et l'on voit en cela qu'ils sont plus proches de la vérité que tous les peuples, puisqu'ils préfèrent adorer Dieu plutôt que ses œuvres. Et ils imitent Dieu, au moyen de cette philanthropie qui est la leur, pratiquant la miséricorde envers les pauvres, rachetant les captifs, ensevelissant les morts, et

---

[27]"Four races of men in the world: the barbarians and the Greeks, the Jews and the Christians." The Greek text from *Barlaam and Josaphat* differs here; as Robinson comments, "the fourfold division of mankind into Barbarians and Greeks, Jews and Christians, was out of place in an Indian court," and replaced with "a triple division—Worshippers of false gods, Jews and Christians." Within this revised division, the first category of idolaters comprises of "Chaldeans, Greeks and Egyptians" (Harris and Robinson, *Apology of Aristides*, 70). This study defaults to the Syrian MS as preserving the original division (for which see also William C. Rutherford, "Reinscribing the Jews: The Story of Aristides' Apology 2.2-4 and 14.1b–15.2," *Harvard Theological Review* 106 [2013]: 84-85), and while some adopt the Greek division (e.g. Denise Kimber Buell, *Why This New Race? Ethnic Reasoning in Early Christianity* [New York: Columbia University Press, 2005]), for the purposes of this study the division of Jews and Christians into competing γένη is the same.

[28]"Let us then come also, O king, to the question of the Jews, and let us see what is their conception of God." This introduction is followed in the Greek text by a passage, well described by Pouderon as "très sévère envers les juifs," which recounts the Jews' killing of the prophets and finally the Son. It is an open (and difficult) question whether this passage, which is missing from the Syriac, belongs to the original apology; Alpigiano regards it as a later interpolation and removes it, while Pouderon wishes to restore it to the primitive text. While the discordance in tone between this evaluation of the Jews and the relatively positive one offered in the Syriac text makes the interpolation theory attractive, neither judgment directly affects the interpretation of our main text in question, which commentators commonly agree to be a part of the original apology. See Alpigiano, *Aristide di Atene*, 112-13, 180; Pouderon, *Aristide: Apologie*, 285n2.

accomplissant d'autres (œuvres) du même genre, agréés de Dieu et belles aussi pour les hommes, qu'ils ont reçues de leurs pères d'autrefois.[29]

4. Or donc, ils se sont eux aussi écartés de la connaisance exacte, pensant en conscience rendre un culte à Dieu. Car dans leur genre de pratiques, c'est aux anges et non à Dieu qu'ils rendent culte, observant les sabbats et les néoménies, les azymes et le grand jeûne, le jeûne,[30] la circoncision et la pureté des aliments—toutes choses que d'ailleurs ils n'observent pas parfaitement. (14.1-4)[31]

Here it can be seen that the practices rejected by Aristides are those of the Torah, including Sabbaths and other Jewish calendar observances (new moons, Passover, feasts), circumcision, and regulations regarding food.[32] By such observances, the Jews think to "rendre un culte à Dieu,"[33] but instead "se sont . . . écartés de la connaissance exacte,"[34] directing their worship "aux anges et non à Dieu" (14.4).[35] Aristides distinguishes these works from other Jewish practices that are praised by him as right imitation of God (and are also prescribed by the Torah), such as having compassion on the poor, ransoming the captive, and burying the dead. These latter works are characterized as "agréés de Dieu et belles aussi

---

[29]"Thus the Jews say that there is only one God, creator of everything and all-powerful, and that it is not appropriate to love anything other than this one God. And we see in this that they are more near to the truth than all the peoples, since they prefer to love God rather than his works. And they imitate God, by means of this philanthropy which is theirs, practicing mercy towards the poor, redeeming captives, burying the dead, and accomplishing other (works) of the same kind, agreeable to God and beautiful as well for men, which they have received from their fathers of old."

[30]The meaning of this repetition is unclear: "Peut-être dittographie, ou oubli du signe du pluriel" ("Perhaps dittography, or oversight of the plural sign") (Pouderon, *Aristide: Apologie*, 235n5).

[31]"Now then, they too have departed from exact knowledge, thinking in their hearts to render worship to God. Since in their kind of practices, it is to angels and not to God that they render worship, observing the sabbaths and the new moons, the unleavened and the great fast, the fast, circumcision and the purity of foods—all things which, moreover, they do not observe perfectly."

[32]Though it lies outside the context of direct comparison with the Jews, cf. also *Arist.* 1.2, where the description of God as not needing sacrifices or libations echoes Is 1:11-12, an important passage in early Christian opposition to the Jewish law (cf. Barn. 2.5; Diog. 3.4).

[33]"Render worship to God."

[34]"Have departed from exact knowledge."

[35]"To angels and not to God." Lieu notes the proximity of this passage to Diognetus, which (while adopting a harsher tone) similarly "warns against 'worshipping according to the Jews' who, although they rightly take God to be one and lord of all, worship him wrongly" (Lieu, *Image and Reality*, 170). Cf. Lindemann, *Paulus im ältesten Christentum*, 352n62: "Die Kritik gilt wie in Dg 4 in erster Linie den jüdischen Zeremonien (14,4 S)" ("As in Dg 4, the critique primarily applies to Jewish ceremonies").

pour les hommes,"[36] and by such practices the Jews appear to be "plus proches de la vérité que tous les peuples" (14.3).[37]

A comparison can also be drawn between these Jewish practices and those mentioned in the following section that characterize the Christians (*Arist.* 15-16), who have received from God "les commandements qu'ils ont inscrits sur leur conscience[38] [τὰς ἐντολὰς αὐτοῦ . . . ἐν ταῖς καρδίαις κεχαραγμένας[39]] et qu'ils observent dans l'espérance et l'attente du monde à venir"[40] (15.3). These include practices such as avoiding adultery,[41] honoring one's parents,[42] rejecting idol worship,[43] doing good to one's enemies,[44] treating slaves as brothers,[45] and caring for the orphan (15.4-6).[46] Interestingly, most of the works mentioned in this section are also given in the Torah, though some are distinctly Christian (such as freeing those suffering on account of Christ's name, 15.7), and others reflect language of the New Testament writings (such as the reference to finding and concealing a treasure, 16.2, cf. Mt 13:44). Aristides identifies the works in this section as "les commandements de leur Christ" and "le commandement de la loi des chrétiens et leurs mœurs" (15.8-9).[47] Apart from the aforementioned works (such as circumcision) with which Jews mistakenly imagine to "rendre un culte à Dieu" (14.4),[48] there is widespread agreement between Jewish and Christian practices and laws;[49] as

---

[36]"Agreeable to God and beautiful as well for men."

[37]"More near to the truth than all the peoples." It is noteworthy that along with the more positive tone toward Judaism, Aristides carries none of the *argumentum ad hominem* elements of Diognetus (cf. Diog. 3.1, 4.1). If the thesis is correct that Diognetus and Aristides's *Apology* are both delivered to Hadrian, Aristides would be seen as adopting a different approach than the speaker in Diognetus (if not indeed holding to a more positive overall view of Judaism himself).

[38]"The commandments which they have had written on their hearts."

[39]Cf. Rom 2:15; Jer 31:31-34.

[40]"And which they observe in the hope and expectation of the world to come."

[41]Cf. Ex 20:14.

[42]Cf. Ex 20:12.

[43]Cf. Ex 20:4-5; Deut 5:8-9.

[44]Cf. Ex 23:4; Prov 25:21.

[45]Corresponding with Philem 16; cf. Bockmuehl, *Jewish Law*, 210.

[46]Cf. Ex 22:22; Deut 10:18; Is 1:17.

[47]"The commandments of their Christ" and "the commandment of the law of Christians and their customs."

[48]"Render worship to God."

[49]The cultic practices of Christians are not outlined in the apology, though Aristides remarks that the king can learn of "le prestige de leur culte" ("the prestige of their worship") in their writings (*Arist.* 16.3).

Grant comments, the apology's prior "vigorous attack on the gods of paganism" here gives way to what is essentially "an extended defense of Jewish and Christian morality."[50]

Significance: What does the practice of these works signify? Aristides says little in *Aristides* 14 regarding the significance of practicing the Jewish feasts, circumcision, and food regulations, though this can be inferred from statements elsewhere in the apology. In 2.1, the apologist outlines his project by inviting the king to examine "la race des hommes"[51] (γένος, used interchangeably with ἔθνος in *Arist.* 2) to see to what degree each race partakes in the truth. The people of the world are divided into four races (2.2, 4),[52] with the Jews attributing "l'origine de leur race à Abraham"[53] and Christians doing the same with Christ (2.3-4). After describing the practices that characterize the Barbarian and Greek races in 3–13, Aristides briefly treats the Jewish people in *Aristides* 14 before moving on to the Christian race in 15–16. While one should not assume univocal equation between ethnicity/race language in antiquity and contemporary usage,[54] it can be said that the practices outlined in *Aristides* 14 are those that characterize the Jewish race. For Aristides, then, to perform these practices represents identification with this γένος of the Jews, just as (from his perspective) worshiping the sun identifies one as a Barbarian (6.1).

Opposition: Why are these works not necessary for the Christian? Like Diognetus, Aristides is relatively terse on the reasons why these particular Jewish practices are not observed by Christians. While the Jews' other works in demonstrating love for their neighbors are praised as right imitation of the one benevolent God, their practices of calendar observances, circumcision, and food regulations are characterized as

---

[50]Grant, *Greek Apologists*, 38.

[51]"The race of men."

[52]On the divergence between the Syriac and Greek texts on the number of races, see n27 above.

[53]"The origin of their race to Abraham."

[54]While contemporary notions of ethnicity/race often revolve around skin color and geographical origin, Buell notes that religious practices could function as a similar defining characteristics in antiquity, and "for Aristides' Apology, religious practices are the primary means for differentiating *genē*." See Buell, *Why This New Race?*, 36-37; cf. also Marcel Simon, *Verus Israel: A Study of the Relations Between Christians and Jews in the Roman Empire (135–425)*, trans. H. McKeating (New York: Oxford University Press, 1986 [1948]), 108.

worship directed "aux anges et non à Dieu" (14.4).[55] Though charges
along these lines are not unheard of in this period,[56] and indeed have
some Pauline correspondence (Col 2:18; cf. Gal 3:19),[57] one is forced into
conjecture in determining the origins or underlying significance of this
charge. On top of the mistaken direction of this worship toward angels,
the Jews do not observe their aberrant practices perfectly (14.4), though
it does not appear that perfect observance would be of particular merit
in any case. From what is explicitly stated in this passage, perhaps the
best that can be inferred are the general conclusions that unlike the
works of mercy and compassion praised at the beginning of the passage,
these works do not reflect the character of the one God or represent what
he desires from humanity.

As with Diognetus, one can deduce additional reasoning for why these
particular Jewish practices are rejected by comparing this passage with
the next section that describes the works of Christians, though the substantial overlap between Jewish and Christian practices means that this
comparison affords less material than in Diognetus.[58] Perhaps the most
suggestive passage is *Aristides* 15.3, which describes the commandments
observed by Christians as being written on their hearts. This distinctive
feature of the Christian γένος evokes the new covenant language of
Jeremiah 31:31-34 (and its NT counterparts, cf. Rom 2:15, 29; 2 Cor 3:3),
a passage that describes God's renewing and reconstituting of Israel
("I will be their God and they will be my people").[59] This work of God in
fashioning a people with a new covenant may constitute reasoning—
though indeed only implicit—for why the works that are distinctive to
the old race are rejected. As Aristides writes, Christians are "vraiment un

---

[55]"To angels and not to God."

[56]See Celsus in *Cels.* 1.26; 5.6; *KP* Fr. 4a (in *Strom.* 6.5.4); cf. also Acts 7:42, 53. On angels at the law's delivery, see also Josephus *Ant.* 15.136, Liber Antiquitatum Biblicarum 11.5.

[57]Vona notes the proximity of this passage to Col 2:16-18, with its similar rejection of food regulations, Sabbaths and feasts, and the worship of angels (Vona, *L'apologia di Aristide*, 66); see as well
the rejection of fleshly circumcision in Col 2:11-13. Cf. Lieu, *Image and Reality*, 170-72.

[58]As Lieu observes, "There is in Aristides' predominantly ethical presentation of Christianity little
that would not be at home in a Jewish Apology" (Lieu, *Image and Reality*, 174).

[59]As Vona comments, this idea of Christians as a new γένος and ἔθνος has perhaps more correspondence with the writings of Peter (1 Pet 2:9-10) than Paul (Vona, *L'apologia di Aristide*, 74),
though influence from Rom 9:25-26 is possible as well.

nouveau peuple, dans lequel se mêle quelque chose de divin" (16.3),[60] while other peoples lacking this divine admixture remain in error (τὰ δὲ λοιπὰ ἔθνη πλανῶνται καὶ πλανῶσιν ἑαυτούς, 16.6).[61]

While the reasoning for rejecting these Jewish practices is limited in *Aristides*, the apology does make certain arguments against them appear less likely. These works are not rejected because of a Christian opposition to either law or works in general, as Christians are described as being under the commandment of the law of Christians (15.9), and *Aristides* 15–16 is filled with examples of works that Christians perform in the hope of the world to come, awaiting "du salaire dont ils seront rétribués, chacun selon son œuvre propre, dans l'autre monde" (16.3).[62] Nor does striving after righteousness appear to be problematized, as Aristides attests that Christians "s'efforcent de devenir justes" (16.2).[63] Indeed, apart from the practices of Sabbaths and feasts, circumcision and food laws that characterize the Jewish people, there is very little difference between the Jewish and Christian approaches to works or to law in general. As Grant observes, "Christianity, for [Aristides] as for the other apologists, is essentially a new law," and this "loi des chrétiens"[64] reaffirms much of the Jewish law (15.9).[65]

CONCLUSION

The works opposed by Aristides in the *Apology*'s section on the Jews are those of the Torah, including Jewish calendar observances (such as Sabbath, new moons, Passover, and feasts), circumcision, and food regulations. Aristides contrasts these practices with those by which the Jews imitate God (which the Torah also prescribes), such as showing mercy to the poor, freeing the captives, and burying the dead, as well as

---

[60]"Truly a new people, in which something divine is mixed."

[61]Cf. *Arist.* 17.2: "Vraiment, bienheureuse est la race des chrétiens, plus que tous les humains qui sont sur la face de la terre!" ("Truly, blessed is the race of Christians, more than all the humans who are on the face of the earth!")

[62]"The wages with which they will be remunerated, each according to his own work, in the other world." Cf. *Arist.* 15.3, 9; 16.2-3.

[63]"Strive to become righteous."

[64]"Law of Christians."

[65]Grant, *Greek Apologists*, 38.

the precepts of Christ and the law of Christians. While not made explicit in *Aristides* 14, it can be inferred from the apologist's project of describing different γένη that practicing these works signifies identification with the Jewish people. Aristides offers little reasoning for opposing these works, commenting that these works are directed to angels, and possibly suggesting that such markers are left behind because God's new covenant has created a new people with the law written on their hearts (15.3). While Aristides's uncertain usage of Paul means that his perspective represents only circumstantial evidence for the understanding of works of the law in this period, the presence of material in the *Apology* that is shared in common with Romans makes it possible that Aristides is similarly drawing on tradition influenced by this epistle, if not indeed Romans itself, in rejecting these Jewish practices.

EXCURSUS II

THE EBIONITES, MARCION, AND PTOLEMY

This excursus attempts to reconstruct the understanding of works of the law in three nonmainstream or "heretical" parties in this period—the Ebionites, Marcion, and the Gnostic Ptolemy—which appear to hold the closest parallels with Paul's debates in Romans and Galatians.[1]

---

[1]Concepts of heresy and orthodoxy have been problematized in the twentieth century, most famously with Bauer's thesis that in many locations heresy preceded orthodoxy (Walter Bauer, *Orthodoxy and Heresy in Earliest Christianity*, ed. Robert A. Kraft and Gerhard Krodel [Philadelphia: Fortress Press, 1971 {1934}]). While the details of Bauer's argument have been subjected to substantial critique, it is noteworthy that his account bears at least some resemblance to Origen's; while Celsus assumes a "traditional" view of a unified early orthodoxy that only later fell into factionalism, Origen subverts this simple narrative, countering with examples of disagreements and varieties of interpretation that existed "from the outset" (*Cels.* 3.10-11). The complexities related to early "orthodoxy" are indeed explored a century before Bauer in John Henry Newman, *An Essay on the Development of Christian Doctrine* (New York: Longmans, Green, 1949 [1845]), particularly 1.Intro.10-20. At the same time, these complexities do not discount the existence of a recognizable "mainstream" Christianity in this period. As Wilken notes, while Celsus's attack on Christianity (ca. 178) includes a critique of Christian factionalism, what is noteworthy is how none of these factions are made subject of Celsus's attack on the faith. "When he wishes to offer substantive criticism of Christianity, he does not discuss the Gnostics or the Marcionites; Celsus assumes he knows what Christianity is, and he does not identify it with one of these parties. Instead he aims his attack at the 'great church' [Celsus's terminology in *Cels.* 5.59], the centrist party if you will" (Robert Louis Wilken, "Diversity and Unity in Early Christianity," *Second Century* 1 [1981]: 107; cf. also Rowan Williams, "Does It Make Sense to Speak of Pre-Nicene Orthodoxy?," in *The Making of Orthodoxy: Essays in Honour of Henry Chadwick* [New York: Cambridge University Press, 1989], 1-23). Further challenges to the concept of heresy have been inspired by the work of Michel Foucault, who occupies a position similar to that previously held by Marx in many circles of early Christian studies. While not discounting the insights of Foucauldian analysis, applications of his schema can carry many of the same risks as earlier Marxist criticism, in that the concerns of sources can be artificially homogenized by relating them to totalizing narratives of power, foregrounding the social dynamics between different parties while leaving the ideas they fought over in the background. Among applications of Foucault, the account of Royalty is to be preferred over that of Le Boulluec, with the latter arguing that the idea of heresy is an invention of Justin Martyr, and the former countering that Justin only gives completion to a "process of discursive formation of orthodox heresiology" that is tracable back to the Gospels and post-Pauline literature (Alain Le Boulluec, *La notion d'hérésie dans la littérature*

Reconstructing the views of these parties is a difficult undertaking, as we are reliant for information on the accounts of early heresiologists, who write within polemical contexts that guarantee neither the fullest nor the most charitable representations of their adversaries' views.[2] Further, while some of this information comes from opponents who followed within a century of the parties in question (such as Justin, Irenaeus, and Tertullian), much of the more expansive reporting comes from later writers like the fourth-century Epiphanius, whose accounts are acknowledged to be partially based on hearsay and are of limited historical value.[3] While the combined witness of such accounts allows only tentative sketches of these sources' views on works of the law to be formed, these sketches merit examination as possible witnesses to early interpretation on this subject.

THE EBIONITES

An early Jewish-Christian group, the Ebionites take their name either from a founder named Ebion, or (more likely) a derivation from the Hebrew word for "poor."[4] Though first noted by Irenaeus around 180, patristic sources tend to place their origins in the first century (often following Cerinthus), and Origen's testimony from the third century appears to reflect personal contact with them.[5] The Ebionites are of

---

grecque, IIe–IIIe siècles [Paris: Études Augustiniennes, 1985], 110; Robert M. Royalty, *The Origin of Heresy* [New York: Routledge, 2015], 172).

[2]On the difficulties of this task, see John M. G. Barclay, "Mirror-Reading a Polemical Letter: Galatians as a Test Case," *Journal for the Study of the New Testament* 10 (1987): 73-93.

[3]Cf. Epiphanius, *Pan.* Proem. II.2.4. This section prioritizes earlier witnesses in its reconstructions, only supplementing with Epiphanius where his testimony is widely taken as credible.

[4]Cf. Tertullian, *Praescr.* 33.5; Origen, *Cels.* 2.1; *Comm. Matt.* 16.12; *Princ.* 4.3.8. While Epiphanius identifies Cerinthus as their forefather, Hill demonstrates that the attribution of Ebionite characteristics to Cerinthus comes from misinterpreting Irenaeus's statement regarding their similar Christology as a wholesale equation of their views (Charles E. Hill, "Cerinthus, Gnostic or Chiliast? A New Solution to an Old Problem," *Journal of Early Christian Studies* 8 [2000]: 143-47). The Nazoreans, first noted in Epiphanius, also practice the law without a similar repudiation of Paul mentioned (*Pan.* 29.7-9), though their late attestation prevents them from being analyzed here. For an overview of scholarship on the Ebionites, see Gregory C. Finley, "The Ebionites and 'Jewish Christianity': Examining Heresy and the Attitudes of Church Fathers" (PhD diss., Catholic University of America, 2009).

[5]Though not mentioned by name, many identify correspondence with Ebionite positions in Trypho's statements in Justin, *Dial.* 49.1; 67.2-5.

particular interest for this study for their widely attested opposition to Paul and their continued practice of the law, with Tertullian identifying Paul's opponents in Galatians who "observe and defend circumcision and the law" as holding to "the heresy of Ebion" (*Praescr.* 33.5).[6] Such an identification, attested relatively early among these sources at the beginning of the third century, illustrates the significance of the Ebionites as possible witnesses to the points in conflict between Paul and his Jewish interlocutors.

The securest sources for Ebionite thought are their early patristic opponents, as no certain writings of the Ebionities are extant.[7] Irenaeus offers the earliest testimony regarding the Ebionites, writing that they reject Paul as an apostate from the law, and continue to follow the law's customs (such as circumcision) and the Jewish way of life, "even adoring Jerusalem as if it were the house of God" (*Haer.* 1.26.2). Tertullian, as noted above, identifies the Ebionites with Paul's opponents in Galatians based on their practice of circumcision and the law (*Praescr.* 33.5). Hippolytus, who is suspected to be dependent on Irenaeus's testimony,[8] writes that the Ebionites "live conformably to Jewish customs" (ἤθεσιν Ἰουδαϊκοῖς ζῶσι) and claim to be justified according to the law of Moses (κατὰ νόμον φάσκοντες δικαιοῦσθαι, *Ref.* 7.34.2; identified as νόμον Μωϋσοῦ in 10.22.1). This is related to their Christology, as they believe Jesus himself to

---

[6]Texts and translations in this section (Tertullian, Hippolytus, Pseudo-Tertullian, Origen) are taken from A. F. J. Klijn and G. J. Reinink, eds., *Patristic Evidence for Jewish-Christian Sects* (Leiden: Brill, 1973). As Finley notes, this identification does not mean Tertullian thought "Ebion" to be practicing this heresy in Paul's time (any more than he thought Marcion, whose heresy he identifies John as countering, was present in the first century), but rather refers to the early existence of the teachings themselves (Finley, "Ebionites and 'Jewish Christianity,'" 124); similarly Klijn and Reinink, *Patristic Evidence*, 21.

[7]Although the Pseudo-Clementines (particularly the *Anabathmoi Iakobou* in *Rec.* 1.27-71) and an "Ebionite gospel" mentioned by Epiphanius are sometimes associated the Ebionites, these attributions originate in the late fourth century and cannot be held with confidence; cf. James Carleton Paget, "The Ebionites in Recent Research," in *Jews, Christians and Jewish Christians in Antiquity*, WUNT 251 (Tübingen: Mohr Siebeck, 2010 [1991]) 327-43; Oskar Skarsaune, "The Ebionites," in *Jewish Believers in Jesus: The Early Centuries*, ed. Reidar Hvalvik and Oskar Skarsaune (Peabody, MA: Hendrickson Publishers, 2007), 457-61. The most substantial treatment of the Ebionites is found in Epiphanius, *Pan.* 30, though it has "all the trappings of a literary construction" rather than reflecting personal acquaintance (Carleton Paget, "The Ebionites in Recent Research," 332; cf. Skarsaune, "Ebionites," 461).

[8]Cf. Klijn and Reinink, *Patristic Evidence*, 22.

have been justified by performing the law (τὸν Ἰησοῦν λέγοντες δεδικαιῶσθαι ποιήσαντα τὸν νόμον); he is only named as Christ because he fulfilled the law (ἐτέλεσε τὸν νόμον), which indeed anyone else could have done, and the Ebionites hope to be made Christs in the same way (7.34.2). Pseudo-Tertullian's testimony adds little new information: Ebion puts forward the law as binding on the grounds that Christ observed it and "no servant is above [his] master" (cf. Mt 10:24), which Ebion argues "for the purpose of excluding the gospel and vindicating Judaism" (*Adv. Omn. Haer.* 3.3). Origen appears to have had firsthand contact with the group,[9] and attests to there being two kinds of Ebionites that are distinguished by Christology, with both living according to the Jewish law and refusing to admit Paul's epistles (*Cels.* 5.61, 65; cf. *Hom. Jer.* 19.12).[10] Origen also writes that the Ebionites understand Christ's statement about being sent "only to the lost sheep of the house of Israel" (Mt 10:6) to mean that Christ dwells especially "among the carnal Israelites" (τοὺς σαρκίνους Ἰσραηλίτας), which he counters with Paul's assertion that it is not the children of the flesh who are the children of God (cf. Rom 9:8; *Princ.* 4.3.8). Finally, Eusebius (who may also have known the Ebionites firsthand[11]) repeats much of the same material, adding that the Ebionites celebrate both Sunday and the Sabbath (*Hist. Eccl.* 3.27.5), and writing in summary of their views that they "strongly maintain that the law ought to be kept in a more strictly Jewish fashion" (τὸν νόμον χρῆναι Ἰουδαϊκώτερον φυλάττειν ἀπισχυριζομένων; *Hist. Eccl.* 6.17.1).

Based on Tertullian's testimony and the Ebionites' twofold description as upholding the law and rejecting Paul as an apostate, it appears that the Ebionites were engaging with Paul's discussions on works of the law, but finding themselves on the opposing side of the argument. By the testimony

---

[9]Cf. Skarsaune, "Ebionites," 440-45. The fact that Origen's personal testimony largely corresponds with Irenaeus's picture of the Ebionities makes it less likely that Irenaeus has essentially created them as a sect, *pace* Skarsaune, "Ebionites," 422.

[10]Elsewhere in *Contra Celsum* Origen uses "Ebionite" in a more general way as describing Jewish Christians who continue to obey the law, which included Peter prior to the Cornelius encounter, and perhaps even Paul himself (!) with his offering in Acts 21:26 (*Cels.* 2.1). This general usage is to be distinguished from the parties described by Origen in *Cels.* 5.61, 65 (which, in rejecting Paul's epistles, ostensibly did not count him among their membership!).

[11]Cf. Skarsaune, "Ebionites," 445-50; this is denied by Klijn and Reinink, *Patristic Evidence*, 28.

preserved in the early patristic heresiologists, the works of the law in dispute are those of the Mosaic law, including specific practices of circumcision,[12] Sabbath observance,[13] a focus on Jerusalem,[14] the regulations regarding pure and impure foods attested in Leviticus and Deuteronomy,[15] and celebrating the Passover and the feast of unleavened bread in accordance with Jewish custom.[16] Hippolytus identifies these practices of the law as "Jewish customs" (ἤθεσιν Ἰουδαϊκοῖς ζῶσι, κατὰ νόμον φάσκοντες δικαιοῦσθαι, *Ref.* 7.34.2), and Eusebius summarizes the Ebionites' view as an insistence on the necessity of observing the law's worship (τῆς νομικῆς θρησκείας) and the "Jewish ceremonial" (Ἰουδαϊκὴν ἀγωγὴν; *Hist. Eccl.* 3.27.2, 5).

For the Ebionites, it appears that the observance of the Mosaic law signifies both identification with Jewish people and the path to righteousness: as Hippolytus writes, the Ebionites understand Jesus to have been justified by fulfilling the Mosaic law, so that they too must fulfill this law in the same way. In this respect there is minor correspondence between the Ebionites and Calvin, who similarly regards Jesus as being justified by his perfect obedience of the law, though the Ebionites regard their sharing in this righteousness as coming by way of *imitatio* rather than imputation, and the works they insist on all appear to be cultic or related to Jewish identity rather than ethical or general good works.[17] The practice of these works also signifies association with the Jews: Irenaeus characterizes their practices as being "Judaic in their style of life" (*Haer.* 1.26.2), and Origen describes them as desiring to live "according to the law of the Jews like the multitude of the Jews" (κατὰ τὸν Ἰουδαίων νόμον ὡς τὰ Ἰουδαίων πλήθη; *Cels.* 5.61).

From the Ebionites' perspective, the works of the law are *not* to be rejected, with such treatment reserved instead for the apostle to the Gentiles. As Irenaeus writes, the Ebionites "repudiate the Apostle Paul,

---

[12]Irenaeus, *Haer.* 1.26.2; Origen, *Hom. Gen.* 3.5.
[13]Eusebius, *Hist. Eccl.* 3.27.5.
[14]Irenaeus, *Haer.* 1.26.2.
[15]Origen, *Comm. Matt.* 11.12.
[16]Origen, *Comm. ser. Matt.* 79.
[17]Hippolytus, *Ref.* 7.34.2; Origen, *Comm. ser. Matt.* 79; cf. Skarsaune, "Ebionites," 439.

maintaining that he was an apostate from the law" (*Haer.* 1.26.2), as
Origen and Eusebius similarly testify.[18] According to Eusebius, the reason
Ebionites insist on complete observance of the law's worship and "the
sabbath and the rest of the Jewish ceremonial" is that they think it impossible to be "saved by faith in Christ alone and by a life in accordance with
it" (διὰ μόνης τῆς εἰς τὸν Χριστὸν πίστεως καὶ τοῦ κατ᾽ αὐτὴν βίου
σωθησομένοις), since Christ's justification came through the Mosaic law
(*Hist. Eccl.* 3.27.2, 5). Further, if Jesus dwells especially with people of
Israel according to the flesh (τοὺς σαρκίνους Ἰσραηλίτας), it follows that
observing the practices that denote one's inclusion in this people is altogether necessary (*Princ.* 4.3.8).

In summary, the works in dispute for the Ebionites are those of the
Mosaic law, including circumcision, Sabbath observance, a focus on Jerusalem, food regulations, and the observance of Jewish feasts. The
practice of these works signifies both the path to righteousness (by which
Jesus himself was justified), and identification with the people of Israel.
Pace the apostle Paul, these works *are* necessary for the Christian; faith
in Christ and a corresponding life are not sufficient for salvation, and
since Christ was sent only to the lost sheep of Israel, Christians must be
members of this people by observing the Mosaic law. Though composite
from the fragments of the later patristic testimony, the Ebionites' perspective represents a fascinating possible witness—if Tertullian's identification is correct—to the arguments of Paul's Galatian opponents.

MARCION

The son of a bishop in Pontus, Marcion is attested to have travelled to Rome
around AD 140 bearing a substantial financial gift for the church in the
city.[19] Having come under the influence of the Gnostic Cerdo, according to
Irenaeus and the succeeding heresiologists,[20] Marcion began teaching a du-

---

[18]*Cels.* 5.65; *Hom. Jer.* 19.12; *Hist. Eccl.* 3.27.4.

[19]Tertullian, *Marc.* 4.4.3 (Tertullian, *Adversus Marcionem*, ed. Ernest Evans, 2 vols. [Oxford: Clarendon Press, 1972]); *Praescr.* 30.2; Epiphanius, *Pan.* 42.1.4.

[20]*Haer.* 1.27.1; 3.4.3; cf. Tertullian, *Marc.* 1.2, 1.22.10, 3.21.1; Hippolytus, *Ref.* 10.15; Eusebius, *Hist. Eccl.* 4.10.1. On Cerdo and Marcion, cf. Sebastian Moll, *The Arch-Heretic Marcion*, WUNT 250 (Tübingen: Mohr Siebeck, 2010), 41-43.

alistic doctrine whereby Jesus was not the Messiah of the Jews' creator god (who was yet to come), but rather was sent for the salvation of all nations by a good and previously unknown god.[21] Marcion claimed his teaching to be a restoration of true Christian doctrine that had been corrupted by an early Judaizing conspiracy, to which Paul attested in his rejection of the "pillars" and "false brethren" in Galatians 1–2.[22] Though excommunicated by the church in 144 and operating for only a relatively short period before his death around 160, Marcion's reform project appears to have caught on like wildfire: Justin's *Apology* from the early 150s describes his movement as having reached many of every nation,[23] and despite provoking an unprecedented level of opposition from ecclesiastical writers,[24] Epiphanius describes his sect as still widespread at the end of the fourth century.[25]

Marcion's main works appear to have been his *Antitheses*, which juxtaposed Old Testament and New Testament passages to show the incompatibility of their respective gods, and his redacted versions of Luke's Gospel and the Pauline corpus (the "Apostolikon"). Marcion's Pauline corpus consisted of ten epistles (leaving out the Pastorals but including Philemon, much to Tertullian's confusion[26]), with the key epistle to the Galatians placed at the beginning of his collection. These works are all lost, and while attested in Justin, Irenaeus, and Clement of Alexandria,[27] it is Tertullian's five books *Against Marcion* (*Marc.*) that preserve our best testimony for Marcion. These books are an imperfect witness to Marcion's thought; one cannot be certain that his positions are always represented accurately,[28]

---

[21]*Haer.* 1.27.2-4; 3.12.12. Cf. Tertullian, *Marc.* 4.6. As Moll notes, earlier witnesses to Marcion regard this dualism as between a good god and the evil creator god, which is later articulated as a good versus a "just" god (Moll, *Arch-Heretic Marcion*, 47-63).

[22]*Marc.* 1.20.1-3; 5.3.2-3; cf. Adolf von Harnack, *Marcion: The Gospel of the Alien God*, trans. Lyle D. Bierma and John E. Steely (Durham, NC: Labyrinth Press, 1990 [1921]), 25. On Marcion's movement as (attempted) recovery, see Judith Lieu, *Marcion and the Making of a Heretic: God and Scripture in the Second Century* (Cambridge: Cambridge University Press, 2015), 416-17.

[23]*1 Apol.* 26, 58.

[24]Cf. von Harnack's comment that "in the last third of the second century every teacher in the church who could lift a pen seems to have written against Marcion and his church" (Adolf von Harnack, *Marcion: das Evangelium vom fremden Gott*, 2nd ed. [Leipzig: J. C. Hinrichs, 1924], 315).

[25]*Pan.* 42.1.1-2.

[26]*Marc.* 5.21.1.

[27]*Stromata* 3.3; 4.7-8; 5.1; 7.16-17.

[28]Cf. Judith Lieu, "As Much My Apostle as Christ Is Mine: The Dispute over Paul Between Tertullian and Marcion," *Early Christianity* 1 (2010): 45-46.

and as Riches observes, Tertullian's discussion of Marcion's views "tells us more about Tertullian than Marcion."[29] Furthermore, as Barclay notes, Tertullian's "object of attack may be as much the Marcionites of Tertullian's time and place of writing (c. 210 CE in Carthage) as the Marcion who established his alternative church in the 140s to 160s in Rome," leaving us potentially one step further removed from the second-century figure in question.[30] All the same, the wide-ranging engagement and relatively early date of Tertullian's books against Marcion make them the most useful resource for reconstructing his ideas, and are the primary sources used here.[31]

In light of the comparisons between Marcion and Luther over the centuries—often inspired by Tertullian's refrain that "separatio legis et evangelii proprium et principale opus est Marcionis,"[32] from which von Harnack's identification of Marcion as "der erste Reformator" understandably follows[33]—one might expect Marcion to be an especially valuable early witness to works of the law. These expectations are left substantially unmet, however, as the faith/works of the law antithesis, which is clearly a major concern for both Paul and Luther, does not to appear to hold a similar significance for Marcion. Rather, Paul's antithesis appears to be important for Marcion insofar as it can be employed in the service of a substantially dissimilar project, that of rejecting the creator god in favor of the revelation of the unknown god.[34] As Rensberger observes,

---

[29]John Riches, *Galatians Through the Centuries* (Oxford: Blackwell, 2007), 11; cf. Lieu, *Marcion and the Making*, 51.

[30]John M. G. Barclay, *Paul and the Gift* (Grand Rapids, MI: Eerdmans, 2015), 80.

[31]Cf. Lieu, *Marcion and the Making*, 7; Andreas Lindemann, *Paulus im ältesten Christentum: das Bild des Apostels und die Rezeption der paulinischen Theologie in der frühchristlichen Literatur bis Marcion* (Tübingen: Mohr Siebeck, 1979), 383. Another valuable witness to Marcionite theology is the third or fourth-century *Dialogue of Adamantius* (*Rect. Fide*), though as a later debate with contemporaneous Marcionites it is less secure as a witness to Marcion's own thought (cf. von Harnack, *Marcion*, 106).

[32]"The separation of law and gospel is the proper and primary work of Marcion."

[33]"The first reformer." *Marc.* 1.19.4; cf. 1.21.5; 4.1.1; 4.6.1, 3; cf. the title of von Harnack's first publication, *Marcion: Der Moderne Gläubige des 2. Jahrhunderts, der erste Reformator*. Balás rightly observes that in von Harnack's writings, "Marcion is repeatedly presented as a Luther before Luther; a Luther, moreover, whose image has been molded by the theology of Harnack" (David Balás, "Marcion Revisited: A 'Post-Harnack' Perspective," in *Texts and Testaments: Critical Essays on the Bible and Early Church Fathers*, ed. W. Eugene March [San Antonio, TX: Trinity University Press, 1980], 96).

[34]Cf. Tertullian's comment in *Marc.* 1.3.1: "The principal, and consequently the entire, matter of discussion is one of number, whether it is permissible to suggest the existence of two gods."

The precise contrast of Law and *Gospel* does not occur in Paul, and clearly what Marcion meant was the separation of the revelation and the scripture of the Creator from those of the unknown God, not the separation of two kinds of religion or two ways to salvation. The question of reliance on works of the law or on faith in Christ so characteristic of Paul was simply not what Marcion was thinking of. . . . The Antitheses opposed Old Testament *texts* to New Testament *texts* in order to establish their utter incompatibility and so their provenance from different Gods.[35]

Marcion's antithesis between the two gods governs his readings of Paul, witnessed in examples like Paul's rejection of τὰ στοιχεῖα in Galatians 4:3 being a rejection of the creator of the elements (*Marc.* 5.4.5), and Romans 2:21 as Paul's repudiation of the Old Testament god who hypocritically commanded the despoiling of the Egyptians (5.13.6). Verses discussing works of the law appear to be employed in service of Marcion's project in the same way: judging by Tertullian's counterexegesis, Marcion's argument in Galatians 2:16 has to do with neither faith nor the law, but rather the *object* of faith being different from the god of the law (5.3.8-9). Similarly, Paul's discussion of the curse of the law in Galatians 3:10-13 serves as an argument for Marcion that "Christ belongs to another god," rather than the one who had cursed him (5.3.10; cf. *Rect. Fide* 2.9). Thus, while parallels can still be drawn between these figures[36]—Marcion and Luther both reject the idea of Christ as a judge or lawgiver, for example—Marcion represents somewhat of a false positive for this study; his fundamental opposition is not to works, or even to the law, but rather to the creator god who gave the law.[37]

---

[35]David Rensberger, "As the Apostle Teaches: The Development of the Use of Paul's Letters in Second-Century Christianity" (PhD diss., Yale University, 1981), 154-55. As Balás notes, Marcion's desire to dissociate from Judaism may follow from reflection on the disastrous Jewish war of 132–135, in which the Jews indeed expected a warlike messiah to come from their God (Balás, "Marcion Revisited," 99).

[36]Though perhaps understating Paul's influence on Marcion, Moll's recent study notes that Marcion's fundamental ideas are not inspired by Paul, but that Paul rather serves to corroborate insights Marcion has arrived at from dwelling on Jesus' words and the Old Testament (Moll, *Arch-Heretic Marcion*, 85-86).

[37]So rightly Lieu, *Marcion and the Making*, 256: "Marcion's complaint was not against the Law as such so much as against the inconsistencies of character displayed by its author, the Creator." It is noteworthy that a search through Lieu's expansive volume on Marcion finds that *works of the law* is not once found in its 400-plus pages.

Insofar as an understanding of works of the law can be reconstructed for Marcion, the law in dispute would include the entire body of the Jewish Scriptures. According to Irenaeus, Marcion describes Jesus as "abolishing the prophets and the law, and all the works of that God who made the world" (*Haer.* 1.27.2)—which Marcion himself enacts by erasing allusions to the prophets in his redacted gospel and "Apostolikon"—and Tertullian writes that Marcion interprets the voice from heaven to "hear him" (Lk 9:35) as the unknown god's warning "to hear not Moses and the prophets, but Christ" (*Marc.* 4.34.15). While Marcion points out a variety of contradictions in the law's prescriptions,[38] these do not appear to be used for objections to any particular practices, but rather serve as evidence that the system in total reflects the work of an inferior deity. It seems from Epiphanius's witness to Marcion's "Apostolikon" that Marcion has replaced ἐξ ἔργων νόμου with ὑπὸ νόμον in Galatians 3:10, which makes it seem unlikely that works or "working" in general were targets emphasized by Marcion (though there are questions regarding Epiphanius's possession of Marcion's text).[39] These works are fundamentally rejected because they come from the inferior creator god, whose law Jesus has abolished in revealing the good god, his father (cf. *Marc.* 1.21; 5.4.13; *Rect. Fide* 2.7). Unlike other patristic sources, Marcion does not appeal to the prophetic witness of Scripture (since Christ is not the subject of prophecy, *Marc.* 3.4; 4.6.1), nor Jesus' identity as the Messiah who brings the new law (since Christ is neither the Messiah nor brings a new law, 4.1).[40] Instead, Marcion's arguments all relate back to the

---

[38]Cf. *Marc.* 2.21-22; as one example, note the prohibition of images and the command to make the brazen serpent, similarly discussed by Justin in *Dial.* 94-95.

[39]*Pan.* 42.11.18 (Karl Holl, ed., *Epiphanius [Ancoratus und Panarion]*, 3 vols. [Leipzig: Hinrichs, 1915–1922]; Frank Williams, ed., *The Panarion of Epiphanius of Salamis [Sects 1–46]*, vol. 1, 2nd ed. [Leiden: Brill, 2009]). Cf. John James Clabeaux, *A Lost Edition of the Letters of Paul: A Reassessment of the Text of the Pauline Corpus Attested by Marcion* (Washington, DC: Catholic Biblical Association of America, 1989), 65; see the similar usage by Irenaeus in *Epid.* 35 below. On the complicated (and not clearly consistent) views on the law witnessed by Marcion's various preservations and deletions from his texts, cf. von Harnack, *Marcion*, 75n21 (156).

[40]On Marcion's nonchristological readings of the Old Testament, cf. Moll, *Arch-Heretic Marcion*, 159-60; Lieu, *Marcion and the Making*, 77. As Lieu notes, Marcion's apparent principle of "then the Law, now the righteousness of God through faith in Christ" (5.13.8) may indicate some sequential reasoning for opposing the law, though it is unclear how this would integrate with his arguments elsewhere; cf. Lieu, *Marcion and the Making*, 256, 413.

revelation of the good god, in favor of whom the wicked creator (along with his legislation) is to be entirely rejected. Mirror reading from Tertullian's testimony, Marcion portrays Paul's conflict with the "false brethren" in Galatians as entirely based on this diversion of faith from Jesus and his unknown father to the Jews' creator god and his warlike Messiah, and not any dispute in particular over the law or its practices (1.20.4-6).

In summary, Marcion regards the law in conflict as the Jewish Scriptures, a corpus he rejects in total without focusing his objections on particular works or a principle of "working." Little can be said about the significance of practicing these works, besides an identification with the creator god to which they attest. Marcion rejects these works and law because they belong to the creator god, an inferior deity whose system Christ does away with in revealing the good god, his previously unknown father.

PTOLEMY

Ptolemy is paradoxically both the best and worst-preserved source in this section. Though we possess what appears to be a full copy of his *Letter to Flora*, it is first attested and preserved within the *Panarion* of the late fourth-century Epiphanius,[41] which has already been seen to be a work of limited historical value.[42] Fortunately, what Epiphanius has preserved is widely regarded as authentic, making this letter our securest example of Valentinian thought on the Mosaic law within this period.

Very little is known about the life of Ptolemy, whose letter usually dated around AD 150.[43] According to Irenaeus, Ptolemy was a student of Valentinus,[44] though it is unclear how closely Ptolemy follows the famous Gnostic.[45] Valentinus claimed to be a hearer of Theudas, who was said to

---

[41]Epiphanius, *Pan.* 33.3-7.

[42]Traces of Ptolemy's thought are also preserved in Irenaeus and Hippolytus, though these provide no information for the current question.

[43]There is debate as to whether this Ptolemy is the same whose martyrdom in the early 150s is noted by Justin in *2 Apology* 2. Though distinctions between mainstream early Christian thought and what we know of Ptolemy's ideas—for example, on the number of gods—makes this seem unlikely in an a priori sense, a strong circumstantial case can be made for it; cf. Moll, *Arch-Heretic Marcion*, 14-15.

[44]*Haer.* 1.praef.2: Ptolemy's school "may be described as a bud from that of Valentinus."

[45]Cf. Epiphanius, who while identifying him as a Valentinian and a gnostic, adds that "he has suppositions which are different from his teachers" (*Pan.* 33.1.1). Hippolytus similarly identifies Ptolemy as descended from Valentinus and locates his school in Italy.

be a disciple of Paul (*Strom.* 7.17), and while previous generations of scholarship had given a high estimation of Paul's place in Valentinian theology, this assessment has been substantially revised with the works of Lindemann, Dassmann, and Rensberger.[46] While Ptolemy does appeal to an (ostensibly secret) line of apostolic tradition in explaining the true origins of the Mosaic law,[47] his fundamental appeal to logic suggests that Räisänen is correct in identifying the letter as an intellectual, almost academic proposal by one detached from existential commitment to the Old Testament.[48]

Ptolemy begins his letter by identifying two positions on the law, which appear to be those of the mainstream Christians and the Marcionites: while "some say the law has been laid down by God the Father," others hold that it was given by the evil adversary who created the world (*Pan.* 33.3.2).[49] For Ptolemy, it is evident that both options are incorrect, since this law contains ordinances that are unworthy of the perfect God, but also cannot be the evil god's work because it abolishes iniquity (33.3.4-5). Ptolemy proposes a sort of a mediating position in relation to these two, whereby the law—specified as the five books of Moses—is to be understood as originating from three different sources: God, Moses, and the elders (33.4.1-2). The law originating with Moses is witnessed in Christ's contradiction of Moses' divorce concession (Mt 19:6-8); though contrary to God's law, Moses gave this law out of necessity because of the peoples' weakness (33.4.4-10). The law of the elders is identified by Jesus, who notes it in Matthew 15:4-9 (the "law of Corban"; 33.4.11-13). Taking up the first category (the law of God),

---

[46]Cf. Lindemann, *Paulus im ältesten Christentum*, 298-306; Ernst Dassmann, *Der Stachel im Fleisch: Paulus in der frühchristlichen Literatur bis Irenäus* (Münster: Aschendorff, 1979), 192-222; Rensberger, "As the Apostle Teaches," 364-75.

[47]*Pan.* 33.7.1 (Holl, *Epiphanius*; Williams, *Panarion of Epiphanius*); cf. Ptolemy's opening comment that "not many before us have understood the Law given through Moses" (*Pan.* 33.3.1). According to Irenaeus, it was common for Valentinians to allege that the apostles taught one set of doctrines in public—held by the "vulgar" or "ecclesiastic" multitudes—and the Gnostic doctrines in private, appealing to passages such as 1 Cor 2:9 ("we speak wisdom among the mature"); cf. *Haer.* 3.2.1, 3.15.1-2.

[48]Cf. *Pan.* 33.3.4; Heikki Räisänen, *Paul and the Law*, WUNT 29 (Tübingen: Mohr Siebeck, 1983), 224-26.

[49]On the second position referring to Marcion, cf. Räisänen *Paul and the Law*, 224n125; Moll, *Arch-Heretic Marcion*, 16-17.

Ptolemy further subdivides it into three parts: the pure law, the law mixed with injustice, and the typological law (33.5.1-2). The pure portion—though itself not actually perfect—is the Decalogue, which Christ came to fulfill (33.5.3). The mixed portion is the *lex talionis*: while appropriate for the weak, it is abolished by Christ as being inconsistent with the nature of the Father (33.5.4-7). The typological portion includes practices such as circumcision, Sabbath keeping, and feasts, which, though no longer to be observed literally, are nevertheless are still to be followed in a spiritual sense (such as circumcision of the heart) now that Christ has transformed them (33.5.8-15, cf. Rom 2:29). Following his prior appeals to Christ, Ptolemy here invokes the apostles for these divisons:

> The Saviour's disciples have given proof of these divisions, and so has the apostle Paul. For our sakes he gave proof of the part which consists of images with (his remarks about) the Passover and Feast of Unleavened Bread, as we have said already (cf. 1 Cor 5:7). And of the part which consists of the law which is mixed with injustice by saying, 'The law of commandments contained in ordinances is abolished' (Eph 2:15). And of the part which consists of the law with no admixture of inferior matter by saying, 'The Law is holy, and the commandment holy and just and good' (Rom 7:12).[50]

Ptolemy concludes that imperfections in God's law point to it being the work of neither the perfect God nor the devil, but rather a morally ambiguous demiurge called "the Intermediate" (τὸ τῆς μεσότητος ὄνομα, 33.7.3-4; cf. Gal 3:19). The letter closes with a strong claim to the apostolicity of Ptolemy's doctrine, identifying it as "the apostolic tradition [τῆς ἀποστολικῆς παραδόσεως] which I have received in my turn [ἐκ διαδοχῆς]" (33.7.9).

Though Ptolemy's letter engages the question of the ongoing relevance of the Mosaic law (and indeed invokes Paul in doing so),[51] it is not clear

---

[50]*Pan.* 33.6.6; translation from Williams, *Panarion of Epiphanius.*

[51]Cf. Rensberger on the Paulinism of Ptolemy's letter: "The passages from Paul are cited (usually out of context) as support for Ptolemy's own ideas, which really have no organic connection with Pauline thought on the Law. . . . The Epistle to Flora suggests that Ptolemy had a high regard for Paul's authority—the letters are clearly treated as authoritative—and expected a proof from them to carry conviction. Yet though Paul is among the apostolic witnesses, the thing 'attested' is no

where the works of the law mentioned in Romans 3 and Galatians 2–3 would fit in this scheme.[52] There is little evidence of conflict with Jewish parties in this epistle, and as a result one is forced into conjecture as to which category or subcategory these works would fit in. Circumcision is present in both the Romans and Galatians passages, and with it being mentioned in the typological law (along with the possible reference to Rom 2:29, *Pan.* 33.5.11), it is tempting to assume that the works of the law would have fit in this third subdivision. However, such a conclusion must be read into the text as much as derived from it, and while perhaps less likely, cases can be made for the other two options as well: Ephesians 2 is sometimes viewed as a cognate passage with Romans 3 and Galatians 2, and is invoked here against the law mixed with injustice, and Ptolemy's only clear Romans citation (Rom 7:12) is made in relation to the pure law (*Pan.* 33.6.6). It is similarly difficult to determine the significance of practicing these works, since there is little discussion of practicing the works themselves in the text, and in any case the identity and categorization of the works in question is still unsettled. If the works of the law are indeed within this typological category, they would be relativized from a physical standpoint because the spiritual reality to which they point has arrived with Christ's advent, such as offering sacrifices of praise and kindness rather than animals, practicing heart circumcision instead of physical, and keeping the true Sabbath by avoiding evil works (33.5.10-12). Regardless of which division they fit in, these works come from a different source than the good Father (either "the Intermediate," Moses, or the elders), though how this might serve as an objection is not made explicit. While making a strong appeal to an apostolic tradition, it is difficult to find internal or external substantiation for Ptolemy's claim (a potential Paul-Theudas-Valentinus-Ptolemy connection notwithstanding, which

---

more Pauline than it is apostolic" (Rensberger, "As the Apostle Teaches," 225). Räisänen offers a similarly low estimation of Ptolemy's relation to Paul (while favoring Ptolemy!): "In purely intellectual terms his account of the law is consistent and clear and far more impressive than Paul's" (*Paul and the Law*, 226).

[52] Cf. Bultmann's judgment in assessing Ptolemy's relevance to this subject: "The problem of the way to salvation, or the problem of legalism, is not raised here either" (Rudolf Bultmann, *Theology of the New Testament*, trans. Kendrick Grobel, 2 vols. [London: SCM, 1952], 1:113).

in any case is not mentioned here). Rather than a historically derived interpretive framework, Ptolemy's proposal seems to be a self-conscious exercise in theological triangulation in relation to prominent views of his time.

In short, while Ptolemy's letter offers a fascinating example of Gnostic interpretation of the Mosaic law, there is disappointingly little it can suggest about the specific points of conflict in Paul's debates over works of the law. Perhaps the best conjecture is that these works are understood as typological, and are made relative from a physical standpoint with the arrival of the spiritual realities that they prefigured (in addition to originating from a different god, "the Intermediate"). These connections are uncertain, however, and Ptolemy's confident claims to the apostolicity of his framework are no more so.

CONCLUSION

Our attempted reconstruction of three relevant nonmainstream sources in this period produces a somewhat varied picture. On the one hand, the testimony regarding the Ebionites—whose positions Tertullian identifies as the same held by Paul's Galatian opponents—is clear and particularly pertinent for our question. The Ebionites regard the law in dispute as the Mosaic law, including the practices of circumcision, the observance of Sabbath and Jewish feasts, food regulations, and a focus on Jerusalem. Practicing these works signifies both an identification with Israel and the path to righteousness, as Jesus himself is regarded as being justified by these works. Thus, works of the law *are* necessary for the Christian, as faith in Christ and a corresponding life are not sufficient for salvation by themselves. Furthermore, since Christ was sent only to Israel according to the flesh, Christians must become members of this people by observing the Mosaic law. Rather than rejecting works of the law, then, the Ebionites reject Paul and regard him as an apostate. On the other hand, there is little evidence to be derived from Marcion and Ptolemy for our particular question. While Marcion appears to regard the subject under discussion in Paul's disputes as the Jewish Torah, for him the apostle's fundamental objections focus on neither works nor the law, but rather the creator god who gave the law. It is difficult to identify where the "works of the law" would fit in the tripartite schema outlined in Ptolemy's *Letter to Flora*; our best estimation is that these are Jewish practices originating from a morally ambiguous demiurge, which (if correct) would represent an outlier in relation to other sources in this period.

9

JUSTIN MARTYR (A)

Dialogue with Trypho

□

INTRODUCTION

Introduction and background. The study's next source is Justin Martyr, whose journey through various philosophical schools led to him becoming a convert to the faith and the first Christian philosopher, and who is hailed by Grant as "the most important second century apologist."[1] Such a view appears to have been shared in his own time: Tatian, Irenaeus, and Tertullian all make direct appeal to him in the late second and early third centuries,[2] Chadwick suspects Celsus's *True Discourse* to be written in response to Justin,[3] and Eusebius finds space for his name twenty times in the early chapters of his *History*.[4] Justin is also a figure of particular interest for this study, as one of his extant works, *Dialogue with Trypho*, contains a vast amount of material that corresponds with passages discussing works of the law in Romans and Galatians. However, the question of Justin's relation to Paul has been much debated over the past centuries, and will be treated at length below.

Justin was born into a pagan family in Samaria around the turn of the century in Flavia Neapolis (contemporary Nablus), and a number of

---

[1]Robert M. Grant, *Greek Apologists of the Second Century* (Philadelphia: Westminster Press, 1988), 50.
[2]*Orat.* 18-19; *Haer.* 4.6.2; 5.26.2; *Val.* 5.
[3]Henry Chadwick, "Justin Martyr's Defence of Christianity," *Bulletin of the John Rylands Library* 47 (1965): 283-84.
[4]Cf. *Hist. Eccl.* 2-5.

details from Justin's *Dialogue* suggest that he would have encountered
Jewish traditions in passing from Samaritan religious practice.[5] As he
describes at the beginning of the *Dialogue*, Justin embraced Platonism at
the end of a philosophical quest that led him through brief stints in Stoic,
Peripatetic, and Pythagorean schools.[6] After encountering an old man
who deconstructed his Platonism and commended to him instead the
Hebrew prophets and the Christ of whom they spoke, Justin testifies that
"my spirit was immediately set on fire, and an affection for the prophets,
and for those who are friends of Christ, took hold of me; while pon-
dering on his words, I discovered that his was the only sure and useful
philosophy."[7] Retaining his philosopher's cloak, Justin opened a school of
Christian philosophy in Rome and wrote an apology to the emperor and
senate on behalf of the Christians around AD 153,[8] as well the *Dialogue
with Trypho* and a number of other now-lost works, including a *Syntagma Against All Heresies* that appears to have had Marcion as a primary
target.[9] He is attested to have been tried and beheaded for his faith
around 165, an account of which is preserved in the *Acts of Justin and
Companions.*[10]

The nature and audience of Justin's *Dialogue with Trypho* have been
widely debated, and because these issues are relevant for understanding
Justin's relation to Paul they will be discussed at some length here. The

---

[5]As Stylianopoulos notes, "in certain instances Justin seems unconsciously to include practices of
the oral Law in his understanding of νόμος," which Stylianopoulos terms "Samaritanisms," "Jus-
tinian errors regarding post-biblical practices which actually entail Samaritan customs," such as
requirements regarding tassels and the similarity of the goats on the Day of Atonement. Cf.
Theodore Stylianopoulos, *Justin Martyr and the Mosaic Law* (Missoula, MT: Society of Biblical
Literature, 1975), 48-50.

[6]*Dial.* 2.1-6.

[7]*Dial.* 8.1. Often considered a literary device, Osborn suggests that the "old man" is not purely
fictional: "It is unlikely that Justin would approach the story of his conversion with an excursion
into fantasy. He was not an idealist fascinated by the conflict of ideas. He was writing a defence
of his whole life before the hostile criticism of the Jews" (Eric Francis Osborn, *Justin Martyr*
[Tübingen: Mohr Siebeck, 1973], 7; cf. Kwame Bediako, *Theology and Identity* [Oxford: Regnum
Books, 1992], 40). For the suggestion that the old man is Christ, see Andrew Hofer, "The Old
Man as Christ in Justin's 'Dialogue with Trypho,'" *Vigiliae Christianae* 57 (2003): 1-21.

[8]Justin claims to be writing 150 years after the birth of Christ in *1 Apol.* 42; cf. Dennis Minns and
Paul Parvis, *Justin, Philosopher and Martyr: Apologies* (Oxford: Oxford University Press, 2009),
44.

[9]See Eusebius, *Hist. Eccl.* 4.18; cf. *1 Apol.* 26.8; *Haer.* 4.11.2.

[10]See Minns and Parvis, *Justin, Philosopher and Martyr*, 32-33.

Dialogue itself is an account of a lengthy debate between Justin and a Jew, Trypho, that purports to have taken place over a two-day period near the time of the catastrophic second Jewish revolt in AD 132–135, from which Trypho and his companions attest to have recently fled. However, identifying the *Dialogue* as a simple account from this period is complicated by inconsistencies in the *Dialogue*'s internal clock, with Justin making reference in *Dialogue* 120.6 to his *Apology* to Caesar, written some twenty years after this war. Opinions on the nature of the *Dialogue* have ranged from seeing it as representing a more-or-less verbatim account of an historical encounter in Ephesus, to a pure fiction (along the lines of similar literary dialogues in antiquity) in which Trypho serves as no more than a straw man.[11]

In seeking to understand the *Dialogue*'s nature, one valuable study is the recent thesis of Horner (*Listening to Trypho*).[12] According to Horner, assessments that dismiss a historical basis for Justin's *Dialogue* have failed to fully account for the character of Trypho, whom Horner identifies as often portrayed more attractively than Justin himself in the *Dialogue*, with his Socrates-like questioning forcing Justin into playing the part of the Sophist.[13] Horner accounts for these qualities, as well as the *Dialogue*'s curious internal clock, by identifying an initial "Trypho Text" that preserves Justin's original encounter with Trypho during the time of the Jewish War, which Justin expanded over time and eventually circulated in the form of the present *Dialogue*. According to Horner, seeing an authentic encounter within the *Dialogue* explains the instances in which Justin appears to be confused or frustrated,[14] seems to miss Trypho's point,[15] loses his temper,[16] and suffers damage to his argument at Trypho's hands.[17] As Horner summarizes, "it is clear that the

---

[11]The first position appears to be that of Eusebius, with the second represented by commentators such as Hyldahl and Donahue; cf. Timothy J. Horner, *Listening to Trypho: Justin Martyr's Dialogue Reconsidered* (Leuven: Peeters, 2001), 16-29.

[12]Horner, *Listening to Trypho*.

[13]Horner, *Listening to Trypho*, 73-77, 116-19.

[14]*Dial.* 39.8, 68.1; Horner, *Listening to Trypho*, 115, 156-57, 162.

[15]*Dial.* 89.2; Horner, *Listening to Trypho*, 151.

[16]*Dial.* 67.3; Horner, *Listening to Trypho*, 159.

[17]*Dial.* 87.3, 67.5-6; Horner, *Listening to Trypho*, 158, 162.

intricacies of Trypho's depiction could not be due entirely to Justin's literary skill. It is implausible and inappropriate to imagine Justin crafting his Jewish disputant in such a way as to erode some of the basic tenets of his Christian argument."[18] Horner's thesis, at minimum, is successful in achieving his stated goal of shifting the burden of proof "onto those who would discount the authenticity of the exchange,"[19] with readers such as Boyarin offering similar endorsement,[20] and his explanation of a two-part developmental process that preserves an account of an original discussion is adopted here. This view accords with the previous judgments of Chadwick,[21] Barnard,[22] Lieu[23] and Pelikan, whose terse conclusion can be reaffirmed: "The form of the *Dialogue* is literary, the debate a fact."[24]

The intended audience of Justin's *Dialogue* has been a subject of considerable debate over the past century, with scholars such as Goodenough and Hyldahl suggesting that rather than the traditionally assumed Jewish and Christian audiences, Justin is writing primarily for pagans who are considering becoming Jews (with Trypho's companions consisting of such pagans).[25] This view has become somewhat less prominent in recent decades, brought about not least by Stylianopoulos in an appendix to his 1975 thesis.[26] In this, Stylianopoulos notes that Justin's *Dialogue* "presupposes a familiarity with, even intimate knowledge of, both Judaism and Christianity which cannot be presupposed of a wider Graeco-Roman readership," and that the *Dialogue*'s extensive use of the Hebrew Scriptures and lack of pagan

---

[18]Horner, *Listening to Trypho*, 12.

[19]Horner, *Listening to Trypho*, 197.

[20]Cf. Daniel Boyarin, *Border Lines: The Partition of Judaeo-Christianity* (Philadelphia: University of Pennsylvania Press, 2004), 38.

[21]Chadwick, "Justin Martyr's Defence," 280.

[22]L. W. Barnard, *Justin Martyr: His Life and Thought* (London: Cambridge University Press, 1967), 39.

[23]Judith Lieu, *Image and Reality: The Jews in the World of the Christians in the Second Century* (London: T&T Clark, 1996), 104.

[24]Jaroslav Pelikan, *The Christian Tradition: A History of the Development of Doctrine. The Emergence of the Catholic Tradition (100–600),* 5 vols. (Chicago: University of Chicago Press, 1971), 1:15, in Horner, *Listening to Trypho*, 19; cf. also Jon Nilson, "To Whom Is Justin's Dialogue with Trypho Addressed?," *Theological Studies* 38 (1977): 540-41.

[25]Cf. E. R. Goodenough, *The Theology of Justin Martyr* (Jena: Frommann, 1923); Niels Hyldahl, *Philosophie und Christentum: Eine Interpretation der Einleitung zum Dialog Justins* (Kopenhagen: Munksgaard, 1966); see also Nilson, "To Whom Is Justin's Dialogue."

[26]Stylianopoulos, *Justin Martyr*, 169-95.

apologetic connections (such as the *logos spermatikos* from the *Apology*) render a pagan audience far less likely.[27] Rather, Stylianopoulos observes that "in contrast to other extant ancient Christian writings against the Jews . . . there is a conciliatory tone in the Dialogue, an earnestness of appeal, an irenic spirit," suggesting that "the author is writing not only for the benefit of those who are already on his side, the orthodox Christians, but also of those to whom he seems to appeal, the Jews."[28] Writing from a Jewish standpoint, Rokéah's study has reaffirmed Stylianopoulos's arguments, observing that "the *Dialogue* differs in style from all other *Adversus Iudaeos* works from Barnabas to Chrysostom," with Justin and Trypho consistently identifying one another as friends (and for Justin even brethren, *Dial.* 58.3, 137.1) and Justin openly and earnestly pursuing Trypho's conversion.[29] Rokéah thus concludes with Stylianopoulos that "unlike other *Adversus Iudaeos* works written for internal-Christian purposes, the *Dialogue* intended not only to preach to converted Christians and strengthen their spirits, but also to influence the Jews."[30] Considered in light of Justin's repeated commitments to argue on grounds accepted by the Jews (cf. *Dial.* 28.3, 120.5),[31] these arguments for *Dialogue*'s genuine apologetic appeal to the Jews appear to be sound, and while Justin's concerns in the *Dialogue* are broad enough to accommodate Christian, pagan, and Jewish audiences,[32]

---

[27]Stylianopoulos, *Justin Martyr*, 192-95. Along with these points, Stylianopoulos notes how Justin's usage of plural imperatives suggests Trypho's companions to be Jews like him rather than God-fearing pagans (Stylianopoulos, *Justin Martyr*, 173-76). In my view, Justin's exhortation to "stay as you were at birth" at *Dial.* 23.3 leaves open the possibility that potential Jewish proselytes are among Trypho's companions, though the *Dialogue*'s broader qualities (noted by Stylianopoulos above) show them to be less likely as the primary literary audience.

[28]Stylianopoulos, *Justin Martyr*, 36.

[29]David Rokéah, *Justin Martyr and the Jews* (Leiden: Brill, 2002), 8-9.

[30]Rokéah, *Justin Martyr and the Jews*, 9. See also S. G. Wilson, *Related Strangers: Jews and Christians, 70–170 C.E.* (Minneapolis: Fortress Press, 1995), 261-65; Craig Allert, *Revelation, Truth, Canon, and Interpretation: Studies in Justin Martyr's Dialogue with Trypho* (Leiden: Brill, 2002), 61; Lieu, *Image and Reality*, 106.

[31]Cf. Oskar Skarsaune, "Justin and His Bible," in *Justin Martyr and His Worlds*, ed. Sara Parvis and Paul Foster (Minneapolis: Fortress Press, 2007), 73n88: "[Justin] has committed himself to only quoting texts considered authoritative and authentic by his Jewish interlocutor (*Dial.* 28.2, 32.2, 39.7, 55.3, 56.16, 58.1, 68.1, and esp. 71.2-3), and when he once breaks this principle by quoting three saying of Jesus (*Dial.* 17.3-4), he excuses himself after the fact (*Dial.* 18.1)."

[32]So Miroslav Marcovich, *Iustini Martyris Dialogus cum Tryphone* (Berlin: De Gruyter, 1997), 64-65; Stylianopoulos, *Justin Martyr*, 184-85, though Marcovich remains with the view that pagans leaning towards Judaism are the primary audience.

it appears to be the Jewish and Christian readerships that are most strongly implied.

In summary, Justin's *Dialogue* is best understood as a literary retelling and expansion of an encounter that took place near the conclusion of the second Jewish revolt in AD 135, with Justin's final written text being completed in the years following the *Apology* referenced by Justin in *Dialogue* 120.6, likely around 155–160.[33] While Justin's audience is not limited to one particular group, his conciliatory tone and adoption of grounds that will appeal to Jewish readers indicate that the work intends to serve as an apologetic to Jews, with a Christian readership (both what Justin would consider orthodox and heretical) likely in view as well.

Text and translation. The text of Justin's *Dialogue* is poorly preserved, with the single fourteenth-century manuscript that contains the text (*Parisinus gr* 450) suffering at least one lacuna of substantial length at *Dialogue* 74.[34] A number of reconstructions of the Greek text have been undertaken, and this study follows the recent edition of Marcovich.[35] The Falls English translation is the most fluid English rendering, and is used except where otherwise indicated;[36] on some occasions the *Ante-Nicene Fathers* translation more closely follows the Greek, with ANF marked where these translations are used.[37]

JUSTIN AND PAUL

Knowledge and use of Paul. Determining Justin's proximity to Pauline "works of the law" disputes is perhaps the most difficult such judgment within this study, as the relationship between the apostle and the apologist has been debated for centuries in biblical studies, with their connection

---

[33]Cf. Marcovich, *Iustini Martyris Dialogus*, 1.

[34]For the quality and condition of the *Parisinus gr* 450, see Marcovich, *Iustini Martyris Dialogus*, 1-6. The size of the missing text is difficult to estimate, though Marcovich marks it with the flag of "<Huge lacuna.>" (44).

[35]Marcovich, *Iustini Martyris Dialogus*.

[36]Thomas Falls, trans., *Dialogue with Trypho*, ed. Thomas Halton and Michael Slusser (Washington, DC: Catholic University of America Press, 2003 [1965]).

[37]Alexander Roberts and James Donaldson, eds., *The Ante-Nicene Fathers: Translations of the Writings of the Fathers down to A.D. 325*, vol. 1, *The Apostolic Fathers with Justin Martyr and Irenaeus* (Peabody, MA: Hendrickson, 1994 [1885]).

often serving as a linchpin in various reconstructions of the development of early Christianity.[38] On the one hand, Justin does not mention Paul or his letters, nor (for the specific purposes of this study) does he use the phrase *works of the law*,[39] and some commentators have gone so far as to argue that Justin sees Paul as in some way antithetical to the Christian mission.[40] On the other hand, a number of more recent studies have argued that Justin's wide variety of parallels with Paul's epistles is evidence that the apologist uses them extensively, with commentators such as Lindemann identifying Justin as a "champion" of Pauline theology, and Rokéah viewing Paul as even more formative for Justin than Jesus himself.[41] If these latter assessments are accurate, then the *Dialogue* would represent a gold mine of early Pauline reception and interpretation on works of the law, as discussions over the Christian's relation to the law occupy arguably the greatest amount of space in Justin's lengthy debate, and a wide range of apparent allusions can be identified to relevant sections in Romans and Galatians. These include passages discussing the justification of Abraham (Rom 4, Gal 3; cf. *Dial.* 11, 23, 92 and 119),[42] the universal sinfulness of Israel (Rom 3; cf. *Dial.* 27),[43] circumcision of the

---

[38]On this, see Rensberger's very useful summary in Rensberger, "As the Apostle Teaches," 3-22.

[39]Arnold's recent suggestion that δικαιοπραξίας ἔργον in *Dial.* 137.1 is "used to conjure up Paul's memorable, but controversial, phrase ἔργα νόμου" is not clear from the evidence; see Brian John Arnold, "Justification One Hundred Years After Paul" (PhD diss., Southern Baptist Theological Seminary, 2013), 229.

[40]On Justin and the "Pauline captivity," cf. chapter one, "The Early Reception of Paul."

[41]See Andreas Lindemann, *Paulus im ältesten Christentum: das Bild des Apostels und die Rezeption der paulinischen Theologie in der frühchristlichen Literatur bis Marcion* (Tübingen: Mohr Siebeck, 1979), 353; Rokéah, *Justin Martyr and the Jews*, vii.

[42]See, for example, Rom. 4:9-11: Ὁ μακαρισμὸς οὖν οὗτος ἐπὶ τὴν περιτομὴν ἢ καὶ ἐπὶ τὴν ἀκροβυστίαν; λέγομεν γάρ· ἐλογίσθη τῷ Ἀβραὰμ ἡ πίστις εἰς δικαιοσύνην. πῶς οὖν ἐλογίσθη; ἐν περιτομῇ ὄντι ἢ ἐν ἀκροβυστίᾳ; οὐκ ἐν περιτομῇ ἀλλ᾽ ἐν ἀκροβυστίᾳ· καὶ σημεῖον ἔλαβεν περιτομῆς σφραγῖδα τῆς δικαιοσύνης τῆς πίστεως τῆς ἐν τῇ ἀκροβυστίᾳ.

Cf. *Dial.* 23.4: καὶ γὰρ αὐτὸς ὁ Ἀβραὰμ ἐν ἀκροβυστίᾳ ὢν διὰ τὴν πίστιν, ἣν ἐπίστευσε τῷ θεῷ, ἐδικαιώθη καὶ εὐλογήθη, ὡς ἡ γραφὴ σημαίνει· τὴν δὲ περιτομὴν εἰς σημεῖον, ἀλλ᾽ οὐκ εἰς δικαιοσύνην ἔλαβεν (similarly *Dial.* 92.3). Among other examples, see also Abraham's fatherhood of many nations (*Dial.* 11.5; Rom 4:17); and those of faith being Abraham's children (*Dial.* 119.5-6; Gal 3:6-7).

[43]See Rom 3:11-17: οὐκ ἔστιν ὁ συνίων, οὐκ ἔστιν ὁ ἐκζητῶν τὸν θεόν. πάντες ἐξέκλιναν ἅμα ἠχρεώθησαν· οὐκ ἔστιν ὁ ποιῶν χρηστότητα, [οὐκ ἔστιν] ἕως ἑνός. τάφος ἀνεῳγμένος ὁ λάρυγξ αὐτῶν, ταῖς γλώσσαις αὐτῶν ἐδολιοῦσαν, ἰὸς ἀσπίδων ὑπὸ τὰ χείλη αὐτῶν· ὧν τὸ στόμα ἀρᾶς καὶ πικρίας γέμει, ὀξεῖς οἱ πόδες αὐτῶν ἐκχέαι αἷμα, σύντριμμα καὶ ταλαιπωρία ἐν ταῖς ὁδοῖς αὐτῶν, καὶ ὁδὸν εἰρήνης οὐκ ἔγνωσαν.

heart (Rom 2–3),[44] and the curse of the law (Gal 3; cf. *Dial.* 95–96).[45] Among these, the last is particularly noteworthy for Justin's apparent usage of Galatians 3:10 at *Dialogue* 95.1, a verse in which Paul uses the phrase "works of the law" (with Justin employing "the law of Moses," τὸν νόμον Μωσέως).[46]

Though studies that identify Justin as drawing on Paul constitute a majority in the field, the fact that some commentators maintain a negative or agnostic position on the question means that any categorization will be open to critique, and to further complicate matters, it would appear that all three possible ratings are in play in Justin's case. If Justin's apparent textual and theological correspondences with Paul are actually due to overlapping traditional materials and not dependence on the apostle himself, a C categorization ("circumstantial evidence") would be most appropriate. Conversely, if Paul is indeed used by Justin, then his overlap with passages that discuss works of the law would make an A rating ("direct evidence") seem difficult to avoid. In such a context, a B rating would seem attractive as a safe middle

---

Cf. *Dial.* 27.3: καὶ πάντες γὰρ ἐξέκλιναν, βοᾷ, πάντες ἄρα ἠχρειώθησαν· οὐκ ἔστιν ὁ συνίων, οὐκ ἔστιν ἕως ἑνός. ταῖς γλώσσαις αὐτῶν ἐδολιοῦσαν, τάφος ἀνεῳγμένος ὁ λάρυγξ αὐτῶν, ἰὸς ἀσπίδων ὑπὸ τὰ χείλη αὐτῶν, σύντριμμα καὶ ταλαιπωρία ἐν ταῖς ὁδοῖς αὐτῶν, καὶ ὁδὸν εἰρήνης οὐκ ἔγνωσαν.

[44]See Rom 2:28-29 in *Dial.* 43.2, 92.3-4, and 113.7.

[45]See Gal 3:10-11, 13: Ὅσοι γὰρ ἐξ ἔργων νόμου εἰσίν, ὑπὸ κατάραν εἰσίν· γέγραπται γὰρ ὅτι ἐπικατάρατος πᾶς ὃς οὐκ ἐμμένει πᾶσιν τοῖς γεγραμμένοις ἐν τῷ βιβλίῳ τοῦ νόμου τοῦ ποιῆσαι αὐτά (Deut 27:26). ὅτι δὲ ἐν νόμῳ οὐδεὶς δικαιοῦται παρὰ τῷ θεῷ δῆλον . . . Χριστὸς ἡμᾶς ἐξηγόρασεν ἐκ τῆς κατάρας τοῦ νόμου γενόμενος ὑπὲρ ἡμῶν κατάρα, ὅτι γέγραπται· ἐπικατάρατος πᾶς ὁ κρεμάμενος ἐπὶ ξύλου (Deut 21:23).

Dial. 95.1-96.1: Καὶ γὰρ πᾶν γένος ἀνθρώπων εὑρεθήσεται ὑπὸ κατάραν ὂν κατὰ τὸν νόμον Μωσέως· Ἐπικατάρατος γὰρ εἴρηται πᾶς ὃς οὐκ ἐμμένει ἐν τοῖς γεγραμμένοις ἐν τῷ βιβλίῳ τοῦ νόμου τοῦ ποιῆσαι αὐτά (Deut 27:26). καὶ οὐδεὶς ἀκριβῶς πάντα ἐποίησεν . . . εἰ οὖν καὶ τὸν ἑαυτοῦ Χριστὸν ὑπὲρ τῶν ἐκ παντὸς γένους ἀνθρώπων ὁ πατὴρ τῶν ὅλων τὰς πάντων κατάρας ἀναδέξασθαι ἐβουλήθη . . . Καὶ γὰρ τὸ εἰρημένον ἐν τῷ νόμῳ, ὅτι Ἐπικατάρατος πᾶς ὁ κρεμάμενος ἐπὶ ξύλου (Deut 21:23).

Paul and Justin's close agreement in their citations of Deut 27:26; 21:23 diverges from the LXX: Ἐπικατάρατος πᾶς ἄνθρωπος ὅστις οὐκ ἐμμενεῖ ἐν πᾶσιν τοῖς λόγοις τοῦ νόμου τούτου ποιῆσαι αὐτούς (Deut 27:26 LXX); ὅτι κεκατηραμένος ὑπὸ θεοῦ πᾶς κρεμάμενος ἐπὶ ξύλου (Deut 21:23 LXX, italics mine). On this parallel, cf. Oskar Skarsaune, *The Proof from Prophecy: A Study in Justin Martyr's Proof-Text Tradition* (Leiden: Brill, 1987), 118; I follow Skarsaune's text in this case rather than Marcovich's emendations.

[46]Other common parallels include the close paraphrase of Elijah's story in Rom 11:3-4 at *Dial.* 39.1 (using a non-LXX citation of 1 Kings 19:10, 14, 18), and Rom 9:7 in *Dial.* 25.1, 44.1-2, and 140.2.

ground; but such a categorization, while convenient, would be arrived at by a mediating impulse rather than by attempting to answer the question of whether Justin indeed draws on Paul—because if he does, then he almost certainly belongs within the A category, since it is precisely the parallels with "works of the law" passages in Paul that are the strongest in Justin's *Dialogue*. For this reason, a B categorization (whereby Justin is dependent on Paul's epistles, but not directly on verses discussing works of the law) seems the least plausible of the options. This leads to a choice between A and C level influence, and in light of the importance of this judgment for this study, it is valuable to examine a range of views over the past decades on the question; while not exhaustive, the survey that follows will provide a broad sampling of the conclusions of recent commentators and common arguments that are employed on each side.

Among studies that do not hold Justin to have drawn on Paul (or maintain that such usage cannot be demonstrated with confidence), Rensberger's balanced analysis is paradigmatic and takes into account a number of common arguments. After examining the most significant passages that are taken as influenced by the apostle, Rensberger concludes that "the preserved works of Justin simply do not tell us enough to judge how he regarded Paul," and that "while Justin may have made some direct use of the letters of Paul, there are no grounds for a really confident assertion either that he did or that he did not."[47] This echoes the earlier judgment of Smit Sibinga's study on Justin's OT quotations; while conceding that since "Justin is the only one among the early Christian writers *adversus Judaeos* who, like Paul, combines Deut 27:26 and 21:23 [cf. Gal 3:10-13, *Dial.* 95.1, 96.1], there must be some relation to them," he ultimately finds the evidence to be inconclusive and suggests that Justin may be dependent on a source that knows Paul.[48] Von Campenhausen foregrounds the use of Paul by the Gnostics, suggesting that his writings were of little use to "ward off the gnostic attacks" due to Paul's "peculiar doctrine of the multiplication of sin by the Law," so that it is "understandable that Justin logically ignores

---

[47]Rensberger, "As the Apostle Teaches," 191.
[48]Joost Smit Sibinga, *The Old Testament Text of Justin Martyr* (Leiden: Brill, 1963), 97-99.

Paul altogether."[49] Barrett's brief assessment identifies "a measure of mistrust" toward Paul by Justin's failure to mention him: "Paul was the heretics' apostle, and it was wise to be cautious in using him."[50] Frend, himself no great admirer of Justin, offers the terse statement that "there is no evidence that [Justin] was influenced by any of the writers of the New Testament," though he adduces no arguments for or against.[51] Koester briefly restates the view common to the "Pauline captivity" thesis, that due to Marcion's use of the Pauline epistles, "it seems that Justin deliberately avoided these letters."[52] Finally, Foster's recent survey reaches the vivid conclusion that in contrast to other apostolic figures and writings, "when it comes to Paul, and to the use of his writings, there is a strange, almost deathly, silence."[53] Attributing the passages that appear to indicate Pauline dependency to Justin's use of *testimonia* collections that were likely influenced by Paul, Foster speculates that Justin's silence may be due to his not knowing Paul, a reluctance to use Paul because of his association with Marcion, or his not viewing Paul's writings "as a secure basis for advancing his own arguments," though he concludes that "the answer is simply unknown."[54]

Among commentators who view Justin as drawing on Paul, one might begin with the surprising example of Barnett. While still holding to the second-century "Pauline captivity" thesis (for which Justin's nonengagement with Paul was usually the key evidence), Barnett nevertheless views Justin's usage of Paul as frequent and clear, with Romans and Galatians cited numerous times, and the important passage of *Dialogue* 95–96 (citing Gal 3:10, 13) classed as "A" (certain).[55] Massaux's survey of the

---

[49]Hans von Campenhausen, *The Formation of the Christian Bible* (Philadelphia: Fortress Press, 1972), 98.

[50]C. K. Barrett, "Pauline Controversies in the Post-Pauline Period," *New Testament Studies* 20 (1974): 237.

[51]W. H. C. Frend, *The Rise of Christianity* (Philadelphia: Fortress Press, 1984), 237.

[52]Helmut Koester, *History and Literature of Early Christianity*, vol. 2 of *Introduction to the New Testament*, 2nd ed. (New York: Walter de Gruyter, 2000), 9.

[53]Paul Foster, "Justin and Paul," in *Paul and the Second Century*, ed. Michael F. Bird and Joseph R. Dodson (New York: T&T Clark, 2011), 123.

[54]Foster, "Justin and Paul," 124-25.

[55]Albert Barnett, *Paul Becomes a Literary Influence* (Chicago: University of Chicago Press, 1941), 241, 247. On Barnett's scale of confidence, citations of Romans stand at 8 as "A," 2 as "B," and one as "C"; for Galatians the figures are 2 as "A," 2 as "B," and 2 as "C."

question concludes that Justin was "particularly familiar" with Paul's
writings and "drew inspiration" from them, though "very rare are the
cases in which a literary dependence is certain"; among such instances,
Massaux identifies Justin as drawing on Galatians 3:6-7 at *Dialogue* 119
and Romans 4:9-10, 17 at *Dialogue* 119.5-6, 23.4, and 92.3.[56] Falls's translation of the *Dialogue* offers no commentary on the question, but identifies Justin as reliant on Romans 3 at *Dialogue* 27.3 and Galatians 3 at
Dialogue 95.1.[57] Shotwell's thesis on this subject finds that "in matters of
exegesis, Justin was a direct descendant of his illustrious predecessor,"
Paul, whom he chose "as his mentor."[58] Paul's influence can be seen in
Justin's engagement with the law, such as *Dialogue* 94.5–95.2, where "he
states the same argument that Paul uses in Gal. 3.10-14."[59] Barnard sees
Justin as drawing on most of Paul's epistles, including Romans and Galatians, though Justin's apologetic purpose "prevented his appealing to
purely *Christian* teachers and writings as authorities," reserved by Justin
only for the words of the incarnate Logos.[60] Donahue's thesis on Justin's
Dialogue finds Justin to "clearly reflect Paul's argument in Romans 4" at
Dialogue 23.4, and identifies Justin as a "Paulinist" more broadly by his
kerygmatic emphasis.[61]

Stylianopoulos's thesis notes that "Justin could not but have known
the Pauline Letters, at least indirectly, through writing against Marcion
whom he must have read, or must have known about, before refuting" in
his now-lost *Syntagma*.[62] Stylianopoulos finds Justin's arguments on
Abraham's justification to rely on Paul's reasoning in Romans 4 and
Galatians 3, which "no other Christian writer prior to Justin reproduces
. . . as fully as Justin does," though unlike figures such as Ptolemy, Justin
"does not quote [Paul] nor does he mention him because the Dialogue is

[56]Edouard Massaux, *The Influence of the Gospel of Saint Matthew on Christian Literature Before Saint Irenaeus*, ed. Arthur J. Bellinzoni, vol. 3 of 3 (Macon, GA: Mercer, 1993 [1950]), 97-100.
[57]Falls, *Dialogue with Trypho*, 188, 298.
[58]Willis Shotwell, *The Biblical Exegesis of Justin Martyr* (London: S.P.C.K., 1965), 55, 12.
[59]Shotwell, *Biblical Exegesis of Justin*, 46, 12.
[60]Barnard, *Justin Martyr*, 62-63.
[61]Paul J. Donahue, "Jewish-Christian Controversy in the Second Century: A Study in the Dialogue of Justin Martyr" (PhD diss., Yale University, 1973), 121-22, 213.
[62]Stylianopoulos, *Justin Martyr*, 70.

written for Jews and the authority of the discussion with Trypho is the Old Testament."[63] Lindemann's study similarly finds that "Justin hat paulinische Briefe, jedenfalls Röm, I Kor und Gal, gekannt und bei der Abfassung des Dial zu Rate gezogen,"[64] and that Paul not being expressly mentioned "ist Folge seines theologischen Prinzips: Die Wahrheit des Christentums wird aus dem Alten Testament erwiesen."[65] Further, Lindemann counters the idea that Justin would have avoided Paul on account of Marcion by noting that Marcion's placement of Luke's Gospel at the front of his canon does not prevent Justin from using it either (cf. *Dial.* 103.8; Lk 22:42-44).[66] Dassmann comments that in light of Justin's correspondences with Paul (such as *Dial.* 27 and 39), "wird man die Kenntnis und Verwendung des paulinischen Römerbriefes nicht bestreiten können," with traces of many other Pauline letters (including Galatians) found as well.[67] Dassmann offers a modified version of von Campenhausen's thesis, seeing Justin as the first writer after the author of Acts to address the question of the validity of the Jewish law, and writing that "obwohl diese Antwort paulinisch inspiriert war, konnte sie nicht im Namen des Apostels gegeben werden; denn die ebenfalls von Paulus vertretene Auffassung von der Mehrung der Sünde durch das Gesetz wäre zu Abwehr der gnostischen Angriffe gegen das Gesetz ein schlechter Helfer gewesen."[68] Skarsaune's wide-ranging analysis of OT citations concludes that Justin draws directly on Paul rather than intermediary sources, finding that "within the *corpus Paulinum*, Justin seems to have made special use of Romans and Galatians," with Justin "no doubt" having "Galatians 3 before his eyes when writing *Dial.* 95f."[69] According

---

[63]Stylianopoulos, *Justin Martyr*, 116-18, 168.

[64]"Justin knew the Pauline letters, at least Romans, 1 Corinthians and Galatians, and consulted them when drafting the Dialogue."

[65]"Is a consequence of his theological principle: the truth of Christianity is proven from the Old Testament." Lindemann, *Paulus im ältesten Christentum*, 366.

[66]Lindemann, *Paulus im ältesten Christentum*, 367. Cf. Massaux, *Influence of the Gospel*, 3:101, who ranks Luke as second in influence behind Matthew among NT books in Justin's writings.

[67]"The knowledge and use of the Pauline epistle to the Romans cannot be disputed." Dassmann, *Der Stachel im Fleisch*, 245.

[68]"Although this answer was inspired by Paul, it could not be given in the name of the apostle; for the view Paul presents of sin's increase through the law would have been a bad helper to repulse the gnostic attacks against the law." Dassmann, *Der Stachel im Fleisch*, 246.

[69]Skarsaune, *Proof from Prophecy*, 97-100, 118-19, 216-20.

to Skarsaune, "not only are Pauline quotations frequently borrowed by Justin," but in "crucial passages of the *Dialogue* [such as *Dial*. 91–95, 119–121] Justin states Pauline points of view with considerable insight and emphasis."[70] These findings are reaffirmed in Skarsaune's later study on "Justin and His Bible," where he concludes that "there is no reason to doubt that Justin made extensive use of Paul's letters, especially Romans and Galatians," which stands in contrast to his engagement with nearly all other NT writings: Justin appears "strikingly independent of the scriptural proof in Acts," James "may be echoed once in Justin," 1 Peter "possibly on three occasions, none of them certain," with 1 John carrying "only one possible allusion in Justin, far from certain."[71]

Cosgrove, while still inhabiting the "Pauline captivity" paradigm, nevertheless comments that dependence on the apostle is evident in "Justin's salvation-history approach to the law, which so parallels Paul's," particularly in the passages of *Dialogue* 95–96 (Gal 3) and *Dialogue* 11 and 23 (Rom 4).[72] Koch's brief analysis of *Dialogue* 27 and 95–96 concludes that Justin relies not on preexisting *florilegia*, but rather directly on Paul in Romans 3:11-17 and Galatians 3:10-13.[73] Siker's study follows Stylianopoulos in concluding that "Justin did know Paul's letters firsthand," which he uses but does not directly cite due to the Marcionite crisis and his desire to appeal to authorities Trypho recognizes: Justin draws on even Jesus' sayings only with hesitation and "only as corroborating evidence," and for Trypho, "Paul's letters would have been even less convincing."[74] Hill's brief study on Justin and the New Testament writings rebuts Koester's minimalist conclusions, commending instead those of Barnard and Osborn on Justin's positive usage of Paul.[75] Marcovich's

---

[70]Skarsaune, *Proof from Prophecy*, 430.

[71]Skarsaune, "Justin and His Bible," 74-75.

[72]Charles Cosgrove, "Justin Martyr and the Emerging Christian Canon: Observations on the Purpose and Destination of the Dialogue with Trypho," *Vigiliae Christianae* 36 (1982): 225.

[73]Dietrich-Alex Koch, *Die Schrift als Zeuge des Evangeliums: Untersuchungen zur Verwendung und zum Verständnis der Schrift bei Paulus* (Tübingen: Mohr Siebeck, 1986), 251.

[74]Jeffrey Siker, *Disinheriting the Jews: Abraham in Early Christian Controversy* (Louisville, KY: Westminster John Knox Press, 1991), 250-51.

[75]Charles E. Hill, "Justin and the New Testament Writings," in *Studia Patristica*, vol. 30, ed. E. A. Livingstone (Leuven: Peeters Press, 1997), 42-48; cf. Osborn, *Justin Martyr*, 136.

critical edition of the *Dialogue* identifies a multitude of Pauline parallels, including thirty-seven references to Romans and eleven to the third chapter of Galatians alone.[76] Werline's study on Justin and Paul finds that Justin "certainly knows Paul's writings in detail and uses them," with the *Dialogue* providing "a perfect occasion for him to employ Paul because in it he addresses the relationship between Judaism and the church, a central topic in both Romans and Galatians."[77] Within these letters, Justin focuses especially on Romans 2–4 and 9–11 and "probably has Galatians 3 before him as he composes *Dialogue* 95–96," though the apostle is not explicitly mentioned since "Paul . . . is not an authority figure for Trypho, and, consequently, it is futile to cite him in this regard."[78] Rokéah goes so far as to identify Justin as more influenced by Paul than Jesus (who is seen as less anti-Jewish than Paul), asserting that "Justin understood and correctly interpreted Paul's stance" and "fulfilled Paul's vision."[79] Beginning in *Dialogue* 11, "Justin follows the exegetical path laid down by Paul, citing Abraham, among others, as proof for the unimportance of circumcision,"[80] and similarly draws on the apostle "on the issues of the Torah, Abraham and the status of the Gentiles" throughout the *Dialogue*.[81] According to Lincicum, Justin uses Paul as a guide toward reading the Old Testament—including the "particularly striking" example of *Dialogue* 95–96, where Justin is "almost certainly indicating his dependence" on Galatians 3:10-13—and while Justin transforms Pauline arguments in a supersessionist direction, "this change in interpretation cannot be used as an argument against Pauline derivation."[82] Finally, Arnold's recent thesis reaches a clear affirmative conclusion: Justin "goes straight to the heart of Paul's theology, attacking Judaism along the same lines that the Apostle did," so that "in all the treatment of the Law in the Dialogue,

---

[76]Marcovich, *Iustini Martyris Dialogus*, 329-30.

[77]Rodney Werline, "The Transformation of Pauline Arguments in Justin Martyr's 'Dialogue with Trypho,'" *Harvard Theological Review* 92 (1999): 79-80.

[78]Werline, "Transformation of Pauline Arguments," 80-81.

[79]Rokéah, *Justin Martyr and the Jews*, vii.

[80]Rokéah, *Justin Martyr and the Jews*, 4.

[81]Rokéah, *Justin Martyr and the Jews*, 30.

[82]David Lincicum, "Learning Scripture in the School of Paul: From Ephesians to Justin," in *The Early Reception of Paul*, ed. Kenneth Liljeström (Helsinki: Finnish Exegetical Society, 2011), 164.

one cannot help but hear loud echoes of Paul reverberating through Justin's arguments."[83]

With opinions on Justin's usage of Paul ranging from a "deathly silence" on one end to engagement that "goes straight to the heart of Paul's theology" on the other, how might one attempt to adjudicate between these views? To begin, in assessing the arguments against Justin's usage of Paul, it can be seen that many on this side are influenced by unmet expectations for Paul to be explicitly named and cited if he is used, along with prior assumption of the second-century "captivity" narrative, and it is noteworthy that one need look no farther than Rensberger's own analysis for these ideas to be contested. With regard to Justin not explicitly naming Paul, Rensberger notes the importance of accounting for the genre and audience of Justin's extant writings; taking the example of a student of Justin's, Tatian, Rensberger notes that although his apology "neither mentions Paul nor has any really certain echoes of his letters . . . he is known from other sources to have been intensively engaged with the epistles when writing for fellow Christians."[84] This trend, observed in other writers like Theophilus, suggests that when apologists have outsiders as a primary audience, "no occasion is found to speak of Paul, and little to make use of his letters; it is only when Christians are being addressed that he, and they, become significant as objects of discussion, debate, and exegesis, and as authorities on which teachings are to be based."[85] Indeed, as Rensberger observes, "that an apologist's failure to say anything about Paul is a nonissue should already be evident from the fact that whole apologies can be written (Tatian; Theophilus) without once mentioning Christ!"[86] Rather than an anomaly, then, Rensberger concludes that "since [Justin's] extant works are both apologetic," an absence of explicit appeal to Paul "represents

---

[83] Arnold, "Justification One Hundred Years After," 202, 210.
[84] Rensberger, "As the Apostle Teaches," 336.
[85] Rensberger, "As the Apostle Teaches," 336-37. These same points are made by Lightfoot, who speculates that in contrast to these of Justin's extant apologetic works (written for outsiders), Justin's treatise against Marcion would naturally contain much more explicit appeal to Christian authorities; see J. B. Lightfoot, *Essays on the Work Entitled Supernatural Religion* (London: Macmillan and Co., 1893), 33, cf. Hill, "Justin and the New Testament Writings," 43.
[86] Rensberger, "As the Apostle Teaches," 336n5; note also Minucius Felix's *Octavius*.

more or less what one would expect."[87] In addition to this, Rensberger's thesis questions the presupposition of a captivity of Paul's epistles, since it is Justin's nonusage of Paul that constitutes the key evidence for this theory, and here Justin's usage of these epistles is precisely the point in question. Instead, Rensberger reaches the conclusion that "there is no reason to ascribe [Justin's] failure to use them (if such is the case) to anxieties about Marcion or gnosticism. Any such interpretation remains purely hypothetical, and quite arbitrary as well, since it has neither a basis in the works of Justin nor parallel in the procedure of other anti-Marcionite and antignostic writers."[88] Rather, in light of the tendencies of other antiheretical writers, "if we must speculate about Justin's reaction to the use of Paul by Marcion and other adversaries, the most plausible hypothesis would be that he studied the letters and explained them, not that he thrust them into a corner."[89]

This leaves the issue of whether the correspondences between Paul and Justin are strong enough to conclude that the apologist is drawing directly on Pauline texts. Here Rensberger's agnostic position, while not untenable, does represent a minority among current studies, and it is one that he himself holds with reservations. Though he follows Smit Sibinga's tentative conclusion that an intermediary source lies between Paul and Justin at *Dialogue* 95–96 (Gal 3:10-13), Rensberger concedes that "the evidence is hardly compelling" for this hypothesis,[90] and his objection that Justin's line of reasoning differs from Paul's in this passage seems less problematic in light of other patristic citations—such as Diognetus's use of 1 Corinthians 8:1—where not even the topic of discussion appears to correspond with the passage cited.[91] As with Deuteronomy in *Dialogue* 95–96, Rensberger recognizes that Justin's use of Abraham at *Dialogue* 23 "certainly represents a move beyond the Genesis text to the Christian world of Paul," as do *Dialogue* 92, 11, and 119.[92] Indeed, Rensberger

---

[87]Rensberger, "As the Apostle Teaches," 337.
[88]Rensberger, "As the Apostle Teaches," 361.
[89]Rensberger, "As the Apostle Teaches," 363.
[90]Rensberger, "As the Apostle Teaches," 182.
[91]See Diog. 12.3-5.
[92]Rensberger, "As the Apostle Teaches," 184-85.

acknowledges that in certain passages "the combination and form of the cited [OT] texts are so like Paul, and so unlike the Septuagint, that at first glance one can only think that Justin has borrowed them from him."[93] Rensberger continues, "Yet why should Justin, in all the length of the Dialogue with Trypho, never copy out a passage from Paul, except for quotations from the Old Testament?"[94] But further on he appears to find two answers for this question as well.

First, in relation to the Dialogue's audience, Rensberger notes that "Otto and C. Semisch already suggested the Jewish addressees of the Dialogue as a sufficient reason for not bringing up Paul,"[95] and continues, "One wonders what Justin would have said about Paul if he had spoken of him: that he was a Pharisee and persecutor of the church, who however became a Christian and taught us not to observe the Law? Trypho no doubt knew of one or two such persons himself (cf. Dial. 39.2), and is unlikely to have been impressed by the example."[96] Rensberger's suggestion that a Jewish audience would make explicit reference to Paul less likely[97] indeed finds attestation as far back as the second century: as Clement of Alexandria writes regarding Paul's authorship of Hebrews, "in writing to Hebrews who had conceived a prejudice against him and were suspicious of him, [Paul] very wisely did not repel them at the beginning by putting his name."[98] Second, as Rensberger recognizes (with reference to Stylianopoulos), Justin is consistent in his promise to Trypho to engage only agreed-on authorities, so that "even [Jesus] is not appealed to in the Dialogue" as an authority.[99] This accounts for the lack of explicit Pauline appeal, and while it is possible that Justin could "copy out a passage from Paul" (as he appears to do with his OT citations) and introduce it into the discussion without attribution, such a move would

---

[93]Rensberger, "As the Apostle Teaches," 168.
[94]Rensberger, "As the Apostle Teaches," 168.
[95]Rensberger, "As the Apostle Teaches," 188.
[96]Rensberger, "As the Apostle Teaches," 189.
[97]The same suggestion is made by von Harnack, who comments that Paul's name would have been a "disgusting hindrance" to the Jews; see Adolf von Harnack, Judentum und Judenchristentum in Justins Dialog mit Trypho (Leipzig: J. C. Hinrichs, 1913), 50, cited in Stylianopoulos, Justin Martyr, 71n61.
[98]Preserved in Hist. Eccl. 6.14.3.
[99]Rensberger, "As the Apostle Teaches," 189; cf. Stylianopoulos, Justin Martyr, 165.

seem likely to undermine the apologist's credibility with his readers in a
text where he pledges to refrain from "basing my arguments about Christ
upon writings which you [Trypho] do not recognize," and rather "only
upon those writings recognized by you until now as authentic"
(*Dial.* 120.5, translation adjusted; cf. 28.2, 71.2).

This proves to be the final piece of the puzzle: Justin's frequent echoes
of Paul—which even most agnostics admit to hearing, even if they believe them to come via secondary sources—must be allusive, and not
verbatim citation of texts, if Justin is to remain within the agreed-on
grounds of his debate. Justin's concern to remain within these grounds
can be witnessed throughout the *Dialogue*, beginning with his reticence
to mention the words of Jesus, which he does only briefly and apologeti-
cally at *Dialogue* 18.1, stating that to do so seems οὐκ ἄτοπον on the
grounds that Trypho had previously introduced them into the discussion
and attested to reading them (*Dial.* 10.2).[100] Similarly, Justin refuses to
engage on nonshared grounds in his discussion of disputed OT texts:
while stating his confidence in the LXX texts and translation, he continues, "But, since I know that all you Jews deny the authenticity of these
passages, I will not start a discussion about them, but I will limit the
controversy to those passages which you admit as genuine" (*Dial.* 71.2).[101]
Trypho attests elsewhere to the importance of Justin's consistency in
basing his arguments "only upon those writings" that his interlocutors
"recognize as authentic" (*Dial.* 120.5), admitting that he has only continued listening to Justin because of his strict focus in referring everything back to the Hebrew Scriptures (σοῦ λέγοντος οὐκ ἠνειχόμεθα, εἰ
μὴ πάντα ἐπὶ τὰς γραφὰς ἀνῆγες, *Dial.* 56.16). While one who considers
this debate to be fictional might counter that these ground rules are
themselves an invention of Justin, such an objection fails to recognize
that the written text of the *Dialogue* seeks to persuade not Trypho, but
rather Jews like Trypho who will encounter the text, and for whom strict
adherence to the authority of the Hebrew Scriptures—as Trypho makes

---

[100]Cf. Stylianopoulos, *Justin Martyr*, 71-72; Siker, *Disinheriting the Jews*, 251; Skarsaune, "Justin and
His Bible," 73n88.
[101]Cf. Allert, *Revelation, Truth, Canon*, 44.

clear in *Dialogue* 56.16—provides the only possible grounds for engage-ment.[102] If Justin is already carefully limiting the grounds of the debate to common authorities, to the point of even avoiding disputed OT texts, then direct citations of Paul's epistles would be among the very last sources one would expect Justin to introduce.

Such a recognition validates the observation of Rensberger and others that while so many passages appear tantalizingly close to Paul, the overlap between the texts curiously never appears to represent direct citation. Indeed, even if one follows the assertion of Skarsaune and others that Justin must have Galatians 3 before him in composing *Dialogue* 95–96 (which in my view is likely), it remains true that even here Justin avoids straightforward citation. What commentators have largely overlooked is that this avoidance is *deliberate* on Justin's part, and is indeed necessary for the integrity of Justin's argumentation—which he has agreed to base solely on common authorities—to be maintained.[103] Such an explanation affirms both the contention of the majority of commentators that Justin does draw on Pauline arguments, as well as the dissenting view that Jus-tin's usage does not constitute direct citation.[104] Rather, what one finds in the *Dialogue* is that Justin has absorbed the content of these Pauline ar-guments and restated them with his own words and arrangement, with much of the language and logical sequence naturally holding correspon-dence with Paul's own.

In summary, given the wide array of instances of apparent overlap with Pauline texts in the *Dialogue*, no a priori reasons—without prior assumption of the captivity narrative—to doubt Justin's usage of Paul, and clear positive reasons why Justin would not explicitly introduce or cite Paul within such a debate, such an explanation—whereby Justin draws on Pauline material without using direct citation, and instead

---

[102]Cf. Rokéah, *Justin Martyr and the Jews*, 9: "The sole and absolute authority of the Hebrew Bible is the common ground of the two parties (cf. 120: 5, 28: 2); the controversy between them is only over its correct interpretation."

[103]As Stylianopoulos notes, such a principle of exclusively citing the Old Testament is similarly adopted in Tertullian's *Against the Jews* (Stylianopoulos, *Justin Martyr*, 72).

[104]Cf. Foster, "Justin and Paul," 108: "Nowhere in Justin's extant writings . . . is there any direct citation of Paul's epistles unambiguously referenced by acknowledging the title or recipients of the letters."

restates the content of his arguments with his own words and arrangement—offers the fullest account for all the available evidence. This does not mean that every argument Justin uses in the *Dialogue* is Pauline, and attention is given in the following analysis to identify those areas that most clearly evidence Paul's influence. Nevertheless, for the purposes of this study, this analysis affirms the majority position that Justin's *Dialogue* does draw on relevant verses in Romans and Galatians, thus placing it within category (A).

Justin as Pauline interpreter. As with his usage of Paul, Justin's aptitude as a Pauline interpreter has been the subject of considerable debate, not least because Paul's meaning in many of the passages that Justin draws on is itself widely disputed among commentators. As a result, assessments of Justin as an interpreter of Paul are somewhat more varied than other patristic figures whose engagement with Paul centers on less controversial areas (such as the author of Diognetus), with more depending on the prior outline of Pauline theology held by the reader.[105] As an illustration, it is useful to examine two sides of one particular topic in recent debate: the relation between Jews and Gentiles and the question of supercessionism.

On the one hand, a number of contemporary readers identify Justin as drawing on Paul's arguments, but transforming them in a supersessionist and anti-Jewish direction. One prominent example is Werline, who holds that Justin uses Paul's arguments regarding Abraham in conjunction with other material in a way that alters Paul's meaning. For example, while beginning with Paul's arguments in Romans 4, Werline sees Justin as introducing Isaiah 63 at *Dialogue* 24 to show that "the Jews would reject Jesus and the Gentiles would accept him," and Matthew 8 at *Dialogue* 119–20 to "Mattheanize" Paul and demonstrate that Gentiles will inherit the promises to Abraham.[106] Further, with the twin phenomena of the two disastrous Jewish wars with Rome and the now-predominantly Gentile character of the church, Justin now interprets within a sociohistorical environment that differs significantly from Paul's

---

[105]Cf. especially Lindemann, *Paulus im ältesten Christentum*, 354-55.
[106]Werline, "Transformation of Pauline Arguments," 84, 86-87.

own context. As a result, whereas "Paul's writings discuss how both Jew and Gentile are on an equal footing," Justin shifts these arguments "to exclude Jews from the promises and God's mercy."[107] On the other hand, commentators who believe that Paul does not argue for an equal Jew-Gentile footing, but rather that Jews are disinherited apart from Christ, find far greater affinity between Justin and Paul. As one example, Rokéah's study finds Justin to be a very good Pauline interpreter (which for Rokéah is his chief demerit[108]), and contends that the change in sociohistorical environment has only allowed Justin to state Paul's theology more openly and explicitly than Paul could.[109] Justin thus "fulfilled Paul's vision," as "both claimed that the Gentiles are the heirs to the promises made by God to Abraham, while the Jews have fallen from their elevated status and been dispossessed because of their refusal to believe in Jesus as the Messiah."[110] Such an evaluation of Justin's Paulinism differs significantly from Werline's, illustrating the difficulty of making overarching statements regarding Justin's interpretive ability: Justin transforms Werline's Paul, but correctly exegetes the Paul of Rokéah.

However, while consensus on Justin's merit as a Pauline interpreter is difficult to arrive at, some general comments can be offered on Justin's usage of Paul's writings and the apostle's place in his theology. As Werline and Rokéah observe, Justin writes from a different context than Paul's own: while Paul operated within a Jewish movement that had begun incorporating Gentiles, Justin writes within a predominantly Gentile movement with a century of opposition from the Jews, who have themselves been defeated in two disastrous uprisings. This transition brings themes of God's judgment of the Jews to the foreground in Justin's writings in a more prominent manner than is found in Paul. Werline is also correct that Justin does not interpret Paul in isolation: the fact that

---

[107]Werline, "Transformation of Pauline Arguments," 92-93. Werline's argument requires balance from passages in Justin that emphasize Christ's welcome to the Jews, cf. *Dial.* 33.2: "Those circumcised persons who approach him with faith in their hearts and a prayer on their lips for his blessings will be welcomed and blessed by him." Cf. also *Dial.* 26.1.

[108]See Rokéah, *Justin Martyr and the Jews*, vii-viii.

[109]Cf. Rokéah, *Justin Martyr and the Jews*, vii.

[110]Rokéah, *Justin Martyr and the Jews*, vii. As with Werline, such an argument must be balanced by Justin's statements of the Messiah's continuing welcome of the Jews, cf. *Dial.* 33.2.

Justin can sometimes conjoin his restatements of Pauline arguments with prophetic texts or statements from Jesus hinders the search for a "pure" Paulinism, and not all of Justin's arguments about the law have direct correspondence in Paul's writings.[111] Nevertheless, Justin's value as a witness to Pauline theology should not be understated either. As Skarsaune observes, Justin's usage of Paul's epistles appears to far surpass his use of any other NT writings apart from Matthew and Luke.[112] Justin's proximity to Paul appears even in disputed matters regarding Jews and the law, such as Justin's conviction that those who are "weak" with respect to continued law observance should nevertheless be accepted by the strong (*Dial.* 47.2; cf. Rom 14:1-2).[113] In addition, Justin's own traditionalist instincts—witnessed especially in antiheretical passages like *Dialogue* 35—makes him a valuable witness to earlier Christian sources.[114] As Goodenough notes, "in his exposition of Christianity Justin's aim is not to expand or elaborate, but to reproduce the doctrines of Christianity as he had received them,"[115] and Barnard similarly concludes that Justin's self-understanding is not that of an innovator, but rather of "a traditionalist who was handing on the faith which had come down to him."[116]

THE LAW AND WORKS IN *DIALOGUE WITH TRYPHO*

Meaning: What works of what law? In Justin's *Dialogue*, the works in question between he and Trypho are those of the Mosaic law, which is first witnessed in Trypho's response to Justin's conversion story. After declining Justin's invitation to become acquainted with Christ, Trypho counters, "If you will listen to me (indeed I already think of you as a friend), first be circumcised, then observe the precepts concerning the

---

[111]See, for example, *Dial.* 23.5 on the gender limitation of circumcision.

[112]Skarsaune, "Justin and His Bible," 74-75.

[113]Dial. 47.2: ἀσθενὲς τῆς γνώμης . . . προσλαμβάνεσθαι; Rom 14:1: Τὸν δὲ ἀσθενοῦντα τῇ πίστει προσλαμβάνεσθε; cf. n123 below.

[114]See, for example, Skarsaune on Justin's exegesis: "When Justin expounds the OT, he does so as a pupil of the apostles; he is carrying on the OT exegesis they learnt from Christ. . . . Justin's idea [is] that his OT exegesis is something received, a tradition which for him derives from the highest authority" (Skarsaune, *Proof from Prophecy*, 12-13).

[115]Goodenough, *Theology of Justin Martyr*, 262.

[116]Barnard, *Justin Martyr*, 169.

Sabbath, the feasts, and God's new moons; in brief, fulfill the whole written law, and then, surely,[117] you will experience the mercy of God" (*Dial.* 8.3). Justin responds, "My friends, is there any accusation you have against us other than this, that we do not observe the Law, nor circumcise the flesh as your forefathers did, nor observe the Sabbath as you do? Or do you also condemn our customs and morals?" (10.1). Trypho affirms that his difficulty is neither with common accusations against Christians, nor Christ's precepts themselves (though he suspects that they are "so marvelous and great that I don't think that anyone could possibly keep them," 10.2):

> But this is what we are most puzzled about, that you who claim to be pious and believe yourselves to be different from the others do not segregate yourselves from them, nor do you observe a manner of life different from that of the Gentiles, in that you do not keep the feasts or Sabbaths, nor do you practice the rite of circumcision. You place your hope in a crucified man, and still expect to receive favors from God when you disregard his commandments. Have you not read that "the male who is not circumcised on the eighth day shall be eliminated from his people?" (Gen 17:14). This precept was for the stranger and purchased slave alike. But you, forthwith, scorn this covenant, spurn the commands that come afterwards, and then you try to convince us that you know God, when you fail to do those things that every God-fearing person would do. (10.3; translation adjusted from Falls)

These works of the Mosaic law—circumcision, Sabbath ordinances, feasts and new moons and festivals—constitute the basis of Justin and Trypho's disagreement throughout the *Dialogue*, with observances such as the sacrificial system, laws regarding food, and the building of the Temple also noted in the course of the discussion.[118] As with the debates between Paul

---

[117]There is an interpretive question regarding the word ἴσως, which translators render variously as "perhaps," "probably," and "surely." Stylianopoulos's discussion on this question makes a strong case for the third option as the most plausible, and though in my view the lexicographic evidence and the context of Trypho's argument still leaves ambiguity, I have followed his reading in this passage; cf. Stylianopoulos, *Justin Martyr*, 8n4; similarly Graham Stanton, "The Law of Moses and the Law of Christ: Galatians 3.1–6.2," in *Paul and the Mosaic Law*, ed. J. D. G. Dunn, WUNT 89 (Tübingen: Mohr Siebeck 1996), 105n19.

[118]Cf. *Dial.* 19–20, 92.4. In addition to these, Stylianopoulos notes that "in certain instances Justin seems unconsciously to include practices of the oral Law in his understanding of νόμος," such as "that the two goats of the Day of Atonement must be alike (*Dial.* 40.4)," which "is not found

and his interlocutors over works of the law, there is no apparent controversy between Justin and Trypho regarding the works that are in question, nor does explicit definition for Justin's terms seem to be necessary.[119]

As Rokéah notes, Justin exclusively uses the word νόμος to identify these disputed works in the *Dialogue*.[120] Further, Justin consistently avoids using νόμος to refer to other parts of the law, such as its moral precepts or the Pentateuch's narrative sections (for which he uses γραφή or γραφαί).[121] The works denoted by νόμος are further clarified by the contrast Justin sets up between these practices and the righteous deeds that please God. Following Trypho's insistence on physical circumcision and Sabbath observance in *Dialogue* 12, Justin counters that "such practices afford no pleasure to the Lord our God. . . . If there be a perjurer or thief among you, let him mend his ways; if there be an adulterer, let him repent; in this way he will have kept a true and peaceful Sabbath of God" (12.3). Similarly, Justin cites Isaiah 58:1-11 in *Dialogue* 15 to contrast Israel's fasts with the true fasting that God desires ("Share your bread among the hungry, and bring the needy and harborless into your house; when you see one naked, cover him"). Such practices correspond with the true circumcision, that of the heart (15.7), which Justin identifies elsewhere as the "spiritual circumcision" given to Christians in baptism (43.2; cf. Rom 2:29). While circumcision of the flesh benefits neither the Jews nor other circumcised nations for righteousness, Christians have received the "good and useful circumcision," possessed by those who know God and his Christ and keep "his lasting precepts of justice" (τὰ αἰώνια δίκαια, 28.4; cf. Rom 2:26). In *Dialogue* 45, Justin makes clear that his objections are not to the precepts in the Mosaic law that the righteous patriarchs observed, which "in themselves are good, and holy, and just" (τὰ φύσει καλὰ καὶ εὐσεβῆ καὶ δίκαια, 45.3-4). Rather, Justin speaks

---

in Leviticus but in the Mishnah (Yom. 6.1)," and also "with respect to the tassels and the teffilin ('phylacteries,' *Dial.* 46.5) which he treats just as he treats legal precepts of the Pentateuch." Due to his upbringing in Samaria, Stylianopoulos suggests that this "partial and unconscious identification of the written and the oral law is more by default than by intent." See Stylianopoulos, *Justin Martyr*, 48-50.

[119]Cf. Allert, *Revelation, Truth, Canon*, 170; Stylianopoulos, *Justin Martyr*, 59.

[120]Rokéah, *Justin Martyr and the Jews*, 45.

[121]Cf. Stylianopoulos, *Justin Martyr*, 50-51, 59.

specifically of the practices given to Israel following her national apostasy at Sinai, which the righteous patriarchs before Moses were not compelled to observe, but which were added because of the nation's hard-heartedness (45.3, 47.2; cf. 67.4, 8).[122] Though Justin does not believe that the continued practice of these Mosaic works (insofar as is possible with the destruction of the temple) automatically nullifies one's faith, if one insists on them for salvation, they themselves cannot be saved (46.1–47.1).[123]

Paul's influence on Justin's understanding of these works is most clearly seen in Justin's arguments regarding the justification of Abraham, in which his responses to Trypho parallel Paul's engagement with his interlocutors over "works of the law" in Romans and Galatians.[124] After arguing in *Dialogue* 23.3 that since "circumcision was not required before the time of Abraham, and if there was no need of Sabbaths, festivals, and sacrifices before Moses, they are not needed now" following Christ's advent, Justin presents an argument that closely follows Paul's use of Genesis 15 in Romans 4:3-11 and Galatians 3:5-9. "Indeed, while Abraham himself was still uncircumcised, he was justified and blessed by God because of his faith in him, as the Scriptures tell us. Furthermore, the Scriptures and the facts of the case force us to admit that Abraham received circumcision for a sign, and not for justification itself" (23.4). In *Dialogue* 92, Justin again reproduces a Pauline argument regarding Abraham's justification, with circumcision standing in place of "works of the law": "Abraham, indeed, was considered just, not by reason of his circumcision, but because of his faith. For, before his circumcision it was said of him, 'Abraham believed God, and it was reckoned to him as righteousness'" (92.3, translation adjusted; cf. Gen 15:6; Rom 4:3; Gal 3:6).

---

[122]Circumcision is the one work that does not fit neatly into this schema, which singles it out for special attention beginning at *Dial.* 16. Cf. also *Dial.* 93.1-2, where Justin more fully articulates the natural commandments that God has given to all people at all times.

[123]Justin continues that "if some, due to their weakness of mind (ἀσθενὲς τῆς γνώμης), desire to observe as many of the Mosaic precepts as possible . . . while at the same time they place their hope in Christ" and "desire to perform the eternal and natural acts of justice and piety," they should be received as brethren (*Dial.* 47.2, translation adjusted; cf. Rom 14:1-2). For the patristic interpretation of the "weak" in Romans 14 as Jews following the law, cf. Ambrosiaster, *Comm. Rom.* 14.1; Chrysostom, *Hom. Rom.* 14.1 (25); Theodoret, *Comm. Rom.* 14.1.

[124]Abraham is a key figure in Justin's argumentation; as Siker notes, Justin "appeals to Abraham over one hundred times" in the *Dialogue* (Siker, *Disinheriting the Jews*, 163).

This is followed by a commendation of circumcision of the heart in place of physical circumcision, echoing Paul in Romans 2:25, 29, along with a similar rejection of Sabbaths and offerings (92.4-5). In Justin's appropriation of Pauline arguments related to faith and justification from Romans and Galatians, it is these practices that are rejected in the place held by "works of the law."

Significance: What does the practice of these works signify? In Justin's *Dialogue*, the observance of the works of the Mosaic law carries a set of closely related meanings, including separation from the Gentiles, identification with the Jewish people, and participation in God's covenant with Israel. These are first witnessed in Trypho's initial set of objections to Justin in *Dialogue* 10, where he states that Jews are "most puzzled" that Christians "do not segregate yourselves from [others], nor do you observe a manner of life different from that of the Gentiles, in that you do not keep the feasts or Sabbaths, nor do you practice the rite of circumcision" (10.3, translation adjusted). The significance of these works as boundary markers that separate from the other nations and demarcate God's people, the Jews, is reinforced throughout the *Dialogue*, with circumcision being highlighted most frequently in this regard. As Justin states in *Dialogue* 16, "circumcision according to the flesh, which is from Abraham, was given for a sign; that you may be separated from other nations, and from us . . . for you are not recognised among the rest of men by any other mark than your fleshly circumcision" (16.2-3, ANF; see also 19.1-6, 92.3). The function of circumcision as making one a Jew is made explicit in discussion of the proselytes, who are "circumcised in order to be incorporated into the body of your [Trypho's] people like a native-born," while the rest are called Gentiles "because we are uncircumcised" (123.1). This identification as a Jew is closely linked with participation in the covenant that demarcates Israel's identity, with Trypho criticizing how Christians "scorn this covenant" and "spurn the commands that come afterwards" (10.3).[125] These issues—whether Christians need to separate from the Gentiles, practicing the Mosaic law in accordance with

---

[125]As Allert notes, "For Justin the Covenant and the Law belong together. He repeatedly combines the terms 'law' and 'covenant.' [11.2; 24.1; 34.1; 43.1; 122]" (Allert, *Revelation, Truth, Canon*, 169).

God's covenant with Israel and so becoming a part of the Jewish people—represent the substance of Justin and Trypho's disagreement over various works throughout the *Dialogue*. As with the issue of the precise works in question, there does not appear to be substantial controversy between Justin and Trypho regarding what is signified by practicing these works, with the nearest to disagreement being whether they were given for the sake of righteousness; Justin states from the outset that they were not (23.4-5, 46.2-5), and Trypho is eventually compelled to agree (67.4-11).

For the purposes of this study, it merits noting that Trypho's initial statement following Justin's conversion story can be interpreted as corresponding with an "old perspective" understanding of works of the law, with Trypho stating that Justin should receive circumcision and observe Sabbath and feast days, "in brief, fulfill the whole written law," so that "then, surely, you will experience the mercy of God" (8.3). Taken on its own, such a statement can be read as indicating that these works are practiced to gain favor with God as a sort of legalism.[126] Such a reading is difficult to substantiate in the text that follows, however, since (as seen above) the subsequent *Dialogue* indicates that these works are practiced not to win God's acceptance by one's own achievements,[127] but to be incorporated within the Jewish people and covenant (e.g., *Dial.* 123.1). Justin repeatedly characterizes Trypho's perspective as a reliance on ethnic heritage, which he rebuts in strikingly Pauline language in

---

[126]For the jump to "legalism" as Justin's target, see, e.g., Arnold, "Justification One Hundred Years After," 207: "Either Trypho was a legalistic Jew who believed that total obedience to the Law was necessary for salvation or Justin thought that this is what Jews believed and taught." Arnold, following Stanton, raises good questions over Sanders's "getting in/staying in" distinction in relation to this passage, with God's mercy following the adoption of these works in *Dial.* 8.3; see 214-15; Graham Stanton, "The Law of Moses and the Law of Christ: Galatians 3.1–6.2," in *Paul and the Mosaic Law*, ed. J. D. G. Dunn, WUNT 89 (Tübingen: Mohr Siebeck, 1996), 106. This is further complicated by the apparent reversal in sequence at *Dial.* 10.3, where Trypho describes these practices as "the commands that come afterwards" (τῶν ἔπειτα). Note also *Dial.* 95.3, where the sequence Justin presents to Trypho could also be subject to Arnold's charge: if Trypho repents, acknowledges Jesus to be the Christ, and observes his precepts, he will receive remission for his sins.

[127]See, e.g., Bultmann, "Christ the End of the Law," in *Essays Philosophical and Theological* (London: SCM, 1955 [1940]), 60; Douglas Moo, "Justification in Galatians," in *Understanding the Times: New Testament Studies in the 21st Century: Essays in Honor of D. A. Carson on the Occasion of His 65th Birthday*, ed. Andreas J. Köstenberger and Robert W. Yarbrough (Wheaton, IL: Crossway, 2011), 186.

Dialogue 44: "And you deceive yourselves while you imagine that, because you are the seed of Abraham after the flesh, therefore you shall fully inherit the good things announced to be bestowed by God through Christ. For no one, not even of them, has anything to look for, but only those who in mind are assimilated to the faith of Abraham" (44.1-2, ANF; cf. Rom 4:16, Gal 3:7).[128] Further, Justin's perspective on law keeping more broadly militates against the suggestion of legalism as a target, as Justin similarly believes the law is to be observed in its entirety (and reprimands the Jews for not doing so, *Dial.* 12.2-3). The difference between he and Trypho is that Justin understands this law to be Christ and his precepts, which have been delivered for all people and have relativized the old Torah (11.1-4). Justin thus counters Trypho's repeated commendations of the work of circumcision not by objecting to legalism, but rather by commending the work of baptism, which the new covenant prescribes as alone able to wash away sins (14.1-2; cf. 19.1-3, 29.1, 43.1-2), and contrasts the Mosaic law's prescribed fasts with the true fasts of setting the oppressed free, sharing bread with the hungry, bringing the needy into one's house, and clothing the naked (15.1-7; cf. 40.4).[129]

Opposition: Why are these works not necessary for the Christian? In the *Dialogue*, Justin presents a nexus of closely related arguments for why these works of the Mosaic law are not necessary for the Christian to practice. Though these reasons are usually presented in conjunction and are not easily separable, for the purposes of this study they will be distinguished from one another in what follows.

While Justin's reasons for why Christians do not follow the Mosaic law are presented in detail throughout the course of the *Dialogue*, many of them can be observed by examining Justin's opening statement at *Dialogue* 11, in which he responds to Trypho's request for an explanation for

---

[128]See also *Dial.* 125.5: "Expecting with assurance to be saved only because you are descendants of Jacob according to the flesh, you again deceive yourselves, as I have repeatedly shown"; *Dial.* 140.2: "They [the Jewish teachers] suppose that those who are descendants of Abraham according to the flesh will most certainly share in the eternal kingdom."

[129]See as well *Dial.* 141.2-3, where Justin cites Ps 32:2 (cf. Rom 4:8) to rebuke Trypho for thinking that one could attain forgiveness of sins simply by knowing God rather than by repenting with tears and lamentations like David.

why Christians claim to know God without observing the works of his covenant:

> And I answered him, "Trypho, there never will be, nor has there ever been from eternity, any other God except him who formed this universe. Furthermore, we do not claim that our God is different from yours, for he is the God who, with a strong hand and outstretched arm, led your forefathers out of Egypt. Nor have we placed our trust in any other (for, indeed, there is no other), but only in him whom you also trusted, the God of Abraham and of Isaac and of Jacob. But, our hope is not through Moses or through the Law, otherwise our customs would be the same as yours.
>
> "Now indeed, for I have read, Trypho, that there should be a definitive law and a covenant more binding than all others, which now must be respected by all those who aspire to the heritage of God. The law promulgated at Horeb is already obsolete, and was intended for you Jews only, whereas the law of which I speak is simply for all men. Now a later law in opposition to an older law abrogates the older; so, too, does a later covenant void an earlier one. An everlasting and final law, Christ himself, and a trustworthy covenant has been given to us, after which there shall be no law, or commandment, or precept.
>
> "Have you not read these words of Isaiah: 'Hear me, listen to me, my people; and give ear to me, you kings: for a law shall go forth from me, and my judgment shall be a light to the nations. My justice approaches swiftly, and my salvation shall go forth, and nations shall have hope in my arm?' (Isa 51:4-5). And concerning this new covenant, God spoke through Jeremiah thus: 'Behold the days shall come, said the Lord, and I will make a new covenant with the house of Israel, and with the house of Judah: it will not be like the covenant which I made with their fathers, in the day that I took them by the hand to lead them out of the land of Egypt' (Jer 31:31-32).
>
> "If, therefore, God predicted that he would make a new covenant, and this for a light to the nations, and we see and are convinced that, through the name of the crucified Jesus Christ, men have turned to God, leaving behind them idolatry and other sinful practices, and have kept the faith and have practiced piety even unto death, then everyone can clearly see from these deeds and the accompanying powerful miracles that he is indeed the New Law, the new covenant, and the expectation of those who, from every nation, have awaited the blessings of God.
>
> "We have been led to God through this crucified Christ, and we are the true spiritual Israel, and the descendants of Judah, Jacob, Isaac, and Abraham, who,

though uncircumcised, was approved and blessed by God because of his faith and was called the father of many nations. All this shall be proved as we proceed with our discussion." (11.1-5)

From this section, five main arguments can be distilled:

(1) In this passage, the first reason why Christians need not practice these works is the testimony of the Hebrew prophets: Justin attests to have read from them regarding the definitive law and covenant, and appeals to Isaiah 51:4-5 and Jeremiah 31:31-32 regarding God's promises for all nations in the new covenant (11.2-3). Such arguments from prophecy are the most common appeal in Justin's *Dialogue*, and as a category it is nearly impossible to separate it from the others that follow, as Justin adduces prophetic texts to undergird nearly all of his reasons for why Christians do not observe these works. Justin draws widely from across the Hebrew Scriptures for his argumentation, with appeals to Isaiah and the Psalms being especially frequent.[130] As Stylianopoulos notes, Justin "uses the Old Testament far more extensively than any of his Christian predecessors,"[131] and the testimony of its inspired authors is the foundational appeal in all of Justin's argumentation against these practices of the law.

(2) The second argument, established on the testimony of the prophets, is that "a definitive law and a covenant more binding than all others" is now in effect, "which now must be respected by all those who aspire to the heritage of God" (11.2). This means that "the law promulgated at Horeb is already obsolete," since "a later law in opposition to an older law abrogates the older," leaving no more requirement to practice these works of the former law (11.2). Justin commends this new law and its precepts to Trypho repeatedly throughout the *Dialogue*,[132] and often does

---

[130]See e.g. the lengthy citations of Is 52:10–54:6 at *Dial.* 13, Is 55:3-13 at *Dial.* 14, and Is 58:1-11 at *Dial.* 15, as well as Justin's ten-chapter exposition of Ps 22 at *Dial.* 97–106.

[131]Stylianopoulos, *Justin Martyr*, 1.

[132]Cf. *Dial.* 12.2-3, 14.1-5, 15.1–16.2, 34.1, 43.1, 51.3, 67.9-10, 118.3, 122.5. As Stylianopoulos notes, the new law is both Christ himself and his precepts, with Christ being both νόμος and νομοθέτης (cf. *Dial.* 11.2, 12.2-3; Stylianopoulos, *Justin Martyr*, 81-82). Stanton relates Justin's statements to Gal 6:2: in referencing "Christ as 'the new law,'" Justin has "in effect offered a profoundly christological interpretation of Paul's phrase: the 'law of Christ' is Christ himself" (Stanton, "What Is the Law," 317).

so using Pauline language, such as Justin's frequent commendations of the new covenant's prescription of circumcision of the heart through baptism, which God values over fleshly circumcision (cf. Rom 2:29).[133] This category of reasoning is arguably the most important in Justin's *Dialogue*,[134] as it reveals the true crux of the disagreement between Justin and Trypho, which in reality is not the practice of particular works of the Mosaic law, nor the question of whether God has promised a new covenant and law. Rather, as will be revisited later, the crux of the disagreement is whether Jesus is indeed the prophesied Messiah, the legislator of this promised new covenant.[135] The predominance of this question in the second half of the *Dialogue* reflects that this is the real issue that determines whether or not the works of the Mosaic law must still be observed.

(3) Closely linked with the new covenant's advent is the nature of this new covenant as promised to be for the nations, not simply for the Jews, which renders becoming a Jew by observing the Mosaic law unnecessary. As Justin argues in *Dialogue* 11.2, the Mosaic law given at Horeb "was intended for you Jews only, whereas the law of which I speak is simply for all men," with Isaiah cited as prophesying the recipients of this new law: "For a law shall go forth from me, and my judgment shall be a light to the nations" (Is 51:4-5; *Dial.* 11.3). This point is similarly restated and reinforced with prophecy throughout the *Dialogue*, such as Justin's citation of Micah 4:1-7 at *Dialogue* 109.1-3, in which the law goes forth from Zion in the last days, and nations beat their swords into plowshares and walk in the Lord's paths.[136] The universal nature of this new covenant is illustrated and confirmed for Justin by the fitness of its commandments for every nationality (67.10), which contrasts with those of the old covenant, which cannot even be fully observed by the Jewish nation following the destruction of the temple (46.2; cf. 40.5).

---

[133]See e.g. *Dial.* 92.4. On circumcision of the heart, see also *Dial.* 15.7–16.1, 41.2, 43.2, 113.6-7, 114.4.

[134]Cf. Stylianopoulos, *Justin Martyr*, 78.

[135]Cf. Justin's exhortation to Trypho early in the *Dialogue*: πάρεστιν ὁ νομοθέτης, καὶ οὐχ ὁρᾶτε ("The Lawgiver has come, and you do not see him"), *Dial.* 12.2.

[136]See also *Dial.* 42.1 (cf. Ps 19:4; Rom 10:19), 119.3-4 (cf. Zech 2:11; Is 65:1; Rom 4:17; 10:20), 121–22 (cf. Ps 72:17, 2:7-8; Is 49:6; 43:10, 49:8), 130 (cf. Deut 32:43).

(4) The advent of this prophesied covenant and law for all nations is confirmed by the witness of the lives of Christians, to which Justin often appeals in arguing that Christians need not adopt the old covenant and law. After professing his faith in the God of Trypho's ancestors, Justin notes that "our hope is not through Moses or through the Law, otherwise our customs would be the same as yours"; rather, "an everlasting and final law, Christ himself, and a trustworthy covenant has been given to us" (11.1-2). The reality of this reception is witnessed by the fact that through Christ, the nations "have turned to God, leaving behind them idolatry and other sinful practices, and have kept the faith and have practiced piety even unto death," confirming that he is the new law and covenant promised for all nations (11.4). Justin's assertion that "we have been led to God through this crucified Christ" (11.5) is difficult for Trypho to deny, as he attests to being perplexed at these former pagans who, while not obeying the comparatively easy dictates of the Mosaic law, nevertheless are transformed so as to "endure all sorts of tortures" for their faith (19.1).[137] Justin also appeals to the identity of those transformed, who comprise all nations, as fitting the description of those promised to the Messiah. Unlike Solomon, whom the Jews take as the referent of messianic passages like Psalm 72,[138] "you can find men of every nation who, for the name of Jesus have suffered, and still suffer, all kinds of torments rather than deny their belief in him" (121.2). For Justin, transformed lives such as these can only be explained as a work of God, and thus the arrival of the promised new covenant, which is delivered for all nations and abrogates the works of the old.[139]

(5) Finally, Justin appeals in this passage to the precedent of Abraham, "who, though uncircumcised, was approved and blessed by God because of his faith and was called the father of many nations,"[140] and through likeness to whom Christians are heirs and "the true spiritual Israel" (11.5). Paul's influence on Justin is especially evident in his arguments regarding

---

[137]Cf. *Dial.* 10.2-3.
[138]Cf. *Dial.* 34.3-7.
[139]See also *Dial.* 119.5-6, 131.2.
[140]Cf. Gen 15:6, Rom 4:9-10; Gen 17:5, Rom 4:17-18.

Abraham's justification. Like Paul in Romans 4 and Galatians 3, Justin is eager to make the sequential argument that Abraham's justification came by faith before and apart from his circumcision (11.5, 23.4, 27.5, 92.3), the work which stands as a sort of synecdoche in the *Dialogue* for the entire Mosaic legislation.[141] Justin similarly follows Paul in employing Abraham as the precedent for Christians:

> Abraham, indeed, was considered righteous, not by reason of his circumcision, but because of his faith. For, before his circumcision it was said of him, "Abraham believed God, and it was reckoned to him as righteousness" (Gen 15:6; cf. Rom 4:3, Gal 3:6). We also, therefore, because of our belief in God through Christ, even though we are uncircumcised in the flesh, have the salutary circumcision. (92.3-4, translation adjusted)

Just as Abraham was justified by faith apart from his reception of circumcision, so too do Christians exhibit a faith like Abraham's apart from circumcision and the Mosaic law, making them his true descendants, the "true spiritual Israel," with no need to become physical Jews to join his lineage (11.5).[142] Such arguments are restated many times in the *Dialogue*, with Paul's influence especially clear at *Dialogue* 119, where Justin states:

> And we shall inherit the Holy Land together with Abraham, receiving our inheritance for all eternity, because by our similar faith we have become children of Abraham. For, just as he believed the voice of God, and was thereby justified, so have we likewise believed the voice of God (which was spoken again to us by the prophets and the apostles of Christ), and have renounced all worldly things even to death. Thus, God promised Abraham a religious and righteous nation of like faith, and a delight to the Father; but it is not you, "in whom there is no faith." (119.5-6; cf. Deut 32:20, Rom 4:17-21, Gal 3:7-9)

Justin further bolsters his argument by noting the other patriarchs who were righteous apart from the Mosaic law (such as Judah, Jacob, and Isaac in 11.5) and the sign of circumcision (such as Abel, Enoch, Lot, Noah, and Melchisedek, 19.3-4; cf. 46.3). Like Abraham, these figures

---

[141]So rightly Arnold, "Justification One Hundred Years After," 219; Siker, *Disinheriting the Jews*, 164-65.

[142]See also *Dial.* 119.4 (cf. Rom 4:16-18).

demonstrate the lineage of Christians, who are similarly brought to God apart from the law and its works.

(6) Though the arguments witnessed in *Dialogue* 11 form the backbone of Justin's rationale against observing the works of the Mosaic law, a number of other arguments are found in the course of the *Dialogue*, including Justin's identification of the purposes for which these works were given. Justin's first move is to make clear that these works were not given for justification (or righteousness),[143] and here too Justin's links with Paul are evident. Immediately following his introduction of Abraham in *Dialogue* 23.4, Justin continues by restating Paul's argument in Romans 4:3-11: "Furthermore, the Scriptures and the facts of the case force us to admit that Abraham received circumcision for a sign, not for justification itself." This argument is repeated on the second day in *Dialogue* 92.3, where Justin states that "Abraham, indeed, was considered just, not by reason of his circumcision, but because of his faith," before citing the familiar text of Genesis 15:6. Justin similarly notes the many patriarchs before Abraham who were also righteous without these works, further illustrating that the purpose of circumcision and the Mosaic law cannot be to make one righteous before God.[144] Beyond these familiar arguments, Justin demonstrates this point by noting that the female sex is unable to receive fleshly circumcision, and yet God calls them equally to observe everything that is righteous and virtuous, so that logically physical circumcision cannot be a work pertaining to righteousness.[145] This point regarding the purpose of circumcision is further illustrated in *Dialogue* 28.3-4, where Justin cites Jeremiah 9:25-26 in arguing that circumcision does not confer justification to those Egyptians, Moabites, or Edomites who have undergone it either.

Having demonstrated that the works of the law were not given for righteousness, Justin identifies two positive purposes for which these

---

[143]Here Sanders's "righteousing" for δικαιόω may better serve as a verbal counterpart for δικαιοσύνη (righteousness), as the two words are closely linked in the *Dialogue*; see for example *Dial.* 23, 92.

[144]Cf. *Dial.* 19.1-2, 23.1, 27.5, 43.1-2, 67.7-8, 92.2, 137.1.

[145]*Dial.* 23.5. Cohen identifies a similar argument on the exclusivity of circumcision implicit in Gal 3:28; cf. Shaye J. D. Cohen, *Why Aren't Jewish Women Circumcised? Gender and Covenant in Judaism* (Berkeley: University of California Press, 2005), 72.

works were given. First, the Mosaic legislation was given on account of the hardness of Israel's heart: as Justin tells Trypho, "we, too, would observe your circumcision of the flesh, your Sabbath days, and, in a word, all your festivals, if we were not aware of the reason why they were imposed upon you, namely, because of your sins and your hardness of heart" (18.2). This hard-heartedness was demonstrated in the golden calf incident at Sinai, in response to which "God, adapting his laws to that weak people, ordered you to offer sacrifices to his name, in order to save you from idolatry," and "imposed the observance of Sabbaths . . . so that you would be forced to remember him" (19.5-6).[146] Israel's hard-heartedness as the reason for this law is a constant refrain in the *Dialogue*,[147] and one with which Trypho is ultimately compelled to agree (67.8).[148] While the nature of this law is beneficent, prescribing works to prevent Israel from falling into further wickedness,[149] it could not go so far as to actually produce righteousness, which Justin demonstrates in *Dialogue* 27.3 by employing the same catena of OT texts that Paul uses in Romans 3:11-17 to show Israel's sinfulness despite her possession of the law. In contrast to Israel, Christians have been given the new circumcised heart and have no need for these precepts: as Justin argues in *Dialogue* 19.3, "you Jews, who have the circumcision of the flesh, are in great need of our circumcision, whereas we, since we have our circumcision, do not need yours." Second, Justin identifies another specific purpose for the work of circumcision, which antedates the Mosaic legislation: to demarcate and separate the Jewish people from the rest of the nations, so that they alone would suffer the consequences of their rebellions and violence against Christ and

---

[146]Commentators note that this emphasis on the law's historical function for the Jews, vis-à-vis the emphasis of earlier writers like Barnabas on the law's allegorical meaning, is made with an eye toward Marcion's dismissal of the law, cf. Stylianopoulos, *Justin Martyr*, 155; Skarsaune, *Proof from Prophecy*, 259n10.

[147]Cf. Stylianopoulos: "Whenever in his lengthy exposition he brings to the surface the question of why the Law was originally given . . . the answer is always the same: διὰ τὸ σκληροκάρδιον τοῦ λαοῦ ὑμῶν" (Stylianopoulos, *Justin Martyr*, 68). See e.g. *Dial.* 27.2, 43.1, 44.2.

[148]As Justin notes, to say otherwise would be to attribute inconsistency to God, saying that "God does not wish each succeeding generation of humanity to perform the same acts of righteousness" (*Dial.* 23.1, cf. 92.2).

[149]With Stylianopoulos, *Justin Martyr*, 159-60 against Goodenough, *Theology of Justin Martyr*, 117, who had argued that the law was simply a reproach to Israel; cf. *Dial.* 67.8.

Christians (16.2-4; cf. 19.2, 92.2). This "punitive" understanding of circumcision's purpose draws on the recent edict of Hadrian in expelling all Jews from Jerusalem (for which Justin surmises circumcision to be the means of screening, as "the only mark by which you can certainly be distinguished from other men"[150]), and he and Trypho's shared belief in God's foreknowledge and justice (16.3).[151] As Christians have repented of their sins and are not liable for Christ's death, they have no reason to take on themselves this mark of judgment.

(7) Further, and closely related to these arguments, Justin asserts that the prophets themselves foretell that the Jews will come to be rejected by God, which makes becoming a Jew by practicing these works unimaginable for Christians. This theme is witnessed in Justin's citation of Deuteronomy 32:16-23 in *Dialogue* 119.2, in which God rebukes Israel for her idolatry and wickedness and announces that he will turn his face away, moving her to jealousy "with that which is no people" and heaping evils on her. This rejection is revisited in Justin's citations of Isaiah in *Dialogue* 133.2-5, in which the prophet foresees Israel's guilt in binding the Just One (Is 3:9-15 LXX), and how "their corpses became as dung in the middle of the street" because of God's judgment, yet they do not repent (Is 5:18-25). Though the argument is made less frequently and explicitly than others, to become a Jew for Justin is inconceivable after this prophesied rejection has come to pass, a rejection that is manifest in the historical events from which Trypho and his companions have fled, which for Justin and Trypho cannot be outside of God's providential work.[152]

(8) Though less central than other arguments, Justin also points out imperfections in the Mosaic law that indicate it is not the "blameless law" mentioned in Psalm 19:8 (as Trypho supposes), which instead refers to God's promised eternal law and new covenant (*Dial.* 34.1). First, Justin points to the ineffectiveness of the old law: while its baptisms can only cleanse the flesh and body, it is the baptism of Christ prophesied by

---

[150]Stylianopoulos, *Justin Martyr*, 139-40; cf. Falls, *Dialogue with Trypho*, 27n22.
[151]Cf. Werline, "Transformation of Pauline Arguments," 90.
[152]Cf. *Dial.* 92.2

Isaiah "which alone can purify penitents" for the forgiveness of sins (13.1–14.1, Is 52:10–54.6).[153] Next, Justin points to inconsistencies in the Torah's prescriptions that make clear it is not the eternal and perfect law, such as high priests having to sin to perform oblations on the Sabbath, or the contradiction faced when a child is to be circumcised on an eighth day that falls on a Sabbath (27.5; cf. 29.3). Justin describes the old covenant as "delivered to your [Trypho's] ancestors amid such fear and trembling that they could not listen to God," which Justin identifies as a point in which the new covenant promised through Jeremiah is "different from the old one" (67.9-10, cf. Jer 31:32). Finally, Justin identifies "the Law laid down by Moses" as bringing a curse, citing Deuteronomy 27:26 (cf. Gal 3:10, 13), and notes that "not even you [Trypho] will dare to assert that anyone ever fulfilled all the precepts of the Law exactly; some have kept them more than others, some less" (95.1).[154] By contrast, Christ has "shoulder[ed] the curses of the whole human race" and healed humankind by his wounds (Is 53:3), offering remission of sins to those who acknowledge him and observe his precepts (95.2-3).

(9) Justin also presents arguments regarding the need for spiritual understanding to rightly interpret the old law, though these are similarly underdeveloped in the *Dialogue* in comparison to Justin's more prominent arguments. Justin often refers to the need for God's grace to be able to correctly interpret the mysteries of Scripture,[155] a grace which he attests to have received.[156] With such grace, he is able to identify the

---

[153]See also *Dial.* 122.5, where building on their agreement that God has promised a new covenant, Justin asks Trypho, "If the Law had the power to enlighten the Gentiles and all those who possess it, what need would there be for a new covenant?"

[154]Though Justin only views this law and curse as applying directly to Israel, the cursing principle itself can be extended, as he continues, "But, if those who are subject to the Law are certainly under a curse, because they have not kept the whole Law, how much more so will all the Gentiles evidently be cursed, since they commit idolatry, seduce youths, and perform other wicked deeds?" (*Dial.* 95.1). While not strictly under Israel's curse, such deeds are also worthy of a curse (cf. 94.5) that is to be borne by Christ, who brings healing that the Mosaic law cannot provide (95.2-3). The removal of humanity's curses does not mean a removal from the realm of Christ's judgment (cf. 47.5), nor would performing this law perfectly have brought justification (e.g., 23, 92)

[155]*Dial.* 7.3, 30.1, 39.2-5, 92.1, 119.1.

[156]*Dial.* 58.1. This gift of interpretation may be implied in *Dial.* 44.2, though Justin's gift is not yet mentioned in the text.

"symbolic meaning" (τὸ σύμβολον) of practices like the eating of un-leavened bread, which in reality represents an injunction to "not commit the old deeds of the bad leaven" (such as anger, avarice, and jealousy, 14.2). By contrast, Trypho and the Jews "understand everything in a carnal way," and "deem yourselves religious if you perform such deeds, even when your souls are filled with deceit and every other kind of sin" (14.2). Justin's gift of interpretation is also witnessed in matters like the lamb of Passover, which God ordained as a type of Christ until the fore-ordained time when Christ would suffer and the temple be destroyed, thus ending all such sacrifices (40.1-3); the two identical goats offered during the fast, representing the two comings of Christ (40.4); and the offering of flour for those cleansed from leprosy, representing a type of the bread of the Eucharist (41.1). In reprising these interpretations later, Justin complains that Trypho explains these passages "in an earthly manner [ταπεινῶς], imputing to God every sort of weakness, when you interpret them literally [ψιλῶς] without analyzing the spirit of the words" (112.1). However, while it appears that knowing the true spiritual meaning of such practices renders their literal practice unnecessary, the point does not bear significant weight in the course of Justin's *Dialogue*.

Finally, it merits restating that for Justin, the identity of Jesus as the Christ is actually the most fundamental reason why Christians do not obey the works of the Mosaic law. While Justin and Trypho's initial con-flict is over the nonobservance of specific works like circumcision, it be-comes clear in the course of the discussion that both figures agree that God has promised a new law and covenant, to be inaugurated by the new lawgiver, the Messiah. This then means the true point of conflict between Justin and Trypho is whether or not Jesus is the Christ; and if he is, then both agree that his precepts will constitute the new law that will relativize the old.[157] As a result, a conflict beginning over works of the law soon becomes one devoted almost exclusively to the question of whether Jesus is this promised Messiah, a logical progression similarly witnessed in later works like Tertullian's *Against the Jews*.

---

[157]Cf. *Dial.* 67.10-11.

CONCLUSION

In the *Dialogue with Trypho*, the works in question between Justin and Trypho are the precepts of the Mosaic law, such as circumcision, Sabbath keeping, calendar observances like feasts and new moons, sacrifices, laws regarding food, and the building of the temple. Justin is careful to distinguish such works, denoted with the word νόμος, from those natural and universally good practices given "for the worship of God and the practice of virtue" (44.2). The practice of the works of the law in the *Dialogue* represents separation from the Gentiles, identification with the Jewish people, and participation in God's covenant with Israel. Justin's manifold argumentation for why Christians do not observe these works can be divided into nine categories, in roughly descending order of prominence: (1) the witness of the Hebrew prophets; (2) the arrival of the new law and covenant; (3) the new covenant's nature as for all nations; (4) the lives and experiences of Christians in confirming the new covenant's arrival; (5) the example of Abraham, who was justified without such works, and in whose faith Christians now share as his descendants; (6) the law's purpose as given not for justification, but to constrain hard-hearted Israel and identify her for God's judgment; (7) the prophets' testimony that the Jews will be rejected; (8) imperfections in the old law and covenant; and (9) the need for spiritual understanding to rightly interpret the old law. Interestingly, it becomes evident in the course of the *Dialogue* that Justin and Trypho's debate over works of the law is actually subordinate to, and governed by, the question of whether Jesus is the Christ, the new lawgiver. While the *Dialogue*'s function and audience prevent the apologist from directly appealing to Paul (and indeed all other such authorities), the apostle's influence nevertheless pervades Justin's argumentation against the works of the law, providing a fascinating window into Pauline interpretation on this issue in the mid-second century.

10

MELITO OF SARDIS (B)

Peri Pascha

□

INTRODUCTION

Introduction and background. This study's next source is *On the Pascha* (or *Peri Pascha*, *PP*), a paschal homily attributed to Melito, bishop of Sardis. Written around AD 160–170 and rediscovered in the mid-twentieth century, the homily recounts the story of Israel's Passover as typologically prefiguring the events of Christ's death and resurrection. While not using the phrase *works of the law*, Melito draws on distinct Pauline ideas and alludes to Galatians 4 at the close of a section contrasting the law and the gospel (*PP* 35–45), making his homily relevant as supporting evidence (B) for the understanding of works of the law in this period.

Eusebius introduces Melito as the bishop of Sardis, who wrote an apology defending the faith to Emperor Marcus Aurelius, along with numerous other works.[1] Additional details on Melito can be found in Polycrates's letter to Pope Victor in defense of Quartodeciman practice (ca. 190), in which Easter is celebrated on the same day as the Jewish Passover (14 Nisan).[2] After citing a succession of authorities including the apostle Philip, the beloved disciple John, and Polycarp of Smyrna, Polycrates

---

[1]*Hist. Eccl.* 4.26.1-2. Melito's identity as bishop is occasionally questioned (since Polycrates does not note it), though such omissions are not unusual; see Othmar Perler, trans., *Sur la Pâque et fragments*, Sources Chrétiennes 123 (Paris: Éditions du Cerf, 1966), 8-9.

[2]*Hist. Eccl.* 5.24.1-8.

completes his list with "Melito the eunuch, who lived entirely in the Holy Spirit, who lies in Sardis."[3] The first known pilgrim to the holy land, Melito attests to traveling to the east to learn the Jewish canon firsthand and gather testimonies from the law and prophets regarding Christ.[4] Melito was also noted as an orator,[5] and Wilson observes that his homily is "a work of art as well as a work of theological reflection."[6]

Melito's works were only known in fragmentary form until the 1930s, when *Peri Pascha* was discovered among the Chester Beatty papyri, with a second Greek copy being found in the Bodmer papyri shortly thereafter. There are outstanding questions regarding the relation of the rediscovered text to the two books on the Passover reported by Eusebius (τὰ Περὶ τοῦ πάσχα δύο, *Hist. Eccl.* 4.26.2). Hall's argument that the break at *PP* 45 marks the division between the two books attested to by Eusebius, while possible, is not entirely conclusive; though there is a break in the text, the work itself still reads naturally as a unified whole.[7] Pseftogas offers the thesis that *In Sanctum Pascha* (*IP*)—which, like *Peri Pascha*, expounds Exodus 12 and begins with the statement ὁ μὲν γὰρ τύπος ἐγένετο, ἡ δὲ ἀλήθεια ηὑρίσκετο (*IP* 2, *PP* 5)—is actually the first of Melito's two books.[8] While intriguing, the evidence for the theory is too

---

[3]*Hist. Eccl.* 5.24.5. The reference to living "in the Holy Spirit" indicates Melito was regarded as a prophetic figure like the daughters of Philip, who are described in the same way (*Hist. Eccl.* 5.24.2). Tertullian (via Jerome) confirms this picture, writing that many thought Melito to be a prophet (*Vir. ill.* 24).

[4]*Hist. Eccl.* 4.26.13-14.

[5]Tertullian (again via Jerome) satirically notes Melito's "fine oratorical genius" (*Vir. ill.* 24); cf. Campbell Bonner, *The Homily on the Passion by Melito Bishop of Sardis* (London: Christophers, 1940), 20.

[6]S. G. Wilson, *Related Strangers: Jews and Christians, 70–170 C.E.* (Minneapolis: Fortress Press, 1995), 251. On Melito's rhetorical style, see Alistair Stewart-Sykes, trans., *On Pascha: With the Fragments of Melito and Other Material Related to the Quartodecimans* (Crestwood, NY: St. Vladimir's Seminary Press, 2001), 14-17.

[7]Hall's suggestion that the doxology at *PP* 45 marks the break between books is complicated by the presence of identical doxologies at *PP* 10 and 65; see Stuart George Hall, trans., *On Pascha and Fragments* (Oxford: Clarendon Press, 1979), xxii.

[8]*In Sanctum Pascha* is a paschal homily traditionally attributed to Chrysostom or Hippolytus, which Cantalamessa has argued to originate from Asia Minor in the second century (a judgment Pseftogas follows; cf. Raniero Cantalamessa, "Méliton de Sardes. Une christologie antignostique du IIe siècle," *Revue des Sciences Religieuses* 37 [1963]: 1-26). For a summary of Pseftogas's argument, see Vassilios Pseftogas, *Melitonos Sardeon: Ta peri tou Pascha duo* (Thessaloniki: Patriarchikon Hidryma Paterikon Meleton, 1971), 244-47.

fragmentary for it to be adopted with confidence. Cohick doubts that the text is to be identified with Melito at all, pointing to the absence of the introductory chronological note cited by Eusebius from the extant manuscripts.[9] Against this, however, the style of *PP* appears to be consistent with that of Melito's fragments, and commentators have been undeterred in continuing to identify this distinctive example of Christian oratory with the figure whose "fine oratorical genius" Tertullian notes.[10] The safest judgment is that the rediscovered text of *PP* represents at least one of Melito's two books attested by Eusebius, with the second being *PP* 46–105 or another work, whether *IP* or one currently unknown. Eusebius's introductory chronological note would date *PP* "under Servillius Paulus proconsul of Asia," an otherwise unknown figure. However, Rufinus preserves the note as "Sergius Paulus," who was consul in Asia for the second time in 168 (with the first likely earlier in the decade), and Servilius Pudens (who was consul in 166) is also suggested as a possible candidate.[11] These proposed identifications lead commentators to a rough dating of approximately 160–170, which is adopted here.[12]

A number of theories regarding Melito's context and identity have been suggested to provide insight into the homily, and in particular its severe rhetoric against Israel in *PP* 72–99. While each of these holds potential value in shedding light on Melito's text, they are also based on inferences and are widely contested among commentators. Sardis was home to a well-integrated Jewish community and an enormous synagogue (the largest known in antiquity), leading Kraabel to suggest that Melito's rhetoric can be explained sociologically as a reaction by the weaker Christian congregation against the socially influential Jews.[13] However,

---

[9]Lynn Cohick, "Melito of Sardis's 'Peri Pascha' and Its 'Israel,'" *Harvard Theological Review* 91 (1998): 356-57.

[10]Cf. *Vir. ill.* 24. On the chronological note, Perler, *Sur la Pâque*, 19 mentions similar notices at the beginning of Augustine's sermons "qui, pour la plupart, ont été omises par les copistes" ("which, for the most part, have been omitted by the copyists"), though Eusebius's particular interest in chronology would have led him to cite it.

[11]*Hist. Eccl.* 4.26.3; cf. Perler, *Sur la Pâque*, 23-24; Hall, *On Pascha and Fragments*, xxi.

[12]Perler, *Sur la Pâque*, 24; Hall, *On Pascha and Fragments*, xxii.

[13]See, e.g., A. T. Kraabel, "Melito the Bishop and the Synagogue at Sardis: Text and Context," in *Studies Presented to G. M. A. Hanfmann*, ed. D. G. Mitten (Mainz: Zabern, 1971), 77-83; cf. also Josephus, *Ant.* 14.235, 16.171.

Stewart-Sykes notes that the building in question only became a synagogue in the fourth century,[14] and Lieu cautions that social reconstructions such as Kraabel's rely too heavily on "scholarly imagination."[15] Melito's own identity has been suggested as an explanation for the motivations behind his writing, with Stewart-Sykes contending that Melito is a converted Jew, making the conflict in *Peri Pascha* between "a heterodox form of Judaism" and "mainstream Judaism."[16] Others like Cohick reject this as without warrant in the text, and because Stewart-Sykes's argument relies on major inferences from the succession list in Polycrates's letter, a confident assertion either way is not possible.[17] Melito's Quartodecimanism has also been suggested as a key toward understanding his approach toward the Jews. As Wilson writes, Melito "would have been under considerable pressure to distinguish the Christian from the Jewish festival and to avoid the charge of judaizing," with the shared feast day with the Jews leading to "a determined effort to establish distance" in other areas, "to separate the old from the new Passover, the Church from Israel."[18] However, as Cohick observes, "nothing in the homily itself hints at typical Quartodeciman issues, such as interest in fasting or dating Easter,"[19] and Hall further notes that the homily "was dispersed and used in parts of the world where Quartodeciman practice was not found, and was certainly copied and used long after the practice was generally condemned."[20] In

---

[14]Stewart-Sykes, *On Pascha*, 13.

[15]Judith Lieu, *Image and Reality: The Jews in the World of the Christians in the Second Century* (London: T&T Clark, 1996), 228; cf. Alistair Stewart-Sykes, "Melito's Anti-Judaism," *Journal of Early Christian Studies* 5 (1997): 272-73.

[16]Stewart-Sykes, *On Pascha*, 26-27; cf. Stewart-Sykes, "Melito's Anti-Judaism," 278: "The conversion may have been seen by Melito as a move within Judaism."

[17]Lynn Cohick, *The Peri Pascha Attributed to Melito of Sardis: Setting, Purpose, and Sources* (Providence, RI: Brown Judaic Studies, 2000), 14-15. Cohick swings to the opposite extreme, contending that the homily "does not reflect any second- or third-century rivalry between Jews and Christians but rather highlights the developing theological arguments concerning identity among Christians," though the explanation that the author creates "a hypothetical 'Israel' . . . largely for rhetorical purposes" has not won wide support (Cohick, "Melito of Sardis's 'Peri Pascha,'" 371-72).

[18]S. G. Wilson, "Passover, Easter, and Anti-Judaism: Melito of Sardis and the Others," in *"To See Ourselves as Others See Us": Christians, Jews, "Others" in Late Antiquity*, ed. Jacob Neusner and Ernest S. Frerichs (Chico, CA: Scholars Press, 1985), 350.

[19]Cohick, "Melito of Sardis's 'Peri Pascha,'" 355; cf. Perler, *Sur la Pâque*, 20.

[20]Hall, *On Pascha and Fragments*, xxv. Note as well that similar divisions between the church and Israel are not uncommon in other (ostensibly non-Quartodeciman) early sources.

sum, caution should be exercised in placing substantial weight on any of these theories, though it means that questions regarding Melito's context and identity must remain more open-ended than we would like.

Text and translation. The text of Melito's *Peri Pascha* is reconstructed primarily from the fourth-century Chester Beatty and Michigan papyrus (A) and the third or fourth-century Papyrus Bodmer XIII (B). Secondary witnesses include a small Oxyrhynchus fragment and a number of Coptic, Georgian, Latin, and Syriac fragments. This chapter uses Hall's critical edition for the Greek text and follows his English translations, except where noted.[21]

MELITO AND PAUL

Knowledge and use of Paul. Melito's usage of Paul has attracted surprisingly little research: *Paul and the Second Century* does not include a chapter on Melito, Lindemann's study ends just before reaching him, and Rensberger's thesis devotes one page to the question, commenting that it is "rather disappointing to observe that there are no citations or even very clear reminiscences of Paul" in an uncharacteristically cursory overview.[22]

The major exception to this trend is Dassmann's study. In Melito's description of the outworking of Adam's sin in *PP* 50, 53f., Dassmann remarks that "unverkennbar sind die Übereinstimmungen mit Röm 1,21/32, insbesondere mit den Versen 24 und 26f.,"[23] and finds "das Verständnis der Sünde als personifiziert gedachter Unheilsmacht, die als Handlangerin des Todes diesem den Weg bereitet"[24] to be inspired by Paul in Romans 5 and 7.[25] As with his understanding of sin, "ebenfalls von Paulus inspiriert ist Melitons heilsgeschichtliches Denken,"[26] particularly in his

---

[21]Hall, *On Pascha and Fragments.*

[22]David Rensberger, "As the Apostle Teaches: The Development of the Use of Paul's Letters in Second-Century Christianity" (PhD diss., Yale University, 1981), 306: "The best [parallel] is at Pascha 45, where the κάτω and ἄνω Jerusalem are contrasted; cf. Gal 4:26, but the likelihood of an allusion is small."

[23]"Unmistakable are the correspondences with Rom 1:23-32, especially with verses 24 and 26f."

[24]"The understanding of sin considered as a personified damning power, which, as a henchman of death, prepares the way for it."

[25]Ernst Dassmann, *Der Stachel im Fleisch: Paulus in der frühchristlichen Literatur bis Irenäus* (Münster: Aschendorff, 1979), 289-90.

[26]"Likewise inspired by Paul is Melito's salvation-historical thinking."

usage of Adam-Christ parallelism in the homily (cf. Rom 5; 1 Cor 15).[27] According to Dassmann, Melito interprets "die Grundzüge der paulinischen Soteriologie"[28] in conjunction with other sources, particularly John, and similarly relies on Paul and John for his understanding of the law.[29] While cautioning that such correspondences alone do not make Melito "zu einem paulinischen Theologen,"[30] Dassmann writes that Melito nevertheless serves as a prelude to the heralded Irenaeus in his usage of Paul, and may have merited a similarly prominent position in the history of Pauline reception had more of his works survived.[31]

Dassmann's judgment corresponds with the findings of the critical editions of *Peri Pascha*. Bonner's *editio princeps* identifies the most prominent Pauline allusions as Galatians 4:25-26 at *PP* 45; Ephesians 1:7, Colossians 1:14, and 1 Corinthians 5:7 at *PP* 103; and Romans 8:29 and Colossians 1:15 with *PP* 82.[32] In addition to identifying a number of Pauline allusions,[33] Blank's German edition notes the influence of Paul in the structure of Melito's thought, commenting on *Peri Pascha* that "hier wohl erstmalig die bei Paulus (Röm 5, 1 Kor 15) angelegte Adam-Christus-Parallele in systematischem Zusammenhang entfaltet und eine christologische Schau der gesamten Heilsgeschichte versucht [wird]."[34] Blank identifies Paul and

---

[27]Dassmann, *Der Stachel im Fleisch*, 290.

[28]"The basics of Pauline soteriology."

[29]Dassmann, *Der Stachel im Fleisch*, 290-91: "Wenn Meliton vom Gesetz spricht, denkt er ebenfalls paulinisch und johanneisch." ("When Melito speaks of the law, his thought is likewise Pauline and Johannine.") In addition to adopting Paul's typological scheme, Dassmann identifies echoes of Paul at 1 Cor 8:6; Eph. 4.10; Col 1:15-17; and 2 Cor 5:17 (Dassmann, *Der Stachel im Fleisch*, 291-92).

[30]"Into a Pauline theologian."

[31]Dassmann, *Der Stachel im Fleisch*, 292. Dassmann's overall findings echo Tsakonas's prior study, which identified a number of parallels and even explicit Pauline references (such as Rom 8:21 and Gal 4:24, 5:1 at *PP* 45 and 70-71), cf. Basil G. Tsakonas, "The Usage of the Scriptures in the Homily of Melito of Sardis on the Passion," *Theologia* 38 (1967): 614-16.

[32]Bonner, *Homily on the Passion*, 40.

[33]E.g. Rom 10:4; 13:10 at *PP* 40; Rom 8:4 at *PP* 42; Rom 1:21-32 at *PP* 49; Gal 3:13 at *PP* 70; 1 Cor 8:6 at *PP* 5.

[34]"Here for the first time the Adam-Christ parallel developed by Paul (Rom 5, 1 Cor 15) unfolds in a systematic context and a christological exhibition of the whole of salvation-history is attempted." Josef Blank, trans, *Vom Passa: die älteste christliche Osterpredigt* (Freiburg: Lambertus-Verlag, 1963), 44. Cf. 67 on *PP* 46-47: "Offensichtlich folgt hier Meliton jenem 'Schema,' das durch die Adam-Christus-Parallele in Rom 5 (auch 1 Kor 15) von Paulus grundgelegt war." ("Obviously Melito here follows that 'pattern' which was established by Paul's Adam-Christ parallel in Rom 5 [also 1 Cor 15].")

John as Melito's primary theological resources, seeing Melito as using νόμος "im paulinischen und johanneischen Sinn" (*PP* 3-4),[35] and noting "in seiner Theologie sind Tod und Sünde die Unheilsmächte schlechthin, darin steht er in der Linie von Paulus und Johannes."[36] Perler's edition similarly notes Paul's influence on Melito's understanding of sin in *PP* 50: "« Le Péché », principe, puissance du mal qui règne depuis Adam, est personnifié ici et dans la suite . . . Méliton s'inspire visiblement de S. Paul, surtout de la lettre aux Romains, chap. 5-8."[37] In addition, Perler observes Melito to be following Paul (2 Cor 1:21-22; *PP* 67) in his description of baptism and the reception of the Spirit,[38] which are the antitypes of Israel's sealing (ἐσφράγισεν) and anointing (χρίσατε) at the exodus (*PP* 14-17).[39] Perler also identifies Romans 1:26f. as "[l]a source biblique de Méliton" in his tracing of humanity's downward spiral of sexual transgressions in *PP* 53.[40] Ibañez and Mendoza's Spanish edition identifies an array of unclassed parallels with Pauline texts in *Peri Pascha*, including twenty passages from Romans and six from Galatians, though the only passage noted as an explicit citation is the thrice-used doxology of Galatians 1:5 (ᾧ ἡ δόξα εἰς τοὺς αἰῶνας [τῶν αἰώνων], ἀμήν; cf. 2 Tim 4:18; *PP* 10, 45, 65).[41] Finally, Hall's English edition reaffirms Bonner's findings on Melito's usage of Paul, making the common observation that Melito interprets Romans 5:12–6:14 "on the consequences of Adam's sin" at *PP* 48.[42]

---

[35]"In the Pauline and Johannine sense." Blank, *Vom Passa*, 55.

[36]"In his theology death and sin are the damning powers par excellence, in which he stands in the line of Paul and John." Blank, *Vom Passa*, 57-58.

[37]"'Sin,' principle, power of evil which reigns since Adam, is personified here and in the following. . . . Melito is obviously inspired by St. Paul, especially from the letter to the Romans, chap. 5-8." Perler, *Sur la Pâque*, 50.

[38]2 Cor 1:21-22: χρίσας ἡμᾶς θεός, ὁ καὶ σφραγισάμενος ἡμᾶς καὶ δοὺς τὸν ἀρραβῶνα τοῦ πνεύματος ἐν ταῖς καρδίαις ἡμῶν; *PP* 67: καὶ ἐσφράγισεν ἡμῶν τὰς ψυχὰς τῷ ἰδίῳ πνεύματι, καὶ τὰ μέλη τοῦ σώματος τῷ ἰδίῳ αἵματι.

[39]Perler, *Sur la Pâque*, 145-46.

[40]"Melito's biblical source." Perler, *Sur la Pâque*, 165.

[41]Javier Ibañez and Fernando Mendoza, *Meliton de Sardes: Homilia sobre la pascua* (Pamplona: Ed. University of Navarra, 1975), 267-68. Dratsellas's Greek edition similarly notes a wide variety of Pauline parallels without further comment (Konstantinos N. Dratsellas, *Homilia eis to pathos e Peri Pascha* [Athenai, 1971]).

[42]Hall, *On Pascha and Fragments*, 25n15. See also Lightfoot, who identified Pauline influence in Melito solely from Melito's fragments before the discovery of *PP* (J. B. Lightfoot, *Essays on the Work Entitled Supernatural Religion* [London: Macmillan and Co., 1893], 237).

While the evidence for Melito's use of Paul in *PP* is considerable—and, conversely, it is difficult to find a sustained argument against such usage—a measure of caution is nevertheless appropriate. As Rankin notes, "while the author quotes freely from the Old Testament, he makes only allusions to passages from the New," which complicates an assessment of Melito's dependency on any NT author.[43] Nevertheless, it is not without warrant that the critical editions of *PP* are filled with references to Paul's writings. The case for Melito's dependency on Paul is compelling based on both the quantity of these allusions and the strength of select examples, such as Galatians 4:25-26 at *PP* 45, where it is surprising that Rensberger would doubt Melito's allusion to the passage that is the methodological example par excellence for Melito's typological exegesis (ἅτινά ἐστιν ἀλληγορούμενα, Gal 4:24).[44] More compelling, however, is the manner in which key Pauline themes are integrated into the fabric of Melito's theology, such as in his usage of Adam-Christ parallelism (*PP* 46–47) and his account of original sin (*PP* 50), both of which evidence an internalization of Pauline ideas that is reminiscent of Diognetus. To be sure, the density of allusions to Paul in *Peri Pascha* is not as remarkable as one finds in Diognetus; but neither is Dassmann inaccurate in concluding that "Meliton präludiert Irenäus" by his substantial engagement with Paul.[45] Melito's paschal homily is thus placed within category "B" for this study, with evident usage of both Romans and Galatians.[46]

Melito as Pauline interpreter. The relative absence of scholarship on Melito and Paul means that there is little to summarize by way of

---

[43]David Ivan Rankin, *From Clement to Origen: The Social and Historical Context of the Church Fathers* (Aldershot: Ashgate, 2006), 94.

[44]In this context, de Lubac is to be preferred over Daniélou in rejecting a sharp distinction between allegory and typology, which (at least in the case of Paul) is difficult to maintain; cf. Henri de Lubac, "'Typologie' et 'Allégorisme,'" *Recherches de Science Religieuse* 34 (1947): 180-226. Other significant passages for Melito's interpretive methodology include Rom 5:14 (Ἀδὰμ ὅς ἐστιν τύπος τοῦ μέλλοντος, cf. *PP* 54) and 1 Cor 10:11 (ταῦτα δὲ τυπικῶς συνέβαινεν ἐκείνοις, cf. *PP* 85).

[45]"Melito preludes Irenaeus." Dassmann, *Der Stachel im Fleisch*, 289-92; Blank, *Vom Passa*, 55-58.

[46]Some have identified possible correspondence with Gal 3:13 at *PP* 71 (ὁ ἐπὶ ξύλου κρεμασθείς), which completes Paul's argument on works of the law in Gal 3:10, though the overlap between texts is too minor for a confident assertion of dependency. For those noting the correspondence, cf. Perler, *Sur la Pâque*, 99, 169; Cohick, *Peri Pascha*, 95.

assessments of Melito as a Pauline interpreter. As noted above, commentators such as Dassmann and Blank regard Melito as dependent on Paul's theology in his understanding of sin and salvation and his conception of the law,[47] and Perler similarly identifies Melito as "se tenant étroitement à la sotériologie de S. Paul et de S. Jean."[48] However, the frequent linking of John with Paul among commentators illustrates how any search for a pure "Paulinism" in Melito is doomed to failure; and indeed, if any one source is to be identified as most foundational for Melito's theology, it is John who represents the strongest candidate.[49] Further, it can be noted that aspects of Paul's theology are conspicuously absent in Melito; as Blank notes, Paul's hopeful conclusions regarding God's mercy on Israel in Romans 11 are not appropriated in Melito's homily, which instead emphasizes how Israel remains under God's judgment.[50] Nevertheless, Melito's ostensible combination of traditionalism and independence— witnessed in his journeying to the holy land to gain a more certain knowledge of the ancient writings, and his constancy in maintaining Asia's traditional (but less-attested) Passover date—suggests his unique value as a Pauline witness and interpreter, even if his theology is informed by more than the Apostle alone.

THE LAW AND WORKS IN *PERI PASCHA*

Meaning: What works of what law? In *Peri Pascha*, the "old" law that Melito contrasts with the gospel is Israel's Torah (*PP* 4), witnessed in Melito's recounting of the Passover story from Exodus "just as it is written in the law" (καθὼς ἐν τῷ νόμῳ γέγραπται), which was read prior to his address (*PP* 11). Melito specifically refers to Christ's giving of the Mosaic law at Horeb (*PP* 85, 88), though νόμος is also used as a synecdoche for the entire Torah elsewhere in contrasting νόμος with εὐαγγέλιον

---

[47]Cf. Dassmann, *Der Stachel im Fleisch*, 291; Blank, *Vom Passa*, 55.

[48]"Holding closely to the soteriology of St. Paul and St. John." Perler, *Sur la Pâque*, 37.

[49]As Eusebius notes, the Quartodecimans "claimed John as their apostolic guarantor" (Wilson, "Passover, Easter, and Anti-Judaism," 352, cf. *Hist. Eccl.* 5.24.3). On John's influence on Melito, cf. Stewart-Sykes, "Melito's Anti-Judaism," 279-81.

[50]Blank, *Vom Passa*, 85. This emphasis may be influenced by the catastrophic events of 132–135, which are interpreted in other sources of the period as a sign of God's judgment on Israel, cf. *Dial.* 16.2-3.

(cf. *PP* 3–4, 6–7, 39–43).[51] *Peri Pascha* contains no comprehensive discussion of the works of this law that are unnecessary for Christians; rather, as a paschal homily, Melito's attention naturally focuses on the feast celebration of Passover and the sacrifice of the lamb, particularly in the section of *PP* 35–45. This feast and sacrifice are rejected in favor of the true paschal lamb, Jesus, the reality typologically prefigured in the lamb sacrificed by the Israelites, whose presence in the type was the sole cause of its effectiveness (*PP* 32–33).[52] Along with these practices, Melito rejects Israel's focus on the temple, Jerusalem (described in *PP* 94 as πόλει νομικῇ), and the inheritance of the land, which have now been replaced by Christ, the Jerusalem above, and the entire world (*PP* 44–45; cf. Gal 4:26). More broadly, Melito speaks of the law's position now being filled by "the decrees of the gospel" (τὰ τοῦ εὐαγγελίου δόγματα, *PP* 39). Commentators have also noted the text's apparent references to baptism—such as the reference to "illumination" (συνεφωτίζετο) at *PP* 30, the term used by Justin[53]—as the practice that represents the antitype of the paschal events.[54] Though it cannot be said for certain whether baptism would have taken place as part of this celebration itself,[55] the implied contrast between the practices of Israel's pascha and their fulfillment in Christian baptism is likely.

Significance: What does the practice of these works signify? Melito does not devote space to discussing the significance of practicing these works of the law, though from context it appears that doing so represents identification with the λαὸς of Israel that prefigured the reality of the church. In Melito's homily, νόμος and λαός are so closely linked that they

---

[51]Melito also describes God as νομοθετήσας διὰ τῆς ἐντολῆς in commanding Adam to not eat from the tree, though no objections are raised in this instance (*PP* 47).

[52]On this, see similarly Justin in *Dial.* 40.1-3.

[53]Cf. *1 Apol.* 61.13, 65.1.

[54]Cf. Hall, *On Pascha and Fragments*, 17n9: "The guarding and illumination reflect the terminology of Christian baptism and unction"; Perler, *Sur la Pâque*, 151: "C'est l'illumination spirituelle par le baptême" ("This is spiritual illumination by baptism"); J. Ligon Duncan, "The Covenant Idea in Melito of Sardis," *Presbyterion* 28 (2002): 31-32. See also *PP* 13–15, 67, 103.

[55]Perler holds that "notre texte suppose que le baptême était administré à l'occasion de la fête de Pâque" ("our text assumes that baptism was administred on the occasion of the feast of Passover"), citing *PP* 103's invitation to receive the remission of sins, while Hall cautions that this is possible but not certain; cf. Perler, *Sur la Pâque*, 151; Hall, *On Pascha and Fragments*, xxviii.

appear as two sides of the same typological coin, which is itself a prefigurement of the two-sided fulfillment of εὐαγγέλιον and ἐκκλησία that has come in Christ (*PP* 39–40). As Melito writes, "the people [λαός] was precious before the church [ἐκκλησία] arose, and the law [νόμος] was marvelous before the gospel [εὐαγγέλιον] was elucidated," with both types of λαός and νόμος becoming worthless with the arrival of their corresponding antitypes (*PP* 41–43). For Melito, to practice the νόμος is one and the same as being a part of the λαός of Israel (with Melito linking them four times in *PP* 39–43), just as being a part of the ἐκκλησία and observing the decrees of the gospel (τὰ τοῦ εὐαγγελίου δόγματα) are two parts of the same reality (*PP* 39).

Opposition: Why are these works not necessary for the Christian? Melito relativizes these works of Israel's law with two closely related arguments: first, the typological argument that the law and its works were types pointing toward a coming reality; and second, the salvation-historical argument that the reality prefigured by these works has arrived in the person of Christ, thus rendering the types superfluous.

In *PP* 35–36, Melito explains how nothing is made without a "comparison" (παραβολή) or "preliminary sketch" (προκέντημα) or "prefiguration" (προτύπωσις). Though such a prototype is valuable before the arrival of the thing for which it serves as a model, when the reality does arrive, "that which once bore the image of the future thing is itself destroyed as growing useless" (*PP* 37). According to Melito, this is the nature of the law and its practices; the law "was the writing of a parable," a type foreshadowing a coming reality that would be "the recounting and fulfillment of the law" (διήγημα νόμου καὶ πλήρωμα, *PP* 40). And yet Christ as antitype is more than simply a later fulfillment; he is both new and old (*PP* 3, 59), and is himself present in the types: "It is he who in many endured many things: it is he that was in Abel murdered . . . and in the lamb slain" (*PP* 69).[56] It is the antitype's presence in the law's types—and not the practices themselves—that made them precious and rendered them powerful, as seen in the example of the sacrifice of the lamb at Passover:

---

[56]Cf. Judith Lieu, "They Speak to Us Across the Centuries: Melito of Sardis," *The Expository Times* 110 (1998): 44; see similarly *Diog.* 11:4.

Tell me, angel, what did you respect?
The slaughter of the sheep or the life of the Lord?
The death of the sheep or the model of the Lord?
The blood of the sheep or the Spirit of the Lord?
It is clear that your respect was won
when you saw the mystery of the Lord occurring in the sheep,
the life of the Lord in the slaughter of the lamb,
the model of the Lord in the death of the sheep;
that is why you did not strike Israel, but made only Egypt childless.
    (*PP* 32-33)

The natural corollary to the law being a prototype is that Christ's gospel is the reality prefigured by the νόμος and its practices, with its appearance ushering in a new age of salvation history in which the types are left behind. According to Melito, there is a proper season (ἴδιος καιρός) and proper time (ἴδιος χρόνος) for the model and the reality, and the model that "once was precious becomes worthless when what is truly precious has been revealed" (*PP* 37–38). The law belongs to this "old" (παλαιόν) dispensation, which is also characterized as "temporary" (πρόσκαιρον), "perishable" (φθαρτόν), and "mortal" (θνητόν) (*PP* 3). While "the slaying of the sheep, and the distribution of the blood, and the scripture from the law have reached as far as Christ, on whose account were all things in the ancient law" (ἐν τῷ πρεσβυτέρῳ νόμῳ), these practices are worthless now that "the law has become word, and the old new, having gone out together from Zion and Jerusalem," evoking the prophecies of a law coming from Zion in the last days in Isaiah 2:3 and Micah 4:2 (*PP* 6–7).[57] Melito offers a seven-part list contrasting the previous stage in salvation history with the time now inaugurated by Christ: "For once the slaying of the sheep was precious, *but now* it is worthless because of the life of the Lord; the death of the sheep was precious, *but now* it is worthless because of the salvation of the Lord" (*PP* 44, translation and italics mine). Christ's identity as the true antitype is confirmed by his being "proclaimed through the law and the prophets" (*PP* 104), with Melito calling forth testimonies from Moses, David, Jeremiah, and Isaiah that are fulfilled by Christ in his passion (*PP* 61–65).

---

[57]Cf. similarly *Dial.* 109.1-3.

One can also identify an implicit argument for the universality of the gospel as a reason for rejecting the old law's valuation of the temple, Jerusalem, and the inheritance of the land: "For it is not in one place nor in a little plot that the glory of God is established, but on all the ends of the inhabited earth his bounty overflows, and there the almighty God has made his dwelling, through Christ Jesus, to whom be glory for ever" (*PP* 45; cf. Rom 4:13, Gal 1:5). However, this characteristic of the gospel as overflowing to the ends of the earth does not stand as an independent argument, but rather is dependent on the salvation-historical reasoning that Christ's pascha has inaugurated the promised new age (cf. *PP* 6–7).

It should also be noted that Melito does not reject the νόμος and its practices due to a fundamental opposition to law or works as such, since this old law is only made worthless because the realities it prefigured have now arrived (*PP* 43–45).[58] Christ himself is identified as the law in *PP* 9,[59] which as Cantalamessa notes (following Lebreton), may refer to his role as the legislator who gives the new and definitive law, or be meant "dans le sens ontologique et hypostatique (Nomos comme hypostase divine et Fils de Dieu)."[60] While Christ's advent indeed makes the old law's practices obsolete, the νόμος and εὐαγγέλιον are nevertheless closely linked in their relation as type and fulfillment: as Melito writes, "the decrees of the gospel were proclaimed in advance by the law" (*PP* 39), and "the gospel is the recounting and fulfillment of the law" (*PP* 40).[61]

---

[58]Cf. Wilson, "Passover, Easter, and Anti-Judaism," 345; Henry M. Knapp, "Melito's Use of Scripture in 'Peri Pascha': Second-Century Typology," *Vigiliae Christianae* 54 (2000): 370-71.

[59]*PP* 9: ὅς ἐστιν τὰ πάντα· καθ᾽ ὃ κρίνει νόμος; cf *PP* 7. See similarly *KP* Fr. 1.

[60]"In the ontological and hypostatic sense (Law as divine hypostasis and Son of God)." Cantalamessa, "Méliton de Sardes," 13-14. According to Cantalamessa, these possibilities are both present for Melito's usage of λόγος as well.

[61]See Duncan, "Covenant Idea in Melito," 28: "In other words, Melito's contrast between old covenant and new covenant realities is not absolute (that is, between what was not valuable and what is truly valuable), but relative (that is, between what was once valuable and what is now valuable). The type was valuable before the coming of the fulfillment (*PP* 41)." This contrast can also be witnessed in Melito's description of the relation between Judaism and Christianity in *Hist. Eccl.* 4.26.7; cf. Stewart-Sykes, "Melito's Anti-Judaism," 273.

CONCLUSION

In Melito's *Peri Pascha*, the law in question between Jewish and Christian parties is Israel's Torah. As a paschal homily, *Peri Pascha* naturally focuses on the practices of the Passover feast and its accompanying sacrifices, though Israel's focus on the temple, Jerusalem, and the inheritance of the land are noted as well. This feast and sacrifice are rejected in favor of the true paschal lamb, Jesus, and an implied contrast between the initiation of Israel's Passover and the Christian practice of baptism can be noted as well. Melito does not explicitly discuss the significance of practicing these works, though they appear to represent identification with the people of Israel, as Melito frequently links the νόμος and λαός of Israel as types that prefigure the realities of the εὐαγγέλιον and ἐκκλησία that have come in Christ (*PP* 39–43). These works are rejected due to the nature of the νόμος and its practices as types, which are made void now that the realities they foreshadowed have arrived with Christ. The νόμος and the εὐαγγέλιον are nevertheless closely linked, as "the decrees of the gospel were proclaimed in advance by the law" (*PP* 39), and "the gospel is the recounting and fulfillment of the law" (*PP* 40). While not using the phrase *works of the law*, Melito's homily shows influence from Paul and draws on both Romans and Galatians in its argumentation, and thus serves as a supporting witness to the reception of these debates in the mid-second century.

11

IRENAEUS OF LYON (A)

Against Heresies and *Demonstration*
of the Apostolic Preaching

◻

INTRODUCTION

Introduction and background. This study's final source is Irenaeus of
Lyon, the late second-century bishop whom Grant identifies as "the most
important Christian controversialist and theologian between the apostles
and the third-century genius Origen."[1] It is difficult to overstate his influence on the succeeding history of Christian theology: as Behr notes,
"Irenaeus establishes a foundation and identifies Christianity in a manner
that becomes a given for most Christian history thereafter,"[2] and von
Balthasar goes so far as to call him the "founding father" of theology itself.[3] In addition, Irenaeus is often regarded as the first great exegete and
expositor of Paul (at least among those whose writings survive in any
quantity), and for this reason his views on works of the law are especially
significant for our study.

Most of our knowledge of Irenaeus's theology comes from *Against
Heresies* (*Haer.*), a project of five books that seeks to counter second-
century groups that Irenaeus sees as heretical and draw them back to the

---

[1]Robert M. Grant, *Irenaeus of Lyons* (London: Routledge, 2000), 1.
[2]John Behr, *Irenaeus of Lyons: Identifying Christianity* (Oxford: Oxford University Press, 2013), 205.
[3]Hans Urs von Balthasar, *The Scandal of the Incarnation: Irenaeus Against the Heresies* (San
Francisco: Ignatius Press, 1990), 8.

orthodox faith. The scope of *Against Heresies* is massive, and as Osborn notes, "while Irenaeus is provoked by the censures of the heretics, his chief concern is positive; the response far exceeds the stimulus."[4] In addition, Irenaeus's *Demonstration of the Apostolic Preaching* (*Epid.*) was rediscovered in 1904, which is a brief guide to the rule of faith that summarizes much of *Against Heresies*, and which Benedict XVI has called "the oldest 'catechism of Christian doctrine.'"[5] Taken together, Irenaeus's works represent a synthesis of the preceding apostolic tradition on a scale that had been heretofore unseen.[6]

Irenaeus was likely born between AD 130 and 140,[7] and is thought to have been raised in Asia Minor, as he writes of having heard Polycarp, the bishop of Smyrna, as a youth. As he testifies in a letter to Florinus (preserved by Eusebius), Polycarp left an indelible impression on the young Irenaeus, as the bishop relayed to him all his memories of John and the others who were eye-witnesses of Christ.[8] Irenaeus was established at the other side of the empire in Lyon by 177, with the beleaguered church of this city commending him as a man "zealous for the covenant of Christ" in a letter delivered to the bishop of Rome,[9] and Irenaeus taking up the episcopacy left by the martyred Pothinus thereafter.[10] The five books of *Against Heresies* were written during Eleutherus's episcopacy in Rome (ca. 175–189), and their influence appears to have been extensive; a fragment of this work dated to the late second or early third century (and thus perhaps within Irenaeus's own lifetime) was found as far away as Oxyrhynchus in Egypt,[11] and the work was used

---

[4]Eric Francis Osborn, *Irenaeus of Lyons* (Cambridge: Cambridge University Press, 2001), 7.

[5]Benedict XVI, "Saint Irenaeus of Lyons," General Audience, St. Peter's Square, March 28, 2007, www.vatican.va/content/benedict-xvi/en/audiences/2007/documents/hf_ben-xvi_aud_2007 0328.html.

[6]Cf. Grant, *Irenaeus of Lyons*, 1.

[7]Cf. Osborn, *Irenaeus of Lyons*, 2; Andre Benoit, *Saint Irénée: Introduction à l'étude de sa theologie* (Paris: Presses universitaires de France, 1960), 50.

[8]Cf. *Hist. Eccl.* 5.20.5-7.

[9]*Hist. Eccl.* 5.3.4.

[10]Cf. *Hist. Eccl.* 5.1.27. While migration to Lyon from far-off Asia Minor may seem unexpected, temple ruins and inscriptions found in Gaul reveal strong social and economic links between the two regions in the second century; see Grant, *Irenaeus of Lyons*, 4.

[11]P. Oxy. 405; see Bernard Pyne Grenfell and Arthur Surridge Hunt, *The Oxyrhynchus Papyri*, 72 vols. (London: Egypt Exploration Fund, 1903), 3:10.

across the empire in the early third century by Clement of Alexandria, Tertullian in Carthage, and Hippolytus in Rome.[12] Irenaeus's *Demonstration* is generally thought to have been written after *Against Heresies*;[13] prior to its being discovered, the work had no attestation besides as "un simple titre" in Eusebius.[14]

As Briggman's recent study outlines, the late nineteenth- and early twentieth-century works by Wendt, Werner, von Harnack, and Loofs served to create an image of Irenaeus as a muddle-headed and unoriginal compiler, while the second half of the twentieth century saw this trend reversed and Irenaeus's reputation rehabilitated.[15] One charge that has continued to carry force, however, is that of unoriginality; as Benoit writes, "il est donc vain de chercher chez lui une oeuvre personelle: il n'a pas voulu faire un travail de dogmaticien, une oeuvre d'avant-garde: il n'a voulu être qu'un jalon sur la route de la tradition et exposer la foi chrétienne, en face des problèmes concrets qui se posaient de son temps."[16] A similar conclusion is reached by Minns:

> Irenaeus would have been deeply offended had it been suggested to him that he was an original thinker. The original thinkers of his time were the gnostics, Marcion and other heretics. Their originality of thought was, in Irenaeus's view, precisely what was wrong with them, and it was their novel views he attacked, in defence of what he supposed to be the traditional teaching of the Church, handed down unchanged and unchanging.[17]

---

[12]Osborn, *Irenaeus of Lyons*, 6-7, Grant, *Irenaeus of Lyons*, 7. See *Val.* 5; *Ref.* 6.37. The relationship between Irenaeus and Clement is a matter of some debate, with evidence leaning towards Clement using Irenaeus's works; see L. G. Patterson, "The Divine Became Human: Irenaean Themes in Clement of Alexandria," *Studia Patristica* 31 (1997): 497-516.

[13]See, for example, Adolf von Harnack, *Des heiligen Irenäus Schrift zum Erweise der apostolischen Verkündigung* (Leipzig: J. C. Hinrichs, 1907), 55; Adelin Rousseau, *Démonstration de la prédication apostolique* (Paris: Éditions du Cerf, 1995) 352-53; recent challenges to this view include Yves-Marie Blanchard, *Aux sources du canon, le témoignage d'Irénée* (Paris: Éditions du Cerf, 1993), 113n2; Behr, *Irenaeus of Lyons*, 68-69.

[14]"A simple title." Rousseau, *Démonstration de la prédication apostolique*, 1.

[15]Anthony Briggman, *Irenaeus of Lyons and the Theology of the Holy Spirit* (Oxford: Oxford University Press, 2012), 3-5.

[16]"It is thus vain to search in him for a personal work: he did not want to do the labor of a dogmatician, an avant-garde work: he wanted only to be a marker on the road of the tradition and to present the Christian faith, in view of concrete problems that arose in his time." Benoit, *Saint Irénée*, 255.

[17]Dennis Minns, *Irenaeus* (London: G. Chapman, 1994), 132.

While overly simplistic notions of Paul being passed along as an uninterpreted static entity should be avoided,[18] Irenaeus's understanding of the nature of theology and his task as a theologian does signal his value as a source for identifying the church's earliest understanding of works of the law, which could conceivably trace back to Paul himself. As Bockmuehl observes, "Irenaeus affirms a harmony of Scripture and its tradition of interpretation, which the church has inherited from the apostles," which for Irenaeus "is no mere ideological figment of a 'collective memory,' but . . . is vouchsafed by an unbroken and identifiable claim of *personal recollection* reaching back to the apostles themselves (*Against Heresies* 3.1-5)."[19]

While fidelity to the teachings of the apostles is basic to all of Irenaeus's argumentation,[20] the primary intent of his work is not to produce a standalone commentary on biblical texts, but rather to uphold their teachings vis-à-vis what he understands to be the false alternatives of his own time, which for Irenaeus is foremost the Gnostic tendency to separate the God of the Old Testament from the Father of Jesus.[21] As Norris writes, "Irenaeus saw himself confronted by two distinct groups of opponents: the followers of Marcion, who simply repudiated the Jewish scriptures, and the Valentinians, who . . . saw themselves as occupying a middle ground, at least on the subject of the law."[22] In contrast to these groups, "Irenaeus argues that the same God who 'sent his son' into the world is the author of the Mosaic law."[23] The aim of Irenaeus's overall theological project is well illustrated by his reading of Romans 10:4, τέλος γὰρ νόμου Χριστός. Whereas for the heretics, this signifies the end of the

---

[18] As White recognizes, "each individual portrayal of Paul and/or his texts is shaped within a mnemonic community that exerts its own social pressures on how individual pieces of tradition should and should not be remembered." For Irenaeus, White rightly identifies the *regula veritatis* as shaping his own readings and usage of Paul; cf. Benjamin L. White, *Remembering Paul: Ancient and Modern Contests over the Image of the Apostle* (Oxford: Oxford University Press 2014), 164-65.

[19] Markus Bockmuehl, *Seeing the Word: Refocusing New Testament Study* (Grand Rapids, MI: Baker Academic, 2006), 184 (italics original).

[20] See e.g. *Haer.* 3.1-5.

[21] This is not to limit Irenaeus's interest in Paul to countering the Gnostics; cf. Elio Peretto, *La Lettera ai romani cc. 1–8 nell'Adversus Haereses d'Ireneo* (Bari: Istituto di letteratura cristiana antica, Università, 1971), 54.

[22] Richard A. Norris, "Irenaeus's Use of Paul in His Polemic Against the Gnostics," in *Paul and the Legacies of Paul*, ed. William S. Babcock (Dallas: Southern Methodist University Press, 1990), 86.

[23] Norris, "Irenaeus's Use of Paul," 86.

law in general (and for some a repudiation of the God who authored it), for Irenaeus it is a statement that the shadow of the old law has been fulfilled by the reality of the new.

Texts and translations. While Irenaeus wrote in Greek, only fragments of the Greek original of *Against Heresies* remain, and readers are primarily dependent on a third century Latin translation (ostensibly used by Tertullian in *Against the Valentinians*) that is "noted for its slavish literalness."[24] For the *Demonstration*, the only extant copy is the thirteenth-century Armenian text discovered in the early twentieth century.[25] For the text of *Against Heresies* the 1965–1969 Sources Chrétiennes (SC) is used,[26] with translations primarily drawn from *Ante-Nicene Fathers* (ANF) edition,[27] and supplemented by the 1991–2012 *Ancient Christian Writers* (ACW) where noted.[28] While the standard critical text and translation of the *Demonstration* is the French 1995 SC edition,[29] for the sake of clarity I have used Behr's English edition for translations.[30]

IRENAEUS AND PAUL

Knowledge and use of Paul. In his 1946 study, Lawson approvingly cites Seeberg's assertion that "Irenaeus is a Biblicist, and the first great representative of Biblicism," and concludes by identifying Irenaeus as "a Biblical theologian" and "indeed *homo unius libri.*"[31] While such characterizations

---

[24]Dominic Unger, trans., *St. Irenaeus of Lyons Against the Heresies*, edited by John J. Dillon and Matthew Steenberg, 3 vols., Ancient Christian Writers (New York: Paulist Press, 1992–2012), 1:14.

[25]Rousseau, *Démonstration de la prédication apostolique*, 19.

[26]Adelin Rousseau and Louis Doutreleau, eds., *Irénée de Lyon: Contre les hérésies*, 5 vols. (Paris: Éditions du Cerf, 1965–1982).

[27]Alexander Roberts and James Donaldson, eds., *The Ante-Nicene Fathers: Translations of the Writings of the Fathers down to A.D. 325*, vol. 1, *The Apostolic Fathers with Justin Martyr and Irenaeus* (Peabody, MA: Hendrickson, 1994 [1885]).

[28]Unger, *St. Irenaeus of Lyons*. There is currently no ideal English edition of *Against Heresies*, as the recent ACW series lacks books 4–5 and tends to paraphrase the underlying Latin and Greek. While showing its age, the ANF translation remains the best English version, offering the complete text and close (if sometimes wooden) renderings of the original languages. Translations of this edition are sometimes adjusted to remove archaisms.

[29]Rousseau, *Démonstration de la prédication apostolique*.

[30]John Behr, trans., *On the Apostolic Preaching*, Popular Patristics Series 17 (Crestwood, NY: St. Vladimir's Seminary Press, 1997).

[31]"Man of one book." John Lawson, *The Biblical Theology of Saint Irenaeus* (London: Epworth Press, 1948), 23-24, 292; see Reinhold Seeberg, *Lehrbuch der Dogmengeschichte* (Leipzig: A. Deichert, 1908), 290.

are not unproblematic,[32] they do correctly point to the presence of a more developed scriptural canon in Irenaeus, both with respect to concept and content, so that Irenaeus can indeed be regarded as the earliest mainstream theologian who witnesses to a canon of Scripture—and as part of it, a Pauline corpus.[33] Paul and Pauline texts are thus engaged at a new level, with Benoit identifying Irenaeus's works as "l'origine de l'usage intensif de la collection paulinienne."[34]

Pauline influence in Irenaeus is evident before one begins *Against Heresies*; as Grant notes, the work's full title—*On the Detection and Refutation of the Knowledge Falsely So Called*—is itself an echo of 1 Timothy 6:20.[35] With the possible exceptions of Philemon and Hebrews, Irenaeus appears to contain references to all the traditionally ascribed letters of Paul within the five books of *Against Heresies*.[36] According to Peretto's compilation of studies,[37] the number of Pauline references in *Against Heresies* is variously counted by Burgon as 499, Werner as 324, Jacquier as 279, and Hoh as 342.[38] Romans and Galatians are both frequently referred to, with Werner, Jacquier, and Hoh respectively finding 84, 78, and 95 references to Romans

---

[32]The term *biblicist* does not do justice to Irenaeus's understanding of the relation between Scripture and tradition (cf., for example, *Haer.* 3.2.2). Further, Irenaeus does not testify to a unified *unus liber* of Scripture, and his own canon differs from those of later centuries by including books such as 1 Clement and Shepherd of Hermas (cf. *Haer.* 3.3.3, 4.20.2).

[33]On Marcion and his canon, see Excursus 2.

[34]"The origin of the intensive usage of the Pauline collection." Benoit, *Saint Irénée*, 135. "This judgment is based on our extant sources, of course, and the rediscovery of others—such as Justin's lost antiheretical writings—may show Irenaeus's use of Paul against the heretics to be less original (cf. David Rensberger, "As the Apostle Teaches: The Development of the Use of Paul's Letters in Second-Century Christianity" [PhD diss., Yale University, 1981], 363).

[35]Grant, *Irenaeus of Lyons*, 34. On the minor influence of the Pastorals and Acts in Irenaeus's interpretation of Paul, cf. Rensberger, "As the Apostle Teaches," 321 (though this is nuanced by White, *Remembering Paul*, 144-45).

[36]See Norris, "Irenaeus's Use of Paul," 80; Ernst Dassmann, *Der Stachel im Fleisch: Paulus in der frühchristlichen Literatur bis Irenäus* (Münster: Aschendorff, 1979), 296; Grant, *Irenaeus of Lyons*, 34.

[37]These figures leave out Hebrews, which only Jacquier and Hoh view as cited and which Irenaeus does not expressly identify as Pauline.

[38]Peretto, *Lettera ai romani*, 53; see John W. Burgon, *Index of Texts of the New Testament Quoted, or Referred to, by the Greek and Latin Fathers*, 16 vols. (London: British Museum, 1872); Johannes Werner, *Der Paulinismus des Irenaeus. Eine kirchen- und dogmengeschichtliche Untersuchung über das Verhältnis des Irenaeus zu der paulinischen Briefsammlung und Theologie* (Leipzig: J. C. Hinrichs, 1889); Eugène Jacquier, *History of the Books of the New Testament*, trans. J. Duggan (New York: Benziger, 1907); Jospeph Hoh, *Die Lehre des hl. Irenäus über das Neue Testament* (Münster/Westf.: Aschendorff, 1919).

and 27, 23, and 24 references to Galatians.[39] For Irenaeus's *Demonstration*, Rousseau counts 62 Pauline references (excluding Hebrews), including 23 from Romans and 7 from Galatians.[40] While allusions and echoes are still found in Irenaeus's writings, Irenaeus differs from previous sources in this study by often directly citing Paul's epistles, making his usage of Pauline texts considerably easier to trace. As a result, fewer context-based inferences are necessary to identify correspondence with the phenomena of works of the law, with Irenaeus simply using the phrase in citing Galatians 3:5-9 at *Against Heresies* 4.21.1, along with his allusion to Romans 3:20-21 at *Demonstration of the Apostolic Preaching* 35.

Irenaeus as Pauline interpreter. A little over a century ago, Werner's *Der Paulinismus des Irenaeus* spoke of the "Minderwertigkeit"[41] of Paul's writings compared to the rest of Scripture for Irenaeus, an assertion that was reaffirmed by scholars such as Loofs in the following decades.[42] This view began to change toward the second half of the twentieth century, particularly with Lawson's monograph, which countered that Irenaeus's ecclesiology was at the foundation of his understanding of Paul's authority:

> The Church herself is of plenary authority because she has received the truth from the Apostles. The Apostles are therefore collectively a paramount religious authority. Among this august company there are two who occupy so exalted a place that the Church of Rome herself rises to her pre-eminent authority through foundation in their ministry.[43] One of these great ones is the writer of the Epistles. It is but natural to find that in practice S. Paul is quoted in the same authoritative manner as are the Old Testament Scriptures.[44]

---

[39]Peretto, *Lettera ai romani*, 53.

[40]Rousseau, *Démonstration de la prédication apostolique*, 396-97.

[41]"Inferiority."

[42]Werner, *Paulinismus des Irenaeus*, 33. Loofs proves even more dismissive of Irenaeus's "Paulinism" than Werner: "Auch von dem, was Veranlassung gegeben hat, von einem „Paulinismus des Irenaeus" zu reden, stammt vieles schon aus seinen Quellen; was übrig bleibt, ist wohl mehr durch sie als durch eigenes Bibelstudium des Irenaeus angeregt" ("Even in material that caused us to speak of a 'Paulinism of Irenaeus,' much came already from his own sources; what remains is likely more animated by them than by Irenaeus's own Bible study"), *Theophilus von Antiochen Adversus Marcionem und die anderen theologischen Quellen bei Irenaeus* (Leipzig: J. C. Hinrichs, 1930), 434.

[43]Cf. *Haer.* 3.3.2.

[44]Lawson, *Biblical Theology of Saint Irenaeus*, 48.

Though Irenaeus's recognition of Pauline authority has seldom been defended as lyrically since Lawson (for whom Irenaeus "plainly betrays an underlying assumption that S. Paul, when rightly understood, must display the fullness of divine truth in his every word"[45]), his general conclusion has nonetheless been widely reaffirmed.[46] In the most recent full-length study on Irenaeus and Paul in German, the pendulum appears to have swung entirely away from Werner: according to Noormann's 1994 *Irenäus als Paulusinterpret*, "Paulus ist für Irenäus zwar nicht der einzige Apostel—die marcionitische Position eines solus Paulus weist er entschieden zurück—, aber dennoch der Apostel schlechthin: Der absolut gebrauchte Titel ὁ ἀπόστολος bezeichnet Paulus, und kein anderer neutestamentlicher Autor wird so oft zitiert wie er."[47] As Blackwell notes, "the Apostle" is Irenaeus's "most consistent designation of Paul," with the succeeding patristic tradition following Irenaeus's example in making this title a universal appellation.[48] Dunn uses perhaps the strongest language for Irenaeus as a Pauline advocate:

> It is Irenaeus . . . who put Paul at the centre of Christian theology, so that it is in no way surprising that following Irenaeus we find sustained exegetical commentary on and exposition of Paul's letters, beginning with Tertullian and Origen. . . . And it was probably Irenaeus who secured for Paul the adulation in which he was held thereafter by Origen and his successors as expositors of Paul.[49]

Rather than serving as a witness to the inferiority of Paul, Irenaeus is now commonly regarded as playing an important role in confirming Paul's central place in Christian theology.

---

[45]Lawson, *Biblical Theology of Saint Irenaeus*, 31.

[46]See e.g. Benoit, *Saint Irénée*, 136; Dassmann, *Der Stachel im Fleisch*, 296; Osborn, *Irenaeus of Lyons*, 180.

[47]"Paul is certainly not the only apostle for Irenaeus—he decidedly rejects the Marcionite position of a 'Paul Alone'—but he is nevertheless the apostle par excellence: the absolute use of ὁ ἀπόστολος as a title denotes Paul, and no other New Testament author is cited as often as he is." Rolf Noormann, *Irenäus als Paulusinterpret: zur Rezeption und Wirkung der paulinischen und deuteropaulinischen Briefe im Werk des Irenäus von Lyon*, WUNT 2:66 (Tübingen: Mohr Siebeck, 1994), 517.

[48]Ben C. Blackwell, "Paul and Irenaeus," in *Paul and the Second Century*, ed. Michael F. Bird and Joseph R. Dodson (London: T&T Clark, 2011), 195. This usage does not appear entirely original to Irenaeus, however, with the title also appearing at *Diog.* 12.5.

[49]James D. G. Dunn, *Neither Jew nor Greek: A Contested Identity*, vol. 3 of *Christianity in the Making* (Grand Rapids, MI: Eerdmans, 2015), 722-23.

As with other aspects of his thought, Irenaeus's credentials as a Pauline interpreter have been rehabilitated among scholars in recent decades, although the overall picture is still somewhat mixed. As is common with other patristic sources, Blackwell observes that "those who argue that Irenaeus 'got Paul wrong' usually mean Irenaeus disagrees with their own reading of Paul," with his fortunes as a Pauline interpreter generally mapping onto contemporary trends in Pauline scholarship.[50] A sampling of recent assessments is instructive:

Lawson, while critiquing Irenaeus's "incautious attempt to demonstrate the identity of the divine Source of the religions of the Old and New Covenants by means of the doctrine of the New Law," nevertheless concludes that "it is not too much to claim that in general S. Irenaeus was a fairly sound expositor of S. Paul," since Irenaeus "lived in a community which still spoke the same religious language of the Apostle" and thus "had no difficulty in 'making sense of' most parts of Paul's writings."[51] Peretto's evaluation of Irenaeus's use of Romans 1–8 in *Against Heresies* is favorable; while one may speculate whether Irenaeus's understanding "avrebbe potuto essere più profonda e ampia, se invece di un'opera polemica, avesse commentato *Rom* 1–8," nevertheless, "Ireneo si rivela capace di capire Paolo."[52] Dassmann's findings are similar, concluding that the diverse character of Pauline citations found in Irenaeus "verdeutlicht somit nur die außerordentliche Vertrautheit des Irenäus mit dem paulinischen Gedankengut."[53] Balás's survey of the structure of *Against Heresies* concludes that "the place and role of Paul is both quantatitively and qualitatively impressive," which he attributes to "Irenaeus's own conviction (received from an already existing tradition but clarified and strengthened further by him) that the witness of Paul is an integral and substantial part of the

---

[50]Blackwell, "Paul and Irenaeus," 206.

[51]Lawson, *Biblical Theology of Saint Irenaeus*, 81-82, 85.

[52]"Could have been more profound and wide, if instead of a polemical work, he had commented on Rom 1-8," nevertheless "Irenaeus reveals himself capable of understanding Paul." Peretto, *Lettera ai romani*, 243.

[53]"Thus only illustrates Irenaeus' extraordinary familiarity with the Pauline ideas." Dassmann, *Der Stachel im Fleisch*, 297.

apostolic witness to Christ."[54] Noormann's comprehensive study concludes that "Irenäus zeigt sich als ein versierter Paulus-Exeget, der
paulinische Textzusammenhänge und „Konkordanzen" zwischen Par-
allelstellen ebenso wahrnimmt wie theologische Aussageintentionen,
der aber nicht selten anderen als den heutigen Auslegungsregeln folgt
und gelegentlich auch Texte gegen ihren Sinn interpretiert."[55] For his
part, Blackwell is reticent to pass too great a judgment on Irenaeus's
value as an interpreter, concluding modestly Irenaeus is "an interesting and historically significant interpreter of Paul," who "offers a
different emphasis from the Pauline letters" with respect to justification and forgiveness.[56]

It must also be recalled that as with the preceding figures, Irenaeus is
not strictly a Pauline interpreter, and his own usage of a figure like
Abraham, for example, does not solely reflect influence from Paul.[57] John
and Paul emerge as the chief influences in Irenaeus's theology,[58] and as
Dunn and Dassmann observe, Irenaeus often combines Pauline and Johannine perspectives in responding to his adversaries.[59] While this may
arguably dilute Irenaeus's purity as a Pauline witness, Irenaeus objects to
those who seek to interpret Paul atomistically, as "the Lord did not come
to save only Paul, nor is God so poor that He would have only one apostle
who would know the economy of His Son" (*Haer.* 3.13.1, ACW).[60] As
Dassmann notes, according to Irenaeus, "nur Paulus ist in der Theologie
ebenso falsch wie ohne Paulus."[61]

---

[54]David Balás, "The Use and Interpretation of Paul in Irenaeus's Five Books *Adversus Haereses*." *Second Century* 9 (1992): 38.

[55]"Irenaeus shows himself to be an accomplished Pauline exegete, who perceives Pauline textual contexts and connections between parallel passages as well the theological intent of his state-ments, but who not seldom follows principles of interpretation besides those of today and oc-casionally even interprets texts against their sense." Noormann, *Irenäus als Paulusinterpret*, 518-19.

[56]Blackwell, "Paul and Irenaeus," 205.

[57]Cf. Norris, "Irenaeus's Use of Paul," 88.

[58]Osborn, *Irenaeus of Lyons*, 190.

[59]Cf. Dunn, *Neither Jew nor Greek*, 722; Dassmann, *Der Stachel im Fleisch*, 310-13.

[60]Irenaeus continues, "Let Paul himself refute those who assert that he alone had knowledge of the truth [followed by citation of 1 Cor 15:11]: 'Whether then it was I, or they, so we preach and so you believed.'"

[61]"Only Paul in theology is as incorrect as without Paul." Dassmann, *Der Stachel im Fleisch*, 313.

THE LAW AND WORKS
IN *AGAINST HERESIES* AND *DEMONSTRATION*
OF THE APOSTOLIC PREACHING

Meaning: What works of what law? In *Against Heresies*, the law in contention between Jewish and Christian parties is the Jewish Torah, which is first witnessed in Irenaeus's overview of the Ebionites, who are described as regarding Paul as an apostate from "the law." Along with their repudiation of Paul, this group continues to practice circumcision, and "persevere in the observance of those customs which are enjoined by the law, and are so Judaic in their style of life, that they even adore Jerusalem as if it were the house of God" (*Haer.* 1.26.2).[62]

In 4.14, Irenaeus identifies the law Christians are not obliged to observe as that which was given to the unruly people in the desert by Moses. This law includes the specific works of "the construction of the tabernacle, the building of the temple, the election of the Levites, sacrifices also, and oblations, legal monitions, and all the other service of the law," which Irenaeus sees as types of the eternal realities to be revealed in Christ (4.14.2-3). Irenaeus elsewhere calls these obligations the "yoke" or "laws of bondage," which "were one by one promulgated to the people by Moses," and which God has now "cancelled by the new covenant of liberty" (4.15.1, 4.16.5; cf. Gal 4:21-26; 5:1). Irenaeus makes clear that these do not include the works of the Decalogue, which are identified as "the entrance into life," and "which, if any one does not observe, he has no salvation" (4.12.5, 4.15.1). Rather, Irenaeus refers specifically to the elaborate yoke of law that came following Israel's apostasy with the golden calf, in which they placed themselves back in servitude and were given laws suitable to their condition. Regarding this law Irenaeus cites Ezekiel: "And their eyes were after the desire of their heart; and I gave them statutes that were not good, and judgments in which they shall not live" (Ezek 20:24-25; *Haer.* 4.15.1).[63]

---

[62]On the Ebionites, see Excursus 2 above.

[63]See also P. W. van der Horst, "I Gave the Laws That Were Not Good: Ezekiel 20:25 in Ancient Judaism and Early Christianity," in *Hellenism—Judaism—Christianity: Essays on Their Interaction* (Kampen, the Netherlands: Kok Pharos, 1994), 135.

Irenaeus writes at length of how circumcision and Sabbath in particular are not necessary for the Christian,[64] and cites God's rejection in Isaiah 1:11-14 of "holocausts, and sacrifices, and oblations, as likewise the new moons, and the sabbaths, and the festivals, and all the rest of the services accompanying these" as a prophetic anticipation of the new covenant (4.17.1).[65] Such works are to be set aside in favor of the deeds in Isaiah that, according to Irenaeus, "pertained to salvation," such as ceasing from evil ways, relieving the oppressed, and pleading for the widow (cf. Is 1:16-18; *Haer.* 4.17.1, translation adjusted).[66]

Similarly, in discussing the continuity between the old and new dispensations, Irenaeus makes a distinction between those works that were particular to the period of the Mosaic law and those that are greater and necessary for salvation under both. As Irenaeus writes, "the precepts of an absolutely perfect life . . . are the same in each Testament," and while God "has promulgated particular laws adapted for each . . . the more prominent and greatest commandments, without which it is not possible to be saved, He has exhorted [us to observe] the same in both" (sed eminentiora et summa, sine quibus salvari non est, in utroque eadem suasit, 4.12.3; translation adjusted). These greater commandments, which Irenaeus elsewhere calls the "natural precepts of the law" (*naturalia Legis*), appear from his perspective to be part and parcel of justification by faith. As Irenaeus writes, "it is seen from his own words that the Lord did not abrogate the natural precepts of the law, by which man is justified, which also those who were justified by faith, and who pleased God, did observe previous to the giving of the law [per quæ homo justificatur, quæ etiam ante legisdationem custodiebant qui fide justificabantur], but that He extended and fulfilled them" (4.13.1; translation adjusted).[67] Irenaeus illustrates this point with examples from the Sermon on the Mount, in which Christ expands Moses' prohibitions of adultery and murder to lust and anger as well. Contrary to the followers of Marcion, who regard

---

[64]Cf. *Haer.* 4.16.1-2.

[65]Cf. Barn. 2.5; Diog. 3.2-5. It bears noting, to take one example, that Irenaeus does not oppose oblations *qua* oblations, as the new covenant has oblations as well; see *Haer.* 4.18.2, 11.3.3 below.

[66]Cf. Justin, *Dial.* 18.2, 44.4.

[67]Cf. ActPl 8.10.

these differences as "an opposition to and an overturning of the [pre-
cepts] of the past," Christ's words exhibit "a fulfulling and an extension"
of these natural precepts (4.13.1).[68]

Works of the law thus do not appear to be a general category of action
or obedience, as Irenaeus indeed equates faith itself with the action of
obeying God in 4.6.5: "Now, to believe in Him is to do His will" (credere
autem ei est facere eius voluntatem). Love also appears to be outside the
category of works of the law, for without it, even faith—which both Paul
and Irenaeus set in antithesis to works of the law—is of no avail.[69]

In Irenaeus's *Demonstration*, the law under discussion is similarly the
Torah, received by Moses in the desert for the children of Israel and supplemented with Deuteronomy at the end of his life (*Epid.* 26, 28). One
may detect a shift in emphasis outside of the polemical context of *Against
Heresies*, where the continuing value of the Mosaic law (and its author)
were in question; while fewer specific works are mentioned, both the
Decalogue commandments (such as the prohibition of murder) and
other laws (such as those regarding tithes and sacrifices) are portrayed as
superfluous, seeing as they are met and surpassed by Christians (96).
Though this grouping of the Decalogue along with "laws of bondage"
may seem to be in tension with the Decalogue's continuing importance
in *Against Heresies*, these perspectives are compatible in that the necessity
spoken of in the earlier work is for performance of the Decalogue's commandments (quae si quis non fecerit, non habet salutem[70]), which is
similarly affirmed (and attested as being surpassed) in the *Demonstration*
(*Haer.* 4.15.1; *Epid.* 95). Likewise, *Against Heresies* similarly speaks of the
earlier righteous fathers having the Decalogue's righteousness written on
their hearts and thus not needing prohibitionary commandments (vir-
tutem decalogi conscriptam habentes in cordibus et animabus suis
... propter quod non fuit necesse admoneri eos correptoriis literis,
4.16.3), including those of the Decalogue.

---

[68]This passage's content corresponds closely with *Dial.* 43-46.
[69]Cf. *Haer.* 4.12.2.
[70]"Which, if any one does not observe, he has no salvation."

Irenaeus also references a number of relevant sections from Paul that discuss works of the law in *Demonstration* 35, including an allusion to Romans 3:20-21. In this section, Irenaeus places emphasis on the law itself as the crux of Paul's antithesis, so that it is the Torah, rather than any specific works, which is distinguished from the faith of Abraham and of Christians. After testifying to this shared faith with reference to the familiar Pauline citation of Genesis 15:6 (cf. Rom 4:3, Gal 3:6), Irenaeus writes,

> In the same way, we, believing in God, are made righteous, for "through faith shall the righteous live";[71] so "the promise made to Abraham [came] not through the Law but through faith."[72] Since Abraham was made righteous by faith, and "the Law is not laid for the righteous,"[73] likewise, we are not made righteous by the Law, but by faith, which receives testimony from the Law and Prophets,[74] and which the Word of God offers us. (*Epid.* 35)

From the location of these allusions to Romans and Galatians, it is evident that Irenaeus is drawing from sections of Paul's letters that discuss works of the law; however, because it is the law that Irenaeus sees as Paul's target (rather than works or "working" per se), Irenaeus is able to refer to "works of the law" simply with "law," which now stands in for the full phrase.

In summary, the law in question for Irenaeus is the Mosaic legislation given to Israel in the desert, including practices such as circumcision, Sabbath, new moons, and sacrifices, which Irenaeus identifies as the "yoke of bondage" (cf. Gal 5:1). Irenaeus contrasts these practices with the natural precepts of the law and the Decalogue, and though even the Decalogue is made relative in the *Demonstration*, this is because its dictates are now intensified and surpassed by Christ's precepts.

Significance: What does the practice of these works signify? According to Irenaeus in *Against Heresies*, the observance of works of the law represents identification with the race of Abraham, the Jewish people,

---

[71]Hab 2:4; Rom 1:17; Gal 3:11; cf. *Haer.* 4.34.2.
[72]Cf. Rom 4:13.
[73]1 Tim 1:9.
[74]Cf. Rom 3:20-21.

which has the Mosaic legislation as its particular inheritance. As is seen from Irenaeus's description of the Ebionites, the continued practice of circumcision and "the practices which are prescribed by the law" is described as upholding "the Judaic standard of living" (Judaico charactere vitæ), which accompanies their rejection of Paul as an apostate from the law (apostolum Paulum recusant, apostatam eum legis dicentes, *Haer.* 1.26.2, ACW). In discussing the continuity between covenants in 3.12, Irenaeus identifies circumcision in particular as given to distinguish the race of Abraham, which had received the promise of inheritance: "For [God] gave it as a sign, that they [the Jews] might not be like the Egyptians" (3.12.11).[75] The same purpose is restated in 4.16: rather than being a "completer of righteousness" (consummatricem justitiae), circumcision was given "as a sign, that the race of Abraham might continue recognizable" (ut cognoscibile perseverus genus Abrahae), with the same purpose identified for the keeping of Sabbath (4.16.1).

From a salvation-historical perspective, the adoption of works of the law can also be seen as an identification with the period prior to Christ's advent. As the people of Israel were given a "yoke of bondage" as legislation in the wilderness,[76] having chosen to desert God and being "placed for the future in a state of servitude suited to their wish," to continue observing this legislation would be to identify with the people not yet brought to freedom by Christ (4.15.1).[77] As Irenaeus writes later in book 4, "circumcision and the law of works" represent the "intervening period" between Abraham (and the former patriarchs) and the coming of Christ, so that to adopt such works represents an identification with this former period of bondage (4.25.1).

---

[75]There is an obvious tension here with the anachronism of Abraham performing a work of the Mosaic law (circumcision). Irenaeus explains this by stating that both covenants—that of law under Moses, and that of grace under Christ—are prefigured in Abraham, and are represented respectively by Abraham's circumcision and his prior justification by faith; cf. *Haer.* 4.25.1.

[76]Cf. Gal 5:1.

[77]While Irenaeus typically makes a twofold distinction between covenants (that of Moses and that of Christ, both of which are prefigured in Abraham, as in 4.25.1), this usage is not completely uniform. In 3.11.8 Irenaeus speaks of four covenants, and the Latin translation and an extant Greek fragment differ substantially in describing them: the Latin text lists the four covenants as those under Adam, Noah, Moses, and Christ, while the Greek speaks of Noah, Abraham, Moses, and Christ.

Irenaeus makes clear that works such as circumcision do not represent "the completer of righteousness," perhaps contra Jewish interlocutors who, like Trypho in Justin's *Dialogue*, would contend that to adopt such works would complete the Christian's otherwise piecemeal fulfillment of the Mosaic law (4.16.1).[78] While criticizing those who held to practices beyond what the law prescribed (and citing Paul in Romans 10:3 in doing so), "legalism" would not accurately characterize the significance of observing works of the law according to Irenaeus.[79] Indeed, Irenaeus commends those who were scrupulous about the law, contending that "as many as feared God, and were anxious about His law, these ran to Christ, and were all saved. . . . For the law never hindered them from believing in the Son of God; nay, but it even exhorted them so to do" (4.2.8).

In Irenaeus's *Demonstration*, the adoption of works of the law similarly represents an identification with "the former legislation" under Moses, and thus the people of this legislation, the Jews (*Epid.* 95). Along with this, adoption of such works represents identification with humanity's juvenile state before Christ, which needed "the Law as a paedagogue" (96; cf. Gal 3:24), and from a salvation-historical perspective, with the "intervening period" before Christ's advent (8).[80]

Opposition: Why are these works not necessary for the Christian? In *Against Heresies*, the reason that works of the Mosaic law are not necessary for the Christian is straightforward: a new covenant—and hence a new legislation—has come with Christ, the incarnate Word. As Irenaeus explains,

> the law, since it was laid down for those in bondage, used to instruct the soul by means of those corporeal objects which were of an external nature, drawing it, as by a bond, to obey its commandments, that man might learn to serve God. But the Word set free the soul, and taught that through it the body should be willingly purified. Which having been accomplished, it followed as of course, that the bonds of slavery should be removed, to which man had now become accustomed, and that he should follow God without fetters:

---

[78]Cf. *Dial.* 8.3, 10.3, 19.1, 27.1.
[79]Cf. *Haer.* 4.12.4.
[80]Cf. *Haer.* 4.25.1.

moreover, that the laws of liberty should be extended, and subjection to the king increased, so that no one who is converted should appear unworthy to Him who set him free. (*Haer.* 4.13.2)

As Irenaeus describes, the change in human nature wrought by the incarnate Word renders unnecessary the "bonds of slavery," those "laws of bondage" given to the people by Moses (4.16.5). Just as God made a law suitable for the condition of the unruly people in the desert and gave certain precepts in accordance with the hardness of their hearts (such as the multitude of ordinances and the permission of divorce),[81] so too has God given a new law corresponding to the redeemed condition of humanity that has come with Christ's incarnation.[82] While this old law, which was in operation from Moses until John the Baptist,[83] was fit for slaves and those "who are as yet undisciplined," the precepts of the new law are for those who "are free, and have been justified by faith" (liberis autem et fide justificatis congruentia dans præcepta, 4.9.1). The abolition of the old "laws of bondage" is repeatedly and emphatically contrasted with the place of the Decalogue and the "laws of liberty" under the new dispensation;[84] while works such as circumcision and Sabbath, "which were given for bondage and for a sign . . . He canceled by the new covenant of liberty," in the new covenant Christ "has increased and widened those laws which are natural, and noble, and common to all" (4.16.5).[85]

Against those "advocating the cause of the Jews," this new covenant does not correspond with the rebuilding of the temple under Zerubbabel, an idea Irenaeus counters by pointing that the Jews continued using the Mosaic law during that period (4.34.4). However, with Christ's advent, "the new covenant which brings back peace, and the law which gives life

---

[81]*Haer.* 4.14.2, 4.15.2. Irenaeus follows Justin in tying this legislation to Israel's disobedience in the desert with the golden calf; see *Dial.* 19.5, Noormann, *Irenäus als Paulusinterpret*, 396n101.

[82]Irenaeus sees such a principle of accommodation as present in the new covenant as well; see *Haer.* 4.15.2.

[83]Cf. *Haer.* 4.4.2.

[84]Cf. *Haer.* 4.12-13, 16.

[85]Irenaeus also identifies a typological significance for the Mosaic law's works, with "the law typifying, as it were, certain things in a shadow, and delineating eternal things by temporal, celestial by terrestrial" (4.11.4). Thus, works such as circumcision and Sabbath "were given for a sign," as "the circumcision after the flesh typified that after the Spirit," and weekly Sabbath prefigured the Christian's continual service in the kingdom (4.16.1).

(vivificatrix lex), has gone forth over the whole earth," as was prophesied by the prophets Isaiah and Micah (Is 2:3-4; Mic 4:2-3; *Haer.* 4.34.4).[86] No other law and word coming from Zion has produced such transformation among the Gentiles, except for the "law of liberty [*libertatis lex*], that is, the word of God, preached by the apostles," on account of which nations have turned their swords into plowshares (4.34.4). This transformation among the Gentiles fulfills the testimony of the prophets, and confirms that it is Christ and his law to which they were pointing.

It is significant for Irenaeus that this new covenant is not limited to one race; Irenaeus writes that because this legislation of liberty is greater than the legislation of bondage, it therefore "has also been diffused, not throughout one nation [only], but over the whole world" (4.9.2). Irenaeus makes the same point in retelling Jesus' parable of the wicked tenants, in which "God planted the vineyard of the human race when at the first He formed Adam and chose the fathers," then "let it out to husbandmen when He established the Mosaic dispensation," hedging the vineyard with specific instructions for worship and building for it the tower of Jerusalem (4.36.2).[87] With the killing of the prophets and finally the son by these tenants, "the Lord God did even give it up (no longer hedged around, but thrown open throughout all the world) to other husbandmen, who render the fruits in their seasons,—the beautiful elect tower being also raised everywhere. For the illustrious Church is [now] everywhere, and everywhere is the winepress digged: because those who do receive the Spirit are everywhere" (4.36.2). However, this national limitation does not by itself constitute a reason why Christians are exempt from observing the works of the Mosaic law; rather, this point is subordinate to the advent of the promised new covenant in Christ, and does not stand alone as an objection.

Irenaeus additionally writes at length of how the works of the Mosaic law are not necessary because they were not given for humanity's justification,

---

[86]Cf. similarly *Dial.* 109.1-3; *PP* 6–7.

[87]One may note the parallels with Letter of Aristeas 139–42: "[Moses] fenced us round with impregnable ramparts and walls of iron, that we might not mingle at all with any of the other nations, but remain pure in body and soul. . . . He hedged us round on all sides by rules of purity, affecting alike what we eat, or drink, or touch, or hear, or see."

and frequently alludes to Pauline texts to substantiate his arguments. Like Justin, Irenaeus formulates his arguments by referencing Abraham and the righteous patriarchs who lived before him, who lived neither by Sabbath, nor circumcision, nor the rest of the Mosaic legislation:[88]

> And that humanity was not justified by these things, but that they were given as a sign to the people, this fact shows,—that Abraham himself, without circumcision and without observance of Sabbaths, "believed God, and it was reckoned to him as righteousness; and he was called the friend of God" (Gen 15:6; cf. Gal 3:6; Rom 4:3). Then, again, Lot, without circumcision, was brought out from Sodom, receiving salvation from God. So also did Noah, pleasing God, although he was uncircumcised, receive the dimensions [of the ark]. . . . Enoch, too, pleasing God, without circumcision, discharged the office of God's legate to the angels. . . . Moreover, all the rest of the multitude of those righteous men who lived before Abraham, and of those patriarchs who preceded Moses, were justified independently of the things above mentioned, and without the law of Moses. As also Moses himself says to the people in Deuteronomy: "The Lord thy God formed a covenant in Horeb. The Lord formed not this covenant with your fathers, but for you."[89] (Deut 5:2-3; 4.16.2, translation adjusted)

This naturally leads to the question of why the Mosaic legislation was not needed for the earlier fathers, but only for the people under Moses, which Irenaeus explains thus:

> Why, then, did the Lord not form the covenant for the fathers? Because "the law was not established for righteous men."[90] But the righteous fathers had the meaning of the Decalogue written in their hearts and souls,[91] that is, they loved the God who made them, and did no injury to their neighbour. There was therefore no occasion that they should be cautioned by prohibitory mandates, because they had the righteousness of the law in themselves. (4.16.3-4)

According to Irenaeus, while the Mosaic law became necessary "when this righteousness and love to God had passed into oblivion, and became

---

[88]Cf. *Dial.* 19.3-6, 23.1-4, 27.5.

[89]It appears fundamental to Irenaeus's argumentation that justification entails a being or becoming righteous; because the patriarchs before Moses were indeed righteous, it follows logically that their justification (or "righteousing") could not have come by the Mosaic law.

[90]1 Tim 1:9.

[91]Cf. Rom 2:15; 2 Cor 3:2.

extinct in Egypt," Christians finds themselves in the same position of Abraham and these earlier righteous fathers, living by a faith whereby "the meaning of the Decalogue [is] written in their hearts and souls," the words of which "remain permanently with us, receiving by means of His advent in the flesh, extension and increase, but not abrogation" (4.16.4). In this way, Christians—though most are from among the Gentiles—are true heirs of God's promises to Abraham, whose justification by faith apart from the Mosaic law prefigured their own. Irenaeus substantiates this point by citing Galatians 3:5-9:

> But that our faith was also prefigured in Abraham, and that he was the patriarch of our faith, and, as it were, the prophet of it, the Apostle has very fully taught, when he says in the Epistle to the Galatians: "He therefore that ministers to you the Spirit, and works miracles among you, [does he do it] by the works of the law, or by the hearing of faith? Even as Abraham believed God, and it was reckoned to him as righteousness. Know therefore, that they which are of faith, the same are the children of Abraham. But the Scripture, foreseeing that God would justify the Gentiles through faith, announced beforehand unto Abraham, that in him all nations should be blessed. So then they which are of faith shall be blessed with faithful Abraham."[92] For which [reasons the Apostle] declared that this man was not only the prophet of faith, but also the father of those who from among the Gentiles believe in Jesus Christ, because his faith and ours are one and the same. (4.21.1; translation adjusted)

Thus, while "circumcision and the law of works occupied the intervening period" between the time of the patriarchs and the Christians,

> this faith which is in uncircumcision, as connecting the end with the beginning, has been made [both] the first and the last. For, as I have shown, it existed in Abraham antecedently to circumcision, as it also did in the rest of the righteous who pleased God: and in these last times, it again sprang up among mankind through the coming of the Lord. (4.25.1)

Irenaeus also rejects a number of alternative views as to why the works of the Mosaic law do not bind the Christian. Such works are not rejected because the Mosaic legislation "is different from, and contrary to, the

---

[92]Gal 3:5-9.

doctrine of the Gospel," as is judged by "all those who are evil-minded" (3.12.12, ACW). On the contrary, the new lawgiver's command "not only to abstain from things forbidden by the law, but even from longing after them—is not contrary to [the law]," nor is it "the utterance of one destroying the law, but of one fulfilling, extending, and affording greater scope to it" (4.13.1).[93] Comparing the two legislations by the illustration of Christ's comparing himself to the temple, Irenaeus writes:

> But [the words] *greater* and *less* are not applied to those things which have nothing in common between themselves, and are of an opposite nature, and mutually repugnant; but are used in the case of those of the same substance, and which possess properties in common, but merely differ in number and size; such as water from water, and light from light, and grace from grace. (4.9.2)

In addition, while Irenaeus recognizes what one might call a kind of supralegalism as present among some Jews in Christ's time, he does not identify legalism (at least in relation to the actual dictates of the law) as an argument against observing the Mosaic legislation. According to Irenaeus, Christ "does not call the law given by Moses commandments of men, but the traditions of the elders themselves which they had invented," and it is by their adherence to these outside commandments that "they made the law of God of none effect, and were on this account also not subject to His Word" (4.12.4).[94] This devotion to traditions beyond the Mosaic law, according to Irenaeus, is what Paul has in view in Romans 10:3-4: "For this is what Paul says concerning these men: 'For they, being ignorant of God's righteousness, and going about to establish their own righteousness, have not submitted themselves to the righteousness of God. For Christ is the end of the law for righteousness to every one that believes'" (Rom 10:3-4; *Haer.* 4.12.4, translation adjusted).[95] In contrast to such men, however, Irenaeus commends those who were meticulous

---

[93]In addition to instituting the new covenant of freedom, Irenaeus holds that it was Christ himself who appointed the covenant of bondage, but now has made his disciples friends rather than servants (*Haer.* 4.13.4; cf. John 15:15).

[94]See also *Haer.* 4.11.4.

[95]As Noormann notes, Irenaeus's reading of Rom 10:3 has often drawn severe criticism from Protestant interpreters; see Noormann, *Irenäus als Paulusinterpret*, 404-5, e.g. Lawson, *Biblical Theology of Saint Irenaeus*, 75.

with respect to observing the Mosaic law itself: for "as many as feared God, and were anxious about His law, these ran to Christ, and were all saved" (4.2.8).

In the *Demonstration*, Irenaeus similarly argues that the "former legislation" is now surpassed by the precepts of Christ (exemplified particularly in the Sermon on the Mount), which is powerfully illustrated by setting the two in contrast in *Demonstration* 96:

> Therefore we do not need the Law as a paedogogue.[96] . . . For no more shall the Law say, "You shall not commit adultery," to him <to> whom does not <even> come desire for another's wife[97]; nor, "You shall not kill," to him who has removed all anger and enmity from himself[98]; <nor>, "you shall not covet your neighbour's field or his ox or his ass," to those who make no care at all of earthly things, but lay up heavenly fruit[99]; and neither "an eye for an eye and a tooth for a tooth," to him who counts no man an enemy, but all [as his] neighbour, and, for this reason, cannot even stretch out his hand in vengeance.[100] (*Epid.* 96)

As Irenaeus describes, those who have been transformed by Christ and follow his more rigorous injunctions have no need for the previous legislation.

Irenaeus also points to a number of prophecies from Scripture that confirm that the former legislation was meant to be fulfilled and abrogated. Rather than "by the prolixity of the Law," humanity is to be saved by faith and love, which are the fulfillment of Isaiah 10: "He will complete and cut short [His] Word in righteousness; for God will make a concise Word in all the world" (Is 10:22-23 LXX, cf. Rom 9:28; *Epid.* 87).[101] This "concise Word" is attested by Paul to be love, the fulfillment of the law,[102] and the faith represented by Christ's two great commandments, on which hang all the Law and Prophets (87).[103] Isaiah 43 is similarly called as a

---

[96]Gal 3:24.
[97]Cf. Ex 20:13; Mt 5:27-28.
[98]Cf. Ex 20:15; Mt 5:21-22.
[99]Cf. Ex 20:17; Mt 6:19-20.
[100]Cf. Ex. 21:24; Mt 5:38-39, 44-48.
[101]Cf. similarly Ign. *Eph.* 14.1.
[102]Cf. Gal 5:14; Rom 13:8, 10.
[103]Mt 22:37-40.

witness that the redeemed are saved by faith and love toward the Son of God "in the newness by the Word," so that God's words through Isaiah to "forget the old things" means that "He does not want the redeemed to turn back to the Mosaic legislation, for the Law was fulfilled by Christ" (Is 43:18-21, *Epid.* 89).

According to Irenaeus, Scripture's prophecies also indicate that the Gentiles will be accepted into God's new covenant *qua* Gentiles. With a series of Old Testament references, many of which parallel Paul's own citations, Gentiles are identified as the "waterless place" before the Spirit's advent,[104] those who no longer trust in the works of their hands,[105] the people who had not sought God[106] and were called "not my people,"[107] the stones raised up to Abraham who have received hearts of flesh,[108] and the barren woman who now bears more than she who has a husband.[109] Even Moses himself prophesies in Deuteronomy that God would provoke his idolatrous people with what is no nation,[110] and "that the Gentiles are to be at 'the head' and the disbelieving people at 'the tail' (*Epid.* 95; cf. Deut 28:44). Having chronicled the long disobedience of Israel to its covenant, culminating in its killing of the Messiah, Irenaeus concludes:

> [therefore] God was pleased to bestow His inheritance on the foolish Gentiles, who were neither of the citizenship of God nor knew who God is. Since, then, by this calling, life has been given and God has recapitulated in us the faith of Abraham, we should no longer turn back, that is, I mean, to the former legis- lation. For we received the Lord of the Law, the Son of God, and through faith in Him we learn to love God with [our] whole heart and our neighbour as ourselves. (*Epid.* 95)

Having received the author of the Law itself, and being received precisely as "no people" in accordance with Scripture's promises, the Gentile church now has no need to turn back to the Jewish law.

---

[104]Is 43:19; *Epid.* 89.
[105]Is 17:7-8; *Epid.* 91.
[106]Is 65:1; cf. Rom 10:20; *Epid.* 92.
[107]Hos 2:23; cf. Rom 9:25; *Epid.* 93.
[108]Mt 3:9; Ezek 11:19; *Epid.* 93.
[109]Is 54:1; cf. Gal 4:27; *Epid.* 94.
[110]Deut 32:21; cf. Rom. 10:19; *Epid.* 95.

CONCLUSION

In conclusion, Irenaeus's perspective on works of the law is rooted within the debates over the role of the Mosaic law in the new covenant, with specific identity markers such as circumcision and Sabbath coming into particular focus. These works are distinguished from natural and moral precepts, which are necessary for salvation (*Haer.* 4.12.3), such as those of the Decalogue. While Irenaeus can indeed even speak of the Decalogue's commandments as superfluous, it is not because they involve "doing" rather than "believing,"[111] but rather because the "doing" of the Christians so far surpasses the "doing" prescribed in the Torah that the former legislation is simply obsolete by comparison (*Epid.* 95).[112] The practice of these works represents identification with the Jewish people, the old covenant, and the prior unredeemed condition of Adamic humanity. According to Irenaeus, these works are rendered unnecessary by the arrival of the new covenant and law with Christ's advent, which so transforms humanity that it renders the Mosaic "laws of bondage" unnecessary, and allows the "laws of liberty" to be extended so as to increase subjection to God (*Haer.* 4.13.2). As the examples of Abraham and the righteous patriarchs show, these works of the Mosaic law were not given for humanity's justification, but rather to constrain rebellious Israel. By contrast, the new covenant is for all nations, and the testimony of the Hebrew prophets foretells that the Gentiles will be accepted into the new covenant *qua* Gentiles. Irenaeus both cites and alludes to Pauline verses on works of the law in his expositions on this topic, offering direct evidence for the understanding of works of the law at the close of the period of apostolic "living memory."

---

[111]Cf. Douglas Moo, "Justification in Galatians," in *Understanding the Times: New Testament Studies in the 21st Century: Essays in Honor of D. A. Carson on the Occasion of His 65th Birthday*, ed. Andreas J. Köstenberger and Robert W. Yarbrough (Wheaton, IL: Crossway, 2011), 167, 182.

[112]Cf. Iain MacKenzie, *Irenaeus's Demonstration of the Apostolic Preaching: A Theological Commentary and Translation* (Aldershot, UK: Ashgate, 2002), 299.

PART IV

CONCLUSIONS

◻

The idea that any man or writer should be opaque to those
who lived in the same culture, spoke the same language, shared the same
habitual imagery and unconscious assumptions, and yet be transparent
to those who have none of these advantages, is in my opinion preposterous.
There is an a priori improbability in it which almost no argument
and no evidence could counterbalance.

C. S. Lewis, "Modern Theology and Biblical Criticism"
(or "Fern-seed and Elephants")

C. S. Lewis, *Fern-seed and Elephants: And Other Essays on Christianity*, ed. Walter Hooper
(Glasgow: Collins, 1977), 112-13.

12

CONCLUSIONS

◻

EARLY PERSPECTIVES ON WORKS OF THE LAW

This study began with an overview of competing accounts of Paul's meaning by "works of the law" as put forward by the old and new perspectives on Paul, and has now taken us through all of the relevant patristic material on this question up to the time of Irenaeus, the last figure writing within a period of apostolic "living memory." We will here bring together these second-century perspectives with regard to the meaning, significance, and reasons for opposing works of the law.

Category A, direct evidence. We begin with this study's two A-level witnesses, Justin Martyr and Irenaeus, who refer to verses on works of the law within similar discussions to Paul's own in Romans and Galatians. In Justin's *Dialogue with Trypho*, the law in question is the Mosaic law, given at Mount Sinai following Israel's apostasy with the golden calf, with the works rejected including circumcision, Sabbath keeping and Jewish calendar observances (such as feasts and new moons), sacrifices, and laws regarding food. In *Against Heresies* and the *Demonstration*, Irenaeus similarly regards this law as the body of legislation delivered by Moses in the desert, which he calls the "yoke of bondage" (*Haer.* 4.15.1; Gal 5:1), and rejects works such as circumcision, Sabbath, the building of the temple, and the elaborate practices of worship and sacrifice. Both of these figures distinguish these works of the law from good or righteous works more broadly. Justin contrasts the work of circumcision with God's everlasting righteous requirements (cf. Rom 2:26), and makes clear that his objections are not to the works contained in the Torah that "in themselves are good, and holy, and just," which the righteous patriarchs also kept (*Dial.* 44.1–45.4). Irenaeus similarly makes clear that works of the law are not those of the Decalogue, which are "the entrance into life," and "which, if any one does not observe, he has no salvation" (*Haer.* 4.12.5, 4.15.1). Nor are these the natural precepts of the law that the righteous patriarchs observed: Irenaeus sees these works as closely linked with justification by faith, and testifies that Christ fulfills and extends them. Interestingly, even the works prescribed by the Decalogue can be portrayed as unnecessary in Irenaeus's *Demonstration*, though this is because they have now been intensified and surpassed by the precepts of Christ.

For Justin, the practice of these works of the law signifies identification with the Jewish people and covenant, and separation from the Gentiles. Justin comments that to adopt circumcision is to become a Jew, as proselytes are "circumcised in order to be incorporated into the body of your [Trypho's] people like a native-born" (*Dial.* 123.1). For Justin, reliance on these works means supposing that the "descendants of Abraham according to the flesh" will inherit God's promises (*Dial.* 44.1-2; cf. Rom 4:1, 16; Gal 3:3-9). Justin also makes clear in his debate that these practices were not given for the sake of righteousness (cf. Rom 4:9-11), with Trypho eventually being compelled to agree. Likewise, according to Irenaeus, to observe these works identifies one with the Jewish nation and their covenant, with circumcision and Sabbath given to distinguish the Jews from other nations and preserve Abraham's race recognizable, rather than for the fulfillment of righteousness. From a salvation-historical perspective, the practice of this former legislation also represents identification with humanity's juvenile state before its renewal by Christ (cf. Gal 3:24), and with the intermediate period between Abraham's calling and Christ's advent.

Justin and Irenaeus each provide a wide range of arguments for why works of the law are not necessary for the Christian. For Justin, the most prominent reasons for rejecting these works are the testimony of the Hebrew prophets; the arrival of the new law and covenant with Christ, which abrogates the old; the nature of this new covenant as intended for all nations; the lives and experiences of Christians in confirming the new covenant's arrival; and the examples of Abraham and the righteous patriarchs, who were similarly justified by faith without circumcision and the Mosaic law (cf. Rom 4:3-11; Gal 3:5-9). Additional reasons include the law's purpose to identify and constrain hard-hearted Israel, not to justify; the prophets' testimony regarding the rejection of the Jewish people; imperfections in the old law and covenant, which reveal them as provisional and not eternal; and the need for spiritual understanding to rightly interpret Scripture's symbolic meaning. Underlying all these arguments is the question of whether Jesus is indeed the Messiah, since both Justin and Trypho agree that the Messiah's promised new covenant and law will take precedence over the old. Irenaeus's primary arguments against these works relate to the arrival of the new covenant and law with Christ's advent, which so transforms humanity that it renders the Mosaic "yoke of bondage" unnecessary, and allows the "laws of liberty" to be extended so that subjection to God might increase. This "law that gives life" has gone forth from Zion by the apostles' preaching and transformed the Gentile nations, fulfilling Scripture's prophecies and thus confirming the new covenant's arrival. In addition, Irenaeus argues that the works of this law were not given for humanity's justification, as is illustrated by the examples of Abraham and the righteous patriarchs, but rather to constrain rebellious Israel; that the new covenant is for all nations (and not simply the Jews); and that the Hebrew prophets foretell the annulment of these works and the acceptance of the Gentiles *qua* Gentiles.

Category B, supporting evidence. Additional evidence for the second century understanding of works of the law is found in this study's three B-level witnesses—the epistles of Ignatius, the Epistle to Diognetus, and Melito's *On the Pascha*—which make use of Romans or Galatians and contain similar discussions to Paul's in these epistles. In Ignatius's writings against the Judaizers in *Magnesians* and *Philadelphians*, the law in question is the Mosaic law, which he denotes as "the archives." The specific works rejected by Ignatius include Sabbath and the "ancient practices" in *Magnesians*, and a relativizing of circumcision in *Philadelphians*.

Diognetus rejects a number of Jewish practices contained in the Torah (though "the law" is not mentioned), including animal sacrifices, food regulations, the observance of Sabbaths, circumcision, and the new moons, feasts, and fasts of the Jewish calendar. Melito's paschal homily also regards the law in question as the Torah, and naturally focuses its objections on the feast of Passover and the sacrifice of the lamb, with Israel's focus on the temple, Jerusalem, and the inheritance of the land also noted. It is also clear that these three witnesses are not opposing "works" in a general or absolute sense: Ignatius replaces Sabbath keeping with observing the Lord's day, Diognetus contrasts these Jewish works with the universally beneficent practices of Christians, and Melito sees the decrees of the gospel as taking the place of the law's practices.

For Ignatius, the practice of these works signifies "Judaism," the Jews' manner of life and worship according to the Torah. In Diognetus, these works represent the distinctive markers of the Jews and their misguided system of worship. For Melito, adherence to the law's practices represents association with the people of Israel, just as adherence to the gospel represents association with the church.

In *Magnesians*, Ignatius's reasoning against these works includes the Christian's reception of grace apart from them (cf. Gal 5:4), the witness of the Hebrew prophets, the priority of Christ's teaching and the practices he enjoins, the salvation-historical movement from the "old yeast" of Judaism to the "new yeast" of Christianity, and the universality of Christianity. Ignatius's main arguments in *Philadelphians* relate to the primacy of Christ and his teaching over the archives of the law, with the hope of justification found in Christ's cross, death, and resurrection, and the faith that comes from him. These are accompanied by minor arguments regarding the unity of the church and witness of the prophets. Diognetus offers little argumentation against these works, with the apologist briefly echoing common Greco-Roman critiques of Judaism, and possibly implying arguments regarding the universality of Christianity and the establishment of Christians as a new race. Melito identifies Israel's law and its works as types pointing toward coming realities, which have now arrived with Christ's advent, thus rendering the types superfluous.

Category C, circumstantial evidence. Further possible attestation to works of the law is found in the Didache, the Epistle of Barnabas, and the *Apology of Aristides*, three C-level sources that lack clear usage of Pauline texts, but contain similar discussions to Paul's in Romans and Galatians. In the Didache, the works rejected include fasting according to the Jewish calendar and the Jews' manner of prayer, both of which are based on traditions associated with the Torah, along with possible implied rejections of the temple and sacrificial system. In Barnabas, the legislation in question is Israel's law, with the works rejected including sacrifices, circumcision, calendar observances like Sabbaths, new moons and fasts, food regulations, and a focus on the temple. Aristides's *Apology* similarly rejects practices of the Torah, including Sabbaths and other Jewish calendar observances (new moons, Passover, feasts), circumcision, and regulations regarding food. As with the other witnesses, these sources do not reject works in a general or absolute sense. Rather than fasting on Monday and Thursday and praying the *Shemoneh Esreh*, Christians in the Didache are instructed to fast on Wednesday and Friday and pray the Lord's prayer. Barnabas contrasts the rejected works of the Mosaic law with the Lord's righteous requirements (cf. Rom 2:26), such as baptism and the acts of mercy enjoined by the prophets. Aristides distinguishes the works of the law from Jewish practices that constitute right imitation of God, such as having compassion on the poor and burying the dead, as well as the precepts of the Christian law that are inscribed on believers' hearts (cf. Rom 2:15).

In the Didache, the practice of these works identifies one with "the hypocrites," the Jews. For Barnabas, to practice these works signifies the adoption of the Jewish law, and thus association with Israel, the people set in contrast with Christians throughout the epistle. In Aristides's *Apology*, these acts of misguided piety represent identification with the γένος of the Jews, just as (for Aristides) the practice of worshiping the sun identifies one as a barbarian.

The Didache provides very little reasoning for rejecting these works, besides the general charge that they represent hypocrisy and their ostensible replacement with corresponding Christian works. Barnabas, by contrast, provides an array of reasoning for why these works are unnecessary, with the three most prominent arguments being the testimony of the Hebrew prophets; the new law now instituted by Christ, which takes precedence over the old; and Christ's transformative circumcision of the heart (cf. Rom 2:29), brought about in baptism, which allows these laws to be understood and obeyed in their true spiritual sense. Aristides briefly comments that the Jews' works are directed to angels rather than God, with the new covenant's creation of a new people also possibly implied as an argument.

Unclassed sources. Finally, we round out this picture with the fragmentary testimony in our two excursuses. The works rejected in the fragments of the Preaching of Peter are the Torah's calendar observances, which correspond with the Jewish people and their erroneous worship, as well as the old covenant. These practices are rejected because they did not constitute true worship of God. Instead, a new way of worship has been revealed to Christians in the new covenant, which establishes them as a third race in relation to the Greeks and Jews. In the brief fragment of the *Dialogue of Jason and Papiscus*, the work in dispute is Sabbath observance. This work ostensibly represents identification with the Jews and a prior period in salvation history, and is relativized because God, following from the prophetic witness of Scripture, has replaced it with a new day with Christ's advent. The extant Acts of Paul are too fragmentary to contribute anything secure to this picture, besides what appears to be a statement from Paul that one is justified by works of righteousness.

Among the fragmentary reconstructions of nonmainstream sources in this period, it is testimony regarding the Ebionites—whose positions Tertullian identifies as the same held by Paul's Galatian opponents—that is most valuable for our study. The Ebionites regard the law in dispute as the Mosaic law, including the practices of circumcision, the observance of Sabbath and Jewish feasts, food regulations, and a focus on Jerusalem. Practicing these works signifies both an identification with Israel and the path to righteousness, as Jesus himself is regarded as being justified by these works. Thus, works of the law *are* necessary for the Christian, as faith in Christ and a corresponding life are not sufficient for salvation by themselves. Furthermore, since Christ was sent only to Israel according to the flesh, Christians must become members of this people by observing the Mosaic law. Rather than rejecting works of the law, then, the Ebionites reject Paul and regard him as an apostate. The perspectives of Marcion and Ptolemy are less useful witnesses to works of the law: Marcion's objections do not focus on either works or the law, but rather the creator god who gave the law, and Ptolemy's *Letter to Flora* seems to attribute these practices to the work of a morally ambiguous demiurge.

An "early perspective" on works of the law. In summarizing this patristic material, is it possible to speak of an "early perspective" on works of the law? While the testimony of the extant sources is not identical—not every source mentions all of the same works, nor are the same reasons given for rejecting them in each case—there still exists a striking degree of cohesion among these early witnesses, both with regard to the works and law in question and the significance of practicing these works. Though there is a wide range of argumentation regarding why these works are unnecessary for the Christian, these arguments frequently recur between the various patristic sources, and are broadly compatible with one another. Further, there does not appear to be significant variation in the interpretation of works of the law between sources that show stronger influence from Paul's discussions on the topic and those that show less, which suggests that the works and law under discussion in such debates were commonly known in early Christianity (as was implied by Paul's own usage of the phrase in Galatians and Romans, cf. chap. 1 above). This suggestion is strengthened by the absence of any controversy in the patristic sources regarding the law and works in question, or what is signified by practicing them. Indeed, these points appear to be common knowledge among Jewish interlocutors in this period as well, as is witnessed in the arguments of Trypho and the Ebionites.

This early conception of works of the law can be summarized as follows. The law in question is the Mosaic law, which was delivered to the hard-hearted nation of Israel following the apostasy at Sinai. The principal works of this law that come into focus are circumcision, Sabbath and other Jewish calendar observances (such as new moons, feasts, and fasts), sacrifices, and laws regarding food, with a focus on the temple and Jerusalem occasionally noted as well. The practices of the Mosaic law are consistently distinguished from good works more broadly, whether these be the natural and universal pious deeds that were performed by Abraham and the righteous patriarchs, the works of the Decalogue, the acts of mercy enjoined by the prophets, or the commandments of Christ and works of his covenant, such as baptism and keeping the Lord's day.

The practice of these works signifies identification with the Jewish people, the Jewish covenant, and "Judaism," the manner of life and worship prescribed in the Mosaic law. The Jewish nation, covenant, and praxis are so closely linked that each can stand as a synecdoche for the others; to be a part of this nation means to be a member of their covenant, and to live and worship according to its dictates. The practice of these works also represents a corresponding move of separation from the Gentile nations. These works are practiced because salvation is believed to be tied in with the election of the Jewish people, which one enters by observing the Jewish law. From a Christian salvation-historical perspective, it can also be said that practicing these works identifies one with the period before Christ's advent, and with the juvenile and hard-hearted condition of humanity before its renewal by Christ.

It is difficult to create categories for each source's arguments against the necessity for Christians to observe the works of the law, and an even greater challenge to create categories that can apply to all of them. Nevertheless, one can do justice to the patristic material by categorizing these arguments under five major headings:

1. The arrival of the new law and covenant in Christ, the Messiah, whose teachings and ordinances replace those of the Mosaic law

2. The witness of the Hebrew Scriptures, in which the prophets testify regarding the Messiah and this new covenant, and the cessation of these previous works

3. The universal nature of this new covenant, which is promised to be for all nations, and which has its arrival confirmed by the Gentiles receiving grace and turning to God apart from becoming Jews

4. The transformation in humanity wrought by Christ, understood as the new birth or the circumcision of the heart, which renders the laws given to hard-hearted Israel unnecessary, and which allows the types and mysteries of Scripture to be rightly understood

5. The examples of Abraham and the righteous patriarchs, who were similarly accepted by God apart from these practices, and whose righteousness confirms that the Mosaic law and circumcision were not given for humanity's justification

Though less prominent in these early sources, other arguments for not observing these works include the prophets' testimony that the Jews will be rejected; the establishment of Christians as a new race; imperfections in the old law that reveal it as temporary and provisional; the characterization of these practices as old in relation to Christianity's newness; and the unity of the church apart from these boundary markers.

Among these arguments, the understanding that Christ gives a new law within the new covenant is most useful in explaining why particular works of the Mosaic law—like circumcision and Sabbath—are always the points in conflict between Jews and Christians in this period, even while the entire Mosaic legislation is seen as not in effect. This is because Christians are under the law of Christ, which, though it fully replaces the old Mosaic law, nevertheless maintains some of the same precepts—such as on the priority of loving God and neighbor—and indeed intensifies many others, like the prohibitions of adultery and murder now extending to lust and anger. As a result, it is only the points of discontinuity between these laws—the markers of the Jewish people, and the system of legislation regarding purity and worship that God ordained for the nation in its sinful and hard-hearted condition—that come into focus in conflicts between Christian and Jewish parties. The case of Trypho is telling: though he is astonished at Christ's precepts and incredulous that anyone can keep them, he does not object to Christ's intensification of the Torah's moral teachings, since they do not violate the Mosaic law in the process. It is only those points that are left behind in the new covenant that spur Trypho's objections, though he too comes to acknowledge that if Christ is the Messiah, then his legislation indeed takes precedence over the law of Moses. There are thus no objections from Jews regarding moral or good works in this period, and if anything it is the other way round; Justin critiques Trypho for *downplaying* the decisive role of such works, with Jews relying instead on their possession of the old covenant markers that secure their status as God's elect people.

From Irenaeus to Origen. Though properly a subject for another investigation, it is useful to give a brief overview of how these lines of interpretation continue in patristic sources up to Origen, the author of the earliest extant commentary on Romans, whom Luther and Calvin identify as the source of errors on this topic.[1] The Muratorian Fragment (ca. 180–210),[2] though offering only the briefest of commentary, identifies the subject matter of Paul's letter to the Galatians not as works in general, but rather the specific work of circumcision (*Callatis circumcisione*).[3] The *Acts of Peter* (ca. 200) attests that Paul's depature for Spain caused great sadness among the Roman Christians, who recalled how "Paul often quarreled with the teachers of the Jews and had confounded them by saying, 'Christ, on whom your fathers laid their hands, abrogated their Sabbath and their fasting and festivals and circumcision and abolished the teaching of men and other traditions'" (Acts Pet. 1).[4] Bardesanes's *Book of the Laws of Various Countries* (ca. 190–220) parallels Diognetus and *Aristides* in contrasting Jewish law observance with the practices of Christians, who are not subject to the customs of only one race or locale. Just as Christians abstain from polygamy among the Parthians and violent retribution in Edessa, so too do they refrain from

---

[1]Cf. *LW* 26.121, 180, 275; *Comm. Gal.* 38–39.

[2]An excellent summary of recent scholarship and debates on the dating of the Muratorian Fragment is found in Eckhard J. Schnabel, "The Muratorian Fragment: The State of Research," *Journal of the Evangelical Theological Society* 57 (2014): 231-64; see also Christophe Guignard, "The Original Language of the Muratorian Fragment," *Journal of Theological Studies* 66 (2015): 596-624.

[3]As Schnabel notes (following Lindemann), these brief descriptions "presuppose that Christian teachers were still aware of the original historical conditions in which Paul wrote" (Schnabel, "Muratorian Fragment," 255-56; cf. Andreas Lindemann "Die Sammlung der Paulusbriefe im 1. und 2. Jahrhundert," in *The Biblical Canons*, ed. Jean-Marie Auwers and H. J. de Jonge [Leuven: Peeters, 2003], 349).

[4]J. K. Elliott, ed., *The Apocryphal New Testament: A Collection of Apocryphal Christian Literature in an English Translation* (Oxford: Clarendon Press, 1993), 399.

Jewish circumcision even if in Judea. Rather, "in whatever place they are and wherever they may find themselves, the local laws cannot force them to give up the law of their Messiah."[5]

While falling just beyond the scope of living memory, Tertullian offers a wealth of interpretation on works of the law across his writings, with the two most relevant being his works *Against the Jews* and *Against Marcion* (ca. 200-15). In the former, Tertullian follows similar lines of reasoning to those found in Justin's *Dialogue*, expressly identifying the law in question as that given to Moses for the Jews, not the natural law observed by Abraham and the righteous patriarchs (*Adv. Jud.* 2). This law's works, such as circumcision, Sabbath, and sacrifices, were given to serve as distinguishing markers for Israel, and have been abolished by the promised new law given to all nations by the Messiah, Jesus. As in Justin's *Dialogue with Trypho*, it is Jesus' identity as this promised figure that represents the true crux of conflict with the Jews (*Adv. Jud.* 3, 6-7). In the latter work, Tertullian writes that Paul's conflict with the Galatians was based on their "insisting on circumcision, and observing the seasons and days and months and years of those Jewish ceremonies which they ought to have known were now revoked." According to Tertullian, these "antiquated ceremonies" were rejected in accordance with the Creator's new dispensation, which is illustrated with familiar texts from the prophets Isaiah, Jeremiah and Hosea (*Marc.* 1.20.4-6, translation adjusted).[6]

The Syriac *Didascalia Apostolorum* (ca. 200–250)[7] distinguishes between the "First Legislation" of the Ten Commandments and the "Second Legislation," consisting of Mosaic bonds and burdens given to Israel because of her apostasy in the wilderness. While Christ "renews and confirms and fulfils the Ten Words of the Law," Christians are to reject this second law, as "our Saviour came for no other cause but to fulfil the Law, and to set us loose from the bonds of the Second Legislation" (*Didasc.* 2; cf. 26). Finally, references to works of the law are common in Origen's

---

[5]H. J. W. Drijvers, ed., *The Book of the Laws of Countries* (Assen: Van Gorcum, 1965), 61.

[6]Is 43:9; 1:14; Jer 31:31; 4:3; Hos 2:1. See also *Apol.* 21; *Praescr.* 33; *Idol.* 14; *Or.* 1; *Mon.* 6; *Pud.* 6; *Jejun.* 14. Christ's preaching of the new law is so prominent as to be noted in Tertullian's rule of faith (*Praescr.* 13).

[7]Hugh R. Connolly, ed., *Didascalia Apostolorum* (Oxford: Clarendon Press, 1929), cix.

works, with his most important volume for our purposes being his *Commentary on Romans* (ca. 240).[8] Origen writes in this commentary that "the works that Paul repudiates and frequently criticizes are not the works of righteousness that are commanded in the law, but those in which those who keep the law according to the flesh boast; i.e., the circumcision of the flesh, the sacrificial rituals, the observance of Sabbaths or new moon festivals." According to Origen, these works are "the ones on the basis of which [Paul] says no one can be saved" (*Comm. Rom.* 8.7.6). As we have seen, such claims by Origen do not represent an interpretive innovation, but rather show his fidelity to the Christian tradition that precedes him.[9]

EARLY, OLD, AND NEW PERSPECTIVES

To evaluate the correspondence between these early witnesses and the old and new perspectives on works of the law, we might begin by imagining how these patristic figures would react if they overheard a contemporary discussion on this topic. To take a recent shorthand summary of the old and new perspectives by J. V. Fesko, imagine a conversation taking place along these lines:

> According to some new perspective scholars, "works of the law" refer to Sabbath observance, food laws, and circumcision—those things that identified Jews. According to the old perspective, "works of the law" represents the Judaizers' attempt to secure salvation through moral effort.[10]

If we imagine our patristic figures overhearing such a discussion, we can be certain that they would be perplexed, as if the participants were standing on their heads: for a viewpoint recognizable as their own would be termed the "new perspective," and a viewpoint called the "old perspective" would correspond with an idea that none of them had ever heard of.

---

[8]See also *Cels.* 1.22; 2.2-7, 52, 75-76; 4.22; 8.29.

[9]For Origen on works of the law, cf. Thomas Scheck, *Commentary on the Epistle to the Romans, 1–5* (Washington, DC: Catholic University of America Press, 2001), 39-42.

[10]J. V. Fesko, "Old and New Perspectives on Paul: A Third Way?" *The Gospel Coalition.* January 6, 2016. www.thegospelcoalition.org/reviews/old-and-new-perspectives-on-paul-a-third-way/.

Of course, we have seen that Fesko's articulation somewhat oversimplifies the debate, particularly in that it does not engage the important question of why these works are opposed, since much new perspective reasoning in this area would indeed seem novel to these early witnesses. Further, while new perspective figures sometimes limit the works of the law to the particular practices of circumcision, Sabbath, and food laws, the early perspectives see these as the most prominent pieces of the entire Mosaic legislation, which is now left behind with the advent of Christ and his law. Nevertheless, signs that the nomenclature of "old" and "new" might be inverted on this issue can be observed even before one examines these early sources themselves. For example, it is noteworthy that both Luther and Calvin expressly distinguish their views from those of the early church on works of the law, and identify the author of their earliest known commentaries, Origen, as the source of errors on this issue.[11] On the other side, though surprisingly little work has been done in examining the correlation between patristic sources and the new perspective, a hint of this correspondence can be found in Wright's earliest publication. In explaining his reading of Romans 2–3, Wright comments, "For those who are interested in how Paul was read in the second century, it should be noted that this passage has very close links with Justin's dialogue with Trypho."[12]

Early and old perspectives. We observed in part two that the old perspective understands Paul's emphasis in "works of the law" to be on *works* in general, rather than a particular law or subset of practices. As we have seen, it is difficult to identify any general objection to works in similar conflicts with Jewish parties in this early period. Nor do the second-century witnesses provide support for the view that works of the law were performed on an individualistic basis to earn salvation, whether

---

[11]Note also the example of Martin Chemnitz, "the best informed and equipped student of patristics that Lutheranism has ever known," who is straightforward in identifying the early church fathers' understanding of works in relation to justification as "exceedingly unfortunate"; cf. Carl Beckwith, "Martin Chemnitz's Use of the Church Fathers in His Locus on Justification," *Concordia Theological Quarterly* 68 (2004): 283; Martin Chemnitz, *De Loco Iustificationis* 225a, ed. J. A. O. Preus (St. Louis, MO: Concordia Publishing House, 1989), 471.

[12]N. T. Wright, "The Paul of History and the Apostle of Faith," *Tyndale Bulletin* 29 (1978): 82.

under the guise of legalism, works righteousness, or self-powered striving. The passage in the early patristic writings that represents the nearest to support for a conception of Jewish works righteousness is *Dialogue* 8.3, where Trypho exhorts Justin to receive circumcision and practice the Torah so that "then, surely, you will experience the mercy of God." However, we have seen that the remainder of the *Dialogue* does not substantiate such a reading, as Trypho does not exhort Justin to works or "working" per se, but to become a part of the Jewish covenant and nation by observing these practices (cf. *Dial.* 10.1-3; 44.1-2; 123.1). Indeed, as Räisänen similarly observes, Justin regards Trypho as *underestimating* the connection between works and righteousness, with the Jews relying on the presumption of God's grace through fleshly descent from Abraham, without the corresponding works that represent the necessary response to God's grace (*Dial.* 140.2).[13]

In evaluating the correspondence between the old perspective and early patristic arguments against the works of the law, it is easy to envision the two sides talking past one another, since they hold different conceptions of the works under discussion and the significance of practicing them. In the case of Luther, his three arguments against works of the law—that no one can perform them due to humanity's sinful condition, that they do not justify, and that trying to perform them is itself a sinful self-idolatry—do not find close correspondence in the second-century sources. With the first argument, the patristic witnesses do not characterize works of the law as impossible to perform, though they would affirm that the Mosaic law and its practices are unable to address the underlying problem of sinful human nature. As Justin writes, though not strictly under Israel's curse, all of humanity stands cursed by its actions and is in need of healing, which the Torah cannot provide (*Dial.* 95.1-3; cf. Is 53:5). There is difficulty in assessing correspondence with Luther's

---

[13]Cf. Heikki Räisänen, *Paul and the Law*, WUNT 29 (Tübingen: Mohr Siebeck, 1983), 168n39: "Interestingly enough, however, both John the Baptist before Paul (Mt. 3.7 ff. par) and Justin Martyr after him (Dial 44.1-2, 25.1, 102.6, 141.2-3 and, in particular, 140.1-2) regard as a typical fault of the Jews their exaggerated trust on the covenant and the sonship of Abraham—as does Paul himself in Rom 2! It seems that this kind of distortion of the religious ideal was the more characteristic one."

second argument: while the patristic testimony would confirm that the Mosaic law's works are not able to justify, this is not interpreted as an absolute rejection of works in relation to justification. Though itself the subject for another study, the common soteriological pattern of the early patristic sources is that initial justification is completely by grace apart from works of any sort, and that final judgment (or final justification) is based on the outworking of this grace in one's subsequent life.[14] Within this paradigm, the works of the Mosaic law have no role, either as bearers of the grace of salvation (or somehow prerequisites for it), or as criteria that will have any kind of significance at the last judgment. While the second-century sources would affirm with Luther that no works are necessary for initial justification, they would still regard works as the basis for final justification—and in either case, they understand the points in contention within Paul's disputes not as works in general, but the Mosaic law's dictates in particular. Finally, Luther's third argument regarding the sinfulness of attempting to obey the law does not find attestation among the early patristic witnesses; there is no problematizing of moral effort in this period, nor any view that the pursuit of righteousness represents a devaluation or displacement of Christ. Luther himself is often very forthright in his view that, save for Augustine, the patristic tradition failed to understand Paul in matters related to faith, works of the law and justification.[15] In Luther's view, "the same thing would have happened to Augustine if the Pelagians had not eventually exercised his full attention and driven him to the righteousness that is of faith," though even Augustine is not spared from Luther's later objections.[16]

---

[14]See especially the overview of the patristic testimony on this topic in Robert B. Eno, "Some Patristic Views on the Relationship of Faith and Works in Justification," *Recherches Augustiniennes et Patristiques* 19 (1984): 3-27. Here passages like 1 Clem. 30–35 and Pol. *Phil.* 1–2 are especially valuable, illustrating how initial justification comes apart from works of any sort (1 Clem. 32.3-4; Pol. *Phil.* 1.3), while final judgment or justification is still contingent on subsequent obedience (1 Clem. 34–35; Pol. *Phil.* 2.1-3).

[15]As one example, see Luther's warning following his definition of these terms in his Romans commentary: "Without such a grasp of these words, you will never understand this letter of St. Paul, nor any other book of Holy Scripture. Therefore beware of all teachers who use these words in a different sense, no matter who they are, even Origen, Ambrose, Augustine, Jerome, and others like them or even above them" (*LW* 35.372).

[16]*WA* 30II, 650, in Manfred Schulze, "Martin Luther and the Church Fathers," in *The Reception of the Church Fathers in the West: From the Carolingians to the Maurists*, ed. Irena Backus, vol. 2

Calvin's reasoning against works of the law focuses on Luther's first argument above, that these works are rejected because it is impossible for anyone to perform them perfectly due to humanity's sinful condition. As with Luther, this precise argumentation does not find correspondence in the early patristic sources, though they do argue that the Mosaic law in particular is unable to provide redemption from humanity's sinful condition. While Calvin's writings are filled with appeals to patristic sources that substantiate his own positions, such appeals are conspicuously absent on this question. After acknowledging that "it is a matter of doubt, even among the learned, what the works of the law mean," Calvin notes Chrysostom, Origen, and Jerome against his position, and uncharacteristically fails to mention any patristic witnesses that support his own.[17]

As with Luther and Calvin, Bultmann's arguments against works of the law—that sinful humanity is unable to fulfill them in their entirety, and

---

(Leiden: E. J. Brill, 2001), 611. Cf. *LW* 54.49, no. 347: "At first I devoured, not merely read, Augustine. But when the door was opened for me in Paul, so that I understood what justification by faith is, it was all over with Augustine."

Augustine is neither fish nor fowl on our question: while the traditional "early" position can be found in his earlier works (see e.g. *Exp. Gal.* 19; *Faust.* 19.17), he also develops the view that "works of the law" represents all works done apart from God's grace, which are contrasted with those powered by grace (see e.g. *Spir. et Litt.* 50; suggested already in *Exp. Gal.* 15–16). This precise dichotomy is not followed by the later reformers or the "new" perspective, and is also distinct from the preceding tradition. Augustine stresses this interpretation within the context of the Pelagian controversy, in which the prior Jew/Gentile controversy has been superseded by a soteriological debate among Christians. Nevertheless, Augustine's transposition is still compatible with the soteriological pattern witnessed in early Christianity elsewhere (noted above); while no works of the Mosaic law—or indeed any works at all—are necessary prerequisites for receiving God's grace, the outworking of this grace in one's life is the condition for final justification and receiving eternal life (see e.g. *Perf.* 8; *Grat.* 18; *Fid. op.* 40–49). On the compatibility of the "early" and Augustinian views on works of the law, cf. Scheck, *Commentary on the Epistle*, 93. In the medieval period, both of these interpretations are preserved; see, e.g., Aquinas, *Comm. Gal.* 3.4. On the distinctiveness of Augustine's reading of "works of the law" from the preceding tradition, cf. Maurice Wiles, *The Divine Apostle: The Interpretation of St. Paul's Epistles in the Early Church* (London: Cambridge University Press, 1967), 68.

[17]*Comm. Rom.* 3:20, trans. John Owen (University of Virginia, 1849), 130 (cf. *Comm. Rom.*, ed. Ross Mackenzie [Grand Rapids, MI: Eerdmans, 1995 (1965)], 69). While not wishing to get lost in counterfactuals, it is significant that both Luther and Calvin had little to no access to patristic sources prior to Irenaeus (cf. Robert M. Grant, *The Apostolic Fathers: Introduction*, vol. 1 of *The Apostolic Fathers: A New Translation and Commentary* [New York: Thomas Nelson 1964], 1–2; Anthony Lane, *John Calvin, Student of the Church Fathers* [Grand Rapids, MI: Baker Books, 1999], 41). Particularly in the case of Calvin, whose view of the early tradition is generally quite high, it is worth considering how access to these sources would have influenced his understanding of works of the law. On Calvin's aims to return to the early fathers, see e.g. *Reply to Sadolet*.

that the Jews' deeper sin is actually their desire to become righteous by performing them—also find little patristic support. Bultmann recognizes the odd absence within early patristic discussions of what he regards as the views of Paul and the Jews. In Barnabas's polemic against the Jewish law, for example, Bultmann writes that "the real problem of the Law as the way of salvation—i.e. the problem of legalism, the problem of good works as the condition for participation in salvation—escaped the author."[18] Similarly, Bultmann concludes that in his debate with Trypho, "it is apparent that Justin did not attack the problem of legalism, either."[19] Even Ignatius, the only patristic figure whom Bultmann identifies as truly understanding Paul,[20] does not provide substantiation for Bultmann's ideas: "The heresy against which Ignatius struggles is indeed called 'Judaism.' But the 'Judaizing' that he battles consists in certain ritual observances, like keeping the Sabbath, and not in the Jewish 'zeal' to attain righteousness by fulfilling the law."[21] From Bultmann's standpoint, it seems that both Paul's arguments, *and* the arguments of his interlocutors, have disappeared in the postapostolic period.

Moo acknowledges that works of the law are rejected on salvation-historical grounds, but sees humanity's inability to obey the works of the law as Paul's more fundamental reason for rejecting them. Moo's reasoning that the era of Torah ends with Christ resembles the patristic argument that the Mosaic law is superseded by Christ's new covenant, and his observation that requiring continued Torah obedience is effectively to "deny that Christ has come" parallels Justin and Trypho's arguments over Jesus' messiahship in the second half of the *Dialogue with Trypho*.[22] However, Moo's more fundamental anthropological argument does not

---

[18]Rudolf Bultmann, *Theology of the New Testament*, trans. Kendrick Grobel, 2 vols. (London: SCM, 1952), 1:111. See also Bultmann's similar judgment of 1 Clement (Bultmann, *Theology of the New Testament*, 1:112).

[19]Bultmann, *Theology of the New Testament*, 1:114.

[20]Rudolf Bultmann, "Ignatius and Paul," in *Existence and Faith: Shorter Writings of Rudolf Bultmann*, ed. Schubert Miles Ogden (New York: Meridian Books, 1960 [1953]), 267-68.

[21]Bultmann, "Ignatius and Paul," 270.

[22]Douglas Moo, "Justification in Galatians," in *Understanding the Times: New Testament Studies in the 21st Century: Essays in Honor of D. A. Carson on the Occasion of His 65th Birthday*, ed. Andreas J. Köstenberger and Robert W. Yarbrough (Wheaton, IL: Crossway, 2011), 180; cf. 184.

find similar attestation in these early sources. None of these figures see the Torah as problematic because "it involves 'doing' rather than 'believing,'" which Moo regards as a perpetual dichotomy due to humanity's inability to ever perfectly obey the law.[23] Rather, the patristic sources attest that Christ provides the remedy for humanity's sinful condition, doing what Torah could not and enabling an obedience that would be otherwise unimaginable.

Early and new perspectives. As was seen in part two, the new perspective understands Paul's emphasis to be on *the law* in rejecting "works of the law," referring to a particular law, the Torah, and the specific deeds that it enjoins. This reading is corroborated by the early patristic witnesses, with the two references to works of the law passages in this period that use allusion rather than citation, *Dialogue* 95.1 and *Demonstration of the Apostolic Preaching* 35, employing "the law of Moses" and "the law" in place of "works of the law" (cf. Gal 3:10; Rom 3:20).[24] Further, in other allusions or possible references to Pauline texts that carry similar dichotomies regarding Abraham's faith and justification, the place of "works of the law" is filled by the specific works of the Torah in question, principally circumcision (Barn. 13.7; *Dial.* 23.4; 92.3; *Haer.* 4.16.1-2).[25]

In relation to the meaning and significance of the works of the law, there is close correspondence between the new perspective and the early patristic sources, with the Torah viewed as the law in question and the specific works of circumcision, Sabbath (and related calendar observances), and food regulations being the common works in dispute. The early witnesses also frequently reject the sacrifices prescribed in the Mosaic law, which does not find similar attestation among new perspective figures (though the focus on the temple, implied in the Didache and noted by Barnabas, Melito, and Irenaeus, is also mentioned by

---

[23]Moo, "Justification in Galatians," 167.

[24]See also Ignatius's hope for justification in Christ and his faith rather than "the archives" in Ign. *Phld.* 8.2; the Ebionite belief that justification comes by "the law of Moses" (*Ref.* 7.34.2; 10.22.1), on account of which they repudiate Paul; and Marcion's ostensible replacement ἐξ ἔργων νόμου with ὑπὸ νόμου in Gal 3:10 (*Pan.* 42.11.18).

[25]The context prior to *Dial.* 23.4 notes Sabbaths, festivals, and sacrifices, and *Dial.* 92.3-4 also mentions Sabbaths, offerings, and the construction of the temple. Circumcision and Sabbaths are the focus of *Haer.* 4.16.2.

Wright). The early and new perspectives are also closely aligned in seeing these works as group identity markers that incorporate one into the Jewish nation and covenant, and separate them from the Gentiles. However, the closely related function of these practices as the Jews' system of worship,[26] mentioned (and derided) by early sources such as Preaching of Peter, Diognetus, and Aristides's *Apology*, is not similarly indicated by the new perspective.

Regarding the arguments against the necessity of these works for the Christian, Sanders's experiential emphasis does not find strong correspondence among the patristic witnesses. It is true that the reception of grace by the Gentile believers serves as confirmation of the new covenant's arrival, witnessed in passages like Ignatius *Magnesians* 8.1, *Dialogue* 11.4, and *Against Heresies*, 4.34.4. However, this experiential argument does not bear the kind of singular weight in the early perspectives that Sanders identifies, and is rather one piece in a broader nexus of arguments against practicing the Mosaic law. Further, Paul's own experience in being called to the Gentiles is not mentioned as a reason for not observing these works, and Paul himself is not identified as playing a distinct role in their rejection. While it can be said that the law-Christ opposition envisioned by Sanders carries some rhetorical correspondence with patristic sources—one thinks in particular of Ignatius's opposition of Judaism to Christianity in *Magnesians* 10.2-3—this opposition is usually accompanied by further reasoning, and is not simply an assertion that God has saved by some other means. In particular, patristic sources are insistent that the Hebrew Scriptures provide the rationale for not adopting the Mosaic law in the messianic age, rather than simply representing a source from which *post factum* arguments might be drawn.

Dunn's social emphasis, which sees Paul as reacting against an attitude of exclusivism by his rejection of works of the law, does not find support in the patristic sources. While directed against the Jews' ethnocentric nationalism in Paul's time, Dunn holds that the key problem for Paul is not these particular works, but rather "the boundary-drawing attitude

---

[26]On this close relation between "religion" and "race," cf. Denise Kimber Buell, "Rethinking the Relevance of Race for Early Christian Self-Definition," *Harvard Theological Review* 94 (2001): 461.

itself," which means that Paul's principles can be extended to other issues that serve to divide and exclude contemporary Christians as well.[27] While these early sources do attest that these works and law limit God's grace to Israel, this national limitation is rejected insofar as it runs counter to the covenant's promises, and does not stand alone as an objection. Further, there is no patristic evidence that these works are rejected because of their association with a boundary-drawing attitude, or of Paul's debates on works of the law being used as a jumping-off point against "issues that exclude" in general. However, though it plays a less prominent role in his theology, Dunn's salvation-historical reasoning against observing these works does correspond with these early witnesses. In describing how adopting circumcision is a step back into another age and world before Christ's incarnation, for example, Dunn is indeed reminiscent of Irenaeus.[28]

Wright's covenantal reading of Paul—which identifies arguments regarding the universal scope of the covenant's promises, the inability of the Torah to address humanity's sinful condition, and the fulfillment of salvation history in Jesus—holds the greatest amount of correspondence with the early patristic sources. Both Wright and the early perspectives regard the fact that God's promises are intended for all nations —and not simply the Jews—as a reason why the Jews' distinctive markers are unnecessary when this covenant is fulfilled. While Wright focuses more on the universality of the Abrahamic covenant's promises, patristic argumentation in this regard places greater emphasis on the universal scope of the new covenant. Wright and the early sources are also close together on the need for reversal of Adam's sin, with Wright emphasizing the negative element—Israel's history as an indicator that the Torah cannot repair the Adamic condition—and the patristic sources focusing on the positive transformation enacted by Christ, which

---

[27]James D. G. Dunn, *The New Perspective on Paul* (Grand Rapids, MI: Eerdmans, 2005), 25n99.

[28]Cf. Dunn, *New Perspective on Paul*, 329; 92-95. Additionally, the absence of conflict in this period between Jews and Christians regarding the gracious nature of God's acceptance would suggest that Dunn is correct to read passages such as Eph 2:8-9; 2 Tim 1:9; Titus 3:5 as affirmations of Israel's own understanding of divine grace (cf. Deut 9:5), rather than examples of discontinuity with the Jewish tradition (cf. 390-91; "James Dunn: Opposition" in ch. 3).

renders the works given on account of Israel's hard-heartedness unnecessary. Wright's third reason holds correspondence with the patristic arguments that Jesus fulfills the covenant's promises in bringing the new law and covenant. However, whereas the patristic sources emphasize how Christ's law and teachings necessarily take precedence over the old, the law of Christ does not perform the same function for Wright, who instead focuses on Christ's role in fulfilling the covenant promises made to Israel and the world. In short, while both perspectives are rooted in Israel's Scriptures and covenant, Wright places greater emphasis on the Abrahamic covenant, while the patristic sources focus more on the new covenant.

In summary, the early perspectives on works of the law are found to align far more closely with the so-called new perspective than the old perspective, particularly with respect to the meaning and significance of these works. On these issues, the alignment between early and new perspectives is such that one can regard *the "new" perspective as, in reality, the old perspective*, while what we identify as the "old" perspective represents a genuine theological *novum* in relation to the early Christian tradition. However, this close alignment does not hold on the question of why these works are opposed, as the distinctive emphases of Sanders and Dunn find little patristic support, and only Wright's reasoning carries substantial correspondence among these early sources. Moreover, it is noteworthy that, notwithstanding his occasionally undiplomatic language, it is Wright who does the most among new perspective authors to incorporate old perspective concerns in his arguments, particularly with respect to Torah's inability to address the underlying issue of human sinfulness. If an "old perspective" adherent—perhaps more likely from the Reformed than the Lutheran tradition—finds Wright's arguments to sufficiently account for the underlying anthropological reasons why works of the law cannot justify,[29] then they are likely to be satisfied with early perspective reasoning on this issue as well.

---

[29]A possibility suggested, for example, in Moo, "Justification in Galatians," 181n46.

EARLY PERSPECTIVES AND PAUL

Finally, what does this material suggest about Paul's own meaning in rejecting works of the law? It is beyond this book's scope to engage in detailed exegesis of Romans and Galatians in light of these second-century perspectives, though it is my hope that this patristic material will be useful for those who comment more fully on these texts. Rather, I hope to bring together here a few central ideas that the combined testimony of these early witnesses would suggest about Paul's own meaning in the biblical texts.

First, these sources would suggest that in rejecting the works of the law, Paul's focus is on the concrete issue of the place of the Torah in the Christian's life, and not on broader questions of obedience to a moral law or concerns about works in general. Indeed, it is a universal practice in the tradition following Paul to distinguish between the works of the Mosaic law and good works more broadly, with language reminiscent of Paul in Romans 2 often used in doing so (Barn. 2.1, 4.11-12, 10.11, *Dial.* 28.4, 92.4-5; *Haer.* 4.16.1-3). If Paul's conflicts with Jewish parties in Romans and Galatians were related to good works and salvation by moral effort, then the "fire" of these conflicts left no smoke in second-century reception, and was instead universally replaced—both by early Christians following Paul, *and* their Jewish opponents, as the witness of the Ebionites and Trypho testifies —by a steady plume arising from a different location. One might maintain that Paul's arguments carry latent within them a rejection of all works or moral effort that remained obscured from both sides of the argument until later generations. The difficulty with this idea, however, is that it fails to engage satisfactorily with Paul's own context: if Paul's arguments are indeed related to the real views of his readers (as Schreiner maintains), then his early readers testify that these works of the Mosaic law were the critical points in conflict with the Jews. Conversely, the absence of any evidence among his readers that Jews were insisting on good works for salvation suggests that this was not a view he was contending against.

Second, in light of the early patristic testimony, it appears that Paul's rejection of the works of the law was not original to him. On this point, the early patristic testimony cuts against the new perspective on Paul.

Sanders sees Paul as rejecting the works that separate Jews from Gentile on an ad hoc basis as it conflicts with his mission,[30] and Dunn believes that Paul dispenses with the law's requirements where they are interpreted in a way that contradicts the more fundamental love commands.[31] Wright too identifies Paul as redefining and intensifying Jewish praxis,[32] though he does suggest elsewhere that Paul's reasoning may go back to Jesus and John the Baptist.[33] While Paul is the most prominent apostolic figure among patristic sources in this early period, these sources offer very little suggestion that Paul has a unique role in deciding which laws are valid and which are discarded within the new covenant.[34] Rather, it appears that Paul is responding to the law of Christ that is held in common with the other apostles, and though his apostleship means that he indeed acts as a steward of this law, it is Christ who redefines and intensifies, not Paul.[35]

This leads to the third point. A major theme in this study is that the early patristic sources frequently make reference, whether directly or indirectly, to the law of Christ as a primary reason why these works of the Mosaic law are no longer binding. It is noteworthy that, notwithstanding some parallels in Wright's thought, this reasoning is absent from *both* the old and new perspectives on Paul in contemporary debates. While all three new perspective figures recognize Paul to be making distinctions between various laws in the Torah, none of them are able to give a completely clear articulation for what standard Paul uses in doing so.[36] For the early patristic witnesses, it seems that this standard—Christ's law,

---

[30]E. P. Sanders, *Paul* (New York: Oxford University Press, 1991), 91.

[31]Cf. James D. G. Dunn, *The Theology of Paul the Apostle* (Grand Rapids, MI: Eerdmans, 1998), 656; James D. G. Dunn, *The New Perspective on Paul* (Grand Rapids, MI: Eerdmans, 2005), 337.

[32]N. T. Wright, *Paul and the Faithfulness of God* (London: SPCK, 2013), 445.

[33]Wright, "Paul of History," 71.

[34]The one possible instance in this period comes from the reconstructed testimony of the Ebionites, though their rejection of Paul appears to be based on his ostensible apostasy by his apostleship to non-Jews, rather than a distinctive legislative authority. Note their similar rejection of all non-Matthean gospels in Irenaeus, *Haer.* 1.26.2.

[35]If anything, it is Peter's experiences that are decisive for these issues (Acts 11–12; cf. *Haer.* 3.12.7, 14), with Paul's charge of hypocrisy drawing its force from the apostles' prior agreement on the relation of Christ's law to that of Moses (Gal 2:1-10). Cf. similarly Acts 15:1-35, however one interprets this account in relation to Paul's visit to Jerusalem.

[36]Cf. E. P. Sanders, *Paul, the Law, and the Jewish People* (Philadelphia: Fortress Press, 1983), 105; Dunn, *New Perspective on Paul*, 55; Wright, *Paul and the Faithfulness*, 1109.

which replaces the Torah—is as clear as day. Though the "Christian law" passages in Paul (Gal 6:2; 1 Cor 9:21; Rom 3:27; 8:4) are sometimes dismissed in contemporary biblical scholarship as mere rhetorical devices,[37] the reception-historical "smoke" encountered in this study would suggest that Paul's referent is more substantive than this. Interestingly, it is none other than Douglas Moo who provides a reading of Paul on this account that corresponds quite closely with the second-century testimony. As Moo writes on Galatians 6:2, while Paul's referent by the "law of Christ" includes Jesus' love command, it is also more than this: "Precisely because the phrase serves as the new covenant counterpart to the 'law of Moses,' we should expect the reference to include all those teachings and commandments set forth by Christ and by his inspired apostles—including Paul."[38] Such an interpretation goes far to explain the widespread references to Christ's law in this early period,[39] as well as the judicial (and even legislative) office that these sources attribute to the apostles.[40] Though Moo does not employ his argument this way, such a law also explains why particular works such as circumcision, Sabbath, sacrifices, and food regulations recur as the points in conflict with the Jews for both Paul and the early patristic sources. Rather than being rejected because of Paul's experiences or their exclusive social function, these works represent the major points of discontinuity between Moses' law in the old covenant and Christ's law in the new, and thus naturally recur as flashpoints in contexts where the validity of one dispensation or the other is in question.[41]

Finally, these early perspectives would suggest that while these works are indeed flashpoints, the conflicts over works of the law are not, at

---

[37]See e.g. Räisänen, *Paul and the Law*, 81.

[38]Douglas Moo, *Galatians* (Grand Rapids, MI: Baker Academic, 2013), 378.

[39]On the law of Christ (and Christ as himself the new law), see Barn. 2.6; Ign. *Magn.* 2.1; Ign. *Rom.* 1.0; Shep. 59.3; 69.2; *KP* Fr. 1; *Arist.* 15.8-9; *Dial.* 11.2-4; 12.2-3 (etc.); *PP* 6-7; *Haer.* 4.9.2, 4.13.1-4, 4.34.4 (etc.); *Epid.* 86; *Autol.* 2.27.

[40]1 Clem. 42–44; Barn. 8.3; Ign. *Magn.* 7.1, 13.1; Ign. *Trall.* 7.1; *Dial.* 42.1-3; *Haer.* 3.3.1-4, 3.12.14, 4.15.2, 4.34.4.

[41]Studies on the law of Christ in Paul and the early patristic sources were pursued by the late Graham Stanton before the end of his life, and this study suggests that it is an area that is ripe for continued research; see especially Graham Stanton, "What Is the Law of Christ?," in *Studies in Matthew and Early Christianity*, ed. Markus N. A. Bockmuehl and David Lincicum, WUNT 309 (Tübingen: Mohr Siebeck, 2013).

heart, about works of the Mosaic law at all, but rather about the identity of Jesus as the Messiah. It is striking that in Justin's *Dialogue*, both he and his Jewish interlocutor agree that if Jesus is the Messiah, then he is the new lawgiver, whose precepts will take precedence over those of Moses.[42] As Irenaeus makes clear, it is the fact of a new legislation—the *vivificatrix lex* and *libertatis lex* coming forth from Zion[43]—that confirms Jesus' identity and the new covenant's arrival; and the fact that the Mosaic law was still in operation under Zerubbabel disqualifies any idea that he was the Messiah or brought this covenant. Seen from this angle, it is clear how continuing to follow and enforce Mosaic legislation is, in reality, to deny that the Messiah and the new covenant have come, and it is *this* denial that Paul recognizes as necessitating his fiercest polemic in Galatians. *In Jesus Christ*, that is, under his new dispensation, Mosaic practices like circumcision no longer count for anything (Gal 5:6); it is Christ's law that now stands to be fulfilled by those with the Spirit (Gal 6:2), not the former legislation of bondage, and to readopt it is to deny Christ's advent and be cut off from him (Gal 5:4).[44] It is because Jesus *is* the Messiah and has established the new covenant that Paul implores the Galatians to become like him (Gal 4:12), as he similarly describes himself in the cognate passage of 1 Corinthians 9:21—not bound by the old legislation and its works, but yet under the law of God, that is, the law of Christ.

---

[42]See similarly Tertullian's *Apology*, which identifies the question of whether the Messiah's advent has occurred as the only point in contention between Jews and Christians (*Apol.* 21).

[43]Mic 4:2-3; Is 2:3-4; cf. Is 42:4; 51:4.

[44]Following Moo, this law is seen as based in Christ's teachings (Gal 6:2), enacted in his ordinances like baptism (3:27), and administered by his apostles (1:6-9).

BIBLIOGRAPHY

PRIMARY SOURCES

Klijn, A. F. J., and G. J. Reinink, eds. *Patristic Evidence for Jewish-Christian Sects*. Leiden: Brill, 1973.

Roberts, Alexander, and James Donaldson, eds. *The Ante-Nicene Fathers: Translations of the Writings of the Fathers down to A.D. 325*. 10 vols. Peabody, MA: Hendrickson, 1994 [1885].

Acts of Paul

Pervo, Richard I., trans. *Acts of Paul: A New Translation with Introduction and Commentary*. Cambridge: James Clarke & Co, 2014.

Rordorf, Willy, and Pierre Cherix, eds. *Actes de Paul*. In *Écrits apocryphes chretiens*, 1117-88. Vol. 1. Paris: Gallimard, 1997.

Schmidt, Carl, ed. *Acta Pauli, aus der Heidelberger koptischen Papyrushandschrift Nr. 1*. Leipzig: J. C. Hinrichs, 1904.

Apology of Aristides

Harris, J. Rendel, and J. Armitage Robinson, eds. *The Apology of Aristides on Behalf of the Christians: From a Syriac MS. Preserved on Mount Sinai*. 1st ed. Vol. 1. Cambridge: Cambridge University Press, 1891.

Pouderon, Bernard, ed. *Aristide: Apologie*. Sources Chrétiennes 470. Paris: Éditions du Cerf, 2003.

Vona, Constantino, ed. *L'apologia di Aristide: Introduzione versione dal Siriaco e Commento*. Rome: Faculta Theologica Pontificii Athenaei Lateranensis, 1950.

Apostolic Fathers

Holmes, Michael W., ed. *The Apostolic Fathers: Greek Texts and English Translations*. Grand Rapids, MI: Baker Academic, 2007.

Aristo of Pella

Bovon, François, and John M. Duffy, trans. "A New Greek Fragment from Ariston of Pella's Dialogue of Jason and Papiscus." *Harvard Theological Review* 105 (2012): 457-65.

Bardesanes

Drijvers, H. J. W., ed. *The Book of the Laws of Countries*. Assen: Van Gorcum, 1965.

Calvin, John

Battles, Ford Lewis, ed. *Institutes of the Christian Religion*. Philadelphia: Westminster Press, 1960.

Childress, Kathy, ed. *Sermons on Galatians*. Edinburgh: Banner of Truth Trust, 1997.

Mackenzie, Ross, ed. *The Epistles of Paul the Apostle to the Romans and to the Thessalonians*. Grand Rapids, MI: Eerdmans, 1995 [1965].

Park, T. H. L., ed. *The Epistles of Paul the Apostle to the Galatians, Ephesians, Philippians and Colossians*. Grand Rapids, MI: Eerdmans, 1996 [1965].

Didache

Rordorf, Willy, and André Tuilier, eds. *La doctrine des douze apôtres: Didachè*. Sources Chrétiennes 248. Paris: Éditions du Cerf, 1998.

Didascalia Apostolorum

Connolly, Hugh R., ed. *Didascalia Apostolorum*. Oxford: Clarendon Press, 1929.

Epiphanius

Holl, Karl, ed. *Epiphanius (Ancoratus und Panarion)*. 3 vols. Leipzig: Hinrichs, 1915–1922.

Williams, Frank, ed. *The Panarion of Epiphanius of Salamis (Sects 1–46)*. 1st ed. Vol. 1. Leiden: Brill, 2009.

Epistle to Diognetus

Jefford, Clayton N., trans. *The Epistle to Diognetus (with the Fragment of Quadratus)*. Oxford: Oxford University Press, 2013.

Marrou, Henri-Irénée. *À Diognète*. Sources Chrétiennes 33. Paris: Éditions du Cerf, 1951.

Eusebius

Lake, Kirsopp, and J. E. L. Oulton, eds. *The Ecclesiastical History*. 2 vols. Cambridge, MA: Harvard University Press, 2014 [1926].

Irenaeus of Lyons

Behr, John, trans. *On the Apostolic Preaching*. Popular Patristics Series 17. Crestwood, NY: St. Vladimir's Seminary Press, 1997.

Froidevaux, L. M., ed. *Démonstration de la Prédication Apostolique*. Sources Chrétiennes 406. Paris: Éditions du Cerf, 1995.

Rousseau, Adelin, and Louis Doutreleau, eds. *Irénée de Lyon: Contre les hérésies*. 5 vols. Paris: Éditions du Cerf, 1965–1982.

Unger, Dominic, trans. *St. Irenaeus of Lyons Against the Heresies*. Edited by John J. Dillon and Matthew Steenberg. 3 vols. Ancient Christian Writers. New York: Paulist Press, 1992–2012.

Jerome

Helm, Rudolf, ed. *Die Chronik des Hieronymus (Hieronymi Chronicon)*. Berlin: Akademie-Verlag, 1984.

Richardson, E. C., ed. *Nicene and Post-Nicene Fathers: A Select Library of the Christian Church*. Vol. 3: *Jerome*. Peabody, MA: Hendrickson, 1999 [1892].

von Gebhardt, Oscar, trans. *De viris inlustribus in griechischer Übersetzung (der soge-nannte Sophronius)*. Leipzig: J. C. Hinrichs, 1896.

Justin Martyr

Falls, Thomas, trans. *Dialogue with Trypho*. Edited by Thomas Halton and Michael Slusser. Washington, DC: Catholic University of America Press, 2003 [1965].

Marcovich, Miroslav, ed. *Iustini Martyris Dialogus cum Tryphone*. Berlin: De Gruyter, 1997.

Luther, Martin

Pelikan, Jaroslav, and Helmut T. Lehmann, eds. *Luther's Works*. 55 vols. St. Louis: Concordia Publishing House, 1955–1986.

Melito of Sardis

Blank, Josef, trans. *Vom Passa: die älteste christliche Osterpredigt*. Freiburg: Lambertus-Verlag, 1963.

Bonner, Campbell, ed. *The Homily on the Passion by Melito Bishop of Sardis*. London: Christophers, 1940.

Dratsellas, Konstantinos N. *Homilia eis to pathos e Peri Pascha*. Athenai, 1971.

Hall, Stuart George, trans. *On Pascha and Fragments*. Oxford: Clarendon Press, 1979.

Ibañez, Javier, and Fernando Mendoza, eds. *Meliton de Sardes: Homilia sobre la pascua*. Pamplona: Ed. University of Navarra, 1975.

Perler, Othmar, trans. *Sur la Pâque et fragments*. Sources Chrétiennes 123. Paris: Éditions du Cerf, 1966.

Stewart-Sykes, Alistair, trans. *On Pascha: With the Fragments of Melito and Other Material Related to the Quartodecimans*. Crestwood, NY: St. Vladimir's Seminary Press, 2001.

Muratorian Fragment

Schnabel, Eckhard J, ed. "The Muratorian Fragment: The State of Research." *Journal of the Evangelical Theological Society* 57 (2014): 231-64.

New Testament Apocrypha

Elliott, J. K., ed. *The Apocryphal New Testament: A Collection of Apocryphal Christian Literature in an English Translation*. Oxford: Clarendon Press, 1993.

James, M. R., ed. *The Apocryphal New Testament*. Oxford: Clarendon Press, 1924.

Schneemelcher, W., ed. *New Testament Apocrypha*. Translated by R. McL. Wilson. Vol. 2. Cambridge: James Clarke & Co, 1992.

Origen

Chadwick, Henry, trans. *Contra Celsum*. Cambridge: Cambridge University Press, 1953.

Scheck, Thomas, ed. *Commentary on the Epistle to the Romans, 1–5*. Washington, DC: Catholic University of America Press, 2001.

Preaching of Peter

Cambe, Michael, ed. *Kerygma Petri: Textus et commentarius.* Turnhout: Brepols, 2003.

Tertullian

Adversus Marcionem. Edited by Ernest Evans. 2 vols. Oxford: Clarendon Press, 1972.

SECONDARY SOURCES

Aageson, James W. *Paul, the Pastoral Epistles, and the Early Church.* Grand Rapids, MI: Baker Academic, 2007.

Aldridge, Robert E. "Peter and the 'Two Ways.'" *Vigiliae Christianae* 53 (1999): 233-64.

Aleith, Eva. *Paulusverständnis in der alten Kirche.* Berlin: A. Töpelmann, 1937.

Allard, Paul. *Histoire des persécutions.* Vol. 1. Paris: V. Lecoffre, 1885.

Allert, Craig. *Revelation, Truth, Canon, and Interpretation: Studies in Justin Martyr's Dialogue with Trypho.* Leiden: Brill, 2002.

Alpigiano, Carlotta. *Aristide di Atene, Apologia.* Florence: Nardini, 1988.

Andriessen, Paul. "The Authorship of the Epistula ad Diognetum." *Vigiliae Christianae* 1 (1947): 129-36.

———. "L'Apologie de Quadratus conservée sous le titre d'Épître à Diognète." *Recherches de Théologie Ancienne et Médiévale* 13 (1946): 5-39, 125-49, 237-60.

Arnold, Brian John. "Justification One Hundred Years After Paul." PhD diss., Southern Baptist Theological Seminary, 2013.

Audet, Jean Paul. *La didachè: instructions des apôtres.* Paris: J. Gabalda, 1958.

Avemarie, Friedrich. "Die Werke des Gesetzes im Spiegel des Jakobusbriefs: A Very Old Perspective on Paul." *ZTK* 98 (2001): 282-309.

Babcock, William S. "Paul in the Writings of the Apostolic Fathers." In *Paul and the Legacies of Paul*, edited by William S. Babcock, 25-45. Dallas: Southern Methodist University Press, 1990.

Bachmann, Michael. "4QMMT und Galaterbrief, התורה מעשי und ΕΡΓΑ ΝΟΜΟΥ." *Zeitschrift für die Neutestamentliche Wissenschaft und die Kunde der Älteren Kirche* 89 (1998): 91-113.

Balás, David. "Marcion Revisited: A 'Post-Harnack' Perspective." In *Texts and Testaments: Critical Essays on the Bible and Early Church Fathers*, edited by W. Eugene March, 95-108. San Antonio, TX: Trinity University Press, 1980.

———. "The Use and Interpretation of Paul in Irenaeus's Five Books *Adversus Haereses.*" *Second Century* 9 (1992): 27-40.

Balthasar, Hans Urs von. *The Scandal of the Incarnation: Irenaeus Against the Heresies.* San Francisco: Ignatius Press, 1990.

Barclay, John M. G. "Mirror-Reading a Polemical Letter: Galatians as a Test Case." *Journal for the Study of the New Testament* 10 (1987): 73-93.

————. *Paul and the Gift*. Grand Rapids, MI: Eerdmans, 2015.

Barnard, L. W. *Justin Martyr: His Life and Thought*. London: Cambridge University Press, 1967.

————. *Studies in the Apostolic Fathers and Their Background*. New York: Schocken Books, 1966.

Barnett, Albert. 1941. *Paul Becomes a Literary Influence*. Chicago: University of Chicago Press.

Barr, James. 1961. *The Semantics of Biblical Language*. London: Oxford University Press.

Barrett, C. K. "Jews and Judaizers in the Epistles of Ignatius." In *Jews, Greeks and Christians: Essays in honour of W. D. Davies*, edited by R. Hammerton-Kelly and R. Scroggs, 220-44. Leiden: Brill, 1976.

————. "Pauline Controversies in the Post-Pauline Period." *New Testament Studies* 20 (1974): 229-45.

Barth, Karl. "Rudolph Bultman—an Attempt to Understand Him." In *Kerygma and Myth: A Theological Debate*, edited by Hans Werner Bartsch. Vol. 2. London: SPCK, 1962.

Bartlet, J. V. "Barnabas." In *The New Testament in the Apostolic Fathers*, edited by Oxford Society of Historical Theology, 1-23. Oxford: Clarendon Press, 1905.

Bauckham, Richard. "The Acts of Paul as a Sequel to Acts." In *The Book of Acts in Its Ancient Literary Setting*, edited by Bruce Winter and Andrew Clarke, 105-52. Grand Rapids, MI: Eerdmans, 1993.

Bauer, Walter. *Orthodoxy and Heresy in Earliest Christianity*. Edited by Robert A. Kraft and Gerhard Krodel. Philadelphia: Fortress Press, 1971 [1934].

Baur, F. C. *The Church History of the First Three Centuries*. Translated by Allan Menzies. London: Williams and Norgate, 1878.

Beatrice, P. F. "Der Presbyter des Irenäus, Polykarp von Smyrna und der Brief an Diognet." In *Pléroma: Salus carnis: homenaje a Antonio Orbe, S.J.*, edited by Eugenio Romero-Pose, 179-202. Santiago de Compostella: Aldecoa, 1990.

Becker, Adam H., and Annette Yoshiko Reed, eds. *The Ways That Never Parted: Jews and Christians in Late Antiquity and the Early Middle Ages*. TSA 95. Tübingen: Mohr Siebeck, 2003.

Beckwith, Carl. "Martin Chemnitz's Use of the Church Fathers in His Locus on Justification." *Concordia Theological Quarterly* 68 (2004): 271-90.

Bediako, Kwame. *Theology and Identity*. Oxford: Regnum Books, 1992.

Behr, John. *Irenaeus of Lyons: Identifying Christianity*. Oxford: Oxford University Press, 2013.

Benedict XVI. "Saint Irenaeus of Lyons." General Audience, St. Peter's Square, March 28, 2007. w2.vatican.va/content/benedict-xvi/en/audiences/2007/documents/hf_ben-xvi_aud_20070328.html.

Benoit, Andre. *Saint Irénée: Introduction à l'étude de sa theologie*. Paris: Presses universitaires de France, 1960.

Bird, Michael F. "The Reception of Paul in the Epistle to Diognetus." In *Paul and the Second Century*, edited by Michael F. Bird and Joseph R. Dodson, 70-90. London: T&T Clark, 2011.

Bird, Michael F., and Joel Willitts, eds. *Paul and the Gospels: Christologies, Conflicts, and Convergences*. London: T&T Clark, 2011.

Blackwell, Ben C. "Paul and Irenaeus." In *Paul and the Second Century*, edited by Michael F. Bird and Joseph R. Dodson, 190-206. London: T&T Clark, 2011.

Blackwell, Ben C., John K. Goodrich, and Jason Maston, eds. *Reading Romans in Context: Paul and Second Temple Judaism*. Grand Rapids, MI: Zondervan, 2015.

Blanchard, Yves-Marie. *Aux sources du canon, le témoignage d'Irénée*. Paris: Éditions du Cerf, 1993.

Blasi, Anthony J. *Making Charisma: The Social Construction of Paul's Public Image*. New Brunswick, NJ: Transaction Publishers, 1991.

Bockmuehl, Markus N. A. *Jewish Law in Gentile Churches: Halakhah and the Beginning of Christian Public Ethics*. Edinburgh: T&T Clark, 2000.

———. *The Remembered Peter*. WUNT 262. Tübingen: Mohr Siebeck, 2010.

———. *Seeing the Word: Refocusing New Testament Study*. Grand Rapids, MI: Baker Academic, 2006.

———. *Simon Peter in Scripture and Memory*. Grand Rapids, MI: Baker Academic, 2012.

Boer, Martinus C. de. "Images of Paul in the Post-apostolic Period." *Catholic Biblical Quarterly* 42 (1980): 359-80.

Bovon, François, and John M. Duffy. "A New Greek Fragment from Ariston of Pella's Dialogue of Jason and Papiscus." *Harvard Theological Review* 105 (2012): 457-65.

Boxall, Ian. *Patmos in the Reception History of the Apocalypse*. Oxford: Oxford University Press, 2013.

Boyarin, Daniel. *Border Lines: The Partition of Judaeo-Christianity*. Philadelphia: University of Pennsylvania Press, 2004.

Brändle, Rudolf. *Die Ethik der "Schrift an Diognet."* Zürich: Theologischer Verlag, 1975.

Brent, Allen. *Ignatius of Antioch*. London: T&T Clark, 2009.

Briggman, Anthony. *Irenaeus of Lyons and the Theology of the Holy Spirit*. Oxford: Oxford University Press, 2012.

Buell, Denise Kimber. "Rethinking the Relevance of Race for Early Christian Self-Definition." *Harvard Theological Review* 94 (2001): 449-76.

———. *Why This New Race? Ethnic Reasoning in Early Christianity*. New York: Columbia University Press, 2005.

Bultmann, Rudolf. "Christ the End of the Law." In *Essays Philosophical and Theological*, 36-66. London: SCM, 1955 [1940].

———. "Ignatius and Paul." In *Existence and Faith: Shorter Writings of Rudolf Bultmann*, edited by Schubert Miles Ogden, 267-77. New York: Meridian Books, 1960 [1953].

———. "Καυχᾶσθαι." In *Theological Dictionary of the New Testament*, edited by Gerhard Kittel and Geoffrey William Bromiley, 3:645-53. 10 vols. Grand Rapids, MI: Eerdmans, 1966.

———. "Liberal Theology and the Latest Theological Movement." In *Faith and Understanding*, 28-52. Vol. 1. London: SCM, 1969 [1924].

———. "Paul." In *Existence and Faith: Shorter Writings of Rudolf Bultmann*, edited by Schubert Miles Ogden, 111-46. New York: Meridian Books, 1960 [1930].

———. "Romans 7 and the Anthropology of Paul." In *Existence and Faith: Shorter Writings of Rudolf Bultmann*, edited by Schubert Miles Ogden, 147-57. New York: Meridian Books, 1960 [1932].

———. *Theology of the New Testament*. Translated by Kendrick Grobel. 2 vols. London: SCM, 1952.

Bunsen, C. K. J. *Christianity and Mankind*. Vol. 1. London: Longman, Brown, Green, and Longmans, 1854.

Burgon, John W. *Index of Texts of the New Testament Quoted, or Referred to, by the Greek and Latin Fathers*. 16 vols. London: British Museum, 1872.

Campenhausen, Hans von. *The Formation of the Christian Bible*. Philadelphia: Fortress Press, 1972.

Cantalamessa, Raniero. *L'omelia "In S. Pascha" dello Pseudo-Ippolito di Roma: recerche sulla teologia dell' Asia Minore nella seconda metà del II secolo*. Milano: Vita e Pensiero, 1967.

———. "Méliton de Sardes. Une christologie antignostique du IIe siècle." *Revue des Sciences Religieuses* 37 (1963): 1-26.

Carleton Paget, James. "Barnabas 9.4 a Peculiar Verse on Circumcision." In *Jews, Christians and Jewish Christians in Antiquity*, 77-90. WUNT 251. Tübingen: Mohr Siebeck, 2010.

———. "The Ebionites in Recent Research." In *Jews, Christians and Jewish Christians in Antiquity*, 325-79. WUNT 251. Tübingen: Mohr Siebeck, 2010.

———. *The Epistle of Barnabas: Outlook and Background*. WUNT 2:62. Tübingen: Mohr Siebeck, 1994.

———. "The Epistle of Barnabas and the Writings That Later Formed the New Testament." In *The Reception of the New Testament in the Apostolic Fathers*, edited by Andrew F. Gregory and Christopher M. Tuckett, 229-49. Oxford: Oxford University Press, 2005.

———. "Paul and the Epistle of Barnabas." *Novum Testamentum* 38 (1996): 359-81.

Carson, D. A., Peter Thomas O'Brien, and Mark A. Seifrid, eds. *Justification and Variegated Nomism*. 2 vols. Grand Rapids, MI: Baker Academic, 2001.

Chadwick, Henry. "Justin Martyr's Defence of Christianity." *Bulletin of the John Rylands Library* 47 (1965): 275-97.

Clabeaux, John James. *A Lost Edition of the Letters of Paul: A Reassessment of the Text of the Pauline Corpus Attested by Marcion.* Washington, DC: Catholic Biblical Association of America, 1989.

Clark, Kenneth W. "Worship in the Jerusalem Temple After A.D. 70." *New Testament Studies* 6 (1960): 269-80.

Cohen, Shaye J. D. *Why Aren't Jewish Women Circumcised? Gender and Covenant in Judaism.* Berkeley: University of California Press, 2005.

Cohick, Lynn. "Melito of Sardis's 'Peri Pascha' and Its 'Israel.'" *Harvard Theological Review* 91 (1998): 351-72.

———. *The Peri Pascha Attributed to Melito of Sardis: Setting, Purpose, and Sources.* Providence, RI: Brown Judaic Studies, 2000.

Cosgrove, Charles. "Justin Martyr and the Emerging Christian Canon: Observations on the Purpose and Destination of the Dialogue with Trypho." *Vigiliae Christianae* 36 (1982): 209-32.

Coxhead, Steven. "John Calvin's Interpretation of Works Righteousness in Ezekiel 18." *WTJ* 70 (2008): 303-16.

Cross, F. L. *The Early Christian Fathers.* London: G. Duckworth, 1960.

Dassmann, Ernst. *Der Stachel im Fleisch: Paulus in der frühchristlichen Literatur bis Irenäus.* Münster: Aschendorff, 1979.

Davies, W. D. *Paul and Rabbinic Judaism.* London: S.P.C.K., 1948.

Del Verme, Marcello. *Didache and Judaism: Jewish Roots of an Ancient Christian-Jewish Work.* New York: T&T Clark International, 2004.

Despotis, Athanasios. *Die "New Perspective on Paul" und die griechisch-orthodoxe Paulusinterpretation.* St. Ottilien: EOS-Verl, 2014.

Diez, Karlheinz and Eero Huovinen. *From Conflict to Communion: Lutheran-Catholic Common Commemoration of the Reformation in 2017.* Leipzig: Evangelische Verlagsanstalt, 2013.

Donahue, Paul J. "Jewish Christianity in the Letters of Ignatius of Antioch." *Vigiliae Christianae* 32 (1978): 81-93.

———. "Jewish-Christian Controversy in the Second Century: A Study in the Dialogue of Justin Martyr." PhD diss., Yale University, 1973.

Dorner, I. A. *History of the Development of the Doctrine of the Person of Christ.* Translated by W. L. Alexander. Vol. 1. Edinburgh: T&T Clark, 1889.

Draper, Jonathan A. "Torah and Troublesome Apostles in the Didache Community." *Novum Testamentum* 33 (1991): 347-72.

Duncan, J. Ligon. "The Covenant Idea in Melito of Sardis." *Presbyterion* 28 (2002): 12-33.

Dunn, James D. G. *Jesus Remembered.* Vol. 1 of *Christianity in the Making.* Grand Rapids, MI: Eerdmans, 2003.

———. *Neither Jew nor Greek: A Contested Identity.* Vol. 3 of *Christianity in the Making.* Grand Rapids, MI: Eerdmans, 2015.

———. *The New Perspective on Paul.* Grand Rapids, MI: Eerdmans, 2005.

———. "A New Perspective on the New Perspective on Paul." *Early Christianity* 4 (2013): 157-82.

———. *The Theology of Paul the Apostle.* Grand Rapids, MI: Eerdmans, 1998.

———. "Whatever Happened to 'Works of the Law'?" In *Epitoayto*, edited by J. Kerkovsky, 107-20. Praha: Mlyn, 1998.

Dunn, Peter Wallace. "The Acts of Paul and the Pauline Legacy in the Second Century." PhD diss., University of Cambridge, 2006.

Edwards, Mark. "Ignatius, Judaism, Judaizing." *Eranos* 93 (1995): 69-77.

———. "Ignatius and the Second Century: An Answer to R. Hübner." *Zeitschrift für Antikes Christentum* 2 (1998): 214-26.

England, Emma, and William John Lyons, eds. *Reception History and Biblical Studies: Theory and Practice.* London: Bloomsbury T&T Clark, 2015.

Eno, Robert B. "Some Patristic Views on the Relationship of Faith and Works in Justification." *Recherches Augustiniennes et Patristiques* 19 (1984): 3-27.

Evans, Robert. *Reception History, Tradition and Biblical Interpretation: Gadamer and Jauss in Current Practice.* London: Bloomsbury T&T Clark, 2014.

Ewald, Heinrich. *The History of Israel.* Translated by J. F. Smith. Vol. 8. London: Longmans, Green, and Co, 1869.

Fairweather, E. R. "The So-Called Letter to Diognetus: Introduction and Books." In *Early Christian Fathers*, edited by Cyril Richardson, 205-12. Philadelphia: Westminster Press, 1953.

Fesko, J. V. "Old and New Perspectives on Paul: A Third Way?" *The Gospel Coalition*, January 6, 2016. www.thegospelcoalition.org/reviews/old-and-new-perspectives-on -paul-a-third-way/.

Finley, Gregory C. "The Ebionites and 'Jewish Christianity': Examining Heresy and the Attitudes of Church Fathers." PhD diss., Catholic University of America, 2009.

Fitzmyer, Joseph A. *The Biblical Commission's Document "The Interpretation of the Bible in the Church": Text and Commentary.* Subsidia Biblica 18. Rome: Pontifical Biblical Institute Press, 1995.

Flusser, David. "Paul's Jewish-Christian Opponents in the Didache." In *Gilgul: Essays on Transformation, Revolution and Permanence in the History Of Religions; Dedicated to R. J. Zwi Werblowsky*, edited by Shaul Shaked, David Shulman, and Gedaliahu A. G. Stroumsa, 71-90. Leiden: Brill, 1987.

Foster, Paul. "The Epistle to Diognetus." In *The Writings of the Apostolic Fathers*, edited by Paul Foster. London: T&T Clark, 2007.

———. "The Epistles of Ignatius of Antioch." In *The Writings of the Apostolic Fathers*, edited by Paul Foster. London: T&T Clark, 2007.

———. "The Epistles of Ignatius of Antioch and the Writings That Later Formed the New Testament." In *The Reception of the New Testament in the Apostolic Fathers*, edited by Andrew F. Gregory and Christopher M. Tuckett, 159-86. Oxford: Oxford University Press, 2005.

———. "Justin and Paul." In *Paul and the Second Century*, edited by Michael F. Bird and Joseph R. Dodson, 108-25. New York: T&T Clark, 2011.

———. "Peter in Noncanonical Traditions." In *Peter in Early Christianity*, edited by Helen K. Bond and Larry W. Hurtado, 222-62. Grand Rapids, MI: Eerdmans, 2015.

Frend, W. H. C. *Martyrdom and Persecution in the Early Church.* Eugene, OR: Wipf and Stock, 2014 [1965].

———. *The Rise of Christianity.* Philadelphia: Fortress Press, 1984.

Gaca, Kathy L. and L. L. Welborn. *Early Patristic Readings of Romans.* New York: T&T Clark, 2005.

Gadamer, Hans-Georg. *Truth and Method.* New York: Crossroad, 1975.

Galli, Marco. "Hadrian, Eleusis, and the Beginning of Christian Apologetics." In *Hadrian and the Christians*, edited by Marco Rizzi. New York: De Gruyter, 2010.

Gathercole, Simon J. "A Law unto Themselves: The Gentiles in Romans 2.14-15 Revisited." *Journal for the Study of the New Testament* 24 (2002): 27-49.

———. *Where Is Boasting? Early Jewish Soteriology and Paul's Response in Romans 1–5.* Grand Rapids, MI: Eerdmans, 2002.

Goodenough, E. R. *The Theology of Justin Martyr.* Jena: Frommann, 1923.

Grant, Robert M. *The Apostolic Fathers: Introduction.* Vol. 1 of *The Apostolic Fathers: A New Translation and Commentary.* New York: Thomas Nelson, 1964.

———. "The Chronology of the Greek Apologists." *Vigiliae Christianae* 9 (1955): 25-33.

———. *The Formation of the New Testament.* New York: Harper & Row, 1965.

———. *Greek Apologists of the Second Century.* Philadelphia: Westminster Press, 1988.

———. *Ignatius of Antioch.* Vol. 4 of *The Apostolic Fathers: A New Translation and Commentary.* Camden, NJ: Thomas Nelson, 1967.

———. *Irenaeus of Lyons.* London: Routledge, 2000.

Gregory, Andrew F., and Christopher M. Tuckett, eds. *The Reception of the New Testament in the Apostolic Fathers.* Oxford: Oxford University Press, 2005.

———. *Trajectories Through the New Testament and the Apostolic Fathers.* Oxford: Oxford University Press, 2005.

Grenfell, Bernard Pyne, and Arthur Surridge Hunt. *The Oxyrhynchus Papyri.* Vol. 3. 72 vols. London: Egypt Exploration Fund, 1903.

Guignard, Christophe. "The Original Language of the Muratorian Fragment." *Journal of Theological Studies* 66 (2015): 596-624.

Gundry, R. H. "Grace, Works, and Staying Saved in Paul." *Biblica* 66 (1985): 1-38.

Hagner, D. A. *The Use of the Old and New Testaments in Clement of Rome.* Leiden: Brill, 1973.

Harnack, Adolf von. *Des heiligen Irenäus Schrift zum Erweise der apostolischen Verkündigung.* Leipzig: J. C. Hinrichs, 1907.

———. *Judentum und Judenchristentum in Justins Dialog mit Trypho.* Leipzig: J. C. Hinrichs, 1913.

———. *Marcion: das Evangelium vom fremden Gott.* 2nd ed. Leipzig: J. C. Hinrichs, 1924.

———. *Marcion: The Gospel of the Alien God.* Translated by Lyle D. Bierma and John E. Steely. Durham, NC: Labyrinth Press, 1990 [1921].

Hartog, Paul. *Polycarp and the New Testament.* WUNT 2:134. Tubingen: Mohr Siebeck, 2002.

Hasler, Victor. *Gesetz und Evangelium in der alten Kirche bis Origenes, eine auslegungsgeschichtliche Untersuchung.* Zürich: Gotthelf, 1953.

Hays, Richard B. *Echoes of Scripture in the Letters of Paul.* New Haven, CT: Yale University Press, 1989.

Hengel, Martin. *Judaism and Hellenism.* Translated by J. Bowden. Philadelphia: Fortress, 1974.

Hill, Charles E. "Cerinthus, Gnostic or Chiliast? A New Solution to an Old Problem." *Journal of Early Christian Studies* 8 (2000): 135-72.

———. *From the Lost Teaching of Polycarp.* WUNT 186. Tübingen: Mohr Siebeck, 2006.

———. "'In These Very Words': Methods and Standards of Literary Borrowing in the Second Century." In *The Early Text of the New Testament*, edited by Charles E. Hill and Michael J. Kruger, 263-81. New York: Oxford University Press, 2012.

———. *The Johannine Corpus in the Early Church.* Oxford: Oxford University Press, 2004.

———. "Justin and the New Testament Writings." In *Studia Patristica*, edited by E. A. Livingstone, vol. 30:42-48. Leuven: Peeters Press, 1997.

Hoek, Annewies van den. "Techniques of Quotation in Clement of Alexandria: A View of Ancient Literary Working Methods." *Vigiliae Christianae* 50 (1996): 223-43.

Hofer, Andrew. "The Old Man as Christ in Justin's 'Dialogue with Trypho.'" *Vigiliae Christianae* 57 (2003): 1-21.

Hoh, Joseph. *Die Lehre des hl. Irenäus über das Neue Testament.* Münster/Westf.: Aschendorff, 1919.

Horbury, William. "Jewish-Christian Relations in Barnabas and Justin Martyr." In *Jews and Christians in Contact and Controversy*, 127-61. Edinburgh: T&T Clark, 1998.

———. *Jewish War Under Trajan and Hadrian.* Cambridge: Cambridge University Press, 2014.

Horner, Timothy J. *Listening to Trypho: Justin Martyr's Dialogue Reconsidered.* Leuven: Peeters, 2001.

Horst, P. W. van der. "I Gave the Laws That Were Not Good: Ezekiel 20:25 in Ancient Judaism and Early Christianity." In *Hellenism—Judaism—Christianity: Essays on Their Interaction*, 106-18. Kampen, the Netherlands: Kok Pharos, 1994.

Howard, George. "Romans 3:21-31 and the Inclusion of the Gentiles." *Harvard Theological Review* 63 (1970): 223-33.

Hübner, Reinhard. "Thesen zur Echtheit und Datierung der sieben Briefe des Ignatius von Antiochien." *ZAC* 1 (1997): 44-72.

Hvalvik, Reidar. *The Struggle for Scripture and Covenant: The Purpose of the Epistle of Barnabas and Jewish-Christian Competition in the Second Century.* WUNT 2:82. Tübingen: Mohr Siebeck, 1996.

Hyldahl, Niels. *Philosophie und Christentum: Eine Interpretation der Einleitung zum Dialog Justins.* Kopenhagen: Munksgaard, 1966.

Inge, W. R. "Ignatius." In *The New Testament in the Apostolic Fathers*, edited by Oxford Society of Historical Theology, 63-83. Oxford: Clarendon Press, 1905.

Inowlocki, Sabrina. *Eusebius and the Jewish Authors: His Citation Technique in an Apologetic Context.* Leiden: Brill, 2006.

Jacquier, Eugène. *History of the Books of the New Testament.* Translated by J. Duggan. New York: Benziger, 1907.

Jaspert, Bernd, and G. W. Bromiley, eds. *Karl Barth—Rudolf Bultmann: Letters, 1922–1966.* Grand Rapids, MI: Eerdmans, 1981.

Jefford, Clayton N. *The Apostolic Fathers and the New Testament.* Peabody, MA: Hendrickson Publishers, 2006.

———. *Reading the Apostolic Fathers: A Student's Introduction.* Grand Rapids, MI: Baker Academic, 2012.

Kay, D. M. *The Apology of Aristides the Philosopher.* Edited by Allan Menzies and Philip Schaff. Edinburgh: T&T Clark, 1897.

Keith, Chris. *Jesus' Literacy: Scribal Culture and the Teacher from Galilee.* New York: T&T Clark, 2011.

Kieffer, René. *Foi et justification à Antioche: Interprétation d'un conflit (Ga 2, 14-21).* Paris: Cerf, 1982.

Kihn, Heinrich. *Der Ursprung des Briefes an Diognet.* Freiburg: Herder, 1882.

Kirk, Alexander N. *The Departure of an Apostle: Paul's Death Anticipated and Remembered.* WUNT 2:406. Tübingen: Mohr Siebeck, 2015.

Knapp, Henry M. "Melito's Use of Scripture in 'Peri Pascha': Second-Century Typology." *Vigiliae Christianae* 54 (2000): 343-74.

Knight, Mark. "Wirkungsgeschichte, Reception History, Reception Theory." *Journal for the Study of the New Testament* 33 (2010): 137-46.

Knox, John. *Marcion and the New Testament.* Chicago: University of Chicago Press, 1942.

Koch, Dietrich-Alex. *Die Schrift als Zeuge des Evangeliums: Untersuchungen zur Verwendung und zum Verständnis der Schrift bei Paulus.* Tübingen: Mohr Siebeck, 1986.

Koester, Helmut. *History and Literature of Early Christianity.* Vol. 2 of *Introduction to the New Testament.* 2nd ed. New York: Walter de Gruyter, 2000.

———. *Synoptische Uberlieferung bei den apostolischen Vätern.* Berlin: Akademie-Verlag, 1957.

Kraabel, A. T. "Melito the Bishop and the Synagogue at Sardis: Text and Context." In *Studies Presented to G. M. A. Hanfmann,* edited by D. G. Mitten, 72-85. Mainz: Zabern, 1971.

Kraft, Robert. *Barnabas and the Didache.* Vol. 3 of *The Apostolic Fathers: A New Translation and Commentary.* Edited by Robert M. Grant. New York: Thomas Nelson, 1965.

Lahey, Lawrence. "Evidence for Jewish Believers in Christian-Jewish Dialogues Through the Sixth Century (excluding Justin)." In *Jewish Believers in Jesus: The Early Centuries,* edited by Oskar Skarsaune and Reidar Hvalvik, 581-639. Peabody, MA: Hendrickson Publishers, 2007.

Lane, Anthony. *John Calvin, Student of the Church Fathers.* Grand Rapids, MI: Baker Books, 1999.

Lawson, John. *The Biblical Theology of Saint Irenaeus.* London: Epworth Press, 1948.

Le Boulluec, Alain. *La notion d'hérésie dans la littérature grecque, Iie–IIIe siècles.* Paris: Études Augustiniennes, 1985.

Lewis, C. S. *Fern-seed and Elephants: And Other Essays on Christianity.* Edited by Walter Hooper. Glasgow: Collins, 1977.

Lieu, Judith. "As Much My Apostle as Christ Is Mine: The Dispute over Paul Between Tertullian and Marcion." *Early Christianity* 1 (2010): 41-59.

———. *Image and Reality: The Jews in the World of the Christians in the Second Century.* London: T&T Clark, 1996.

———. *Marcion and the Making of a Heretic: God and Scripture in the Second Century.* Cambridge: Cambridge University Press, 2015.

———. *Neither Jew nor Greek? Constructing Early Christianity.* Edinburgh: T&T Clark, 2002.

———. "They Speak to Us Across the Centuries: Melito of Sardis." *The Expository Times* 110 (1998): 43-46.

Lightfoot, J. B. *The Apostolic Fathers.* Edited by J. R. Harmer. London: Macmillian and Co, 1898.

———. "The Epistle of Barnabas." In *The Apostolic Fathers,* 503-12. London: Macmillan and Co., 1890.

———. *Essays on the Work Entitled Supernatural Religion.* London: Macmillan and Co., 1893.

———. *S. Ignatius, S. Polycarp.* Vol. 2 of *The Apostolic Fathers.* 2nd ed. London: Macmillan and Co, 1889.

———. *Saint Paul's Epistles to the Colossians and to Philemon*. London: Macmillan and Co., 1879.

Liljeström, Kenneth. *The Early Reception of Paul*. Helsinki: Finnish Exegetical Society, 2011.

Lincicum, David. "Learning Scripture in the School of Paul: From Ephesians to Justin." In *The Early Reception of Paul*, edited by Kenneth Liljeström, 148-70. Helsinki: Finnish Exegetical Society, 2011.

Lindemann, Andreas. "Paul in the Writings of the Apostolic Fathers." In *Paul and the Legacies of Paul*, edited by William S. Babcock, 25-45. Dallas: Southern Methodist University Press, 1990.

———. "Paulinische Theologie im Diognetbrief." In *Kerygma und Logos: Beiträge zu den geistesgeschichtlichen Beziehungen zwischen Antike und Christentum*, edited by Carl Andresen and Adolf Martin Ritter, 337-50. Göttingen: Vandenhoeck & Ruprecht (1979).

———. *Paulus im ältesten Christentum: das Bild des Apostels und die Rezeption der paulinischen Theologie in der frühchristlichen Literatur bis Marcion*. Tübingen: Mohr Siebeck, 1979.

———. "Die Sammlung der Paulusbriefe im 1. und 2. Jahrhundert." In *The Biblical Canons*, edited by Jean-Marie Auwers and H. J. de Jonge, 321-51. Leuven: Peeters, 2003.

Lona, Horacio E. *An Diognet*. Freiburg: Herder, 2001.

Loofs, Friedrich. *Theophilus von Antiochen Adversus Marcionem und die anderen theologischen Quellen bei Irenaeus*. Leipzig: J. C. Hinrichs, 1930.

Lubac, Henri de. "'Typologie' et 'Allégorisme.'" *Recherches de Science Religieuse* 34 (1947): 180-226.

Luz, Ulrich. *Matthew in History: Interpretation, Influence, and Effects*. Minneapolis: Fortress Press, 1994.

———. *Matthew 1–7: A Commentary*. Edited by Helmut Koester. Translated by James E. Crouch. Minneapolis: Fortress Press, 2007 [1989].

Lyons, John. *Structural Semantics*. Oxford: B. Blackwell, 1963.

MacKenzie, Iain. *Irenaeus's Demonstration of the Apostolic Preaching: A Theological Commentary and Translation*. Aldershot, UK: Ashgate, 2002.

Marguerat, Daniel. "The Acts of Paul and the Canonical Acts: A Phenomenon of Re-reading." *Semeia* 80 (1997): 169-84.

———. "Paul après Paul: une histoire de réception." *New Testament Studies* 54 (2008): 317-77.

Marshall, I. H. "Salvation, Grace and Works in the Later Writings in the Pauline Corpus." *New Testament Studies* 42 (1996): 339-58.

Marshall, John W. "The Objects of Ignatius's Wrath and Jewish Angelic Mediators." *Journal of Ecclesiastical History* 56 (2005): 1-23.

Mason, Steve. "Jews, Judaeans, Judaizing, Judaism: Problems of Categorization in Ancient History." *Journal for the Study of Judaism* 38 (2007): 457-512.

Massaux, Edouard. *The Influence of the Gospel of Saint Matthew on Christian Literature Before Saint Irenaeus.* Edited by Arthur J. Bellinzoni. Vol. 1 of 3. Macon, GA: Mercer, 1990 [1950].

———. *The Influence of the Gospel of Saint Matthew on Christian Literature Before Saint Irenaeus.* Edited by Arthur J. Bellinzoni. Vol. 3 of 3. Macon, GA: Mercer, 1993 [1950].

McGiffert, Arthur Cushman. *Eusebius.* New York: The Christian Literature Co, 1890.

McGrath, Alister E. *Iustitia Dei: A History of the Christian Doctrine of Justification.* 3rd ed. Cambridge: Cambridge University Press, 2005.

Meecham, Henry G. *The Epistle to Diognetus.* Manchester, UK: Manchester University Press, 1949.

Meeks, Wayne. "Why Study the New Testament?" *New Testament Studies* 51 (2005): 155-70.

Milavec, Aaron. *The Didache: Faith, Hope, & Life of the Earliest Christian Communities, 50–70 C.E.* New York: Newman Press, 2003.

Minns, Dennis. *Irenaeus.* London: G. Chapman, 1994.

———. "The Rescript of Hadrian." In *Justin Martyr and His Worlds*, edited by Sara Parvis and Paul Foster, 38-49. Minneapolis: Fortress Press, 2007.

Minns, Dennis, and Paul Parvis. *Justin, Philosopher and Martyr: Apologies.* Oxford: Oxford University Press, 2009.

Moessner, David P., Daniel Marguerat, Mikeal C. Parsons, and Michael Wolter, eds. *Paul and the Heritage of Israel.* London: T&T Clark, 2012.

Moll, Sebastian. *The Arch-Heretic Marcion.* WUNT 250. Tübingen: Mohr Siebeck, 2010.

Molland, Einar. "The Heretics Combatted by Ignatius of Antioch." *Journal of Ecclesiastical History* 5 (1954): 1-6.

Moo, Douglas. *The Epistle to the Romans.* Grand Rapids, MI: Eerdmans, 1996.

———. *Galatians.* Grand Rapids, MI: Baker Academic, 2013.

———. "Justification in Galatians." In *Understanding the Times: New Testament Studies in the 21st Century: Essays in Honor of D. A. Carson on the Occasion of His 65th Birthday*, edited by Andreas J. Köstenberger and Robert W. Yarbrough, 160-95. Wheaton, IL: Crossway, 2011.

———. "'Law,' 'Works of the Law,' and Legalism in Paul." *Westminster Theological Journal* 45 (1983): 73-100.

———. "The Law of Christ as the Fulfillment of the Law of Moses." In *Five Views on Law and Gospel*, edited by Stanley Gundry, 319-76. Grand Rapids, MI: Zondervan, 1993.

Morgan, Robert. *Romans.* Sheffield, UK: Sheffield Academic Press, 1997.

Muilenburg, James. *The Literary Relations of the Epistle of Barnabas and the Teaching of the Twelve Apostles.* Marburg: Yale University, 1929.

Mundle, Wilhelm. *Der Glaubensbegriff des Paulus.* Leipzig: M. Heinsius Nachfolger, 1932.

Murray, Michele. *Playing a Jewish Game: Gentile Christian Judaizing in the First and Second Centuries CE.* Waterloo, Ontario: Wilfrid Laurier University Press, 2004.

Myllykoski, Matti. "Wild Beasts and Rabid Dogs: The Riddle of the Heretics in the Letters of Ignatius." In *The Formation of the Early Church*, edited by Jostein Ådna, 341-74. WUNT 1:183. Tübingen: Mohr Siebeck, 2005.

Newman, John Henry. *An Essay on the Development of Christian Doctrine.* New York: Longmans, Green, 1949 [1845].

Nicklas, Tobias, Andreas Merkt, and Jozef Verheyden. *Ancient Perspectives on Paul.* Göttingen: Vandenhoeck & Ruprecht, 2013.

Niederwimmer, Kurt. *The Didache: A Commentary.* Edited by Harold W. Attridge. Minneapolis: Fortress Press, 1998.

Nielsen, Charles M. "The Epistle to Diognetus: Its Date and Relationship to Marcion." *Anglican Theological Review* 52 (1970): 77-91.

Nilson, Jon. "To Whom Is Justin's Dialogue with Trypho Addressed?" *Theological Studies* 38 (1977): 538-46.

Noormann, Rolf. *Irenäus als Paulusinterpret: zur Rezeption und Wirkung der paulinischen und deuteropaulinischen Briefe im Werk des Irenäus von Lyon.* WUNT 2:66. Tübingen: Mohr Siebeck, 1994.

Norris, Richard A. "Irenaeus's Use of Paul in His Polemic Against the Gnostics." In *Paul and the Legacies of Paul*, edited by William S. Babcock, 79-89. Dallas: Southern Methodist University Press, 1990.

Novensen, Matthew. "Paul's Former Occupation in Ioudaismos." In *Galatians and Christian Theology: Justification, the Gospel, and Ethics in Paul's Letter*, edited by Mark W. Elliot, Scott J. Hafemann, N. T. Wright, and John Frederick, 24-39. Grand Rapids, MI: Baker Academic, 2014.

O'Ceallaigh, G. C. "'Marcianus' Aristides, on the Worship of God." *Harvard Theological Review* 51 (1958): 227-54.

Osborn, Eric Francis. *Irenaeus of Lyons.* Cambridge: Cambridge University Press, 2001.

———. *Justin Martyr.* Tübingen: Mohr Siebeck, 1973.

Osborne, Grant R. *The Hermeneutical Spiral.* Downers Grove, IL: IVP Academic, 2010.

Oswald, Hilton C., Jaroslav Pelikan, Helmut T. Lehmann, and Hans Joachim Grimm, eds. *Luther's Works.* St. Louis: Concordia Pub. House, 1986 [1955].

Owen, John, ed. *Commentaries on the Epistle of Paul the Apostle to the Romans.* University of Virginia, 1849.

Patterson, L. G. "The Divine Became Human: Irenaean Themes in Clement of Alexandria." *Studia Patristica* 31 (1997): 497-516.

Pelikan, Jaroslav. *The Christian Tradition: A History of the Development of Doctrine. The Emergence of the Catholic Tradition (100–600).* Vol. 1 of 5. Chicago: University of Chicago Press, 1971.

Penny, Donald N. "The Pseudo-Pauline Letters of the First Two Centuries." PhD diss., Emory University, 1979.

Peretto, Elio. *La Lettera ai romani cc. 1–8 nell'Adversus Haereses d'Ireneo.* Bari: Istituto di letteratura cristiana antica, Università, 1971.

Pervo, Richard I. *The Making of Paul: Constructions of the Apostle in Early Christianity.* Minneapolis, MN: Fortress Press, 2010.

Prigent, Pierre. *Les testimonia dans le christianisme primitif: l'Épître de Barnabé I–XVI et ses sources.* Paris: J. Gabalda, 1961.

Prostmeier, Ferdinand R. *Der Barnabasbrief.* Göttingen: Vandenhoeck & Ruprecht, 1999.

Pseftogas, Vassilios. *Melitonos Sardeon: Ta peri tou Pascha duo.* Thessaloniki: Patriarchikon Hidryma Paterikon Meleton, 1971.

Räisänen, Heikki. "The Effective 'History' of the Bible: A Challenge to Biblical Scholarship?" *Scottish Journal of Theology* 45 (1992): 303-24.

———. *Paul and the Law.* WUNT 29. Tübingen: Mohr Siebeck, 1986.

Rankin, David Ivan. *From Clement to Origen: The Social and Historical Context of the Church Fathers.* Aldershot, UK: Ashgate, 2006.

Rathke, Heinrich. *Ignatius von Antiochien und die Paulusbriefe.* Berlin: Akademie-Verlag, 1967.

Reagan, Joseph Nicholas. *The Preaching of Peter: The Beginning of Christian Apologetic.* Chicago: The University of Chicago Press, 1923.

Reasoner, Mark. *Romans in Full Circle: A History of Interpretation.* Louisville, KY: Westminster John Knox Press, 2005.

Rensberger, David. "As the Apostle Teaches: The Development of the Use of Paul's Letters in Second-Century Christianity." PhD diss., Yale University, 1981.

Rhodes, James N. *The Epistle of Barnabas and the Deuteronomic Tradition.* WUNT 2:188. Tübingen: Mohr Siebeck, 2004.

Richardson, Cyril. *The Christianity of Ignatius of Antioch.* New York: Columbia University Press, 1935.

Riches, John. *Galatians Through the Centuries.* Oxford: Blackwell, 2007.

Rizzi, Marco. *La questione dell'unità dell' "Ad Diognetum."* Milan: Vita e pensiero, 1989.

Robinson, Thomas. *Ignatius of Antioch and the Parting of the Ways: Early Jewish-Christian Relations.* Peabody, MA: Hendrickson, 2009.

Rokéah, David. *Justin Martyr and the Jews.* Leiden: Brill, 2002.

Roo, Jacqueline de. *"Works of the Law" at Qumran and in Paul.* Sheffield, UK: Sheffield Phoenix Press, 2007.

Rousseau, Adelin. *Démonstration de la prédication apostolique.* Paris: Éditions du Cerf, 1995.

Royalty, Robert M. *The Origin of Heresy.* New York: Routledge, 2015.

Rutherford, William C. "Reinscribing the Jews: The Story of Aristides' Apology 2.2-4 and 14.1b–15.2." *Harvard Theological Review* 106 (2013): 61-91.

Rylaarsdam, David. 2006. "Interpretations of Paul in the Early Church." In *Rereading Paul Together: Protestant and Catholic Perspectives on Justification,* edited by David Aune, 146-68. Grand Rapids, MI: Baker Academic.

Sanders, E. P. *Paul.* New York: Oxford University Press, 1991.

———. *Paul, the Law, and the Jewish People.* Philadelphia: Fortress Press, 1983.

———. *Paul and Palestinian Judaism.* Philadelphia: Fortress Press, 1977.

———. "Paul Between Judaism and Hellenism." In *St. Paul Among the Philosophers,* edited by John D. Caputo and Linda Alcoff, 74-90. Bloomington: Indiana University Press, 2009.

Scheck, Thomas. *Origen and the History of Justification: The Legacy of Origen's Commentary on Romans.* Notre Dame, IN: University of Notre Dame Press, 2008.

Schneemelcher, Wilhelm. "Paulus in der griechischen Kirche des zweiten Jahrhunderts." *ZKG* 75 (1964): 1-20.

Schoedel, William R. *Ignatius of Antioch: A Commentary on the Letters of Ignatius of Antioch.* Philadelphia: Fortress Press, 1985.

Schreiner, Thomas R. "'Works of Law' in Paul." *Novum Testamentum* 33 (1991): 217-44.

Schulze, Manfred. "Martin Luther and the Church Fathers." In *The Reception of the Church Fathers in the West: From the Carolingians to the Maurists,* ed. Irena Backus, 573-626. Vol. 2. Leiden: E. J. Brill, 2001.

Seeberg, Reinhold. *Lehrbuch der Dogmengeschichte.* Leipzig: A. Deichert, 1908.

Shotwell, Willis. *The Biblical Exegesis of Justin Martyr.* London: S.P.C.K., 1965.

Siker, Jeffrey. *Disinheriting the Jews: Abraham in Early Christian Controversy.* Louisville, KY: Westminster John Knox Press, 1991.

Silva, Moisés. *Biblical Words and Their Meaning.* Grand Rapids, MI: Zondervan, 1983.

Simon, Marcel. *Verus Israel: A Study of the Relations Between Christians and Jews in the Roman Empire (135–425).* Translated by H. McKeating. New York: Oxford University Press, 1986 [1948].

Skarsaune, Oskar. "The Ebionites." In *Jewish Believers in Jesus: The Early Centuries,* edited by Reidar Hvalvik and Oskar Skarsaune, 419-62. Peabody, MA: Hendrickson Publishers, 2007.

———. "Justin and His Bible." In *Justin Martyr and His Worlds,* edited by Sara Parvis and Paul Foster, 53-76. Minneapolis: Fortress Press, 2007b.

———. *The Proof from Prophecy: A Study in Justin Martyr's Proof-Text Tradition.* Leiden: Brill, 1987.

Skarsaune, Oskar, and Reidar Hvalvik. *Jewish Believers in Jesus: The Early Centuries.* Peabody, MA: Hendrickson Publishers, 2007.

Smit Sibinga, Joost. *The Old Testament Text of Justin Martyr.* Leiden: Brill, 1963.

Smith, Carl. "Ministry, Martyrdom, and Other Mysteries: Pauline Influence on Ignatius of Antioch." In *Paul and the Second Century*, edited by Michael Bird and Joseph Dodson, 37-56. New York: T&T Clark, 2011.

Snyder, Glenn E. *Acts of Paul: The Formation of a Pauline Corpus.* WUNT 2:352. Tübingen: Mohr Siebeck, 2013.

Sprinkle, Preston M. *Paul and Judaism Revisited: A Study of Divine and Human Agency in Salvation.* Downers Grove, IL: IVP Academic, 2013.

Stanton, Graham. "The Law of Moses and the Law of Christ: Galatians 3.1–6.2." In *Paul and the Mosaic Law*, ed. J. D. G. Dunn, 99-116. WUNT 89. Tübingen: Mohr Siebeck, 1996.

———. "What Is the Law of Christ?" In *Studies in Matthew and Early Christianity*, edited by Markus N. A. Bockmuehl and David Lincicum, 311-22. WUNT 309. Tübingen: Mohr Siebeck, 2013.

Stendahl, Krister. "The Apostle Paul and the Introspective Conscience of the West." *The Harvard Theological Review* 56 (1963): 199-215.

Stewart-Sykes, Alistair. "Melito's Anti-Judaism." *Journal of Early Christian Studies* 5 (1997): 271-83.

Still, Todd D., and David E. Wilhite, eds. *Tertullian and Paul.* New York: Bloomsbury T&T Clark, 2013.

Strawbridge, Jennifer R. *The Pauline Effect: The Use of the Pauline Epistles by Early Christian Writers.* Berlin: De Gruyter, 2015.

Stylianopoulos, Theodore. *Justin Martyr and the Mosaic Law.* Missoula, MT: Society of Biblical Literature, 1975.

Sundkvist, Mikael. *The Christian Laws in Paul: Reading the Apostle with Early Greek Interpreters.* Joensuu: University of Joensuu, 2008.

Thiselton, Anthony C. "Semantics and New Testament Interpretation." In *Thiselton on Hermeneutics: The Collected Works and New Essays of Anthony Thiselton.* Grand Rapids, MI: Eerdmans, 2006 [1977].

Thomas, Matthew J. "Paul and Works of the Law: Perspectives Old and New." *Canadian Theological Review* 1 (2012): 81-86.

Tolley, Harry. "Clement of Alexandria's Reference to Luke the Evangelist as Author of Jason and Papiscus." *Journal of Theological Studies* 63 (2012): 523-32.

Torrance, Thomas F. *The Doctrine of Grace in the Apostolic Fathers.* Grand Rapids, MI: Eerdmans, 1959.

Tsakonas, Basil G. "The Usage of the Scriptures in the Homily of Melito of Sardis on the Passion." *Theologia* 38 (1967): 609-20.

Tuckett, Christopher M. "The Didache and the Writings That Later Formed the New Testament." In *The Reception of the New Testament in the Apostolic Fathers*, edited by Andrew F. Gregory and Christopher M. Tuckett, 83-127. Oxford: Oxford University Press, 2005.

Tugwell, Simon. *The Apostolic Fathers*. Harrisburg, PA: Morehouse Pub., 1990.

VanLandingham, Chris. *Judgment and Justification in Early Judaism and the Apostle Paul*. Peabody, MA: Hendrickson, 2006.

Varner, William. "On the Trail of Trypho: Two Fragmentary Jewish-Christian Dialogues from the Ancient Church." In *Christian Origins and Hellenistic Judaism: Social and Literary Contexts for the New Testament*, edited by Stanley E. Porter and Andrew W. Pitts, 553-65. Leiden: Brill, 2013.

Vermès, Géza. *Christian Beginnings: From Nazareth to Nicaea*. New Haven, CT: Yale University Press, 2013.

Vielhauer, Philipp. *Geschichte der urchristlichen Literatur. Einleitung in das Neue Testament, die Apokryphen und die Apostolischen Väter*. Berlin: De Gruyter, 1975.

Werline, Rodney. "The Transformation of Pauline Arguments in Justin Martyr's 'Dialogue with Trypho.'" *Harvard Theological Review* 92 (1999): 79-93.

Werner, Johannes. *Der Paulinismus des Irenaeus. Eine kirchen- und dogmengeschichtliche Untersuchung über das Verhältnis des Irenaeus zu der paulinischen Briefsammlung und Theologie*. Leipzig: J. C. Hinrichs, 1889.

Westerholm, Stephen. *Perspectives Old and New on Paul: The "Lutheran" Paul and His Critics*. Grand Rapids, MI: Eerdmans, 2004.

White, Benjamin L. *Remembering Paul: Ancient and Modern Contests over the Image of the Apostle*. Oxford: Oxford University Press, 2014.

Whittaker, John. "The Value of Indirect Tradition in the Establishment of Greek Philosophical Texts or the Art of Misquotation." In *Editing Greek and Latin Texts: Papers Given at the Twenty-Third Annual Conference on Editorial Problems, University of Toronto, 6–7 November 1987*, edited by John N. Grant, 63-95. New York: AMS Press, 1989.

Wiles, Maurice. *The Divine Apostle: The Interpretation of St. Paul's Epistles in the Early Church*. London: Cambridge University Press, 1967.

Wilken, Robert Louis. "Diversity and Unity in Early Christianity." *Second Century* 1 (1981): 101-11.

Williams, Rowan. "Does It Make Sense to Speak of Pre-Nicene Orthodoxy?" In *The Making of Orthodoxy: Essays in Honour of Henry Chadwick*, 1-23. New York: Cambridge University Press, 1989.

Wilson, S. G. "Passover, Easter, and Anti-Judaism: Melito of Sardis and the Others." In *"To See Ourselves as Others See Us": Christians, Jews, "Others" in Late Antiquity*, edited by Jacob Neusner and Ernest S. Frerichs, 337-55. Chico, CA: Scholars Press, 1985.

———. *Related Strangers: Jews and Christians, 70–170 C.E.* Minneapolis: Fortress Press, 1995.

Wolff, Robert Lee. "The Apology of Aristides: A Re-examination." *Harvard Theological Review* 30 (1937): 233-47.

Wright, Dudley. *The Eleusinian Mysteries and Rites.* London: Theosophical Publishing House, 1919.

Wright, N. T. *The Climax of the Covenant: Christ and the Law in Pauline Theology.* London: T&T Clark, 1991.

———. "Communion and Koinonia: Pauline Reflections on Tolerance and Boundaries." *NTWrightPage* (blog), 2002. ntwrightpage.com/Wright_Communion_Koinonia.htm.

———. *Justification: God's Plan and Paul's Vision.* London: SPCK, 2009.

———. "Justification and Eschatology in Paul and Qumran: Romans and 4QMMT." In *History and Exegesis: New Testament Essays in Honor of Dr. E. Earle Ellis for His 80th Birthday*, edited by Sang-Won Son, 103-42. New York: T&T Clark, 2006.

———. "The Letter to the Romans: Introduction, Commentary, and Reflections." In *The New Interpreter's Bible*, edited by Leander E. Keck, 10:393-770. Nashville: Abingdon, 2001.

———. *The New Testament and the People of God.* Minneapolis: Fortress, 1992.

———. *Paul: In Fresh Perspective.* Minneapolis: Fortress Press, 2005.

———. *Paul and the Faithfulness of God.* London: SPCK, 2013.

———. "The Paul of History and the Apostle of Faith." *Tyndale Bulletin* 29 (1978): 61-88.

———. "Trevin Wax Interview with N. T. Wright." *The Gospel Coalition.* November 19, 2007. blogs.thegospelcoalition.org/trevinwax/2007/11/19/trevin-wax-interview-with-nt-wright-full-transcript/.

———. *What Saint Paul Really Said.* Grand Rapids, MI: Eerdmans, 1997.

Young, Frances M. *Biblical Exegesis and the Formation of Christian Culture.* Peabody, MA: Hendrickson, 2002.

Young, Stephen E. *Jesus Tradition in the Apostolic Fathers: Their Explicit Appeals to the Words of Jesus in Light of Orality Studies.* WUNT 2:311. Tübingen: Mohr Siebeck, 2011.

Zahn, Theodor. *Ignatius von Antiochen.* Gotha: Perthes, 1873.

AUTHOR INDEX

SUBJECT INDEX

SCRIPTURE INDEX

INDEX OF CLASSICAL
AND JEWISH LITERATURE

INDEX OF PATRISTIC
LITERATURE

INDEX OF MEDIEVAL
AND REFORMATION TEXTS

Finding the Textbook You Need

The IVP Academic Textbook Selector
is an online tool for instantly finding the IVP books
suitable for over 250 courses across 24 disciplines.

_____

ivpacademic.com
_____